INCREASING STUDENT ENGAGEMENT AND RETENTION USING IMMERSIVE INTERFACES: VIRTUAL WORLDS, GAMING, AND SIMULATION

CUTTING-EDGE TECHNOLOGIES IN HIGHER EDUCATION

Series Editor: Charles Wankel

CUTTING-EDGE TECHNOLOGIES IN HIGHER
EDUCATION   VOLUME 6C

INCREASING STUDENT ENGAGEMENT AND RETENTION USING IMMERSIVE INTERFACES: VIRTUAL WORLDS, GAMING, AND SIMULATION

EDITED BY

CHARLES WANKEL
St. John's University, New York, USA

PATRICK BLESSINGER
St. John's University, New York, USA

IN COLLABORATION WITH

JURATE STANAITYTE
NEIL WASHINGTON

Created in partnership with Higher Education
Teaching and Learning

http://hetl.org/

United Kingdom – North America – Japan
India – Malaysia – China

Emerald Group Publishing Limited
Howard House, Wagon Lane, Bingley BD16 1WA, UK

First edition 2012

British Library Cataloguing in Publication Data
A catalogue record for this book is available from the British Library

ISBN: 978-1-78190-240-0
ISSN: 2044-9968 (Series)

ISOQAR certified
Management Systems,
awarded to Emerald for
adherence to Quality
and Environmental
standards ISO 9001:2008
and 14001:2004,
respectively

Certificate Number 1985
ISO 9001
ISO 14001

INVESTOR IN PEOPLE

CONTENTS

v

LIST OF CONTRIBUTORS

Jonathan Becker	Virginia Commonwealth University, Richmond, VA, USA
Francesca Bertacchini	Università della Calabria, Cosenza, Italy
Patrick Blessinger	St. John's University, Queens, NY, USA
Jon Cabiria	Fielding Graduate University, Philadelphia, PA, USA
Maurice Eugene Dawson Jr.	Alabama A&M University, Normal, AL, USA
Stayc DuBravac	University of Kentucky, Lexington, KY, USA
Lorella Gabriele	Università della Calabria, Cosenza, Italy
Steve Gove	Virginia Tech, Blacksburg, VA, USA
Scott A. Johnson	College of Idaho, Caldwell, ID, USA
Jing Luo	University of Greenwich, London, UK
Dale Mann	Virginia Commonwealth University, Richmond, VA, USA; Emeritus, Teachers College, Columbia University, New York, NY, USA
Grace May	Seton Hall University, South Orange, NJ, USA
Danielle Mirliss	Seton Hall University, South Orange, NJ, USA
Denise M. Pheils	Indiana Institute of Technology, Fort Wayne, IN, USA
R. Martin Reardon	Virginia Commonwealth University, Richmond, VA, USA

Michael R. Reich	Virginia Commonwealth University, Richmond, VA, USA
Margarida Romero	ESADE Law & Business School, Sant Cugat del Vallès, Spain
Imad Al Saeed	Colorado Technical University, Colorado Springs, CO, USA
Charol Shakeshaft	Virginia Commonwealth University, Richmond, VA, USA
Wei Lian Tan	Taylor's University, Selangor, Malaysia
Assunta Tavernise	Università della Calabria, Cosenza, Italy
Charles Wankel	St. John's University, Queens, NY, USA
Maxwell K. Winchester	Victoria University, Victoria, Australia
Tiffany M. Winchester	Deakin University, Victoria, Australia
Mary Zedeck	Seton Hall University, South Orange, NJ, USA

PART I
ADOPTION OF IMMERSIVE
INTERFACES: VIRTUAL WORLDS,
GAMING, AND SIMULATION

INNOVATIVE APPROACHES IN HIGHER EDUCATION: AN INTRODUCTION TO USING IMMERSIVE INTERFACES

Patrick Blessinger and Charles Wankel

INTRODUCTION

The chapters in this book focus on three main areas of innovation in teaching and learning in higher education today: virtual worlds, gaming, and simulation. Advancements in both digital technologies and learning theories are transforming the way we teach and learn and those advancements are refining our views of what it means to learn in the contemporary post-industrial age. Both individually and collectively, immersive technologies have become more popular as educational tools across a range of disciplines as a means for educators to engage students more deeply in the learning process. Biggs (2003) advocates deep learning – learning that entails active and devoted engagement with rigorous, high-quality learning activities that is also enjoyable and interesting for the learner.

In a similar manner, Kuh (2009) defines student engagement as a high level of participation and a high quality of effort. With that broad definition in mind, this book presents several studies that illustrate how these

Increasing Student Engagement and Retention using Immersive Interfaces: Virtual Worlds, Gaming, and Simulation
Cutting-edge Technologies in Higher Education, Volume 6C, 3–14
Copyright © 2012 by Emerald Group Publishing Limited
All rights of reproduction in any form reserved
ISSN: 2044-9968/doi:10.1108/S2044-9968(2012)000006C003

three types of immersive technologies are being used as game-based, problem-based, and inquiry-based active learning tools to enable higher levels of participation and a higher quality of effort among students. As such, technology-enriched instruction can assist the instructor to create more interactive learning activities that help foster more self-regulated and personally meaningful learning environments.

These tools are being used in conjunction with a larger set of teaching and learning strategies and educational approaches to (1) increase students' subject matter expertise, (2) increase their higher order thinking and decision-making skills, and (3) develop students' affective and social abilities, which are necessary to function effectively in a globalized world. A key dimension of the tools' power is their ability to create varied, complex scenarios within a mistake-tolerant learning environment. This type of environment provides the learner another way to cultivate multiple perspectives and modes of inquiry needed for complex problem-solving. These tools can be used in both undergraduate and graduate level courses and in many different course contexts and problem-solving learning scenarios.

However, the novelty alone of these technologies is not sufficient to engage learners. As with any teaching and learning tool or strategy, these technologies must be used in a purposeful and thoughtful way and they must be embedded within a theoretical framework that is appropriate to the context of the learning (e.g., educational level, type of course, course objectives, learning outcomes). Using valid and reliable learning theories and principles is important because they form the underlying basis for accurately predicting human behavior and learning outcomes. In addition to relevant theory, it is also essential to understand the pertinent epistemological, ontological, and phenomenological basis for using such technologies.

ADOPTION PRINCIPLES

Thus, two key principles emerge from the findings of the chapters in the adoption section of the book that help frame the book's contents and this set of specific technologies:

(1) immersive environments should be viewed as knowledge-building communities in which diversity (in all its forms), multiple perspectives, multiple modes of inquiry, and collaborative learning are valued and practiced by all participants and where academic engagement and

learning occurs across all domains (affective, behavioral, cognitive), and

(2) community-based environments have the potential to foster a sense of belonging where immediacy, interactivity, and group cohesiveness are important factors in student motivation and in their willingness to participate in co-constructing such communities (Annetta, 2010; Hsu, Wen, & Wu, 2009).

These principles are reflective of the growing level of interdependence and interconnectedness that exists in the post-industrial, globalized world. Thus, these technologies can provide a means where learning environments can be used to mirror complex real-life scenarios and, at the same time, provide a relatively safe and low-risk way to learn in a mistake-tolerant environment. All else being equal, students are more inclined to engage more deeply in learning activities where they know mistakes will be tolerated and where they have a large degree of freedom to experiment with new problem-solving scenarios and explore all the nuances and aspects of the context they are operating within.

If the course is designed appropriately and if the course is facilitated properly, these types of immersive environments can provide an effective way to foster individual and group identities, awareness of individual and group value systems, respect for gender, racial, class, and lifestyle differences, deference for language and culture differences, recognition of historical and political differences, and a better understanding of one's own and others' motivations for learning. These immersive environments can also provide good practice for developing better dialogue and conflict resolution strategies and skills, which are vital in an increasingly interdependent and interconnected world.

Participation with these technologies should be challenging and interesting and the goals (individual and collective) should be feasible and congruent. Intragroup and intergroup relationships in both competitive and noncompetitive environments should be positive and rewarding. Learning within this type of context should be positively stimulating for the learner and should strive to meet the learning needs of each student, which include more effective recognition and feedback mechanisms to encourage performance, a heightened sense of self-regulation and self-efficacy in achieving one's personal goals, and a greater sense of overall accomplishment.

In short, students can be said to be highly engaged when they are deeply immersed in a learning activity and when they are in a state of flow with a personally meaningful experience (Nakamura & Csikszentmihalyi, 2002). This type of flow (absorbing oneself in the activity) requires intrinsic motivation and meaningful, stimulating, and continual feedback. Motivation, which can be described as the personal willingness to engage in a learning activity, is a key ingredient to achieving this state. Therefore, motivation is vital to engagement, and in turn, engagement is vital to learning.

If designed properly and integrated into the course in a purposeful manner, immersive technologies can provide today's learners with a viable means to further enhance their learning experience, especially since today's learners are increasingly accustomed to interfacing with digital, virtual realities. Higher education institutions should therefore seek innovative ways to adapt to this digital world in ways that better suit today's learner.

APPLICATION BENEFITS

As illustrated in the book chapters in the application section and as noted by Aldrich (2009), Annetta (2010), and Rieber, Smith, and Noah (1998) among others, these types of learner-centered immersive environments support:

(1) intragroup and intergroup dialogue and collaboration in a multiplicity of complex situations and contexts,
(2) immediacy, a sense of belonging, and group cohesiveness, which fosters shared identity and culture,
(3) mediation to facilitate learning tasks thereby making learning more enjoyable and interesting,
(4) the development of multiple perspectives and multiple modes of inquiry through role play and personal reflection and through the development of ethical reasoning skills, and
(5) individualized learning that is more personally meaningful to each student and more authentic and conducive to how today's students experience learning in their real life-worlds.

In other words, learning tends to be more effective when students are motivated to construct knowledge in ways that are meaningful to them, and instructors play a vital role in fostering and facilitating this knowledge development. (Lee & Hoadley, 2007; Morse, Littleton, Macleod, & Ewins, 2009; Sun & Rueda, 2012.) In short, the question becomes: how can we create sustainable knowledge-building communities where learning is personally meaningful for students and professionally satisfying for instructors.

In recent decades, the role of teaching and learning has shifted from a passive uni-directional authoritarian instructional paradigm to a more active multi-directional collaborative learning paradigm. Thus, in this emerging paradigm, a key goal of instruction is to facilitate and enable learning and the role of the institution is to become a learning organization. Immersive technologies are beginning to play an increasingly larger part in shaping this emerging paradigm.

THEORETICAL FRAMING

By using different approaches, the authors in this volume operationalize three immersive tools in the spirit of constructivism (cognitive and social) and academic motivation, which are supported by the learning theories of Piaget, Vygotsky, Bandura, and Bruner as well as by several academic motivational theorists (e.g., Anderman, Austin, & Johnson, 2002; Pintrich & Schunk, 2002; Weiner, 1980; Wigfield & Eccles, 2002). Constructivism can be broadly defined as cognitive and social learning wherein the learner constructs new knowledge and meaning based on his/her own experiences − past and present. In other words, deep learning is higher order knowledge building through personal and social meaning making.

Thus, constructivism can provide a plausible framework for designing immersive learning contexts that support engaging students deeply in personally meaningful learning activities. In this model, immersive learning tools allow the learner to more fully engage all their senses and use that sensory input and stimulation to more actively construct personal and social meaning. Personal motivation is a key factor in this process.

Core motivational theories (e.g., expectancy-value theory, goal orientation theory, attribution theory) stress that academic motivation and achievement arise from a nexus of internal (psychological and cognitive) and external (classroom and social) factors, and that motivation is course/ subject specific. Under this set of related learning theories, learners are viewed as active translators and processors of their sensory input and learners naturally reflect on this input in ways that are personally meaningful to them (Gredler, 2009). Learning environments can be structured such that they inhibit or enable this tendency. Hence, the need for more individualized learning contexts that recognize each student's personal values and goals is important.

TECHNOLOGY

One of the tools we focus on in this volume — virtual worlds — is a good example of a technology that facilitates the building of personally meaningful knowledge and provides a platform where students can engage in role play under different scenarios. Virtual worlds are computerized shared social spaces (i.e., knowledge-building communities) that involve immediacy, interactivity, and persistence, and which allow learners to emulate natural social conditions but to do so in a more mistake-tolerant way. Virtual worlds, like Second Life, are used in a variety of disciplines and variety of learning activities such as language learning.

Academic gaming evolved in the late 1990s and games used for academic purposes are commonly referred to as serious games — as opposed to entertainment games. Academic gaming is designed mainly in problem-solving and decision-making scenarios and where the instructor defines specific subject-based learning outcomes for the game players (i.e., students). A desirable skill to be learned in using games is transferability — the ability to take knowledge and skills learned through practicing games and then transfer that knowledge and those skills to more complex and riskier real-life scenarios.

Whereas games tend to be competitive based, simulations tend to be more structured and uniform in nature and often require the learner to assume a specific role. Simulations are designed to parallel the context that one desires to master. So, the learner may, for instance, learn the theory and concepts and principles by way of lecture or textbooks or other sources and then use the simulation to apply that knowledge and develop specific skills and behaviors. A key component of simulation is practice with multiple scenarios until competence is gained. An instructor is vital in helping to assess performance and providing feedback for improvement.

In summary, all three immersive environments — virtual worlds, gaming, and simulations — have the potential to foster a sense of progressing, which is important in motivation and developing competence. Compared with more static methods of learning (e.g., case studies, videos), immersive environments better enable the student to more actively participate in the environment and practice complex decision-making and what-if scenarios in a more forgiving and mistake-tolerant way. In this sense, these technologies support experiential and authentic learning activities that attempt to mirror complex real-world scenarios but have the added benefit of allowing the learner to assume different roles and varied scenarios that might not be possible in their real life-world.

CHAPTER OVERVIEWS

In "Learner Engagement in the Use of Individual and Collaborative Serious Games," by Margarida Romero, the author describes the nature of learner engagement in the use of individual and collaborative Serious Games. Individual engagement is analyzed through their perceptions of the usefulness of the game and the time they spend on task. The collaborative use of Serious Games considers additional mechanisms of engagement related to the intragroup and intergroup relationships, such as the degree of interdependence and the degree of competition. A literature review describes the current research on learner engagement with Serious Games and the author presents a case study where students used the eFinance Game (MetaVals) at the Esade Business School. Finally, the author analyzes iterative design approaches that could allow the game designers and instructors to increase learner engagement using such games.

In "Strategies for Designing Engaging E-Learning Instructions: Know Your Learners' Need," by Wei Lian Tan, describes how e-learning can engage learners in ways not possible in traditional face-to-face settings. The author maintains that instructors need to possess an awareness of learners' need in order to properly motivate them, and thus, to engage them. The author explores two key questions to that end: (1) what motivates and engages learners?, and (2) what are appropriate strategies for designing engaging e-learning instructions based on learners' needs?' The author analyzes factors that engage learners by exploring the value dimension of learners' need by way of their experience with computer games. Based on research findings, the author suggests strategies for designing engaging e-learning instructions that include case studies, problem-based learning and project-based learning.

In "Game Mechanics for Classroom Engagement," by Stayc DuBravac, the describes how educators use games as a way to engage students and keep them on task. The author investigates gamification — the integration of game mechanics into regular classroom activities without destroying routines and ignoring the students' expectations. The author reviews studies that show that in-game rewards are motivational and related rewards such as status, virtual collections, or resources to improve performance increase engagement more than unrelated rewards like bonus points. Just as Activity Theory argues for the progressive removal of help to encourage students to perform on their own, gamification argues for increasingly difficult tasks with fewer rewards as they progress in the course. Too many or too few rewards can lead to an unbalanced system where students experience achievement fatigue, achievement dependence, exhaustion, or dissolution of intrinsic motivation.

In "Increasing Student Engagement Using Client-Based Peer Assessment in Multi-Role, Whole-Enterprise Simulations," by Steve Gove, the author presents two approaches to increase learner engagement: simulations and peer assessment. The author describes how each approach can be used to create active learning environments. An MBA-level course on competitive analysis is used to illustrative how these approaches can yield a highly interactive and engaging course for students. Assessment provides a better understanding of the benefits of the simulation and consequently better performance.

In "Bringing the Classroom to Life: Using Virtual Worlds to Develop Teacher Candidate Skills," by Danielle Mirliss, Grace May, and Mary Zedeck, the authors present a case study in which they explore the creation of simulations in virtual worlds to support teacher candidate education. Teacher candidates are often underprepared for the realities of managing a real-life classroom and the complexities associated with a diverse student population. Student teaching provides an initial glimpse into this community of practice but there are many challenges. For example, some experienced teachers are hesitant to turn over their classroom to teacher candidates during field placements and others consider it unethical to replace an experienced teacher with a novice teacher candidate. Virtual worlds afford teacher preparation programs the ability to create flexible and cost-effective simulations that allow teacher candidates a safe place to develop valuable classroom skills. In this chapter, the authors describe a simulation that was created for the College of Education and Human Services at Seton Hall University. Using Second Life as the virtual world platform, a virtual third grade classroom was created as well as student and teacher avatars. Teacher candidates assumed these various roles as they worked through a classroom scenario involving the accommodation of students with special needs. Results indicate that virtual worlds are a viable platform for creating engaging role play simulations.

In "Engaging Chinese Students and Enhancing Leadership Development through Virtual Simulation: A Cross-Cultural Perspective," by Scott A. Johnson and Jing Luo, the authors explain how engagement is essential to students' successful learning outcomes, psychological adjustment, and multicultural understanding. The authors explain how overseas Chinese students in the United Kingdom face considerable barriers to engagement due to dissimilarities between their own educational backgrounds and communication styles and the expectations driven by traditional Western curriculum and pedagogy. The authors identify key challenges where Chinese student engagement can be enhanced through integrated technology and pedagogy design: (1) application of an interactive simulation (vLeader) that encourages students from Confucian educational cultures to try different communication and leadership styles through experiential learning, (2) progressive achievement through "double-loop" learning that helps Chinese students to build their confidence in intercultural communication, and (3) facilitation of students' critical thinking skills and differentiation from Chinese memory-based teaching methods that help overcome the hesitation to ask questions and help improve understanding across cultures. The authors analyze vLeader's key features that help students overcome barriers to learning that may result from such cultural influences as high collectivism and high power distance. The authors demonstrate how the vLeader technology platform and underlying model are matched to their pedagogical design to facilitate student engagement. They provide an evaluation of their instructional techniques and related student feedback to suggest how these approaches can improve learning outcomes for all students, including the Chinese students studying in Western countries.

In "Engagement in an Online Video Simulation in Educational Leadership," by R. Martin Reardon, Dale Mann, Jon Becker, Charol Shakeshaft, and Michael R. Reich, the authors present an online video simulation of events for a low-performing middle school in the United States. The authors describe how the simulation aimed to engage potential educational leaders by developing their leadership skills, which were derived from various standards-based documents such as the 2008 Educational Leadership Policy Standards issued by the Council of Chief State School Officers. The simulation allowed the authors to gather evidence on engagement and learning and demonstrate how the online format can be used to empower anytime/anywhere learning in a mistake-tolerant setting.

In "Augmenting Engagement: Augmented Reality in Education," by Jon Cabiria, the author discusses the connection between technology and education, and then more specifically, explores augmented reality education and the various ways in which it can be used. The author explains how augmented reality is a visual medium and provides several examples to enhance the text descriptions. The author then looks at the role of cognition in learning and how augmented reality relates to attention, engagement, presence, and immersion. Finally, the author discusses ongoing research and related issues, and the future prospects for augmented reality in education.

In "Bolstering Student Hands-On Experience through the Use of Virtualization," by Denise M. Pheils, the author discusses how virtualization can be used as a viable means for providing students with relevant hands-on experience while synthesizing course content across all delivery systems. The author explains that most courses lack the ability to immerse students fully in the course content. The author explains how providing students with hands-on activities with the content will better empower their problem-solving skills and could foster higher retention and increased student satisfaction. The author concludes that virtualization and customization of the learning experience can foster active learning and increase student success.

In "Use of Open Source Software (Oss) and Virtualization in Academia to Enhance Higher Education Everywhere," by Maurice Eugene Dawson Jr. and Imad Al Saeed, the authors discuss the utilization of Open Source Software (OSS) and virtualization tools that are currently available to educators. The authors discuss how OSS virtual tools have been applied at the university level in graduate course projects to teach the Systems Development Life Cycle. They describe the benefits and challenges of OSS implementation, including how some countries are currently using OSS. The authors maintain that these tools will allow students the opportunity for greater creativity and learning.

In "Active Learning in an Educational Robotics Laboratory: A Case Study with University Students," by Lorella Gabriele, Assunta Tavernise, and Francesca Bertacchini, the authors examine how educational robotics can be used to create engaging and interesting experiences in instructive contexts. The authors explain how the aim of robotics is to improve students' advanced cognitive skills and their constructive experience through laboratories. The authors present a case study on a robotics laboratory where students attended theory-based lecture lessons, and then designed, built and programmed a robot able to perform three differently assigned tasks. The authors analyzed learners' reports and programs to better understand the indicators associated with adopted work/cognitive strategies and engagement. The authors conducted a comparison between an entry questionnaire and a post-treatment questionnaire, and compared the results to a control group that learned robotics content but did not construct or program a robot. The findings show that engaging experiences (like robotic construction and simulations) can provide effective and successful learning outcomes and increase knowledge retention due to feelings of enjoyment and participation.

In "Utilizing the Virtual Learning Environment to Encourage Faculty Reflection and Improve the Student Learning Experience," by Tiffany M. Winchester and Maxwell K. Winchester, the authors discuss the use of weekly student evaluations of teaching (SETs) via the virtual learning environment (VLE). The authors describe the benefits and drawbacks of summative SETs and explain the benefits of using them as a formative evaluation and learning tool. The authors discuss two studies that investigate weekly SETs from faculty and student perspectives, as well as two additional studies that investigate collecting SET data, via the VLE, and found that those instructors who reflected on their SET feedback to a greater degree received higher yearly increases in their summative evaluations.

CONCLUSION

In this collection of chapters, we have presented different perspectives on how to use virtual worlds, gaming, and simulations in order to more fully engage learners in meaningful learning activities. Current research suggests that a key ingredient in learning is motivation so it follows course design should focus on developing ways that triggers this motivation, both externally and internally. These enabling immersive technologies have the potential to increase academic engagement and student learning but they are only one piece of the learning puzzle.

The ultimate goal, regardless of the technology used or the instructional methods employed, is to start students down the path of becoming life-long learners and to instill in them a high value for learning that grows over time. The experiential and immersive nature of the activities highlighted in these chapters helps to achieve this end. Technology is a moving target and it undergoes a constant evolution. Even though new technologies will always appear in the future, it does not follow that they should be viewed as passing fads. Rather, these tools should be viewed as opportunities to expand our definition and concept of teaching and learning in the modern era. Thus, we hope you will join us in exploring the innovative use of these tools to better engage students in an increasingly technological and globalized world.

REFERENCES

Aldrich, C. (2009). Virtual worlds, simulations, and games for education: A unifying view. *Innovate: Journal of Online Education, 5*(5).

Anderman, E. M., Austin, G. G., & Johnson, D. M. (2002). The development of goal orientation. In A. Wigfield & J. S. Eccles (Eds.), *Development of achievement motivation* (pp. 197–222). San Diego, CA: Academic Press.

Annetta, L. A. (2010). The "I's" have it: A framework for serious educational game design. *Review of General Psychology, 14*(2), 105–112.

Biggs, J. (2003). *Teaching for quality learning at university.* New York, NY: Open University Press.

Gredler, M. (2009). *Learning and instruction: Theory into practice* (6th ed.). Upper Saddle River, NJ: Merrill Pearson.

Hsu, S. H., Wen, M., & Wu, M. (2009). Exploring user experiences as predictors of MMORPG addiction. *Computers & Education, 53*(3), 990–999.

Kuh, G. D. (2009). The national survey of student engagement: Conceptual and empirical foundations. *New Directions for Institutional Research, 141*, 5–20.

Lee, J. J., & Hoadley, C. M. (2007). Leveraging identity to make learning fun: Possible selves and experiential learning in massively multiplayer online games (MMOGs). *Innovate: Journal of Online Education, 3*(6).

Morse, S., Littleton, F., Macleod, H., & Ewins, R. (2009). The theatre of performance appraisal: Role-play in second life. In C. Wankel & J. Kingsley (Eds.), *Higher education in virtual worlds: Teaching and learning in second life* (pp. 181–201). Bingley, UK: Emerald Group.

Nakamura, J., & Csikszentmihalyi, M. (2002). The concept of flow. In C. R. Snyder & S.J. Lopez (Eds.) *Handbook of positive psychology* (pp. 89–105). Oxford, UK: Oxford University Press. Retrieved from http://teachingpsychology.files.wordpress.com/2012/02/the-concept-of-flow.pdf.

Pintrich, P. R., & Schunk, D. H. (2002). *Motivation in education: Theory, research, and applications* (2nd ed.). Upper Saddle River, NJ: Merrill/Prentice Hall.

Rieber, L. P., Smith, L., & Noah, D. (1998). The value of serious play. *Educational Technology, 38*(6), 29–37. Retrieved from http://www.coe.uga.edu/~lrieber/valueofplay.html

Sun, J. C.-Y., & Rueda, R. (2012). Situational interest, computer self-efficacy and self-regulation: their impact on student engagement in distance education. *British Journal of Educational Technology, 43*, 191–204.

Weiner, B. (1980). *Human motivation.* New York, NY: Holt, Rinehart, & Winston.

Wigfield, A., & Eccles, J. S. (2002). Introduction. In A. Wigfield & J. S. Eccles (Eds.), *Development of achievement motivation* (pp. 1–11). San Diego, CA: Academic Press.

LEARNER ENGAGEMENT IN THE USE OF INDIVIDUAL AND COLLABORATIVE SERIOUS GAMES

Margarida Romero

ABSTRACT

This chapter aims to advance in the analysis of the learner engagement and performance in the use of computer-based games, also known as Serious Games (SG). The chapter describes the learner engagement in relation to the use of SG in individual and collaborative learning activities. The SG learning experience considers the learner engagement in the individual activities observed through their real use of the game and their perceptions of the usefulness of the game and the time-on-task spent. The collaborative use of SG considers additional mechanisms of engagement related to the intragroup relationships – relationships within the same members of the group – and intergroup relationships – relationships between the different groups – such is the degree of interdependence and the degree of competition in the game. The state of the art in the learner engagement in the use of individual and collaborative SG is based in a literature review, and completed by the study case of the individual and the collaborative use of the eFinance Game or eFG (MetaVals) in ESADE Business & Law School. We analyse the current

Increasing Student Engagement and Retention using Immersive Interfaces: Virtual Worlds, Gaming, and Simulation
Cutting-edge Technologies in Higher Education, Volume 6C, 15–34
ISSN: 2044-9968/doi:10.1108/S2044-9968(2012)000006C004

challenges and transfer the knowledge created through the eFG case for
the practitioners aiming to promote learners' engagement through the
use of individual and collaborative SG.

THE LEARNERS' ENGAGEMENT

The psychologist Csikszentmihalyi (1991, p. 71) asks the question 'why is
playing a game is enjoyable, while the things we have to do every day —
like working or sitting at home — often so boring?'. Similarly, the digital
migrants' parents, teachers and other adults are concerned about the level
of engagement and time-on-task the X and Y Generation spends in playing
video games. Definitively, games are considered both by the younger end-
users and the adults as engaging activities. For parents worrying about the
amount of time their children engages in leisure games, the power of
engagement of the games is a negative attribute of the games that prevents
their children to develop other educative and social activities. The Game-
Based Learning (GBL) approach has considered the engagement potential
of the games for educational purposes. GBL aims to analyse the dynamics
of the game's leading to the player engagement in order to use these
dynamics for the achievement of the learning objectives.

Time-on-task as the amount of time the learners spent in a learning
activity does not ensure their engagement. Learners' attention could be
focused on off-task thoughts or activities that do not ensure their cognitive
engagement. Learners' engagement in a learning activity results from the
combination of the learners' willingness to participate in the learning activities and the efforts the learner engages during the efficient time-on-task.
Coates (2005, p. 26) defines learners' engagement as 'the extent to which
students are actively involved in a variety of educational activities that are
likely to lead to high quality learning'. Coates highlight the active role of
the learner in the activity that is required for achieving the learners'
engagement.

The learners' engagement has been considered as a continuum with
different degrees of engagement, from disengagement to the experience of
flow, considered by Csikszentmihalyi (1991) as the complete engagement
or absorption in an activity. In the state of flow 'the sense of duration of
time is altered; hours pass by in minutes, and minutes can stretch out to
seem like hours' (p. 49). Csikszentmihalyi identifies the playing activity as
one of the activities that helps players' 'achieve an ordered state of mind

that is highly enjoyable' (p. 72). Moreover, the engagement has been related to a compendium of the learners' behaviours (Bulger, Mayer, Almeroth, & Blau, 2008), considered as indicators of their approach, learning strategies and motivation in a specific learning context and activities. For Vinson et al. (2010) the learners' engagement is a key component of student success. The authors studying the influence of engagement in the learning process and outcomes have observed engagement as the students' attitude to show interest and effort (Dewey, 1913), pay attention (Fredricks, Blumenfeld, & Paris, 2004) and invest a certain time-on-task (Berliner, 1979). More recent theories has related the learning engagement to active learning methodologies where the participant is the main agent of the learning process in the context of computer-based environments and video games (Gee, 2003; Jonassen, 1996) and have studied engagement in terms of cognitive presence and cognitive load (Bulger et al., 2008). Reading (2008) has considered three types of engagement including behavioural, cognitive and emotional. Some authors restrict the concept considering only the learners' cognitive engagement (Richardson & Newby, 2004) including their learning strategies and motivation.

In this chapter, the learners' engagement will be considered as the learners' behaviours in the learning activity, including the learning strategies, the perception of the learning activity and the time-on-task.

LEARNING ACTIVITIES SITUATIONS PROMOTING LEARNERS' ENGAGEMENT

Because the learners' engagement is dynamic and contextual, we should consider the degree of engagement the learners' could manifest in different typologies of learning activities. From the teachers' perspective, it is necessary to design learning activities promoting the learners' engagement. Hargreaves (2004) considers the need to increase the active role of the learners' to enhance their engagement. In the context of the first year university students, Krause and Coates (2008) observe learners' engagement is related to their peers' engagement and the academic staff engagement, but also to self-managed and online resources during the courses. The use of the Information and Communication Technologies (ICT) has been related to learners' engagement (Barker, 2002; Reading, 2008). GBL has been considered for the potential to engage the learners (Pivec, Dziabenko, & Schinnerl, 2003). The use of computer-based environments leads to the concept of Digital Game-Based Learning (DGBL), also referred in the last years as SG. According to Prensky (2001, p. 16) 'DGBL is precisely about fun and engagement, and the coming together of and serious learning and interactive entertainment into a newly emerging and highly exciting medium'. Considering the DGBL and SG as one of the learning activities that has been considered as having a potential for developing the learners' engagement, the focus of the next sections will be oriented to identify the individual mechanisms in the learners' engagement in the individual and the collaborative uses of SG.

LEARNERS' ENGAGEMENT IN INDIVIDUAL USE OF SG

GBL methodology has been considered of special interest in the last decades, and it is still being a prolific field of research in education (Pivec, Koskinen, & Tarín, 2011). Researchers and educators have observed that GBL is a pedagogical methodology enhancing the engagements of the students in active learning situations, where the students should apply their knowledge and competencies in scenario-based problem solving and decision making (Gee, 2007; Kiili, 2005; Prensky, 2001). In the context of individual games for educational purposes, the flow theory approach has been considered by Kiili and Lainema (2006) for studying the use of a business game simulation with Higher Education students. The authors observed that the gaming experience in this context allowed engaging the students in the pedagogical objectives of the serious game.

LEARNERS' ENGAGEMENT IN COLLABORATIVE USE OF SG

Collaborative gaming experiences facilitate mutual understanding, contributing to the teamwork orientation (Dieleman & Huisingh, 2006) and to develop the ability to learn with others (Whitton & Hollins, 2008) in a safe environment. The level of the learners' engagement in their collaborative learning task influences their degree of satisfaction with their computer-based activity (Capdeferro & Romero, 2012). According to the indicators of learning engagement developed by Jones, Valdez, Nowakowski and

Rasmussen (1994) and discussed by Fletcher (2005) the learning activity should be organised towards a knowledge-building learning community, developing sharing understanding among individuals in a context of diversity where the different perspectives and strengths of the teammates are valued.

In the following sections, we examine two different types of multi-player relationships that characterise intragroup and intergroup dynamics: positive interdependence and competition.

Positive Interdependence in Multi-Player SG

Learners' engagement in a teamwork activity depends on several factors. One of the aspects that influence the learners' engagement towards the task and the other teammates' is the level of reciprocal interdependence required for the achievement of the task. In interdependent collaborative learning situations, the students are responsible not just for their own learning but also for that of others (Gockhale, 1995). Thus, the success of one student can help others to be successful (R. T. Johnson & Johnson, 1986). In interdependent situations teammates are critically dependent on each other; they need their peers' knowledge to complete their own part of the task and finally reach the group's goal (Dillenbourg, 1999; Lipponen, Rahikainen, Lallimo, & Hakkarainen, 2003). In collaborative learning, individuals may be responsible for their actions, including learning, and need to respect the abilities and contributions of their peers (Panitz, 1997). Help among different groups and information flow can be defined and guided, for instance by multi-player GBL dynamics or by game rules. Positive interdependence is also related to the incentives system implemented in intragroup and intergroup dynamics.

The underlying premise of collaborative learning is based upon consensus building through cooperation among group members (Bruffee, 1995). This is in contrast to competition, in which individuals or groups seek to outplay other individuals or groups in accordance with the game rules proposed by the collaborative GBL environment. We consider the positive interdependence dynamics that could be generated among students involved in a multi-player learning activity in terms of players' need to collaborate with other teams in order to achieve their learning goals. In this respect, multi-player GBL has the potential to enhance collaborative learning by supporting an intragroup dynamic of cooperation and positive interdependence between teammates.

There are multi-player games that are not based on a competitive dynamic. For instance, a game called *Course sans Gagnant* (Moisant, 2005) is a game-based activity played in small groups in which high school students collaborate towards a common final goal, implying that they positively depend on each other. Such a learning approach could lead to positive outcomes in terms of team competences and academic achievement. Developed by a mathematics teacher, this SG simulates a car race and pursues the maximum positive interdependence for a game activity (see Fig. 1); that is, teams can only win if all the players arrive at the finish at the same time. In order to reach this goal, students collaborate within the group and share different strategies and maths knowledge in order to calculate the different speeds required to finish the race together.

Social games or MMOGs also adopt the interdependence mechanism as one of the main aspects for engaging players in the game. Yee (2006) identifies teamwork as a social component of player motivation in MMOGs, where team member derives satisfaction from being part of a group effort and being positively related to teammates. In studies of MOOG addiction,

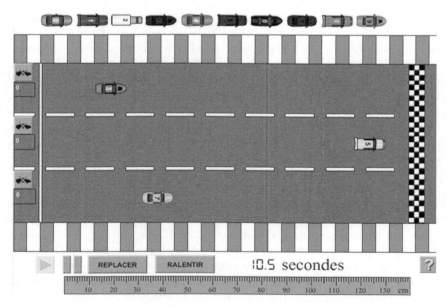

Fig. 1. Course Sans Gagnant. *Source*: Retrieved from http://www.patrickmoisan. net/copains/course_sans_gagnant.html.

the belonging component related to interdependence has been found to be a stronger factor than the competition factor (Hsu, Wen, & Wu, 2009). This suggests that interdependence in the intragroup relationship is one of the strongest motivators for the use of MOOGs. Players in MMOGs may be organised in teams that cooperate together, such as the guilds in the MOOG *Guild Wars* or the clans in the *World of Warcraft* (WoW). Some studies have explored the pedagogical interest of WoW. In their study, Pirius and Creel (2010) proposed students' organising themselves into an interdependent and cooperative clan to investigate the topics of subjective culture, personal and group identity, gender and stereotypes, language, citizenship, and technology. The students showed strong engagement in the game but the professors faced a challenge in managing the class and dealing with the distributed and dispersed knowledge developed through the use of this MOOG. Dubbels (2010) discusses engagement as a committed participation that could be related to interdependence and a belonging feeling the player could develop when playing with other team mates in a multi-player context.

COMPETITION IN MULTI-PLAYER SG

Competition dynamics is considered as one of key element of the explanation of players' engagement experience with games (Vorderer, Hartmann, & Klimmt, 2003; Vorderer, Klimmt, & Ritterfield, 2004). The potential for enhancing collaborative learning through positive interdependence in multiplayer GBL needs to be weighed against situations where students are in a complete win–win position; if the player always and inevitably wins, the resulting lack of challenge could result in a critical loss of engagement. Prensky (2001, p. 106) considers 'conflict, competition, challenge and opposition' components of the game as ways to provide the player with adrenaline, and promote engagement. In order to maintain the principle of competition and the positive interdependence ideally found in multi-player learning situations, we consider both intragroup cooperation and dynamic of competition that can be seen in most commercial games (Moreno-Ger, Burgos, Sierra, & Fernández-Manjón, 2008) played out at the intergroup level. In these situations, members within small teams cooperate together with the objective of beating the other groups. Following Dillenbourg (1999), we define small teams as groups ranging from two peers (dyads) to five students. Bruffee (1983) affirms that competition motivates students to play a game, permits active learning approaches and also encourages collaborative learning in which students can share their knowledge and develop their competences in a safe environment. In the context of collaborative GBL, the dynamic of intergroup competition can enhance group cohesion and coordination, leading to an increase in-group performance (Bornstein, 2003; Erev, Bornstein, & Galili, 1993).

One example of intergroup competition is *eScape*, a SG experience designed by Bluemink et al. (2010). Groups of four students engage in a virtual competition with five other groups through a voice-enhanced activity. The goal of the game is to escape from an ancient prison; in order to win the game, each team must collaborate to solve five problems or quests before the other groups do. These activities were designed to permit positive interdependence among the group members. The authors observed that intergroup dynamics could engage students in a constructive collaborative activity by promoting both cohesion and development of the teams. In addition to intragroup cooperation, intergroup competition can enhance engagement in the activity.

Intergroup competition is one of the basic mechanisms of MOOGs such as World of Warcraft where players are organised in clans that cooperate together against other clans. As mentioned earlier, competition seems to be a less important factor than cooperation for provoking MOOG engagement, and in extreme cases, addiction. We did not manage to identify educational uses of MOOGs where the educational purposes of competition where promoted. However, some studies highlight the existence of competitive behaviour in MOOG. Kristensen (2009) made a discourse analysis study of World of Warcraft , observing that in a male-dominated community discourse is task-oriented and competitive, and woman are perceived as annoying and disturbing. Kristensen discusses competitive male discourse following the work of Holmes (2006), who observed that male humour is competitive and challenging, while feminine humour is supportive.

INTRAGROUP COOPERATION AND INTERGROUP COMPETITION

In multiplayer games allowing the students' to play in groups, the game dynamics could combine both the positive interdependence and the competition in the different levels of the game activity: the intragroup dynamics that is developed between the teammates of the small group and the inter-group dynamics developed between the different small teams engaged in the activity (Fig. 2).

Individuals playing against other individuals are engaged in an inter-individual competition. This dynamic can be considered as extraneous to collaborative GBL, as it entails competition among individuals to reach the final individual goal. In this case, the game provides a multi-player situation, but the game rules of inter-individual competition avoid the collaborative learning dynamics to be developed within the teammates' in situation of rivalry.

As represented in Fig. 3, we could consider this game dynamic as counterproductive for intragroup interdependence and knowledge sharing because of the concurrent game and learning objectives of each individual player in this multi-player GBL situation. Inter-individual competition in this situation is high, as individuals compete against each other.

This is a typical situation of game-play within social network games. An example is the *Play the News* game (Zapusek, Cerar, & Rugelj, 2011). This

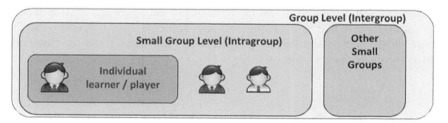

Fig. 2.   Individual Level, Small Group Level and Intergroup Level.
Source: Romero (2011).

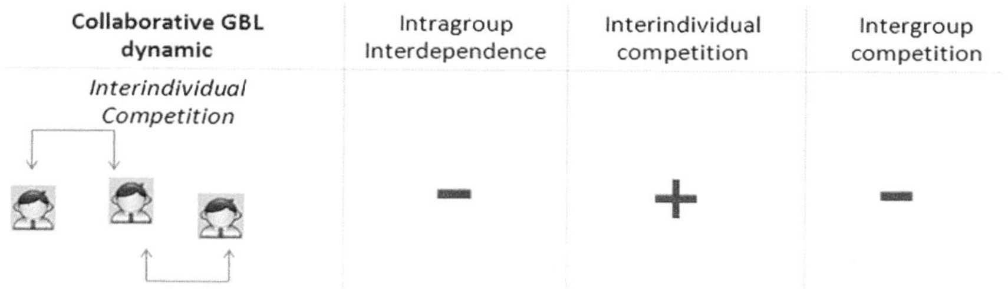

Collaborative GBL dynamic	Intragroup Interdependence	Interindividual competition	Intergroup competition
Interindividual Competition	−	+	−

Fig. 3.   Inter-Individual Competition Dynamics.

multi-player GBL is a web-based activity of interactive gaming on world news. Although users access the game and play it individually, there is a virtual community around the game where players can comment and access their rankings. The game's purpose is to help players create a snapshot of the socio-political profile over time on a range of different issues.

The computer-based design techniques for this SG modality are based on learners' awareness of other players' performance and situation in the game; without these tools, players have the impression of being alone and have no cues for preparing their competitive game strategy. Learners develop awareness of their teammates' knowledge and state, but they compete against each other without developing the sharing meanings and common objectives that requires collaborative learning. For intergroup relationships, the multi-player environments could be used in order implement a complete, focused on enhancing competition aspects through information and knowledge sharing, considering both group history and individual and collaborative game performance. An example of a collaboration-aware environment is *MetaTutor* (Azevedo, 2008; Azevedo, Witherspoon, Chauncey, Burkett, & Fike, 2009), a metacognitive tool for enhancing self-regulated learning. It is based on a reward system which promotes sports-like competition among students (an approach that is increasingly being identified as 'gamification') and aims to foster creativity through the exchange of knowledge.

PLAYING AGAINST OTHER GROUPS

Playing together (intragroup) against other groups (intergroup) is the second dynamics we consider in multi-player GBL. This dynamic corresponds to gaming activities in which students play in a group against other groups, applying the dynamics of intragroup cohesion and the intergroup hostility principle in line with the Realistic Conflict Theory of intergroup relations (LeVine & Campbell, 1972; M. Sherif & Sherif, 1953). Some games are designed to get students to collaborate with their teammates in order to compete against other teams. This type of GBL enables both collaboration and competition processes and is expected to create a higher sense of community inside one's group but also higher motivation for winning the game (Romero, 2011). In this multi-player dynamics, the group pursue collaboration for a final, common objective. That is, there is a totally positive interdependence factor at the intra-group to compete at the inter-group

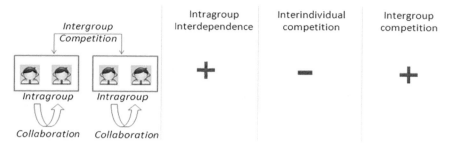

Fig. 4. Intragroup Cooperation and Intergroup Competition Dynamics.

level. As represented in Fig. 4, we could consider this game dynamic as enhancing intragroup interdependence and knowledge sharing within the teammates' of the same group. The inter-individual competition within the members of the group is low, but the intergroup competition is as its peak.

THE EFG CASE: ANALYSIS OF LEARNERS' INDIVIDUAL AND COLLABORATIVE ENGAGEMENT

The eFG or MetaVals is a SG aiming to put into practice finance concepts among non-finance experts at the university context at ESADE Universitat Ramon Llull. The computer-supported collaborative game has by now been played by 70 post-graduate participants enrolled in the introduction to finance course (Romero, Usart, & Almirall, 2011; Usart, Romero, & Almirall, 2011). The eFG pursues two main learning objectives. Firstly, the evaluation of two basic financial concepts: assets and liabilities, which have been introduced by the teacher during the lecture in an individual phase (Fig. 5).

Secondly, the practise of the collaboration competence through the collaborative decision making related to the financial concepts of assets and liabilities. The game begins with an individual phase, where students play individually, but they are invited to collaborate, in dyads, with another student for the second and third phase of the game. At the end of the game, the students receive the correction (feedback) of their answers and could observe their level of achievement relating with the other dyads of their class (Fig. 6).

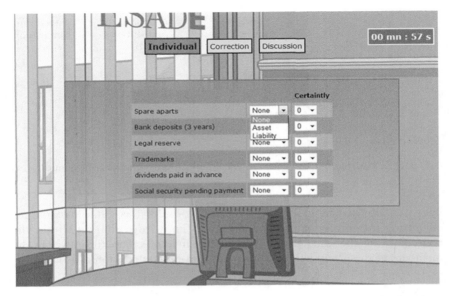

Fig. 5. Individual Decision on Assets/Liabilities and Level of Certainty Declaration.

In this sense, the eFG is a Collaborative game (or GBL environment), aiming to promote collaborative learning by allowing students to observe their peer's answers, to correct them, and finally, to discuss the collaborative decision making before reaching a consensus for the joint answer to the asset/liabilities evaluation. The final decision of the players is and interdependent decision on the identification of each of items as assets or liabilities.

The MetaVals game has been tested and carried out in different modalities depending on the course needs: fully online/face-to-face synchronous/asynchronous (Romero et al., 2012). Whereas in some cases the interaction among dyads was done face-to-face, in some others a chat tool was provided within game to interact on the collaborative part in order to reach final consensus. The competition dynamics with the other couples playing within the same class aims to challenge them to combine a dynamic of intragroup cooperation within the dyad, promoting knowledge convergence, and intergroup competition against other dyads (Romero et al., 2012), which aims to provide the 'conflict, competition, challenge and opposition' components of the game proposed by Prensky (2001, p. 106).

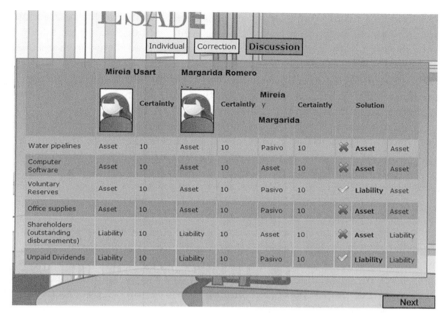

Fig. 6. Dyads Interdependent Decision on Assets and Liabilities.

In terms of game rules incentives for the intragroup dyads cooperation is related to the game assessment. The eFG assessment has been designed considering these two levels. The teacher could observe the individual answers of each of the students, and the overall individual performance. He could also observe the peer evaluation for each student's dyad. Finally, he could also observe the collaborative decision making of the dyad in relation with the previous individual and peer evaluation answers.

TECHNOLOGY SUPPORTING INTRAGROUP INTERDEPENDENCE

From the examples and research outlined herein, we can postulate the need to support intragroup interdependence. This should be achieved through the design of techniques aimed at increasing common knowledge and setting the context for students to share different kinds of information in multi-player GBL activities.

While face-to-face game activities present a natural field for interaction, in computer-mediated multi-player GBL, contextual cues diminish and less information about peers' characteristics is available (Kiesler, Siegel, & McGuire, 1984). Research results in CSCL demonstrate that awareness tools providing information about highly cooperative group members encourage participants to trust one another and minimise the risk of being exploited (Cress & Kimmerle, 2007).

Group Awareness (GA) is an important factor in collaborative online environments; it is defined as (Gutwin & Greenberg, 1995) the updated knowledge of our peers' activities which is required for each individual to coordinate and complete his part of a group task. GA could therefore allow groups to be more effective. For collaborative GBL, small widgets have been specifically designed in order to permit GA (Padrós, Romero, & Usart, 2011; Romero et al., 2011).

The lack of contextual cues in computer-mediated multi-player GBL is a challenge to develop sound GA of teammates' knowledge. Computer-mediated knowledge can be very ambiguous and students tend to mirror their level of knowledge with their peers' knowledge (Nickerson, 1999). These aspects could hamper common learning objectives. Knowledge Group Awareness (KGA) is a representation of peers' knowledge that co-learners build in order to create a shared understanding of a task, a state of being informed about partners' knowledge and sharing this state of being informed. There is a need for compensation cues that can give real information about the knowledge of other group members, thereby providing KGA. KGA tools can also provide feedback about peers' knowledge and provide new insights into both the influence processes of GA and the connection of these processes to specific personality traits with respect to contribution behaviour (Dehler, Bodemer, Buder, & Hesse, 2011). Feedback has a special role to play in effective game-based learning environments, and immediate feedback may be one of the central reasons for efficacy (Dunwell & de Freitas, 2011).

TECHNOLOGY SUPPORTING INTER-INDIVIDUAL AND INTERGROUP COMPETITION

Technology for enhancing the different kinds of awareness possibly involved in successful interactions in computer-mediated multi-player GBL should not be limited to intragroup communication. Awareness of other teams' performance in an intergroup competition environment must also be taken into account in the design and adaptation of SG. In contrast with collaboration tools, intergroup communication widgets are designed with the aim of promoting interaction with opponents, results and feedback, conflict situations including competition, challenge, opposition and conversation (Garris, Ahlers, & Driskell, 2002; Prensky, 2001; Zapusek et al., 2011). The outcomes related to the use of these tools are challenge, selection of an appropriate level of difficulty and better regulation of the probability of success or failure in competitive situations according to the players' competences (Vorderer et al., 2004).

A SG format in which these tools are typically used is races, where awareness of where other players or teams is important in order to know

Fig. 7. EnerCities Ranking.

our own possibilities of winning the game. Additionally, players in virtual world activities often have access to maps and can view the position of the other players. An example can be seen in the multi-player SG *EnerCities* (Fig. 7). This game was first developed for the web, but was ultimately deployed in *Facebook* so as to allow formation of a community of players who compete for the highest scores and share their experiences of the game. It has a scoring system that allows players to compare their scores and rankings with friends and build energy-saving cities.

PRACTITIONERS' RECOMMENDATIONS FOR INCREASING THE LEARNER ENGAGEMENT IN THE USE OF SG

The learners' experience in the use of SG involves a certain degree of engagement that could be promoted both in individual and multi-player games. The learner engagement in the individual activities observed through their real use of the game and their perceptions of the usefulness of the game and the time-on-task spent are mostly related to the flow experience (Csikszentmihalyi, 1991). The collaborative use of SG considers additional mechanisms of engagement related to the intragroup and inter-group relationships, such the degree of interdependence and the degree of competition in the game. Considering the importance of intragroup cooperation and the sense of belonging as one of the key factors of motivation and engagement in multi-player GBL (Bruffee, 1995; Hsu et al., 2009; Yee, 2006), game designers and educators using SG should consider this important mechanism to foster collaborative learning. These practice need to be analysed by researchers in order to better characterise the interdependence mechanisms in the different components of game mechanics, such as group composition, group organisation and role distribution, and the cooperative incentives of game rules. Further research into intragroup collaboration dynamics in SG must focus on design and implementation of tools that foster communication among teammates, both for synchronous and asynchronous scenarios. One aspect that should be taken into account is group history. It has been shown in studies that these are key elements for the solid evolution of a group of persons as a team in a process of team development. Distance between people and team development could be supported through interpersonal communication that promotes immediacy (Annetta, 2010). Therefore, tools designed for collaboration processes could help to improve learning outcomes in intragroup GBL scenarios. Multi-player games used with collaborative learning purposes can be externally regulated by a teacher, or could allow the player to a more self-regulated and co-regulated process during the game. Depending on the collaboration skills of the learners', the teacher should consider the level of external regulation more appropriate for the collaborative learning purposes. Game design should consider more collaborative and interdisciplinary design approaches (de Freitas & Jarvis, 2006) and iterative design approaches in order to further consider the intragroup and intergroup dynamics, the technological support of these dynamics and the analysis of the effective impact of these interdependent and competition dynamics in the learning process and outcomes.

REFERENCES

Annetta, L. A. (2010). The "I's" have it: A framework for serious educational game design. *Review of General Psychology, 14*(2), 105–112.

Azevedo, R. (2008). The role of self-regulation in learning about science with hypermedia. In D. Robinson & G. Schraw (Eds.), *Recent innovations in educational technology that facilitate student learning* (pp. 127–156). Charlotte, NC: Information Age Publishing.

Azevedo, R., Witherspoon, A., Graesser, A. McNamara, D., Chauncey, A., Siler, E., Cai, Z., Rus, V., & Lintean, M. (2009). MetaTutor: Analyzing self-regulated learning in a tutoring system for biology. In V. Dimitrova, R. Mizoguchi, B. du Boulay, & A. Graesser (Eds.) *Building learning systems that care: From knowledge representation to affective modeling* (pp. 635–637). Amsterdam, The Netherlands: IOS Press.

Barker, P. (2002). On being an online tutor. *Innovations in Education and Teaching International, 39*(1), 7–13.

Berliner, D. C. (1979). Tempus educare. In P. Peterson & H. Walber (Eds.), *Research on teaching: Concepts, findings, and implications*. Berkeley, CA: McCutchan Publishing Group.

Bluemink, J., Hämäläinen, R., Manninen, T., & Järvelä, S. (2010). Group-level analysis on multiplayer game collaboration: How do the individuals shape the group interaction? *Interactive Learning Environments, 18*(4), 365–383.

Bornstein, G. (2003). Intergroup conflict: Individual, group and collective interests. *Personality and Social Psychology Review, 7*(2), 129–145.

Bruffee, K. A. (1983). Teaching writing through collaboration. *New Directions for Teaching and Learning, 14*, 23–29.

Bruffee, K. (1995). Sharing our toys: Cooperative learning versus collaborative learning. *Change, 27*(1), 12–18.

Bulger, M. E., Mayer, R. E., Almeroth, K. C., & Blau, S. D. (2008). Measuring learner engagement in computer-equipped college classrooms. *Journal of Educational Multimedia and Hypermedia, 17*(2), 129–143.

Csikszentmihalyi, M. (1991). *Flow: The psychology of optimal experience*. New York, NY: Harper Collins.

Capdeferro, N., & Romero, M. (2012). Are online learners frustrated with collaborative learning experiences? *The International Review of Research in Open and Distance Learning, 13*(2), 26–44.

Coates, H. (2005). The value of student engagement for higher education quality assurance. *Quality in Higher Education, 11*(1), 25–36.

Cress, U., & Kimmerle, J. (2007). A theoretical framework of collaborative knowledge building with wikis – A systemic and cognitive perspective. Paper presented at the 7th International Computer Supported Collaborative Learning Conference, July 16–21, 2007, New Brunswick, NJ.

de Freitas, S., & Jarvis, S. (2006). A framework for developing serious games to meet learner needs. Paper presented at Interservice/Industry Training, Simulation and Education Conference, 2006, Orlando, FL.

Dewey, J. (1913). *Interest and effort in education.* Boston, MA: Riverside Press.

Dehler, Z. J., Bodemer, D., Buder, J., & Hesse, F. (2011). Partner knowledge awareness in knowledge communication: Learning by adapting to the partner. *Journal of Experimental Education, 79*(1), 102–125.

Dieleman, H., & Huisingh, D. (2006). Games by which to learn and teach about sustainable development: Exploring the relevance of games and experiential learning for sustainability. *Journal of Cleaner Production, 14,* 837–847.

Dillenbourg, P. (1999). What do you mean by collaborative learning? In P. Dillenbourg (Ed.), *Collaborative-learning: Cognitive and computational approaches* (pp. 1–19). Oxford: Elsevier.

Dubbels, B. R. (2010). Designing learning activities for sustained engagement: Four social learning theories coded and folded into principals for instructional design through phenomenological interview and discourse analysis. Discoveries in gaming research. In R. E. Ferdig (Ed.), *Discoveries in gaming and computer-mediated simulations: New interdisciplinary applications* (pp. 189–216). Hershey PA: IGI Global Publishers.

Dunwell, I., & de Freitas, S. (2011). Four-dimensional consideration of feedback in serious games. In S. de Freitas & P. Maharg (Eds.), *Digital games and learning* (pp. 42–62). London: Continuum Publishing.

Erev, I., Bornstein, G., & Galili, R. (1993). Constructive intergroup competition as a solution to the free rider problem: A field experiment. *Journal of Experimental Social Psychology, 29,* 463–478.

Fletcher, A. (2005). *Meaningful student involvement: Guide to students as partners in school change.* Olympia, WA: CommonAction.

Fredricks, J. A., Blumenfeld, P. C., & Paris, A. H. (2004). School engagement: Potential of the concept, state of the evidence. *Review of Educational Research, 74*(1), 59–109.

Garris, R., Ahlers, R., & Driskell, J. E. (2002). Games, motivation and learning. *Simulation & Gaming: An Interdisciplinary Journal of Theory, Practice and Research, 33*(4), 43–56.

Gee, J. P. (2003). *What video games have to teach us about learning and literacy* (1st ed.). New York, NY: Palgrave Macmillan.

Gee, J. P. (2007). *What video games have to teach us about learning and literacy* (2nd ed.). Cambridge, MA: New Riders.

Gockhale, A. (1995). Collaborative learning enhances critical thinking. *Journal of Technology Education, 7*(1). Retrieved from http://scholar.lib.vt.edu/ejournals/JTE/v7n1/gokhale.jte-v7n1.html. Accessed on October 2, 2012.

Gutwin, C., & Greenberg, S. (1995). *Support for group awareness in real time desktop confer- ences. Proceedings of the Second New Zealand Computer Science Research Students' Conference,* University of Waikato, Hamilton: New ZealandGame.

Hargreaves, D. H. (2004). *Personalising learning: Next steps in working laterally.* London: Specialist Schools Trust.

Holmes, J. (2006). *Gendered talk at work.* Oxford: Blackwell Publishing.

Hsu, S. H., Wen, M., & Wu, M. (2009). Exploring user experiences as predictors of MMORPG addiction. *Computers & Education, 53*(3), 990–999.

Johnson, R. T., & Johnson, D. W. (1986). Action research: Cooperative learning in the science classroom. *Science and Children, 24,* 31–32.

Jonassen, D. H. (Ed.). (1996). *Handbook of Research for Educational Communications and Technology.* New York, NY: Macmillan.

Jones, B., Valdez, G., Nowakowski, J., & Rasmussen, C. (1994). *Designing learning and tech- nology for educational reform.* Oak Brook, IL: North Central Regional Educational Laboratory.

Kiesler, S., Siegel, J., & McGuire, T. W. (1984). Social psychological aspects of computer- mediated communication. *American Psychologist, 39*(10), 1123–1134.

Kiili, K. (2005). Digital game-based learning: Towards an experiential gaming model. *Internet and Higher Education, 8*(1), 13–24.

Kiili, K., & Lainema, T. (2006). Evaluations of an experiential gaming model: The realgame case. In E. Pearson & P. Bohman (Eds.), *Proceedings of World Conference on Educa- tional Multimedia, Hypermedia and Telecommunications* (pp. 2343–2350). Chesapeake, VA: AACE.

Krause, K., & Coates, H. (2008). Students' engagement in first-year university. *Assessment and Evaluation in Higher Education, 33*(5), 493–505.

Kristensen, M. (2009). *Gendered talk in world of warcraft.* Thesis, Halmstad University, Halmstad.

Leemkuil, H., de Jong, T., de Hoog, R., & Christoph, N. (2003). KM quest: A collaborative internet based simulation game. *Simulation & Gaming, 34*(1), 89–111.

LeVine, R. A., & Campbell, D. T. (1972). *Ethnocentrism: Theories of conflict, ethnic attitudes and group behavior.* New York, NY: Wiley.

Lipponen, L., Rahikainen, M., Lallimo, J., & Hakkarainen, K. (2003). Patterns of participa- tion and discourse in elementary students' computer-supported collaborative learning. *Learning and Instruction, 13,* 487–509.

Moisant. (2005). *Course sans Gagnant.* Retrieved from http://www.patrickmoisan.net/copains/ course_sans_gagnant.html. Accessed on October 2, 2012.

Moreno-Ger, P., Burgos, D., Sierra, J. L., & Fernández-Manjón, B. (2008). Educational game design for online education. *Computers in Human Behavior, 24*(6), 2530–2540.

Nickerson, R. (1999). How we know — and sometimes misjudge — what others know: Imput- ing one's own knowledge to others. *Psychological Bulletin, 125*(6), 737–759.

Padrós, A., Romero, M., & Usart, M. (2011). Developing serious games: From face-to-face to a computer-based modality. *E-learning papers,* 25. Accessed on July 15, 2011.

Panitz, T. (1997). Collaborative versus cooperative learning: Comparing the two definitions helps understand the nature of interactive learning. *Cooperative Learning and College Teaching, 8*(2).

Pirius, L. K., & Creel, G. (2010). Reflections on play, pedagogy, and world of warcraft. *EDUCAUSE Quarterly, 33*(3).

Pivec, M., Dziabenko, O. & Schinnerl, I. (2003). Aspects of game-based learning. *Proceedings of I-KNOW '03*, Graz, Austria, pp. 217–224.

Pivec, M., Koskinen, T., & Tarín, L. (2011). Editorial. *eLearning Papers – Game-Based Learning: New Practices, New Classrooms, 25*(6).

Prensky, M. (2001). *Digital game-based learning*. New York, NY: McGraw-Hill.

Reading, C. (2008). Recognising and measuring engagement in ICT-rich learning environments. In *Australian Computers in Education Conference* (Vol. 1). Presented at the ACEC2008, Canberra.

Richardson, J., & Newby, T. (2004). Students' cognitive engagement in online learning environments: Learning strategies and motivations. In L. Cantoni & C. McLoughlin (Eds.), *Proceedings of World Conference on Educational Multimedia, Hypermedia and Telecommunications 2004* (pp. 4028–4033). Chesapeake, VA: AACE.

Romero, M. (2011, June 20). Supporting collaborative game based learning knowledge construction through the use of knowledge group awareness. NoE games and learning alliance. Lecture at the GaLa 1st Alignment School, Edinburgh.

Romero, M., Usart, M., Ott, M., Earp, J., de Freitas, S., & Arnab, S. (2012). Learning through playing for or against each other? Promoting collaborative learning in digital game based learning. *20th European Conference on Information Systems*, June 10–13, ESADE, Barcelona.

Romero, M., Usart, M., Popescu, M., & Boyle, E. (2012). Interdisciplinary an international adaption and personalization of the MetaVals Serious Games. *The Third International Conference on Serious Games Development and Applications SGDA 2012*, 26–29 September, University of Bremen, Germany.

Romero, M., Usart, M., & Almirall, E. (2011). Serious games in a finance course promoting the knowledge group awareness. *EDULEARN11 Proceedings*, 3490–3492.

Sherif, M., & Sherif, C. W. (1953). *Groups in harmony and tension: an integration of studies on intergroup relations*. New York, NY: Harper.

Usart, M., Romero, M., & Almirall, E. (2011). Impact of the feeling of knowledge explicitness in the learners' participation and performance in a collaborative game based learning activity. *Lecture Notes in Computer Science, 6944*, 23–35.

Vinson, D., Nixon, S., Walsh, B., Walker, C., Mitchell, E., & Zaitseva, E. (2010). Investigating the relationship between student engagement and transition. *Active Learning in Higher Education, 11*(2), 131–143.

Vorderer, P., Klimmt, C., & Ritterfield., U. (2004). Enjoyment: At the heart of media entertainment. *Communication Theory, 14*(4), 388–408.

Vorderer, P., Hartmann, T., & Klimmt, C. (2003). Explaining the enjoyment of playing video games: The role of competition. *International Conference Proceeding Series, 38*, 1–9.

Yee, N. (2006). Motivations of play in online games. *CyberpPsychology and Behavior, 9*, 772–775.

Whitton, N., & Hollins, P. (2008). Collaborative virtual gaming worlds in higher education. *Association for Learning Technology Journal, 16*(3), 221–229.

Zapusek, M., Cerar, S., & Rugelj, J. (2011). Serious computer games as instructional technology. MIPRO, 2011, *Proceedings of the 34th International Convention*, pp. 1056–1058, 23–27 May, Opatija, Croatia.

STRATEGIES FOR DESIGNING ENGAGING E-LEARNING INSTRUCTIONS: KNOW YOUR LEARNERS' NEED

Wei Lian Tan

ABSTRACT

E-learning has the potential to engage learners in ways that is not possible in a conventional classroom environment. Nevertheless, for this unique capability of e-learning to be optimised, a good understanding of learners' need as to what motivate them to be engaged in activities is paramount. This chapter suggests strategies for engaging learners in e-learning based on past empirical studies on computer games characteristics and an exploratory study on values influencing learners' decisions to engage in activities. The exploratory study in this chapter adopted qualitative research methods of Kelly Repertory grid and laddering interview based on the means-end chain (MEC) theory. Based on the exploratory study, value dimension was added to the existing literature. The value dimension of excitement, warm relationship with others *and* sense of accomplishment *were revealed as important to learners in their decision whether to engage in activities. Strategies for e-learning*

Increasing Student Engagement and Retention using Immersive Interfaces: Virtual Worlds, Gaming, and Simulation
Cutting-edge Technologies in Higher Education, Volume 6C, 35–63
ISSN: 2044-9968/doi:10.1108/S2044-9968(2012)000006C005

instructions that promote the revealed values were suggested with the aim of integrating the value dimension with the existing literature as well as proven teaching approaches.

INTRODUCTION

Advancement of computer, digital, multimedia, Internet and Web technologies is transforming teaching and learning in schools, colleges and universities. Advancement of these technologies had made it possible for teaching and learning to be done the *electronic* way, which is commonly referred to as e-learning. The term e-learning used in this chapter broadly refers to asynchronous and synchronous electronic learning that is supported by stand-alone or networked technologies, which include computer-based learning, Web-based learning, online learning, simulations, microworlds and educational games. The potential benefits of e-learning are promising. E-learning has the potential to promote effective learning by providing a more flexible platform for teaching and learning instructions to be customised according to learning styles, pace, and needs of learners (Hiltz & Benbunan-Fich, 1997). E-learning facilitates student-centred learning and collaborative learning anytime and anywhere (Beam & Cameron, 1998; Hiltz & Benbunan-Fich, 1997). Most appealing of all, the unique capabilities of e-learning provide an avenue for learning to be fun and enjoyable with the incorporation of the element of play (Rieber, 1996). However, the extent to which these benefits can be realised depends very much on the instructional design and the innovative use of the unique capabilities of technologies for learning. More often than not, the technology is emphasised more than the design and technology is used merely as a new platform to transfer knowledge the old way. The literature on the effectiveness of e-learning at its various forms is not conclusive and mixed (Ramage, 2002). Contrary to the positive outcomes expected of e-learning, e-learning failed to deliver what is expected of it, learners are often found to be as disinterested as if they were learning in conventional classroom environment and enthusiastic academics are beginning to lose faith in e-learning. Where did it go wrong? Many factors may have contributed to the undesirable outcomes but this chapter argued that one of the main issues lies in poorly designed e-learning instruction that failed to closely meet the needs and wants of learners, and thus failed to get students to be excited about learning, that is failed to motivate and engage learners. This chapter aims to address two issues that are pertinent to the design of engaging e-learning instruction:

1. What motivates learners to be engaged?

   In order to find out what actually motivates learners to be engaged, two critical issues in the author's view are whether we understand the needs of learners enough and what is the best engaging medium to be used to understand the learners. The second issue is not too difficult to address with most of our youngsters in the 21st Century highly attracted to and engaged with computer games. This chapter adopts the engaging elements of computer games as the medium for understanding learners' needs for engagement. In the attempt to understand what learners need to be motivated to be engaged, existing literature on what engaging computer games characteristics (mechanics, elements, and strategies) have informed instructional designers is reviewed. The first issue on whether we understand our learners' needs enough is consequently answered from the literature review. The author is of the view that existing literature does not provide adequate knowledge about what learners' needs to be engaged. Thus, based on what we already know about what learners need to be engaged in activities, an exploratory study is carried out to dig deeper into the personal values of learners. This value dimension of motivation is believed to have direct influence on learners' choice and decision whether to be engaged or not. The main aim of the study is to gain an in-depth understanding of the learners' values that motivated and engaged them by building on what we already know about learners' need (what motivates them). Essentially, the study initiated based on the notion that learners' personal values that influence their decision-making in making life choices, including whether to be engaged in a learning activity/process, enhance our understanding of what actually motivate learners to be engaged. Findings from the study on personal values of learners are integrated with what we presently know about learners' needs to gain in-depth understanding of what motivates them to engage.

2. What are appropriate strategies for designing engaging e-learning instructions based on what we know about what learners need?

   The second issue boiled down to the ability in transferring what we know about what learners want into practical strategies for engaging learners. Past researchers are agreeable on the benefits of integrating games elements in learning, strongly supported by behavioural, constructivist, cognitive learning, social learning and experiential learning theories.

Therefore, vast amount of works concentrated in the drawing up of instructional design strategies, framework and model appropriating knowledge learned from computer games in making learning more engaging. Among others are Dickey (2005) and Keller (1987). Dickey (2005) posed exploratory questions to provide operational guidance for instructional designers based on his examination on the trajectory of player positioning, the role of narrative and methods of interactive design of computer games. Keller in 1979 proposed the ACRS model based on expectancy-value theory that suggests strategies for identifying and solving motivational problems in instructional materials and methods (Keller, 1987, p. 3). Similarly, it is the aim of this chapter to recommend e-learning instructional design strategies that engage learners by focusing on the personal values of learners, which is more direct and accurately inform instructional designers of the needs and wants of learners.

Concisely, the author of this chapter feels strongly that one of the main reasons e-learning failed to realise its full potential is because of poor design of e-learning instruction that failed to incorporate effective strategies to engage learners. This is partly due to diffused and partial understanding of learners' wants and needs. Based on this notion, this chapter attempts to explore the personal values of learners through their experience in playing computer games with the aim of gaining insight into what truly attracts and engages learners, which is then translated meaningfully into strategies for designing engaging e-learning instruction. Specifically, this chapter is presented in three sections. The first section of the chapter discusses how engaging computer game elements had informed instructional designers on what motivates learners to be engaged. Still on the issue of understanding learners' needs, the second section describes a study conducted to explore the personal values of learners. Findings from the study are reported and discussed. The final section of the chapter concludes with recommendations of strategies for designing engaging e-learning instruction informed by past research and findings from this study.

WHAT MOTIVATES AND ENGAGES LEARNERS: TRANSFERRING KNOWLEDGE FROM COMPUTER GAMES DESIGN

Learning cannot take place without the presence of motivation to learn. Learners without the motivation to learn are very unlikely to be engaged in the learning process/activities. In other words, e-learning instructional design will not deliver the desired outcomes without careful consideration and incorporation of strategies for motivating and engaging learners. Motivation and engagement is commonly used interchangeably to mean the desire to do something. In this chapter, the term motivation is used in relation to engagement to refer to the willingness of learners to engage in an activity. Learners who are motivated are assumed to be more willing to engage in the learning process/activities.

As computer game playing evolved as one of the most engaging activities among youngsters in the 21st century, researchers begin to wonder what made those games so captivating and how instructional designers could transfer and harness the powerful ability of computer games in the teaching and learning context. A group of researchers such as Malone (1981), Dickey (2005) and Prensky (2002) just to name a few, had long recognised the great value of captivating and engaging commercial computer game design for instructional design that made it worth investigating. Thus, a large number of works were done in the examination of popular computer game designs, methods, mechanics, devices and strategies that had successfully captured and retained game player engagement. The findings were mixed and over-lapped in many cases. Early examinations of popular commercial computer games had contributed the engaging experience of computer game playing to the game design characteristics that provide clear goals, reinforcing feedback, sensory stimuli, and a non-threatening environment, (Cordova & Lepper, 1996; Lepper & Chabay, 1985; Rieber, 1991; Thurman, 1993). The discussion by the community of researchers then has hovered around externally administered reinforcement that provides extrinsic support and motivation to game players. The interest on examining the intrinsic motivational elements of computer games was initiated by Malone (1980, 1981) that investigated the computer game preferences of youngsters. Malone's (1981) study highlighted challenge, fantasy, and curiosity as a framework for intrinsically motivating instruction. His works are further developed to include the aspects of control, as well as the interpersonal motivations of cooperation, competition, and recognition (Malone & Lepper, 1987). Garris, Ahlers, and Driskell (2002) had neatly categorised the engaging computer game characteristics into six dimensions or categories, namely fantasy, rules/goals, sensory stimuli, challenge, mystery and control, that pulled most of the past research findings together. More recent studies have specifically examined successful game design strategies adopted by commercial computer games in engaging game players such as the point of view (POV), the role of narrative, methods of interactive design and player character engagement in commercial computer games (Dickey, 2005; Lanskoki, 2011). Based on the review of the literature, most of the studies looked at the game characteristics that make the game

Table 1.   Dimensions of Motivation in Computer Game.

Game Characteristics	Motivating Effect of Computer Games	Related Research
Goals, uncertain outcomes, performance feedback, rules, optimal level of difficulty, setting, action and resource hooks (choices), tactical and strategic hooks, time hooks	Challenges	Dickey (2005); Lepper (1985); Lepper and Chabay (1985); Malone (1980, 1981); Malone and Lepper (1987); Thurman (1993) As cited by Garris et al. (2002): Driskell and Dwyer (1984); Ricci, Salas and Cannon-Bowers (1996); Schloss, Wisniewski, and Cartwright (1988); Lepper, Woolverton, Mumme, and Gurtner (1993); Elliot and Harackiewicz (1994); Whitehall and McDonald (1993)
Visual and audio sensory stimuli	Sensory curiosity	Lepper (1985); Malone (1980, 1981); Malone and Lepper (1987); Thurman (1993) As cited by Garris et al. (2002): Hereford and Winn (1994); Rieber (1991); Surber and Leeder (1988); Wishart (1990)
Optimal level of informational complexity, paradoxes, and incompleteness	Cognitive curiosity	Malone (1980, 1981); Malone and Lepper (1987); Thurman (1993) As cited by Garris et al. (2002): Day (1982); Lepper (1985); Loewenstein (1994); Terrell (1990)
Imaginary or fantasy context, themes or characters, first person point of view (POV), branching stories, settings (physical, temporal, environment and emotional dimensions), roles and characters shift	Fantasy	Malone (1980, 1981); Malone and Lepper (1987); Dickey (2005); Cordova and Lepper (1996) As cited by Garris et al. (2002): Driskell and Dwyer (1984); Parker and Lepper (1992)
Active role and control, contingency (responsive learning environment), choices, power to influence, first person point of view (POV), roles and characters, choices, actions, feedback and affordances	Control	Cordova & Lepper (1996); Dickey (2005); Malone and Lepper (1987) As cited by Garris et al. (2002): Hannafin and Sullivan (1996); Kinzie, Sullivan, and Berdel (1988); Reigeluth and Schwartz (1989); Simons (1993); Steinberg (1989); Wishart (1990)

Table 1. (*Continued*)

Game Characteristics	Motivating Effect Relevant for Instructional Design	Related Research
Segmenting activities into interdependent parts, activities require the cooperation with others to progress	Cooperation	Malone and Lepper (1987)
Activities enlist the motivation to compete with others, and competitors' action affect each other	Competition	Malone and Lepper (1987)
Efforts are rewarded by social recognition	Recognition	Malone and Lepper (1987)
Role-playing, non-player character (NPC)	Affiliation with others	Dickey (2005)

fun and engaging with the exception of Malone's (1981, 1987) and Malone and Lepper (1987) that looked into what the motivating effect of computer games. Findings on both of the dimensions are useful for e-learning instructional design and are summarised in Table 1 by integrating Garris et al.'s (2002) six dimensions of game characteristics and Malone and Lepper's (1987) taxonomy of motivational instructional environment.

Researchers had also often attributed the engaging gameplay behaviour to the 'flow' experience propounded by Csikszentmihalyi (1975/2000). The state of flow is achieved in a condition where one is challenged at the appropriate level of one's capacities with clear goals and feedback. Clear goals with instant and unambiguous feedback give players a sense of control and satisfaction in accomplishing an activity at the moment before a subjective state of advancement unfolds (Nakamura & Csikszentmihalyi, 2002). Being in the flow experience resulted in full and focused concentration to the task at the moment that provides an intrinsically rewarding experience. Behaviour of computer game players that showed high motivation and engagement was attributed to the ability of the computer game design to bring players into the state of flow. The concept of the state of flow was confirmed across activities and the flow experience was reported to be similar across lines of culture, class, gender, and age (Nakamura & Csikszentmihalyi, 2002).

Previous works on learner motivation and engagement in computer game design focused mainly on game characteristics (including the game design, mechanics, and strategies) and the motivating effect of the characteristics. While this body of knowledge has meaningfully informed instructional designers on 'what' will motivate learners, it does not address the issue of 'why' these game characteristics motivate game players. Based on the Means-End Theory (Gutman, 1982), it is argued that engaging computer game characteristics researched widely in past research are the *attributes* and the motivating effects of the game characteristics are *consequences*. However, neither attributes nor consequences uncovered in past research explained the underlying reasons as to why they are important, which is referred to in the means-ends theory as *personal values*. An understanding of the rationale underlying the motivating effect of game characteristics, that is the personal value, is argued to be salient for at least two reasons. First, it enhances knowledge about learner needs by an in-depth and direct understanding as to why the attributes or consequences are important to them. Second, the personal values uncovered are more direct needs of learners and thus are more useful to be transferred and applied in e-learning instructional design. The association of attributes, consequences, and values based on the means-end theory are further explained in the next section that describes a study carried out with the aim of understanding the learners better.

UNDERSTANDING LEARNERS' MOTIVATION AND ENGAGEMENT

Values and Motivation from Means-End Theory's Perspective

Rokeach (1973, p. 5) defined values (personal values) as '... an enduring belief that a specific mode of conduct or end state of existence is personally or socially preferable to alternative modes of conducts or end states of existence'. In a simpler form, values are beliefs that people hold that represent their final desired state of existence and these values influence their choices in life, for example whether to consume a product or whether to be engaged in an activity. According to the means-end theory (Gutman, 1982, p. 60), means are objects (products) or activities in which people engage (running or reading) while ends are valued states of being such as happiness, security, and accomplishment. An understanding of the means does not explain the reasons that have motivated a person to engage in an activity. The reasons behind the motivation to engage in an activity are explained by an understanding of the ends, that is the valued states of being. For example, merely knowing that the game characteristic of a

Massively Multiplayer Online Game (MMOG) is desirable because they allow interactions between game players does not provide an in-depth understanding of the players' motivation and engagement unless we know that the MMOG feature fulfilled players' personal needs such as to have warm relationships with others or have a sense of accomplishment (being able to work in teams to win a battle in the game). The rationale for uncovering game players' personal values in the effort to gain in-depth understanding of players' motivation echoed Veludo-de-Oliveira, Ikeda and Campomar's (2006, p. 629) view that it is not the activities' attributes that matter in understanding motives and needs, but the problem solution coming from consequences or subsequent personal values.

Linking Play to Learning

The study to be described in the following section aims to uncover the personal values of learners using a highly engaging entertainment medium, that is a computer game, the question that arises is the relevance of social values uncovered from an entertainment medium to learning in a formal education setting. Although many have reported the effectiveness of computer game characteristics and strategies to teaching and learning contexts, the issue on the validity of transferring motivation in play to formal education is still debated due to the common perceptions that separate play/fun from work/learning. Rieber (1996) described play as voluntary activities that involve some active engagement and are intrinsically motivated in nature with a make-believe quality. In the attempt to link play to learning, Rieber et al. (1998) illustrated the similarities of behaviour between two children at play (building a shopping mall with Legos) and two graphic artists at work (learning a new 3-D graphics application for use on a project). Both of the groups, at play or at work, were highly engaged, engrossed and voluntarily committed great amounts of time and energy to their task at hand despite failure and frustration. Both of the groups learned and had fun. The author argue in that both of the groups gained similar ultimate end states of being (values), that is satisfaction and sense of accomplishment too, whether at play or at work.

THE STUDY

The purpose of this study is to explore the personal values of undergraduate business students that have engaged them in computer game playing.

Based on the argument in the previous section that motivation in playing and learning are somehow very similar, the aim of this study is to understand learner's need better by adding a value dimension to the existing body of knowledge on how computer games have informed instructional designs. This is an exploratory study at its very preliminary stage and the findings are not meant to be generalised to larger applications until studies that are more robust are carried out to confirm the dimension's validity, reliability, and application across gender, age, and cultures. Nevertheless, in this chapter, the author will use the findings of this study to shed more light on learner's needs for designing engaging e-learning instructional strategies. It is the intention of the author in the near future to strengthen the study by conducting more rigorous and extensive study and incorporate the findings of this study and the recommended strategies into interventions to measure the validity and reliability of the dimension in different context, situation and discipline.

Method

This study adopted a qualitative research method using the Kelly Repertory Grid followed by the laddering interview technique based on means-end theory. In this study, the MEC model is used to 'peel further the layers' of the game players' experience in computer game playing. This method is deemed most appropriate in uncovering the personal values of the game players because, as Hetcher (1993) had established in his work, individuals lack a complete awareness of what their values are or what they mean to them. In other words, the participants may not be fully aware of what captivated them to be highly engaged in computer games but the MEC model that was developed with the intention to elicit personal values helped to uncover them.

The Kelly Repertory Grid was used as a tool in this study to explore the constructs people used as a basis for making choices according to their preferences. In this study, the undergraduate business students' constructs, that is computer game characteristics used as a basis for making choices of their preferred computer games, were explored. Bipolar constructs of similarity were identified and compared with 'triadic sort' that revealed the game characteristics of computer games that are organised hierarchically in terms of importance. The game characteristics revealed from the Kelly Repertory Grid exercise were used as a basis for the laddering interview. Laddering is a technique used in interviews that was reported as useful in studies of human behaviour and in investigating personal values (Kahle & Kennedy, 1989, p. 5; Veludo-de-Oliveira, Ikeda & Campomar, 2006, p. 626). Originating from the clinical psychology discipline, laddering refers to an in-depth, one-to-one interviewing technique used to model the concepts and beliefs of people. Laddering involved probing further into the direct needs of participants by asking a series of probing question, typified by the question 'Why is that important to you?' (Reynolds & Gutman, 1988). The process is carried out with the goal of establishing sets of linkages between attributes (A), consequences (C), and values (V). The Lynn Kahle (1983)'s List of Values (LOV) is used in the laddering interview as a key measurement instrument due to its general applications across many disciplines and activities. The Lynn Kahle's LOV comprised of nine key terminal values (Kahle & Kennedy, 1989, p. 7). The description provided by Kahle and Kennedy (1989) was in the context of American consumer behaviour but was adapted for the purpose of this study to the context of undergraduate students. For the purpose of this study, the key values were operationally defined in the context of undergraduate students as below:

i. *Sense of Belonging* — A social value resulted in a feeling that one was part of a social group or community such that one was not perceived as different from the crowd.
ii. *Warm Relationships with Others* — A social value resulted in a feeling that one was endorsed and accepted by others for interactions, sharing, and caring. To have warm relationships with others was closely related to having a sense of belonging but distinct in the sense that it was a social value at a more personal level.
iii. *Excitement* — A personal value that resulted in one feeling thrilled, interested, and curious, wondering what would come next.
iv. *Fun and Enjoyment in Life* — A personal value that involved the appreciation of life. Life was perceived to be enjoyable and fun. The element of relaxation was an important element here.
v. *Self-fulfilment* — A personal value resulted in a feeling of satisfaction upon meeting personal goals and standards set out at an initial stage.
vi. *Sense of accomplishment* — A personal value resulted in a feeling of achievement upon attainment of rewards or ability to successfully complete a task.
vii. *Being well respected* — A social value that related to the need to be acknowledged and looked up to by others.
viii. *Security* — This includes economic and psychological security of feeling safe and secure from economic instability and psychological threats.

ix. *Self-respect* — A personal value on how one sees oneself in terms of self-confidence and self-worth.

Participants

There were a total of nine participants who volunteered to participate in this study based on purposeful sampling. Out of nine participants interviewed, the laddering technique was successfully applied to eight. There is only one female out of the eight participants. All participants are undergraduate business students aged between 18 and 19 years old. They are avid computer game players, spending between 4 to 11 hours per day in playing computer games. All participants are Malaysian-Chinese studying in a private university where English is the main medium of instruction. English is their second language.

Procedures

The Kelly Repertory Grid exercise and laddering interview were carried out in English. The participants were requested to list any six computer games that they were playing. The type of computer games were not confined to any specific genre, as any engaging features of the computer games genre were of interest for exploration in this study. Participants were then asked to choose any three computer games listed and to figure out the game characteristics of the two computer games (of the three chosen) that were similar yet different from the third. The game characteristic was then described with a word/term/phrase. The opposite of the word/term/phrase was identified. Participants were asked to repeat the same exercise three times generating three different features of computer game characteristics, each paired with the contrasting opposite. Interviews using the laddering technique were conducted based on all game characteristics revealed from the Kelly Repertory Grid exercise carried out with the participants. Participants were asked why the game characteristics revealed from the Kelly Repertory Grid exercise were important to them. The laddering interview reached saturation at the ninth participant. Due to the linguistic limitations of participants, the use of dialects (participants first language) for some terms/phrases were allowed, which were then translated to English by the author. All interviews were also video recorded for reference purposes. The Lynn Kahle (1983)'s List of Values was used in the laddering interviews to reach the terminating values.

Data Analysis

Descriptive data collected from the laddering interviews were analysed and interpreted based on Reynolds and Gutman's (1988) and Gengler and Reynolds' (1955) steps for laddering interview content analysis. The steps are integrated and summarised below:

1. Data reduction (data conversion into separated phrases).
2. Content-analyse all of the elements from the ladders.
3. Record the entire set of ladders across respondents on a separate coding form, resulting in a table of linkages from attributes to values.
4. Develop a set of summary codes for all elements elicited.
5. Summation of relations in content codes, resulting in an implication matrix of all paired relationships,
6. Construction of a Hierarchical Value Map (HVM) to meaningfully represent the main implications of the study.

Extra care was exercised in the interpretation of the laddering interview data as well as in the content analysis of data due to the linguistic limitations of the participants as well as the author.

FINDINGS

From the eight successful interviews, attributes that most appealed to participants and that motivated and engaged them in computer games playing were identified in the form of computer game design features. Accordingly, the consequences (external and internal personal effect) of the attributes on the participants were uncovered and finally the underlying values of participants were revealed. The result of the Kelly Repertory Grid method used in this study identified five computer game design features (attributes) deemed most important in participants' choice of computer games. The features identified were strategy game element, multiplayer game, storyline, and graphic display. The laddering interviews that explored deeper and revealed the underlying value for the preferred features uncovered the values of 'warm relationship with others', 'excitement', 'self-accomplishment', and 'fun and

Table 2.   Summary of Codes for Engagement in Computer Games.

Code	Attributes/Game Characteristics	Code	Consequences	Code	Terminal Values
A01	Strategy games	C05	Winning	V16	Excitement
A02	Multiplayer games	C06	Interacting with others	V17	Sense of accomplishment
A03	Storyline of the games	C07	Strategising	V18	Warm relationships with others
A04	Graphic display	C08	Interesting	V19	Fun and enjoyment in life
		C9	Unpredictability		
		C10	Immersion in the virtual world		
		C11	Competing		
		C12	Curiosity		
		C13	Teaming		
		C14	Challenging		
		C15	Powerful		

Notes: A01–A04, attributes; C05–C12, consequences; V13–V16, terminal values.

enjoyment in life' as the underlying values that had engaged participants in computer game playing.

Based on the data reduction and coding exercise, an implication matrix was generated based on the frequency of occurrence of the linkages between the attributes, consequences and terminal values. Table 2 shows the summary of codes for engagement in computer game playing.

The main implications of the study are displayed in an HVM as shown in Fig. 1.

FINDINGS AND DISCUSSION

Kelly repertory grid exercise of the study revealed multiplayer feature as the most desirable computer game characteristic followed by strategy game feature, storyline and graphic display. In-depth laddering interview that prompted participants' rationale for finding these game characteristics highly desirable led to the discovery of participants' personal values fulfilled from computer games playing. *Excitement* was revealed as the most important value satisfied from computer games playing followed by two equally important values, that is *warm relationship with others* and *sense of*

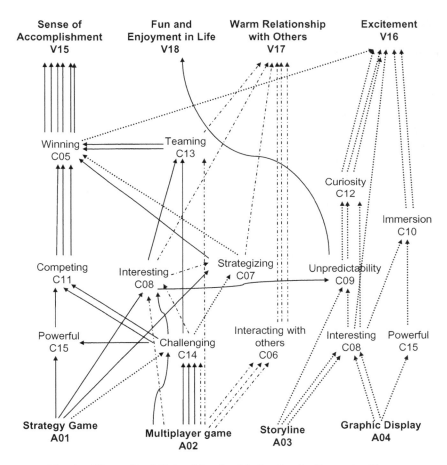

Fig. 1. Hierarchical Value Map for Motivation in Computer Game.

accomplishment. The findings of the study are discussed in this section complemented with richer description from the interviews.

EXCITEMENT

Excitement was the most sought after end value by game players, without which there is little motivation for them to engage in game playing. Almost all game characteristics mentioned by participants were found linked to the personal value of excitement except the multiplayer feature. A closer analysis of the threads and linkages is summarised in the HVM in Fig. 1 (threads of linkages using →) revealed further that most apparent consequences that gave rise to excitement were the opportunity to strategise and win a game as in a battle or a mission. Other game characteristics (consequences) that were also found to lead to excitement were the elements of *interesting, curiosity, unpredictability* and *immersion*. Attributes (game characteristics) that contributed to these consequences were strategy game design, storyline and graphic display.

Excitement was defined in the *Merriam-Webster's Learner's Dictionary* as 'a state of being excited, a feeling of eager enthusiasm and interest'. For the purpose of this study, the term was operationally described as 'a personal value that resulted in one feeling thrilled, interested, and curious, wondering what would come next'. Within the context of computer game playing, the ability of the game design to create interest out of curiosity and unpredictability was paramount.

This was found in this study to be due to the storyline or the graphic display of the game and this was validated in the interviews with the comments below:

Comment 1:
'The story (in the game) was unpredictable and you keep on imagining the ending of the story. That made you curious and you keep on playing to uncover the ending'.
Comment 2:
'No one likes to play a computer game with dull graphics anymore. It's so boring. I prefer 3D graphics but a 2½ graphic display is good enough for me'.

Malone and Lepper (1987) referred to this curiosity as sensory and cognitive curiosity. According to them, the sensory curiosity could be enhanced by variability in audio and visual effects while cognitive curiosity may be prompted by instructional techniques that cause learners to be surprised and intrigued paradoxes, incompleteness or potential simplifications (pp. 248–249). This may pose a challenge to game players due to uncertainty of outcomes as suggested by Malone and Lepper (1987). Uncertainty of outcomes was suggested by Malone and Lepper (1987) to be produced using variable difficult goals, multiple levels of goals, selectively revealed hidden information and randomness (pp. 248–249).

The ability of the game to create immersion in the virtual world was also commented on by participants as one of the attracting elements that excites them in game playing. This was influenced by the 3D graphic design as commented on below:

Comment 1:
'In a 2D graphic environment, I feel restricted and not real but in a 3D graphic environment the game world was more real to me as I didn't feel restricted like in a game box'.
Comment 2:
'The graphic display was so nice and beautiful that I fell in love with the (virtual) world and I wanted to own the beautiful and mystical items in the world'.

This can be loosely mapped to Malone and Lepper's (1987) elements of emotional fantasy (p. 249) that involve fantasies that appealed to the emotional needs of learners.

The aspect of excitement that was commented on by participants from the interview as the most important consequence but was not apparent in Malone and Lepper's (1987) taxonomy is the opportunities to strategise and win a battle/game. Participants directly attributed these consequences to the strategy game design that required game players to understand their own and the opponents' weaknesses and strengths as well as the environment to determine the best strategy to win a battle/game. This element of the game was not apparent in Malone and Lepper's (1987)'s taxonomy but could be seen indirectly from the elements of goals and self-esteem. This study thus shed more lights into the understanding of what excites game players (learners). The participants also revealed in the interview, as in the comment below, one important aspect of games that drove them to continue to play:

'The longer you play, the smarter you become because you have more experience and you know the game, the environment, and your opponents better. That made you smarter in predicting (your opponents' move) and strategizing to win'.

WARM RELATIONSHIP WITH OTHERS

The social need of having warm relationships with others was found to be equally important for game players. It was the second most frequently mentioned personal value fulfilled through computer game playing. The multiplayer design feature of computer games is the sole attribute to this effect.

A closer analysis of the threads and linkages is summarised in the HVM in Fig. 1 (threads of linkages using) uncovered that this social value was ful- filled in computer game playing when game players interact among them- selves (within as well as outside the game environment), team up to analyse and strategise to win, or exchange items and information in the game to win the game. This is reflected in some of participants' comments below:

Comment 1:
'The games become our common topic of communication and we become closer just because we play games. I had more friends because of the games and I became more sociable'.
Comment 2:
'We know our friends better from computer game playing'.
Comment 3:
'I feel great when we manage to team up and win in the game. The cohesiveness we built and the feeling of comradeship that we shared were great'.

The value of having warm relationships with others matches closely with Malone and Leppers's (1987) interpersonal motivations of coopera- tion, competition, and recognition. This value was operationally described in this study as a social value resulting in feeling that one was endorsed and accepted by others for interactions, sharing and caring. This value was identified by participants as a crucial value achieved through the ability of the evolving game design such as MMOG to connect people in the most natural setting. In the game, they cooperate by exchanging information, items and strategies to win the game, building the cohesiveness and com- radeship that may not be possible out of the game. The connection and build of the game seem to also flow out of the game, creating a feeling of social acceptance and increasing the opportunities for interactions (com- mon topic of discussion). The aspect of social recognition was not clear (not frequently mentioned) in the study but was rightly pointed out by Malone and Lepper (1987) as one of the aspects of motivation where a participant did make the comment below:

'If I get the rare item that is very difficult to obtain, I will feel very good and proud because I am the only one who has it. There is only one on the whole server'.
'If I am ranked higher than the other players, I feel good because only a smart person can get to the highest rank. That means I am the best among the others'.

SENSE OF ACCOMPLISHMENT

Sense of accomplishment was ranked third in the line of value sought by game players. The two design features attributed to this terminal value are the strategy game element and multiplayer element. A closer analysis of the threads and linkages is summarised in the HVM in Fig. 1 (threads of linkages using →) revealed further that this personal value is fulfilled from the game characteristics that allowed game players to team up and strategise to win the game. The consequences aroused from these attributes were identified by participants to be the opportunity to win together as a team, interact with others, strategise with others and have fun from doing all of these. The value of sense of accomplishment was operationally described for the purpose of this study as a personal value resulting in a feeling of achievement upon the attainment of rewards or the ability to successfully complete a task. This aspect was not specifically discussed in Malone and Lepper's (1987) taxonomy but somehow related to the interpersonal motivations. This study found that game players' sense of accomplishment was obtained in a social context in active interaction and cooperation with others. This is clearly expressed by comments such as:

Comment 1:
'We have friends in the game that play specific roles of the game. We know our roles and will take appropriate actions as a team to win a clash (war) in the game. When we managed to win the war together, we feel we have achieved something great'.
Comment 2:
'To win alone is satisfying and fun. To win after fighting with a team of friends is more satisfying'.

To summarise, the findings of this study showed that the three main personal values sought by game players who are also learners are excitement, warm relationships with others and a sense of accomplishment. These personal values are the primary, direct and most basic needs of learners accordingly fulfilled from computer games playing. Computer games design provides the opportunity for learners to build a community with shared and common concern as well as to collaborate to achieve goals in the game. The game characteristics revealed from this study have also offers learners excitement stems from unpredictability and curiosity stimuli. The ability of computer games to immerse participants into imaginary worlds through audio, visual, social, emotional, as well as cognitive stimuli fulfilled participants' need for fantasy.

LIMITATIONS OF THE STUDY

As this is an exploratory study at a very preliminary stage, there are limitations as outlined below:

1. A small number of participants interviewed and the absence of other studies to confirm the findings means that the value dimension identified from the study cannot be generalised and used for larger applications.
2. All participants in this study are vivid computer games players spending 4–11 hours of gameplay a day. Therefore, the findings of this study may not apply to learners who have little interest in computer playing.
3. There is evidence that there is a difference in preferences between male and female computer game players. The participants are mainly male with only one female. Therefore, the findings may be biased towards the preferences of male participants.

STRATEGIES FOR DESIGNING ENGAGING E-LEARNING INSTRUCTIONS: INTEGRATING THE VALUE DIMENSION TO THE EXISTING BODY OF KNOWLEDGE

E-learning will never deliver what was expected of it if it is merely about the hype of advance technologies. Most critical in any effective e-learning instruction is the motivation and engagement of learners (Dickey, 2005; Keller, 1987; Malone, 1981; Malone & Lepper, 1987). E-learning, supported by powerful technologies, has unique capabilities to engage learners in ways that is not possible in a conventional classroom environment. Many engaging strategies and activities not doable in classroom environments can be easily and effectively executed in e-learning environments.

This book chapter aims to suggest strategies for designing engaging e-learning instructions based on better understanding of learners needs. This is achieved with the integration of the dimension of value (from the study described) into the existing dimensions of game characteristics and motivating effect of game summarised in Table 1 of this chapter in the previous section (Garris et al., 2002; Malone 1981, Malone & Lepper, 1987). The three dimensions of motivation of computer game are summarised in Table 3. Note that terms deduced from the study were in *italic*. Built on

Table 3.   The Value Dimensions of Motivation in Computer Game.

Game Characteristics Dimension	Motivating Effect Dimension	Value Dimension
Goals, uncertain outcomes, performance feedback, rules, optimal level of difficulty, setting, action and resource hooks (choices), tactical and strategic hooks, time hooks, *strategy game*	Challenges, *strategising*	*Sense of accomplishment, excitement*
Visual and audio sensory stimuli, *3D graphic*	Sensory curiosity, *curiosity*	*Excitement*
Optimal level of informational complexity, paradoxes and incompleteness	Cognitive curiosity, *unpredictability*	*Excitement*
Imaginary or fantasy context, themes, or characters, first person POV, narrative arc, branching stories, settings (physical, temporal, environment and emotional dimensions), roles and characters shift, *interesting and unpredictable storyline*	Fantasy, *immersion,*	*Excitement*
Active role and control, contingency (responsive learning environment), choices, power to influence, first person POV, roles and characters, choices, actions and affordances	Control, *powerful*	*Sense of accomplishment*
Segmenting activities into interdependent parts, activities requires the cooperation with others to progress, *multiplayer*	Cooperation, *teaming*	*Warm relationship with others, fun and enjoyment in life*
Activities enlist the motivation to compete with others, and competitors' action affect each other, *multiplayer*	Competition, *competing, winning*	*Warm relationship with others, sense of accomplishment*
Effort are rewarded by social recognition, *multiplayer*	Recognition	*Warm relationship with others, sense of accomplishment*
Role-playing, NPC, *multiplayer*	Affiliation with others, *interacting with others*	*Warm relationship with others, fun and enjoyment in life*

NPC, non-player character.

the existing body of knowledge about game characteristics that motivates learners, the concept of flow (Csikszentmihalyi, 1975/2000) and the new insights from the exploratory study described in this chapter, effective engaging e-learning strategies are crafted and described in this section.

The discussion of the recommendation of strategies will be structured based on the value of learners, that is the value of *excitement, warm relationship with others, sense of accomplishment* and *enjoyment of life.* These values are recommended to be integrated into pedagogically proven teaching approaches such as case studies, problem-based learning and project-based learning. The e-learning instructional strategies suggested are strategies that aim at fulfilling values of learners, which is deemed important by learners in deciding what activities/process to engage voluntarily, without externally administered enforcement. It is crucial to note that the values are not independent of each other but are closely related. Thus, some of the strategies recommended may overlaps across the values to reflect the inter-relationship of the values.

EXCITEMENT

Excitement was operationally defined in the study as 'a personal value that resulted in one feeling thrilled, interested, and curious, wondering what would come next'. Based on the findings of the study, learners' need for excitement is fulfilled with the consequences of interesting, powerful, curiosity, unpredictability and immersion. These motivating effects were found to be stimulated by the game characteristics of graphic and storyline game. Strategies and technology supports for creating opportunities for learners to fulfil the value of *excitement* in the effort to engage them in the learning process in an e-learning environment are listed below:

I. *Variability of visual and audio effect.* This involves the display of content, information, feedback and any other relevant interventions in the learning process with visual and audio sensory stimuli that appeal to learners. Malone (1980, 1981) and Malone and Lepper (1987) termed this type of curiosity as sensory curiosity that can be enhanced by introducing variability of the stimuli in activities that promote interactive exchange with learners. Strategies in a typical e-learning environment that supports this strategy are:
   a. Use of video cases to set the scenario or backdrop for discussion and analysis of cases/problem.
   b. Use of real life interviews (video or audio) or multimedia presentation for introduction of new information.
   c. Use of social media platforms such as the Facebook, Blogs and Skype for interaction and learning. These platforms appeals to learners because they provide attractive visual outlook and support audio effect.

    d. Use of multimedia effect to provide feedback on learners' progress and achievements. For example, Flash multimedia effect in short clips can be released into using a web-based or networked e-learning platform to provide feedback to learners in a more attractive manner. This strategy is most effective after learners had accomplished a task in groups as they will be more excited to find out how they have fared in an a more interesting manner.

II. *Provide paradoxes, incomplete or potential simplifications of information.* According to Malone and Lepper (1987, p. 249), cognitive curiosity may be promoted by instructional techniques that cause learners to be surprised and intrigued by paradoxes, incompleteness or potential simplifications based on topics that learners is already interested.

    a. Feeding of new information intermittently throughout the group project provides the element of unpredictability and it surprises learners as well as challenges learners' ability to respond to the new information (Csikszentmihalyi, 1975/2000). E-learning platform that allow the new information to be programmed and released at appropriate level of learners' progress will be ideal. Learning Activities Management System (LAMS) is an example of e-learning platform that support such feature.

    b. Ill-structured problem is posed to learners in a problem-based learning environment, which stimulate cognitive curiosity of learners. Data and information (in text and multimedia forms) is scattered within any e-learning platform such as Blackboard, Moodles or LAMS under different folders representing real life sources of information such as the library, news archive, the board room, the coffee shop gossips, etc. The incomplete and sometimes conflicting information given to the learners stimulate learners' curiosity to find out the main issue by gathering the bits and pieces from the e-learning platform and matched them together as in a jigsaw puzzle.

III. *Use of storyline/story branching.* Design a series of activities along a storyline that unfolds as students accomplished tasks assigned, made a decision or take actions. This strategy is most appropriate in a case study learning or project-based learning approach where students' action and decision will be rewarded with consequences presented in the form of story, be it in narrative or rich multimedia format. This feature is supported by LAMS sequencing.

IV. *Assign roles to create the effect of immersion.* Assigning roles to learners and shifting learners' positioning to first person Point of View (POV) gives learners a sense of immersion in the problem/case's world (in the case of using problem-based learning or case study learning approaches) that creates more engaging experience to learners (Dickey, 2005). Strategies in the e-learning environment that supports this strategy are:

a. Design projects or activities with *multiple roles* and learners are put into the shoe of the roles so that they will see from the point of view of the role given. In an e-learning environment, the element of immersion can be created with animated characters (Flash or any other animation software) attached with profile of the role.

b. Technologies in an e-learning environment also allow the creation of *virtual environments* that mimic closely the real world. The problem/case becomes real when learners gain access to real people (such as experts, suspects, managers, etc.), environment (such as the coffee shop, the library, the office, etc.) and real documents (company policies statement, complaint report, marketing reports, etc.). In an e-learning environment, the databases of information can be stored into folders that are titled using common terms used in the real world, which is then retrieved by learners to learn about the issue of the problem/case. Simple technology such as e-mail or instant messenger can be used to enable learners to communicate with mock characters (such as director, scientist or employees) to create a sense of reality.

WARM RELATIONSHIP WITH OTHERS

Warm Relationship with others was operationally defined in the study as 'a social value resulted in a feeling that one was endorsed and accepted by others for interactions, sharing, and caring. To have warm relationships with others was closely related to having a sense of belonging but distinct in the sense that it was a social value at a more personal level'. Based on the findings of the study, learners' need for warm relationship with others is fulfilled when they have the opportunity to communicate, share and work together. The opportunity for learners to team up and compete with others is also found to be an essential element for this value to be satisfied. Strategies and technology supports for creating opportunities for learners to fulfil the value of *warm relationship with others* in the effort to engage learners in the learning process in an e-learning environment are listed below:

I. *Provide a platform for interaction, discussion and exchange of ideas.* Learning Management Systems (LMSs) such as Blackboard and Moodle support synchronous and asynchronous collaborative learning. Features such as discussion forum and chat room provide a platform for learners to interact, exchange information and collaborate online without constrains of time and distance.

II. *Design activities that require learners to cooperate to achieve goals.* Borrowing from the jigsaw puzzle approach to cooperative learning, the e-learning activity can be designed with the feature of restricted access by each group member to information that reside in the database depending on the role they play. This will force learners in the same group to work closely with each other to make sense of the issue/problem. A careful design of LAMS sequence may allow the strategy.

III. *Design activities that require learners to compete with other groups to achieve goals.* While learners have to work together as a group, a competitive environment among groups will provide a sense of urgency and need for good decision making and action. Endogenous competitive environment in which competitors' actions affect each other will also create the need to strategise.

IV. *Create an environment where learners are required to strategise whether to cooperate or compete with other groups to achieve set goals.* The activities are designed for groups to cooperate as well as to compete, depending on the strengths of the groups and the strategy they decide to adopt.

SENSE OF ACCOMPLISHMENT

Sense of accomplishment was operationally defined in the study as 'a personal value resulted in a feeling of achievement upon attainment of rewards or ability to successfully complete a task'. Based on the finding of the study, learners' sense of accomplishment is optimally fulfilled when they are actively interacting and cooperating with others to compete with others to win and achieve desired goals. Strategies and technologies support for creating opportunities for learners to fulfil the value of *sense of accomplishment* in the effort to engage them in the learning process in an e-learning environment are listed below:

I. *Clear progressive milestones that lead to the achievement of the achievement of final goal.* Set clear goals to be achieved by groups in a competitive environment. Both milestones and final goal are essential to retain learners' motivation. Milestones are short term, small achievements that groups compete to achieve throughout the process/activity period. The achievement of these milestones affects the achievement of the final goal.

II. *Real time and instant feedback.* Real time progress tracking and feedback enabled by most LMSs will also provide a sense of accomplishment each time learners take an action as they can measure their success or failure instantly. A progress dashboard reflecting students' progress as well as other groups' progress will keep students momentum going. This will not only create excitement but a sense of accomplishment upon completion of the whole process.

III. *Recognition of individual and group achievement.* Frequent recognition is essential to retain the momentum of effort of learners in the activity. In an e-learning environment, advance technologies allow 'cut scenes' to be built into the system to provide event triggered release of animation, slides or any form of recognition for the achievement of milestones throughout the process/activity. The ability of technologies to provide real time feedback displayed in a dashboard that can be viewed by all groups will also provide learners the sense of accomplishment of their groups' efforts.

CONCLUSION

As mentioned at the beginning of this chapter, e-learning's potential benefits will not ever be optimally actualised if it is merely about another technology solution to conventional teaching and learning model. It cannot be overemphasised here that the need to weave together the underlying pedagogies of learning and technologies through careful instructional design is paramount for effective e-learning. The focus of this chapter is the element of motivation and engagement, which is one of the biggest challenges in any instructional design, regardless whether it is in a face-to-face learning or e-learning. However, e-learning has advantages over the conventional classroom learning. E-learning that is supported by technologies has unique capabilities to motivate and engage learners in ways that is not possible in a conventional classroom environment. The challenge is in understanding what learners' need to be motivated and optimise the unique capabilities of technologies to meet the learners' need. This requires careful design of e-learning instructions that emphasise on strategies to engage learners in the learning process/activities. This chapter attempted to address these issues by crafting strategies for engaging e-learning instructions based on learners' value that are integrated into pedagogically proven teaching and learning approaches of problem-based learning, case teaching and project-based learning. However, the effectiveness of these strategies is yet to be proven. More robust studies on the learners' value and the strategies as interventions will have to be carried out to establish a more structured framework for practical applications.

REFERENCES

Beam, P., & Cameron, B. (1998). But what did we learn...? Evaluating online learning as process. In *Proceedings on the sixteenth annual international conference on computer documentation*, September 24–26, Quebec, Canada, pp. 258–264. Retrieved from http://delivery. acm.org/10.1145/300000/296391/p258-beam.pdf?ip = 203.176.151.253&acc = ACTIVE% 20SERVICE&CFID = 128190961&CFTOKEN = 79450663&__acm__ = 1350434085_ f064e78bb95cdb56e26d81c39a72.

Csikszentmihalyi, M. (2000). *Beyond boredom and anxiety.* San Francisco, CA: Jossey-Bass (Original work published 1975).

Cordova, D. I., & Lepper, M. R. (1996). Intrinsic motivation and the process of learning: Beneficial effects of contextualization, personalization, and choice. *Journal of Educational Psychology, 88,* 715–730. doi: 10.1037/0022-0663.88.4.715

Dickey, M. D. (2005). Engaging by design: How engagement strategies in popular computer and video games can inform instructional design. *Educational Technology, Research and Development, 53*(2), 67. Retrieved from http://www.jstor.org/stable/30220429?seq = 1

Garris, R., Ahlers, R., & Driskell, J. E. (2002). Games, motivation, and learning: A research and practice model. *Simulation & Gaming, 33,* 441. Retrieved from http://scottsdale. brainadvantage.com/PDF/Games,%20Motivation,%20and%20Learning.pdf

Gengler, C. E., & Reynolds, T. (1995). Consumer understanding and advertising strategic translation of laddering data. *Journal of Advertising Research, 35*(4), 19–32.

Gutman, J. (1982). A means-end chain model based on consumer categorization processes. *Journal of Marketing, 46*(2), 60–72. Retrieved from http://www.jstor.org/stable/ 10.2307/3203341

Hechter, M. (1993). Values research in the social and behavioural sciences. In M. Hechter, L. Nadel & R. Michod (Eds.), *The origin of values* (pp. 1–28). New York, NY: Aldine De Gruyter.

Hiltz, S. R., & Benbunan-Fich, R. (1997, April 28). Supporting collaborative learning in asynchronous learning networks: Software engineering or symbolic interactionism [online].

Invited Keynote Address for the UNESCO/ Open University Symposium on Virtual Learning Environments and the Role of the Teacher, Milton Keynes, England. Retrieved from http://web.njit.edu/~hiltz/

Kahle, L. (1983). *Social values and social change: Adaptation to life in America.* New York, NY: Praeger Publishers.

Kahle, L. R., & Kennedy, P. (1989). Using the list of values (LOV) to understand consumers. *Journal of Consumer Marketing, 6*(3), 1–11. doi: 10.1108/EUM000000002549

Keller, J. M. (1987). Development and use of the ACRS model of instructional design. *Journal of Instructional Development, 10*(3), 2–10. Retrieved from http://www.jstor.org/stable/10.2307/30221294

Lanskoski, P. (2011). Player character engagement in computer games. *Games and Culture, 6*(4), 291–311. doi: 10.1177/1555412010391088.

Lepper, M. R., & Chabay, R. (1985). Intrinsic motivation and instruction: Conflicting views on the role of motivational processes in computer-based education. *Educational Psychologist, 20*(4), 217–230.

Malone, T. W. (1980). *What makes things fun to learn? A study of intrinsically motivating computer games.* Palo Alto, CA: Xerox. Retrieved from http://delivery.acm.org/10.1145/810000/802839/p162-malone.pdf?ip=203.176.151.253&acc=ACTIVE%20SERVICE&CFID=102880121&CFTOKEN=87788540&_acm_=1336994432_869da907f1aa2997 28f25dc76f7b7872

Malone, T. W. (1981). Toward a theory of intrinsically motivating instruction. *Cognitive Science, 4*, 333–369. Retrieved from http://www.coulthard.com/library/Files/malone_1981_towardtheoryintrinsicallymotivatinginstruction.pdf

Malone, T. W., & Lepper, M. R. (1987). Making learning fun: A taxonomy of intrinsic motivations for learning. *Aptitude Learning and Instructions, 3*(3), 223–253. Retrieved from http://tecfa.unige.ch/~szilas/nestor/ressources/motivation_malone.pdf

Nakamura, J., & Csikszentmihalyi, M. (2002). The concept of flow. In C. R. Snyder & S. J. Lopez (Eds.), *Handbook of positive psychology* (pp. 89–105). Oxford, UK: Oxford University Press. Retrieved from http://teachingpsychology.files.wordpress.com/2012/02/the-concept-of-flow.pdf.

Prensky, M. (2002). The motivation of gameplay or, the REAL 21st century learning revolution. On The Horizon, *10*(1). Retrieved from http://www.marcprensky.com/writing/prensky%20-%20the%20motivation%20of%20gameplay-oth%2010-1.pdf.

Ramage, T. R. (2002). *The "no significant difference" phenomenon: A literature review.* Dr. Thomas R. Ramage Publications. Paper No. 1. Retrieved from http://spark.parkland.edu/cgi/viewcontent.cgi?article=1000&context=ramage_pubs

Reynolds, T. J., & Gutman, J. (1988). Laddering theory, method, analysis, and interpretation. *Journal of Advertising Research,* (February/March), pp. 11–31. Retrieved from http://www.uta.edu/faculty/richarme/MARK%205338/Reynolds%20and%20Gutman%20laddering%20article.pdf

Rieber, L. P. (1996). Seriously considering play: Designing interactive learning environments based on the blending of microworlds, simulations, and games. *Educational Technology Research and Development, 44*(2), 43–58. Retrieved from http://www.jstor.org/stable/pdfplus/30221022.pdf?acceptTC=true

Rieber, L. P., Smith, L., & Noah, D. (1998). The value of serious play. *Educational Technology, 38*(6), 29–37. Retrieved from http://www.coe.uga.edu/~lrieber/valueofplay.html

Rokeach, M. (1973). *The nature of human values.* New York, NY: The Free Press.

Thurman, R. (1993). Instructional simulation from a cognitive psychology viewpoint. *Educational Technology Research & Development, 41*(4), 75–89. doi: 10.1007/BF02297513

Veludo-de-Oliveira, T. M., Ikeda, A. A., & Campomar, M. C. (2006). Discussing laddering application by the means-end chain theory. *The Qualitative Report, 11*(4), 626–642. Retrieved from http://www.nova.edu/ssss/QR/QR11-4/veludo.pdf

PART II
APPLICATION OF IMMERSIVE
INTERFACES: VIRTUAL WORLDS,
GAMING, AND SIMULATION

GAME MECHANICS FOR CLASSROOM ENGAGEMENT

Stayc DuBravac

ABSTRACT

Gamification, the integration of game mechanics to influence behavior and engagement, is a much-touted method of improving participant action. Characteristics of online video games (e.g., World of Warcraft, Farmville, The Sims) have been shown to improve motivation, sustain learner engagement, and increase satisfaction. Gamification is used in websites, businesses, medicine, law enforcement, and increasingly in education. However, gamification is only beneficial to an activity if the relationship between the activity and the final goal are understood. This chapter looks at the gamification in education, in particular second language acquisition, and examines seven basic game mechanics: achievement, appointment, rewards, leaderboards, privacy, social engagement loops (or viral mechanics), and modifiers. The discussion describes implementation of game mechanics and potential pitfalls of gamification.

Increasing Student Engagement and Retention using Immersive Interfaces: Virtual Worlds, Gaming, and Simulation

Cutting-edge Technologies in Higher Education, Volume 6C, 67–94
ISSN: 2044-9968/doi:10.1108/S2044-9968(2012)000006C006

INTRODUCTION

Congratulations! You have just unlocked the "gamification badge" for beginning this chapter! An increasing number of websites, businesses, and social networking hubs are using cutting-edge technologies and game mechanics to increase loyalty and productivity. The field of education has also increasingly investigated the value of integrating game mechanics (Gee, 2003) and a number of areas in education are using game mechanics to engage their students (Dignan, 2011). Gamification is the integration of game mechanics into normal activities in order to influence participant behavior and engagement. The infusion of game mechanics into existing systems has been shown to motivate individuals to attain personal goals, solve communal problems, and direct systemic activity (Hobson, 2001; McGonigal, 2011; Reeves & Read, 2009). The integration of game mechanics into language classes can enable a holistic view of how emerging technologies can contribute to overall learner engagement. Technologies such as social bookmarking, photosharing, online language labs, blogs, wikis, vodcasts and podcasts, twitter, forums, and ePortfolios are incapable of engaging users simply because of their novelty − in fact, they are no longer novel for many of today's students. Rather it is the *use* and *function* of these technologies that engages learners because they explore, achieve, and socialize within an environment where they can earn and display important accomplishments.

This chapter examines how characteristics of online video games (e.g., World of Warcraft, Farmville, The Sims, Sorority Life) can be incorporated into classes in order to improve motivation, sustain learner engagement and increase satisfaction. Since the early 1980s, computers have increasingly been implemented to engage learners in virtual worlds, games, and simulations. The task for educators is not to create a new game − there are thousands of game design companies that have attempted this and failed − but rather to incorporate game mechanics into the core content. The key questions that educators must answer first and foremost is: What is my core content? What is good learner behavior? What are the projected outcomes for my course?

In order to portray an accurate example of how game mechanics can facilitate learner engagement, this chapter traces the history of research approaches to emerging technologies and examines some key elements in Activity Theory that contribute to language acquisition. The bulk of the chapter focuses on specific game mechanics and how their integration contributes to education in terms of increasing loyalty, motivation, and satisfaction.

SETTING THE STAGE: EMERGING TECHNOLOGIES, APPROACHES, AND ROUTES TO ACCEPTANCE

Virtual worlds, games, and simulations, though significantly studied from a variety of perspectives are still in their nascent stage and can be considered emerging technologies. Over the years, emerging technologies have demonstrated a consistent pattern of how they are investigated. While gamification is not necessarily an emerging technology per se, it is certainly an emerging *concept* as far as educator familiarity and implementation. Hence, it makes sense to describe a short history of Computer assisted-language learning (CALL) research and how emerging technologies have and will continue to be investigated in regards to the field of second language acquisition (SLA).

Levy (2007) argues that a researcher's goal differs according to whether the technology is established or emerging. Krathwohl (2004) presents four approaches to research that align with four stages of investigation: acceptance, evaluation, application, integration. During the initial stage, SLA researchers investigated emerging technologies in a somewhat explorative manner. Professors assumed that the use of computers was beneficial to learning and the academy simply needed to explore the possibilities. We assumed the new technologies were better; we just needed to promote the possibilities and identify shifts in attitude that facilitated their uses. Most of the studies done during this time were pilot studies or investigations of attitudes and perceptions about using computers (e.g., Beauvois, 1994; Osuna & Meskill, 1997).

After using computers for several years, researchers began to look at the potential benefits of and drawbacks to the tool in question. These studies generally compared computer-mediated communication and face-to-face discussions (e.g., Pelletieri, 2000, Warschauer, 1996) or online glosses and in-book glosses (e.g., Lyman-Hager & DuBravac, 1996). These types of comparisons make less sense as emerging technologies become established technologies. For example, comparing digital glosses to print glosses is not useful since a significant number of traditional college-age students read online anyway and they're glossing or Googling unknown words by themselves (Rainie & Fox, 2012). In other words, the technologies exist in a context and current research tends to focus more on the context of use rather than forcing the comparison of non-competing phenomena.

The next phase of research (scholarly or otherwise) tends toward anecdotal accounts of how instructors integrate the technology in courses (i.e., what can one do with emerging technologies to learn the language using computers). These accounts describe experiences with the emerging technology and depict successes and failures with their application in the classroom setting (e.g., Lan, Sung, & Chang, 2007; Parks, Huot, Hamers, & H.-Lemonnier, 2003).

When computers became commonplace both in and out of the classroom, studies investigated SLA through the use of the emerging technology, rather than investigating the emerging technology in the context of SLA (Table1). Studies of this nature tend to look at how SLA occurs while students are engaged with the new technology (e.g., Dooly, 2011; Kessler, Bikowski, & Boggs, 2012).

One of the issues with the developmental stages of investigation mentioned above is that the presentation is much cleaner than the actual practice because of two important variables: the researcher and the technology. Two different researchers are never at the same level of familiarization so

Table 1. Approaches to Researching Emerging Technologies.

	Approach	Type of Research	Examples
Stage 1	Acceptance and exploration of what can be done using the technology	Attitude and perception studies	Osuna and Meskill (1997). Examined attitudes toward using the web to learn Spanish language/culture.
Stage 2	Evaluation old and new methods of instruction	Comparative studies	Biesenbach-Lucas and Weasenforth (2001) compared email and word-processed texts.
Stage 3	Application and discussion successes and failures	Anecdotal studies of how technologies are applied in a context	Parks et al. (2003) investigated what teachers did in networked classrooms equipped with laptop computers.
Stage 4	Integration and investigation of how and why tools are beneficial	Studies on SLA phenomena and the use of tools	Kessler et al. (2012) looked at collaborative writing techniques using google docs.

even while there are trends in the field overall, the approach that one researcher may take may be further along the continuum than what another may take simply because of his or her experience with the technology. For example, many instructors have been using digital video for many years (e.g., French in Action had online videos in the 1990s), while others are just exploring digital video twenty years later (e.g, mainly with Youtube, Teachertube, or video sharing). Different experiences lead researchers to take different approaches to investigating the uses of emerging technology.

Similarly, some types of technology may take a while to emerge while others may move quickly into the mainstream. The rate of emergence influences how quickly research in a given technology moves toward the last stage of investigation mentioned above. For example, speech recognition software began in the 1930s and developed through some significant advancements in the 1980s. However, it has yet to find a prominent acceptance and use in language instruction; it remains an emerging technology for many instructors. Email was welcomed much more quickly. Email found wide-spread acceptance in the late 1980s and within a decade email was no longer considered new technology. Other forms of technology have moved even more quickly from *emerging* to *accepted*. Blogs, for example, began in the early 2000s (Livejournal.com and Blogger.com both launched in late 1999). Blogs and bloggers moved into the mainstream within two years and today a number of teachers us blogs to disseminate information (DuBravac, 2012).

The rate which new technologies are accepted varies from technology to technology, but the path to acceptance has been relatively predictable and is depicted by Gartner's *hype cycle* (2011). The hype cycle has five stages beginning with the technology trigger and progressing to the plateau of productivity. The first stage, the *technology trigger* denotes the discovery of the technology. As users discover new technologies, the excitement about the potential of the technologies inevitably creates unrealistic expectations for its use. The second stage is called the *peak of inflated expectations* or the height of the hype cycle. As users implement the emerging technology on a larger scale, they realize that potential does not match their initial projections which lead to the third stage of the hype cycle: *the trough of disillusionment*. Eventually, those using the technology begin to work with the new technology in ways that solve some problematic issues while identifying the most beneficial uses for the technology. This fourth stage of progression is called *the slope of enlightenment*. Finally, the emerging technology is no longer new and is eventually adopted by a majority of users as it enters the *plateau of productivity*.

Gartner's (2011) hype cycle indicates that gamification is reaching the peak of inflated expectations. Many in business, gaming, and website design are investing significant time and energy to gamify their products and the applications are impressive. Prize linked savings (PLS) accounts, for example, offer lower interest rate but the possibility of receiving cash prizes for their investments. This "no-lose lottery" dubbed "save-to-win" has received support in a number of states (e.g., Michigan, Nebraska) and countries (e.g., United Kingdom, South Africa) (Dubner, 2012). San Francisco installed a Speed Camera Lottery device to encourage safe driving (Schultz, 2010). The camera took pictures of all drivers passing beneath it. Fines levied against the offenders would be pooled to provide a cash prize. The winner of the prize would be randomly drawn from the group of speed-adherents. Finally, video games have been used as a substitute for drugs in burn victims. Maani et al. (2008) describe how a virtual reality video game where soldiers throw snowballs is so engaging that it acts as a "nonpharmacologic analgesic" (p. 193). The instances mentioned above are excellent examples of how the integration of game mechanics into a system has increased engagement. One South African bank indicates that they opened about 500,000 bank accounts for individuals who had never had a bank account in a span of about 6 months by offering PLS accounts. (Dubner, 2012). Over a three-day test period, the speed camera lottery reduced average speeds from 32 km/hour to 25 km/hour even though no fines were levied. Soldiers indicated that "pain unpleasantness" ratings dropped from severe (7/10) to none (0/10) while playing video games.

For the most part, organizations are currently in a phase of exploration to determine how much can be gamified and how effective gamification is in the short and long term. Gamification of education can only occur effectively once designers have determined which learner behaviors contribute to learning and which learner behaviors detract from learning. These behaviors can then be incentivized or discouraged through the design of the system in which the participants operate. Without a clear idea of how languages are learned or which learner behaviors actually increase acquisition among language learners, gamification only leads to sporadic reward system. This type of disconnected reward system at best gets students through the system but may actually confuse them or de-motivate them (Pink, 2009) in the long run. The intended goal of gamification must be clear before initiating the process.

A THEORETICAL FOUNDATION AND SOME PRINCIPLES OF SLA

The Vygostkian (1978) version of sociocultural theory (SCT) provides a solid foundation for an investigation in gamification and SLA. In fact, SCT lends itself to both the study and the teaching of a second language (L2) in ways unavailable from other theoretical perspectives (e.g., interactionist, cognitivist, linguistic). The main advantage to SCT is that it "offers a framework through which cognition can be systematically investigated without isolating it from the social context" (Lantolf & Thorne, 2006, p. 1). There are two important characteristics of SCT in regard to Computer-Assisted Language Learning (CALL). First, it perceives tools (e.g., language, computers) as mediational means and considers how these tools fundamentally change the way humans think. Rather than examine how tools facilitate tasks, SCT, through the lens of activity theory, investigates how tools actually transform tasks. Second, SCT emphasizes the need for social learning. Where interactionist and cognitivist perspectives analyze individual progress manifested by performance, socioculturalist approaches focus on developmental potential observed in interactions with other speakers that occur within the zone of proximal development, or ZPD. The ZPD is simply a theoretical construct that describes the distance between the development level as determined by independent problem solving skills (i.e., no help or guidance) and potential development level as determined by what learners can do in collaboration with more capable peers.

SCT has a significant following in studies of SLA and there are a number of points to consider in SCT (e.g., private speech, microgenesis, mediation, activity theory) but this chapter focuses on the interplay of gamification and activity theory. Activity theory is not a *theory* per se, that is, it does not strive to predict behaviors. Rather, it offers a set of descriptive principles upon which other theories can rely as it attempts to explain why and how humans and organizations accomplish tasks. Activity theory posits five main principles: object-orientedness, hierarchical structure, internalization/externalization, development, and mediation (Kaptelinin, 1996). At the risk of oversimplifying relatively complex conceptualizations of human consciousness and social activity, these terms are defined below.

- Object-oriented means that human activity is goal driven. There may be any number of reasons or goals that second language learners have such as to speak to friends, to write messages, to meet friends, or to impress the instructor. These goals help to determine which actions they must take along the way to accomplish them.

- Hierarchal structure relates to the fact that language acquisition is sequential (i.e., there are steps that come first and steps that come last). In the same way that humans operationalize goals as short-term, mid-term, and long-term, language learners must speak first in discrete words, then phrases and sentences.
- Internalization/externalization refers to the feedback loop that enables both receptive understanding and productive abilities. For SLA to be efficient there must be a feedback loop. The acquisition process for most learners entails hearing, understanding, creating with the language, monitoring comprehension, identifying miscomprehension, and reformulating, negotiate, and repairing meaning. In short, the a feedback loop helps students recognize that their current language is simultaneously insufficient but improving.
- Development refers to the progression that one perceives as he or she acquires a second language. As one gains proficiency in a language, it not only becomes easier to *speak*, but it also gets easier to *learn* the language. The development of language skills improves the efficiency of language learning. Progression also includes social progression. For example, those who speak a second language are more likely to accommodate or understand those non-natives who speak poorly.
- Mediation refers to how learners use tools. Mediation is a key concept in SCT and is critical in the implementation of game mechanics, particularly for procedural engagement. Mediation means that individuals use things (private speech, dictionaries, etc.) to facilitate tasks. For example, sometimes students speak to themselves (to practice the language), sometimes they peek at the answers, and sometimes they request help or clarification. They variety of available tools is endless and extends beyond the purview of this chapter.

Activity theory also makes a very strong case for a task-based teaching methodology, which lends itself nicely to gamification since tasks are at the heart of most games. We assume then, that students learn best when they are performing tasks in the language. There has been some important research on these concepts in SLA (particularly in mediation) but for most of the concepts, the research is still in its nascent stage.

On the other hand, the financial importance of online gaming has led to significant study on how game mechanics influence engagement, motivation, and learning processes. This process of introducing game mechanics into a system is called gamification. Even though gamification is currently at the height of the hype cycle (and thus has more-than-realistic expectation for most), many of these practices have become mainstream for online services. For example, foursquare.com allows users to sign up and visit real-world locations in order to win points, gain reputation, and possibly become mayor of that location (e.g., my local Starbucks, the pool, a local bar). The user's mobile device tracks their location and enables him or her to "check-in" as they visit participating locations. Users can receive badges, awards, and discounts according to the frequency and consistency of their check-ins. Another site, groupon.com, gives discounts only if enough people sign up for it (calling on the viral nature of online gaming). LinkedIn.com lets users know which tasks to complete next and what friends are doing through a status bar and continuous updates. Increasingly more services are incorporating some game mechanics to augment engagement. However, because gamification is not well understood, it is often reduced to the most familiar characteristics.

Gamification is more than earning points, winning badges, or gaining reputation. Gamification implies the use of game mechanics to guide participant behavior toward autonomy, mastery, and purpose. Pink (2009) argues that these three concepts lead to increased engagement, more efficient improvement, and higher achievement. There are well over 100 different game mechanics and this chapter will not address all of them. The game mechanics discussed in this chapter are achievements (e.g., points, badges), appointments, questing or fixed ratio and combo rewards, leaderboards, privacy, social engagement, and modifiers.

Achievement

Achievement is the most recognizable game mechanic in many online games. Players move up levels, gain badges, or earn points. For most foreign language classrooms, achievement has traditionally been the grade that students get on their homework, tests, or participation; however, unlike popular online games, grades do not give any information about progression, only past performance. Popular online games like World of Warcraft, Cityville, or Tetris use the technique of achievement very well. In World of Warcraft, for example, you work your character up to a level-20 Paladin by earning experience points through actions performed in the game. In Tetris, the best-selling game of all time (Dredge, 2011), players progress from level 1 to level 35, for example, (the game does not have an end level), and their level is constantly displayed for them to monitor their progress. Farmville awards achievements with ribbons; websites like four-square.com gives badges; Points, levels, and badges are the primary methods used to help players assess their performance in the game. For many academic subjects, even if students are aware of their performance, they are often unsure of their level. For example, in a French or Italian class, students know what level they are by what course they registered for: French 101, Italian 203. The problematic issue with the course indicating the level-status of the student is that the rewards are few and far between. The standard practice in online gaming is to make the first several levels easy to accomplish. Rapid advancement has the tendency to engage the player more readily. A rapid succession of rewards is called a *boost* and tends to produce intense engagement for short periods of time and increase loyalty. A series of boosts at the beginning of a game is a technique called "onboarding" and Zynga's Farmville serves as the model on how to do this. Farmville begins with a farmer in an empty field with a dialogue box tutorial. The tutorial teaches players how to harvest, plow, and plant crops by telling the player exactly where to click and showing the results of each click. Before completing the tutorial most players have reached level 3 or 4. This rapid acquisition of points or badges tends to encourage players to stay in a game to either explore the possibilities, complete the collection of awards that they began in the onboarding experience, or simply not lose what they have already acquired.

In gaming systems, one or all of three different types of points might exist: XP (experience) points, skill points, or reputation points (Kim, 2011). XP points come from participation and generally lead to level advancement. Generally players cannot lose XP points. Farmville, for example, uses XP points and coins. XP points cannot be spent, lost, sold, or traded. XP points help show the amount of engagement a player has had in a given game, because they are method of showing progress toward the next level (e.g., "200 more points to level 55! Plant crops now!"). They do not indicate skill or any major accomplishments but they may be an indicator of how long a player has played a game or how much money a player has spent on a game. They are particularly useful for personality types that need to explore and they tend to encourage procedural engagement (i.e., actively doing tasks) but may not encourage substantive engagement (i.e., interaction with the material). In Farmville, the ability to plant certain crops, buy certain farm implements, or open new territories is dependent on reaching a certain number of XP points (called a level-requirement). XP points are good at rewarding behaviorally beneficial actions. Importantly, XP points never max out; once the player reaches the next level, the XP points start all over again providing endless game play. While XP points do not figure prominently in education, professors may often grade homework as XP points; if students completed the homework they get the points, regardless of the correctness of the homework. Sadly, however, these individual homework assignment points flaunt many of the principles of game mechanics: players tend to lose points rather than gain points, there is often no relationship between points and level advancement, and points normally max out for each assignment – a trifecta that can easily lead students to feel like the homework is...pointless.

Skill or score points come from interacting with the system in specific ways. Unlike XP points, score points can go up and down (e.g., players often lose skill points when they die in a game). Skill point help to portray rank in a certain system compared to other players or compared with previous accomplishments. Foursquare.com unlocks badges for participation (an XP points system) such as checking in at five different locations, but they also offer mayorships for the highest tally of check-ins at a location. Mayors can be ousted if someone else checks in more than they do and then the ousted player will no longer have access to their discount at the location. Unlike XP points that are rewarded for desired behavior, skill points are rewarded for mastery of the activity or game. Skill points tend to encourage substantive engagement more than XP points do. Professors often treat tests or projects as skill points; students must achieve a certain level in order to receive all the points.

Influence points (often called rank or reputation) differ from XP and scores because they do not originate from interaction with the system but rather from the actions of other players. StackOverflow.com is a good example of this type of system. Individuals post and answer questions and these postings are rated by other participants. A user's reputation is derived from how much help they provide to others in both quantity and quality. Their reputation depends solely on the actions of other players voting for or against them. As users give good answers or rephrase questions to help gain better answers, their rating/reputation increases.

It would be unrealistic, and quite overwhelming, to include all three of these point systems in education, but which should we choose? Point systems in games serve the following important purposes:

- As an onboarding technique to help players understand the rules and routines of the game and to guide appropriate behavior in the game.
- As a self-assessment instrument to enable players to gauge their improvement.

- As a device to encourage competition among players
- As a method of encouraging peer evaluation and cooperation among participants.
- As a motivational tool for those who wish to explore

As in games, points in education could help class management, motivate students, encourage self-assessment, and inspire competition and cooperation. A few simple practices might help the novice instructor/game-designer. First, count up the points and not down. Many students believe that they start the semester with an A (the default grade) and work their way down to a B or C (Roosevelt, 2009). Video games make it clear that their players are moving forward (sometimes even if all they do is log in). McGonigal (2011) makes the argument that we are optimized for productivity and this sense of moving forward or producing things is incredibly rewarding to the human psyche. In fact, the building aspect may be one reason why Farmville, Tetris, and other building games tend to have longer lives and more participants than destruction games such as Doom or Bejeweled Blitz. Counting up points is easier said than done since many students see the starting point in their courses as 100%. The instructor's task is to reinforce from the beginning through continuous feedback to the student that points are going up and failure to participate means a stagnant D and not a falling A.

Second, and more importantly, instructors should offer status indicators (badges/awards) to students at clear intervals. Very few systems in education give clear indicators of a student's level in regard to his or her overall development. One tool for language learners, Linguafolio online (http://www.linguafolio.uoregon.edu), provides an excellent example of what could be done to enable students to monitor their own progress. Students login and track their progression through "can do" statements (e.g., "I can greet someone," "I can order food in a café") and they can see their progression in status bars on the welcome page (Fig. 1). The solid green bar indicates achieved mastery where all tasks are completed without help. The bubble bar indicates tasks that are completed with help or tasks that have been identified as goals. The clear bar indicates areas that learners have not investigated.

This type of point system enables students to see where they are, what they are working on, and clearly identifies their language achievements in an XP-like system. The achievement game dynamics included in LinguaFolio encourages engagement by enabling learns to have autonomy, strive for mastery and maintain purpose. Learners have autonomy because they can

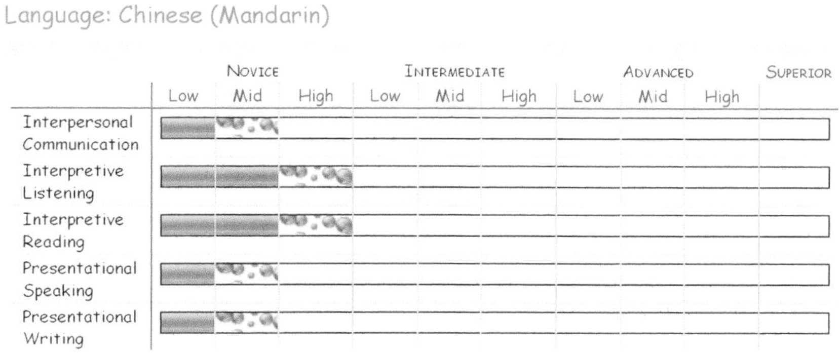

Language: Chinese (Mandarin)

	NOVICE			INTERMEDIATE			ADVANCED			SUPERIOR
	Low	Mid	High	Low	Mid	High	Low	Mid	High	
Interpersonal Communication										
Interpretive Listening										
Interpretive Reading										
Presentational Speaking										
Presentational Writing										

Fig. 1. LinguaFolio Passport: Description of Competencies.
Source: Retrieved from http://www.linguafolio.uoregon.edu/learner/passport.

decide which "can do" statements they want to work on. The "can do" statements allow them to have a clearly identifiable definition of mastery to which they can measure themselves. Finally, the LinguaFolio system allows students to maintain their own purposes as they learn the language; the learners set and meet their own goals in language learning. The achievement dynamic gives learners easily identifiable method for self-assessment.

Achievements can be consumable (e.g., groupon.com) where students get a hall pass or candy bar or they can be collectable (e.g., Foursquare. com) where students acquire online recognition. Achievements can enable students to form collections as in Guitar Hero where players can collect all the single-player badges or in Scouting (not a video game) where scouts collect all the outdoor badges. In a classroom it would be easy for instructors to offer badges such as "over 80% on tests," "90% attendance," or "90% target language spoken in class."

Two negative issues to consider with achievements and learner development are achievement fatigue and achievement dependence. Achievement fatigue occurs when players perceive so many points and awards that the achievements cease to have meaning for them, or the amount of rewards detracts from the "fun" of playing the game. The gaming industry watches these statistics closely because achievement fatigue leads to gamer attrition. Jane McGonigal (2011) makes this point when she argues that humans like to receive awards for difficult tasks more than they do for easy tasks. New accomplishments are not necessarily easy — thus the need for onboarding techniques — but too frequent rewards for common tasks tends to detract from the task. A number of online games have attempted to overcome this by giving fewer and fewer rewards as players progress in the game. Rewards and recognition in education could mirror the gaming industry by providing numerous and frequent rewards at the beginning of the semester with fewer rewards as the semester progresses.

Achievement dependence is related to the moral hazard of game play mentioned later in the chapter and appears to contradict achievement fatigue. Achievement dependence occurs when gamers grow to expect the reward and cease to put forth the effort to accomplish a task if the rewards for that task are no longer attainable. For example, if badges are given for attendance until mid-semester, after which no rewards are given. Some students may find that they have no motivation to come to class. As a rule, once instructors decide to put a reward system that includes points, badges, or levels they must follow through with the system to the end of the semester.

Visible achievements encourage object-orientedness among learners. The achievement mechanic offers important benefits:

- Early and frequent rewards serve as an onboarding technique to help learners understand the rules and routines of the class and encourages them to behave appropriately (e.g., attend class, study for quizzes, complete homework).
- Goals and achievements enable autonomy by encouraging self-assessment that enables learners to gauge their own performance and improvement.
- Status indicators provide a device that enables competition (with one's past performance or with peers).
- Achievements can be a method of encouraging peer evaluation and cooperation among learners with similar goals.
- Achievements constitute a motivational tool for those who wish to explore. For example, if certain tasks are only available to those at level 32, then curious students want to reach level 32 so they can discover the next experience.

For the most part, points should count up rather than down since a focus on progression helps learners concentrate on goals rather than failures. Achievements facilitate engagement by encouraging learners to attend to the essential aspects of the targeted learning, however, they also have the ability to detract from learning when achievements are too numerous or if learners become dependent on them. Finally, as with all game mechanics, consistency is a crucial element. The appointment mechanic provides an excellent example of the importance of consistency.

Appointment

The second game mechanic that is relatively easy to incorporate into a language class is *appointment*. Educators have traditionally valued the appointment mechanic. Appointments in education have usually been referred to as *attendance*. Students come to class and are rewarded with attendance points. When students do not come to class, they lose the points associated with that action. In video games, the appointment mechanic gives rewards to players for coming back at specific times. Ma-bimbo.com encourages players to login daily. Each player has a character — *a bimbo* — that they must feed, bathe, and clothe. When players login, they get paid (from their job and from their boyfriend). If users do not login, their character cannot take a shower, eat, or drink so her hygiene goes down and her hunger and thirst go up. After a couple of days of not logging in to feed her, the character dies of hunger and thirst. In short, players are rewarded for regular activity and punished for lack of activity. Webkinz virtual pets works the same way. Once into the system, game developers are able to guide users to play games, complete tasks, and purchase other items. The appointment mechanism is vital because it enables daily contact with the user base. Farmville, is probably the king of the appointment dynamic. Players plant crops that ripen in a set amount of time, if users do not return after that time to harvest their crops, the crops wither and die and they must plant new crops without reaping the benefits (coins and points).

In language learning, regular contact with the language usually enables more acquisition than periods with significant time between contact, so the appointment dynamic is of particular use to language teachers. Beyond attendance and in order to curb tardiness, a short opening quiz can encourage not only physical attendance but also engagement with the material. The topic of the quiz is announced in the previous class and the quiz deals directly with new material that is in the homework. Quizzes are taken and peer-graded in the first two minutes of class. The essential message is that if students come to class on time they receive easy points. Moreover, when students review the homework, they receive more easy points. Once past the initial groaning, students show annoyance when quizzes were not given as has been apparent in some games that have removed some of their appointment dynamics (e.g., Perfect World, World of Warcraft) — players complain on forums and in public chat about disappearing quests.

The appointment dynamic can be used beyond simply showing up to class. All major language textbooks have accompanying online workbooks. With this plethora of online workbooks, appointments could be used to encourage frequent returns to the workbook. For example, students login once a day to read a paragraph and answer some questions. The daily exercise refreshes every 6—8 hours for a total of 3—4 points per day. In this way, students engage throughout the day with the material on a voluntary basis.

The appointment dynamic in SLA relates to the concept of being goal-driven or object oriented, facilitating development, and providing a regular, predictable feedback loop to the students. These principles not only encourage learners to use the language more frequently, but they also direct the learners' overall systemic activity. It is of particular use for distance and independent courses where students may benefit substantially from impetus to interact with the language on a frequent basis. Appointments differ from quests also known as ratio awards and combo awards in that points are awarded for consistent behavior (called *loyalty* in the game design industry) and not for progression or task accomplishment.

Questing or fixed-ratio, variable-ratio, and combo awards

Fixed-ratio, variable-ratio, and combination, or combo, awards are the fundamental methods of rewarding players for performing certain in-game tasks. Accomplishing tasks to get a reward is normally referred to as *questing*. Fixed-ratio quests reward players after they complete a specific task (e.g., kill 20 orcs, get a new sword). Variable-ratio quests offer a random rate of reward while accomplishing a task. For example, a task may be described as "collect 20 teeth from orcs" and teeth are randomly collected from orcs that are killed (i.e., sometimes a reward is given, sometimes no reward is given). In a fixed-ratio reward schedule players would only kill 20 orcs to complete the task. In a variable-ratio reward schedule, players may need to kill 70—80 orcs to complete the task. Combo awards give additional awards for completion of a set of fixed ratio rewards (e.g., kill 20 orcs, pick 20 mulberries, fly to destination x, y, and z, and then receive an extra reward). Combo awards can consist of fixed- or variable-ratio rewards. In any given game system there are normally several different reward schedules in place.

Activity rate and engagement depend on the type of award players are expecting (Zichermann & Cunningham, 2001). Fixed-ratio rewards tend to produce a pause and then a burst of activity until a reward is given because the reward schedule is consistently predictable. Variable-ratio rewards tend to produce a steady flow of activity without the significant burst of activity. Combination awards tend to encourage players to play longer or harder to complete the set of activities even when the final reward is not relatively equal to the effort required. Of all the types of reward schedules, variable-ratio rewards tend to produce the highest level of consistent game play (Hopson, 2001).

Quests and awards are the basic building blocks for tasks. Questing exploits two of the main elements of activity theory mentioned earlier — object-orientedness and internalization/externalization — humans tend to be more efficient when they have a goal and a feedback loop. There are several significant advantages to questing.

- questing clarifies the tasks to be completed
- questing can be a solo or a social activity
- questing compensates accomplishment more than mere activity

In an educational setting task clarification often occurs through home-work, papers, or tests assigned on the syllabus. The syllabus, then, repre-sents the collection of *quests* to be accomplished during the semester. In schools, many of these tasks are individual (tests, homework, quizzes) with increasingly more social quests (group projects). Yet many of these so-called social activities are merely individual activities that are done in groups, rather than activities that require social interaction for their accomplishment. For example, when organizing a soccer game, it is not difficult to get a ball and a goals; the difficult part is getting players to show up and play. The socialness of the task is much more difficult to cre-ate than the task itself. Few online video games capitalize on the socialness of the task. MMORPGs tend to be good examples of this because different characters have different skills (e.g., clerics heal, wizards attack with magic, knights attack physically) that are required by the rest of the group in order to conquer the "Boss," or large monster at the end of a quest. The problem in education arises because instructors may feel that all students should be acquiring the same skill set, rather than contributing to a project according to each individual's strengths. Finally, fixed-ratio rewards com-pensate accomplishments such as high scores on tests, creative products, or insightful analyses rather than meager attendance.

Assignments on the syllabus generally represent fixed-ratio rewards since students know exactly when they are due, how much they are worth, and when they occur. Predictably, as with all fixed-ratio reward schedules, many students show a pause of activity (what some professors call procrastination) and a surge of activity as the due date (reward) approaches. This process appears to be "cramming for the exam" or "pulling an all-nighter." Yet, this type of engagement is consistent with the systems that game designers have used for many years. The crux of the matter is how to create a variable reward system while being fair to students.

Some real life examples of variable-ratio rewards are slot-machines (the payout is consistent, but the number of lever pulls varies), scratch cards, and lottery systems. Much like the example of the traffic light mentioned earlier, instructors might consider lottery systems for homework or tests. For example, students who turn in the composition early, or those who score above a certain level on a test might have their names entered in a weekly or monthly drawing. When students know that each time they perform an action their names are entered into a drawing, they are more likely to perform that action to improve their perceived chance of receiving a reward. Even when the reward might be limited to the specific activity and a virtual reward (e.g., an *excellent test* badge or a *writer's guild* badge), the reinforcement would still be encourage more consistency over time.

Combo awards usually give a reward that is more valuable than the contributing fixed-ratio rewards. In an educational setting, for example, students with greater than 90% attendance, greater than 85% participation, no homework grades below 90%, might earn a combo award for maintaining consistently good marks across several areas. Combo awards can be smaller. For example, students who are on time for a month, have missed no missed homework, and are among the first five to post on the online discussion board might receive an extra virtual badge.

A point that bears mentioning concerning reward schedules (whether fixed, variable, or combo) is that they are, by nature, all related to the task. Tasks that detract from the purpose of the activity tend to encourage gamers to disengage. For example, when a gamer kills a monster, he or she generally expects in-game coins, gear, or points. When the reward is out-of-game benefits (such as badges displayed on an accompanying website or free credits on another game), gamers tend to bypass the quests or quit short of completing them. There should be a clear and immediate link between the task and the award.

The use of awards is fraught with difficulties. In order for them to work correctly in class the associated quest or quests must be transparent to the students ahead of time and the rewards must be motivating, clear, and consistent. That is to say that students must be aware of which quests lead to which awards (allowing for some fuzziness with variable-ratio awards). The three major dangers with reward systems are *exhaustion, extinction* and the *moral hazard of game play*.

Exhaustion occurs when prizes are so frequent and easy to win that they lose all value (similar to achievement fatigue mentioned previously). If students receive separate awards for coming to class, sitting down, writing their names on papers, speaking in class, and turning in assignments throughout the week, their sense of what offers valuable returns gets obfuscated. When students lose their sense of which activities are valuable, they cease to perceive any of them as fun or meaningful and then they lose interest and disengage from the activity. Game designers strive to prevent reward exhaustion by offering awards for activities that players would not normally perform or for difficult activities that require an increase in activity.

Extinction occurs when the rewards for a specific quest are no longer distributed or when the rewards that are distributed are no longer valuable. When students cease to receive in-game awards for actions, the in-game actions are no longer beneficial, and students lose interest and discontinue the activity. For example, PerfectWorld has a daily quest where players buy a certain number of gems and take them to a NPC (non-playing character) for a XP point reward. At lower levels, players receive the reward for buying only a few gems but at higher levels more gems are required to complete the quest. At higher levels, the cost of the quest increases to about 10 times its cost at the lower levels. Few players continue to complete the daily quest at the high levels because the cost outweighs the benefits.

The moral hazard of game play is related to extinction in that players may cease to do activities that would benefit them simply because a clear reward is no longer available to them. For example, if children were paid a dime every time they brushed their teeth they would develop a habit of brushing their teeth. If they stopped receiving the dime, the moral hazard of game play predicts that most of them would stop brushing their teeth and then their teeth would rot and fall out. Educators should be mindful of how and when rewards influence the behavior of students toward dependence on points and rewards rather emphasizing autonomy, mastery, and purpose. Very little has been done in this arena so there is much research needed on how to avoid this pitfall.

Reward schedules are at the heart of gamification and key to engaging students in three major ways: (1) they clarify the task to be completed, (2) they allow for both individual and social activity, and (3) they compensate engagement toward accomplishment rather than unengaged activity. The form of reward schedule influences the type of engagement instructors can expect. Fixed-ratio rewards encourage bursts of engagement near a deadline. Variable-ratio rewards encourage sustained engagement over extended periods. Combo awards encourage prolonged engagement to complete sets of tasks. Nonetheless, instructors should be wary of the long term effects of reward schedules such as exhaustion, extinction, and the moral hazard of game play. Other potentially beneficial methods of increasing engagement through social game mechanics include cross-situational leaderboards.

Cross-situational leaderboards

Cross-situational leaderboards are popular in almost all games that focus on competition or cooperation. Numerous online communities have formed around cross-situational leaderboards. In cross-situational leaderboards, players are ranked according to different criteria and there are often different rankings depending on your characteristics. So, for example, one could be the highest level barbarian, or the assassin with the fastest attack rate on the server. Farmville, as with most Facebook games, offers a micro-leaderboard where players are ranked only according to their friends who are also playing the same game. These structures generally only encourage those students who are highly competitive and are motivated by seeing their character or avatar improve compared to other players.

Instructors have attempted leaderboards for many years without formalizing them. Some professors simply write the highest test score on the board. Others congratulate a particular student for the "best paper" in the class. Unlike gaming leaderboards, academic pseudo-leaderboards are not continually updated and while they may provide motivation to some in the class, there is no evidence to suggest that all students are motivated by it. Cross-situational leader boards publish the top scorers on different events (scores on tests, papers, best attendance, most progress on project, greatest number of points, least dumb mistakes, etc.) so that all students have the opportunity to feel that they are succeeding in some aspect of the class. One important note is that cross-situational leader boards do not rank the entire class, they simply rank the top few for each category of ranking.

Leaderboards can create some significant problems simply because there is very little evidence to indicate how they motivate students. Moreover, many of the leaderboard features can be replaced by using badges; where continuously updated leaderboards highlight dominance which is good for some learners, badges tend to emphasize achievement which tends to have a wider reach as far as motivation is concerned. Another concern that surfaces in discussions on the publication of student achievement is privacy.

Privacy

The game mechanic *privacy* refers to the idea that some information should not be shared with the entire class. Shared information can be motivational or demotivational depending on the nature of the information. Many students are motivated by public acknowledgment of successes, yet, if students view widespread recognition as a negative reward, high achievement in the public sphere can incite some students to disengage from the activity in order to avoid the notoriety associated with public success.

Lack of privacy can also serve as a significant motivator. For example, an instructor's in class comment such as "oh, you didn't do your homework today?" can cause enough unwanted attention to ensure that future homework assignments are completed on time. FERPA (The Family Educational Rights and Privacy Act) prohibits the improper disclosure of personally identifiable information derived from educational records. In many cases, instructors infer from FERPA regulations that students must sign-on to be part of the leaderboards and that they have the opportunity to opt out at any point in the semester.

These two concepts, cross-situational leaderboards and privacy relate to the need for goal-driven tasks and feedback in order to improve the efficiency of language acquisition. Cross-situational leaderboards can also tap into the sequential nature of language learning if those higher on the leaderboard are performing higher-level tasks than those lower on the leaderboard. These mechanics also help to emphasize the social nature of learning.

Social engagement loops

Social engagement has been a buzz word for the past couple of years in games, particularly online games that claim Web2.0 status. An enormous number of Facebook games encourage users to invite friends to play a part in their gaming network. A social engagement loop rewards players who drive adoption and retention of other players. Social engagement loops generally take advantage of other external social networks (e.g., Twitter, Facebook, LinkedIn) to encourage engagement with the game. Zichermann and Cunningham (2011) identify four aspects of a good engagement loop: motivating emotion, player reengagement, social call to action, and visible progress/reward.

This social loop is evident in a number of Facebook games. First, players begin the game or win an award in the game. Next, the award elicits an emotion which engages them in play. Then, they are encouraged to share this award (e.g., news, badge, virtual gift, request) with friends. When players share awards, they gain new awards and as their friends join the game they receive additional awards. Finally, they receive points (progress) and items (reward) as their friends become engaged in the game. This viral social mechanic encourages players to proselytize their friends, reactivate those whose interests are waning, and promote greater activity among those who are already enthusiastically playing the game.

Second language classes have been focusing on social aspects of communication since the 1980s and it would seem that a social engagement loop would be in place for most courses. However, aside from forced peer-editing there are very few mechanisms that encourage the viral sharing of course content in colleges around the world. Again, LinguaFolio could offer an excellent example of social loops, even though its current interface is clunky and does not facilitate viral sharing. The online LinguaFolio allows members of the class to upload evidence that they can do certain tasks (e.g., a video of them ordering food in a Chinese restaurant, an audio recording of the student saying their name). Other students can validate the claim as *can do well, can do, can do with help,* and *cannot do* by listening to or viewing the uploaded evidence. The social loop would be complete if students had push technology to see who has uploaded and wants evaluation, and then receive rewards for offering advice or helpful feedback (much like StackOverflow.com). In this way, students would be rewarded for completion of their own tasks and they would also gain reputation for helping others complete their tasks by offering help and feedback, sharing awards, and evaluating feedback given by others.

Flurry.com (2011), the iPhone app metric company, indicates that after six months of having downloaded an app, usage shrinks to about 14%. After a year, only 4% continue to use the app. Viral social engagement loops are increasingly important for sustained activity and retention in the gaming world and will be key to increasing activity and retention in education. They leverage social pressure to provide boosts during periods of inactivity and they push players/students to reengage.

Modifiers

The final game mechanic that tends to have the most effect for boosting engagement is the modifier. Modifiers are tools that students can use to increase their achievements or rewards. Online games often offer special $2 \times$ weekends where players can get double points, or twice the rewards (like coins, prizes) for killing the same number of mobs. Farmville has modifiers that enable you to plant more crops or harvest them more quickly. Bejeweled blitz has jewels that slow down the game. World of Warcraft and Call of Duty have weapons and armor to help players survive longer or kill faster. Some modifiers are transferrable to other players (tradeable) while others are bound to the player. Farmville does not allow you to let someone borrow your tractor, for example. On the other hand, World of Warcraft allows players to buy, sell, or trade weapons and armor.

Modifiers are used infrequently in academic settings. Modifiers are items that would help students perform better on tests, score higher on projects, complete homework more quickly, or gain greater rewards for doing any of the above. High school teachers may often use modifiers as a method of both encouraging better grades while allowing certain liberties. Teachers may give a limited number of hall passes throughout the year that can be used in emergencies. Students who do not use the hall passes for going to the restroom, can cash them in for extra points on tests or quizzes or as a method of allowing them to drop a quiz grade. These are not modifiers in the true sense of the terms since students do not receive extra skills or rewards for achievements; they simply receive forgiveness for a lack of accomplishment.

True modifiers would enable students to perform better on the test. A math class, for example, might allow students who have passed a particular quiz to use a calculator on the next test. In this case, the calculator is a modifier because it helps the student perform mechanical tasks more quickly.

I have experimented with several modifiers with varying results. In one course, students could win $2 \times$ coupons (from a variable-ratio task) for use during any week they chose. If they chose to use the coupon they would receive double points during that week for quizzes, attendance, and homework (all of which were XP points and not skill points for this particular class). For the most part, students used these coupons poorly. Two students used the coupons and then were absent for two days of the week. Three students used the coupon during weeks when few assignments were due. Only one student took full advantage of the coupons by matching the syllabus and making significant effort to maximize engagement for the week. Unfortunately, two students expressed displeasure for what appeared to be unfair to them. In other classes, I allowed students to purchase lifeline cards where they could ask me for a limited number of answers on any test. Other students could purchase the opportunity to use a dictionary for an essay test. In a literature class, students could win the opportunity to take the test in teams rather than individually. None of these experiments produced the anticipated results of higher engagement. However, modifiers are theoretically important to SLA as student recognize that tools are essential to facilitating production. It is important for students to learn to use tools that facilitate their production and comprehension of a second language. One major difficulty with modifiers is the unclear distinction between tools for production and devices for cheating. Even today many students may feel that taking the test in groups or using tools unavailable to others creates an unfair advantage and thereby discredits the individual work they can do with no help.

CONCLUSION

This chapter began by discussing the history of how individuals approach a study of emerging technology. The fact is, for most millennials (i.e., those born after 1990), emerging technology is uninteresting, cumbersome, or distracting. In other words, technologies such as social bookmarking, photosharing, online language labs, Twitter, Facebook, and ePortfolios are incapable of engaging users simply because of their novelty. Most digital natives (those who grew up with computers) have already made the conscious choice to use the technology or not; forcing students to use technology that they would not normally use for language learning has not convincingly been shown to have significant benefits to students. Nevertheless, there is a significant research base investigating how students use the technologies that they do to accomplish certain tasks, particularly in the realm of online gaming. In fact, recent studies indicate that the average gamers spend about 20 hours a week (the equivalent of a part time job) working on developing their character (gaining attributes, achievements, questing, etc.) (McGonigal, 2011). Wouldn't it be wonderful if your students were spending 20 hours a week on your class?

Yet, gamification targets more than just increase of time on task. The use of game mechanics with a reliance on Activity Theory aims to increase learner autonomy, socialization, competition, self-expression, and discovery. Weaving game mechanics into the classroom helps to satisfy learner needs of object-orientedness, hierarchical structure, internalization/ externalization, development, and mediation. Gamification also facilitates a task-based teaching methodology. Additionally, game mechanics help to identify tasks (both in the mind of the students and the mind of the instructors). This clarification of task focuses learners' attention on the essential aspects of the task and thereby facilitating completion rather than necessitating task definition.

There are a number of pitfalls and points to consider in gamification. Currently at the height of the hype cycle, gamification will shortly descend into the trough of disillusionment where designers realize that a good engagement system requires more than a blend of game mechanics. Particularly in education, gamification presents numerous hurdles mentioned in this chapter. These obstacles can be summarized as *context* and *dilution*.

Context refers to the idea that gamification of education lends itself more readily to online, distance, and independent study courses. These courses tend to have most of their data and interaction online and the inclusion of game characteristics such as badges, appointments, quests, and social engagement are both easily produced by instructors and more readily accepted among students. For example, an individual's achievement badges are more easily displayed on their online profile than on a classroom wall, in most cases; traditional students already have appointments to come to class at a certain time, whereas independent study courses might benefit more from specific online engagements that provide additional exposure for students.

Dilution refers to the idea that gamification distracts learners from what is really at stake. In some cases, this is a good thing. Math Ninja, for example, requires players to respond to timed flashcard-type math problems in order to win ammunition (more correct responses equals more cash for ammunition). Users are distracted from the fact that they are simply doing mundane, albeit disguised, math flashcards. Other games like Pioneer trail, encourage users to spread the news about their achievements or needs such that users will often post more than 50 comments on a friend's Facebook wall. An activity that distracting them from the facts that (1) they are sending too many messages (and thereby disturbing their friends) and (2) they are losing multiple productive hours looking under digital rocks or building virtual buildings that serve no purpose. The worry is, for many instructors, that students lose sight of the fundamental study of the discipline.

From another perspective, instructors often see points as bonus points that can conceal the fact that students are not gaining proficiency in the targeted skills. That is to say that if there are points for every student action then the course ceases to be a measure of skill and becomes a measure of how well students can play the game. This case, however, raises more concerns for the implementation of the mechanics than the fact that there are additional points.

The second element of dilution is the fact that students experience fatigue from the peripheral elements and fail to engage in the target skills. This concept was described earlier as achievement fatigue (too many badges), achievement dependence (frustration when rewards are not forthcoming), exhaustion (rewards for too many actions), extinction (not enough rewards), or the moral hazard of game play (dissolution of intrinsic motivation). All of these can come into play in an unbalanced system.

Gamification dovetails with Activity Theory in determining which goals are appropriate for instructed language acquisition and how to get there. Zichermann and Cunningham (2011) list status as one of the most desirable and most *sticky* (i.e., for retaining players) reward available to players. Students are really no different in this than others and status can be determined by points, badges, levels, or leaderboards. The inclusion of game mechanics into the classroom facilitates the construction of an environment where students can earn and display status and these rewards have been shown to impact directly motivation, learner engagement, and satisfaction. In conclusion, it is clear that these game mechanics will be increasingly included in courses at all levels. The challenge, then, is to determine the long-term effects and how best to incentivize procedural and substantive engagement with the course materials and class members.

REFERENCES

Beauvois, M. H. (1994). E-talk: Attitudes and motivation in computer-assisted classroom discussion. *Computers and the Humanities, 28,* 177–190.

Biesenbach-Lucas, S., & Weasenforth, D. (2001). E-mail and word processing in the ESL classroom: How the medium affects the message. *Language Learning & Technology, 5*(1), 135–165.

Dignan, A. (2011). *Game frame: Using games as a strategy for success.* New York, NY: Simon & Schuster.

Dooly, M. (2011). Divergent perceptions of telecollaborative language learning tasks: Task-as-workplan vs. task-as-process. *Language Learning & Technology, 15*(2), 69–91.

Dredge, S. (2011). Tetris still top-earning US mobile game. *PocketGamer.biz.* Retrieved from http://www.pocketgamer.biz/r/PG.Biz/Tetris/news.asp?c = 10747

Dubner, S. (2012). Lottery loopholes and deadly doctors. *Freakonomics Radio,* http://www.freakonomics.com/2012/01/18/lottery-loopholes-and-deadly-doctors/

DuBravac, S. (2012). *Technology in the L2 Curriculum.* Upper Saddle River, NJ: Pearson.

Gartner, Inc. (2012). *The Gartner hype cycle special report: what's hot for* 2012 [video webcast]. Retrieved from http://www.gartner.com/technology/research/methodologies/hype-cycles.jsp

Gee, J. P. (2003). *What video games have to teach us about learning and literacy.* New York, NY: Palgrave Macmillan.

Hopson, J. (2001). *Behavioral game design. Gamasutra: The art of making games.* Retrieved from http://www.gamasutra.com/view/feature/131494/behavioral_game_design.php

Kaptelinin, V. (1996). Activity theory: Implications for human-computer interaction. In B. Nardi (Ed.), *Context and consciousness: Activity theory and human-computer interaction* (pp. 53–59). Cambridge, MA: MIT Press.

Kessler, G., Bikowski, D., & Boggs, J. (2012). Collaborative writing among second language learners in academic web-based projects. *Language Learning & Technology, 16*(1), 91–109.

Kim, A. J. (2011). MetaGame design: Rewards systems that drive engagement. Game Designers Conference, March 9, 2010. Retrieved from http://www.gdcvault.com/play/1012242/Meta_Game_Design__Reward_Systems_that_Drive_Engagement.

Krathwohl, D. R. (2004). *Methods of educational and socialscience research: An integrated approach* (2nd ed.). Long Grove, IL: Waveland Press.

Lan, Y.-J., Sung, Y.-T., & Chang, K.-E. (2007). A mobile-device-supported peer-assisted learning system for collaborative early EFL reading. *Language Learning & Technology, 11*(3), 130–151.

Lantolf, J. P., & Thorne, S. L. (2006). *Sociocultural theory and the genesis of second language development.* Oxford: Oxford University Press.

Levy, M. (2007). Research and technological innovation in CALL. *Innovation in Language Learning and Teaching, 1*(1), 180–190.

Lyman-Hager, M. & DuBravac, S. (1996). Multimedia templates for reading and listening. *Proceedings of the Congrès du Multimédia Enseignement des Langues. Actes du 10 Janvier 1996.* Paris: Congrès International de Technologie, pp. 167–170.

Maani, C., Hoffman, H. G., DeSocio, P. A., Morrow, M., Galin, C., Magula, J., et al. (2008). Pain control during wound care for combat-related burn injuries using custom articulated arm mounted virtual reality goggles. *Journal of CyberTherapy & Rehabilitation, 1*(2), 193–198.

McGonigal, J. (2011). *Reality is broken: Why games make us better and how they can change the world.* New York, NY: Penguin Press.

Osuna, M. M., & Meskill, C. (1997). Using the world wide web to integrate Spanish language and culture: A pilot study. *Language Learning and Technology, 1*(2), 71–92.

Parks, S., Huot, D., Hamers, J., & H.-Lemonnier, F. (2003). Crossing boundaries: Multimedia technology and pedagogical innovation in a high school class. *Language Learning & Technology, 7*(1), 28–45.

Pelletieri, J. (2000). Negotiation in cyberspace: The role of chatting in the development of grammatical competence in the virtual foreign language classroom. In M. Warschauer & R. Kern (Eds.), *Network-based language teaching: Concepts and practice* (pp. 59–86). Cambridge, England: Cambridge University Press.

Pink, D. H. (2009). *Drive: The surprising truth about what motivates us.* New York, NY: Riverhead Books.

Rainie, L. & Fox, S. (2012). *Just-in-time information through mobile connections.* Pew Internet and American Life Project. Retrieved from http://pewinternet.org/Reports/2012/Just-in-time.aspx

Reeves, B., & Read, J. L. (2009). *Total engagement: Using games and virtual worlds to change the way people work and businesses compete.* Boston, MA: Harvard Business School Press.

Roosevelt, M. (2009). Student expectations seen as causing grade disputes. *New York Times* [Online]. Retrieved from http://www.nytimes.com/2009/02/18/education/18college.html

Schultz, J. (2010). Speed camera lottery wins VW fun theory contest. *The New York Times*, November 30, 2010. Retrieved from http://wheels.blogs.nytimes.com/2010/11/30/speed-camera-lottery-wins-vw-fun-theory-contest/

Warschauer, M. (1996). Comparing face-to-face and electronic discussion in the second language classroom. *CALICO Journal, 13*(2), 7–26.

Vygotsky, L. (1978). *Mind in society: The development of higher psychological processes.* Cambridge, MA: Harvard University Press.

Zichermann, G., & Cunningham, C. (2011). *Gamification by design: Implementing game mechanics in web and mobile apps.* Sebastopol, CA: O'Reilly.

INCREASING STUDENT ENGAGEMENT USING CLIENT-BASED PEER ASSESSMENT IN MULTI-ROLE, WHOLE-ENTERPRISE SIMULATIONS

Steve Gove

ABSTRACT

This chapter presents two established pedagogical techniques to increase student engagement, simulations and peer assessment. The use of each technique, its benefits and drawbacks, and how content knowledge and student engagement increase are detailed. While each of the approaches can be utilized independently to create active learning environments, this chapter illustrates the potential to extend these approaches further. An overview of an MBA-level elective on competitive analysis structured around a simulation and peer assessment is presented. The result is a highly interactive and engaging course where the simulation and peer

Increasing Student Engagement and Retention using Immersive Interfaces: Virtual Worlds, Gaming, and Simulation
Cutting-edge Technologies in Higher Education, Volume 6C, 95–128
ISSN: 2044-9968/doi:10.1108/S2044-9968(2012)000006C007

assessments achieve symbiotic benefits. Learning and performance in the simulation is enhanced by the application of competitive analyst reports which are used by peer "clients." Assessment in turn leads to greater insights to the simulation, and subsequently higher levels of performance on both the simulation and future analysis work. Insights on these instructional methods, their limitations, and potential barriers to adoption are offered with the hope of inspiring others to utilize and experiment with novel approaches for further enhance learner engagement.

INTRODUCTION

The facilitation of student engagement is a contributing factor for achieving student learning goals and satisfaction. Student engagement is broadly defined as the level of involvement and quality of effort in learning an environment (Kuh, 2009). A variety of active learning techniques are available for achieving this in standard in-person classroom settings. Development of a course design to facilitate engagement in settings where a large portion of learning occurs outside of the classroom, such as part-time evening MBA programs or distance learning environments, is more daunting. This chapter presents a review of two approaches to enhance engagement in such settings: computer-based whole-enterprise simulations and peer assessment techniques. Each can be used independently to increase student engagement for in-person, geographically dispersed, and temporally asynchronous distance learning settings.

This chapter is structured into three sections. The first section provides a general overview of active learning approaches, primarily from an adult learner perspective, and their influence on student engagement. The focus of this section is on simulations and peer assessment as active learning techniques. Whole-enterprise computer simulations, where students take on the role of top managers setting strategy, analyzing competitive environments, and making decisions in virtual organizations are emphasized. The use of these simulations in management education, particularly as part of strategic management course where they are widely used is reviewed. Finally, the use of peer assessment techniques, where students take partial responsibility for the evaluation of work created by fellow students, is reviewed.

The second section provides an overview of an elective graduate-level course on competitive analysis that incorporates simulations and peer assessments as core structural course elements to encourage and facilitate engagement. Engagement can be greatly influenced by course design (Fink, 2003). This overview illustrates how the basic forms of whole-enterprise computer simulations and peer assessment can be adapted, expanded, and integrated within a course structure to create student engagement situations outside of the classroom. The extensions include the incorporation of multiple simulations and assessment of analyst work by fellow students in the position of client (i.e., the recipient who is the actual end user) of these analyses.

As outlined in this section, students engage in a whole-enterprise computer simulation where they are tasked with managing a simulated firm and monitoring competitors. The use of two simulations provides common yet unique learning contexts. Within one simulation, the student is a user of the products of competitive analysis. In the second simulation, the student is the creator of competitive analysis products. Each week, several competitive analysis tools are introduced along with an explanation of their principles and applications. Students then select and apply one competitive analysis tool to the context of the simulation.

These weekly competitive analyst reports are prepared for fellow students who act as clients who use them to aid their decision making. Grading is completed by both the instructor and student clients. While peer assessment itself is a relatively common form of active learning, the analyst/client distinction creates a sense of hierarchical separation which parallels the analyst/client relationship within real organizations. The result of incorporating and extending these active learning approaches is a highly immersive learning environment centered on the creation, use, and evaluation of competitive analyses within organizations.

Lastly, the third section details the limitations experienced in the adoption and integration of simulations and peer assessment approach.

SIMULATIONS AND PEER ASSESSMENT FOR STUDENT ENGAGEMENT

Student engagement is widely recognized as a desirable aspect of the education process that aids student learning. As Kuh details, higher levels of engagement yield multiple benefits to students.

> The engagement premise is straightforward and easily understood: the more students study a subject, the more they know about it, and the more students practice and get

feedback from faculty and staff members on their writing and collaborative problem
solving, the deeper they come to understand what they are learning and the more adept
they become at managing complexity, tolerating ambiguity, and working with people
from different backgrounds or with different views. (2009, p. 5)

A variety of educational techniques can encourage student engagement
(see, e.g., Harrington & Schibik, 2004). Most take some form of "active
learning" – a generic phrase encompassing a range of instructional
approaches that go beyond instructor-centered lectures and elicits the student's desire for knowledge to direct learning. Active learning is especially
relevant for adult learners who are more independent and seek knowledge
for more specific purposes than non-adult learners (Knowles, 1990).
Within adult learner settings, learning techniques based on andragogy
(Knowles, 1990) as opposed to pedagogy, are appropriate.

Under andragogous approaches, the instructor creates situations to
facilitate learning as opposed to being the primary provider of knowledge.
The instructor's role shifts from provision and delivery to creating a setting
of guidance and technical expertise as needed (Knowles, 1990). In this
model, effective course environments are multifaceted, recognizing and
seeking a position along the continuum between teacher-directed and
learner-directed approaches as appropriate at different points in time.

Many business school students, especially those in upper division
undergraduate-level and graduate-level elective courses, have very specific
interests and expectations that influence their decision to enroll in a particular course. They seek knowledge that can be readily applied to current or
expected future settings. Two instructional techniques that promote
applied learning and engagement through active learning are simulations
and peer assessment. Each is an active learning technique that offers great
potential to enhance learner engagement and meet student expectations for
application.

In the following section, an explanation of simulations and peer assessment as learning techniques, a brief history of their development and use,
and evidence of their efficacy in achieving educational objectives and promoting student engagement are provided.

Simulations

Computer-based simulations are not new educational technologies. Their
use, in various forms, extends back to the 1950s with the introduction of a
logistics simulation by the RAND Corporation for the U.S Air Force

(Faria & Wellington, 2004). The use of simulations was once limited to a few enthusiastic faculty due to the predominance of large scale, centralized computer systems. However, the emergence of the personal computer and Internet has greatly expanded the ease of use and subsequent adoption of simulations.

All simulations can be classified as games, but not all games are simulations. The distinction rests on three aspects. First, simulations are synthetic learning environments (Cannon-Bowers & Bowers, 2010, p. 287) which "place individuals in learning environments that are physically and/or socially similar to their work environment." They are isomorphic, corresponding closely to a context or topic one wishes to understand. Simulations are usually used for application or illustration. Content knowledge is gained from other sources. Second, games are for enjoyment. While simulations may be enjoyable, their primary purpose in an academic setting is to aid learning. Third, performance in a simulation is monitored and used for evaluation. Beyond these factors, virtually any game could potentially be used as a simulation.

The use of simulations has increased dramatically. Among Association to Advance Collegiate Schools of Business (AACSB) member business schools, those that reported using business games increased from 72% in the early 1960s to more than 90% by the end of the decade (Faria & Nulsen, 1996). In the 1970s, the methodology became the subject of considerable pedagogical and research attention with the formation of the Association for Business Simulation and Experiential Learning (ABSEL), the launch of an annual conference, and the journal *Simulation & Gaming (S&G): An International Journal of Theory, Practice and Research*. By the mid-1990s, more than 95% of AACSB schools reported using one or more simulations (Faria & Nulsen, 1996). So widespread are simulations that one researcher remarked "Once a novel and cutting-edge teaching technology, this method's use has reached the point of relative saturation in various American business course applications" (Wolfe, 1993, p. 446).

Simulations are effective active learning techniques (Knotts, & Keys, 1997; Wolf, 1997). In many disciplines outside of business schools, the pedagogical value of simulations is long established. Flight simulators, for example, have long been used extensively for pilot training and certification. The use of simulations is expanding in fields such as medicine, law enforcement, and the military. Within business disciplines, there are a wide range of simulations and usage varies. In operations management, for example, simulations are largely modeling techniques, used to examine specific processes or aspects of a firm, such as a specific order system, process flows, and other queuing systems, manipulated or stressed with the intent of process design or management. These simulations bear little resemblance to those used in other areas. In organizational behavior, simulations may illustrate one interaction between the participant and an employee. In labor relations, simulations may illustrate a series of negotiations to resolve one labor dispute. In marketing, there is great variability in simulations, ranging from the effect of price changes on demand for individual products to decision sets surrounding multiple marketing channels, medium, products, and other aspects.

The use of simulations is highest in management and marketing, 41% in both. Use is lowest in accounting at 11%, followed by economics, management science, and finance, with ranges of 15–22% (Faria & Wellington, 2004). The ability of a simulation to represent the encounters and systems within a discipline and the scope of individual topics versus breadth of topics within a course may explain different usage rates. Adoption rates are higher when multiple topics can be combined within a single simulation and the topics warrant coverage throughout a course as opposed to being covered during brief, specific instances.

Within management, strategic management faculty were the early adopters of simulations. By 1986, 53% of schools surveyed reported use of a simulation in strategic management courses (Faria, 1986). Just 10 years later, use of simulations had climbed to two-thirds of institutions (Faria & Nulsen, 1996; Wolfe & Roge, 1997). In 2004, 70% of faculty in strategic management were using or had used a simulation, with 50% of faculty active users (Faria & Wellington, 2004). The main type of simulation used in strategic management is a whole-enterprise simulation in which participants take the role of company managers, responsible for a wide range of decisions affecting firm performance. Most whole-enterprise simulations take a similar form: Students are top managers of a company which operates within an industry in competition with several other student-managed companies. This type of simulation captures the complexity of managing a full range of organizational functions to achieve firm-level performance while competing with others firms seeking to maximize their performance.

The allocation of time to whole-enterprise simulations in strategic management courses attests to their importance. When used, whole-enterprise simulations are major course components. Faria and Nulsen (1996) report simulation users dedicate an average of one quarter of in-class time over the semester to the use of simulations, up to a high of 80%. Similarly, performance and involvement on simulation related activities averages one quarter of course grade criteria among users.

Whole-enterprise simulations are immersive, requiring a high level of active engagement. They are perhaps best described as ongoing, interactive living case examples (Wolfe, 1976). A large portion of the concepts common across strategic management textbooks are incorporated into whole-enterprise simulations (Wolfe & Roge, 1997). Students set and implement strategic direction through budgetary actions in the area of finance, sales and marketing, production, and other activities. Decisions are made based on a comparison of planned strategy to actual performance and in light of actions taken by competitors. Simulations include a variety of pro forma mechanisms so that students can see best case effects of these decisions. Once all teams have entered their decisions, the round is processed. Students then see the results of their decisions. Generally each round represents one year in the life of an organization and using six to eight rounds during a course is common.

A variety of reports are then produced which correspond to a firm's annual report (e.g., income statement, balance sheet, statement of stockholder equity, and cash flow statement), key managerial information (e.g., product inventory, production capacity, effectiveness of marketing practices, etc.), key financial ratios and performance metrics (e.g., stock price performance, liquidity, leverage, and performance ratios, etc.), and similar information for competing firms. The results of decision in one round leads to the starting conditions for the team in the next (i.e., high performance leads to higher levels of cash and more options for borrowing; low performance restricts resources and available options).

Whole-enterprise simulations are unique in several important ways that affect student engagement. First, simulations elicit complexity that comes from managing multiple interrelated functional areas such marketing, finance, and production. This complexity creates the need for students to expend considerable time and effort to assess and understand direct causal associations between individual functions and firm performance as well as the interconnections. Second, participants take on the roles of senior company managers such as the chief executive officer or functional vice president. The context puts students in roles central to organizational success, roles that students seek to occupy upon completion of their degrees. Third, whole-enterprise simulations always incorporate competitive environments, typically in the form of multiple firms engaged in direct competition within a product space. The desire to perform well results in active participation, creating competition between students in different teams. The desire to perform well provides intrinsic motivation to spend time on tasks. Fourth, simulations incorporate temporal components of multiple time periods and path dependency. The firms exist and compete over multiyear periods, with the resources and options available to the firm the result of performance in prior periods as assessed against competing firms. It is not uncommon for students to participate in the simulation across eight to ten rounds spread across a semester. This repeated exposure to the simulation allows for a deeper understanding of cause and effect relationships than a single exposure would allow.

A substantial body of evidence suggests whole-enterprise simulations are valid and effective pedagogical techniques, resulting in high learner engagement with a variety of positive outcomes. The most basic element of strategic management is that the primary objective is firm performance. Students commonly begin their understanding of the simulation by stumbling through the first round making minor decisions and changes and, after the round is processed, ask "how did we do?" They quickly find that answering that question is remarkably complex. Firm performance is a latent phenomenon involving multiple stakeholders, each with a variety of indicators. Performance is also relative, only truly evaluated in a relative sense against comparable firms. To answer the "how did we do?" question, the student must seek out answers, understand measures, find peers, and make relative comparisons. Only then can the student proceed to making causal connections as to why a given level of performance was achieved and seek information and make decisions for future rounds. Future performance is predicated on either luck, which typically is not enduring, or the development of comprehensive solutions based on understanding causal mechanisms, evaluation of relative merit, and the selection and successful implementation of an idea. Thus simulations create an environment that facilitates great depth of understanding, a central objective of active engagement.

The progression of student learning from basic terminology to application and understanding causal relationships is the hallmark of applied fields. While understanding field-specific definitions and concepts is a critical step in the learning process, it is insufficient for managing a company in a simulation. This can be illustrated using Bloom's (1956) learning taxonomy. In a survey or introductory course, definitions (Bloom's level 1) and comprehension (level 2) may be course objectives. However in an applied setting, which is a common attribute of most MBA courses, the emphasis is the ability to use tools and concepts. In the context of Bloom's (1956) taxonomy, any meaningful student involvement in a simulation begins at an advanced learning level involving cause and effect relationships (level 4), synthesizing to develop possible solutions (level 5), and evaluating options (level 6).

Business education, especially at the graduate level, deals with decision making in complex environments. Training at this level is as focused on analytical thinking and decision making processes as on actual decisions. With no clearly right or wrong answers, the development of confidence in one's abilities can be challenging. Simulations require active strategy making and goal setting while involving personal-level and group-level aspects of organizational decision making (Wolfe, 1976). A limited body of evidence suggests simulations are more effective at building student's decision-making self-efficacy (Bandura, 1997) than alternative approaches. Tompson and Dass (2000) compared changes in self-efficacy resulting from learning strategic thinking and analysis using case studies and simulations. While self-efficacy increased under both conditions, it increased significantly more through the use of a simulation ($p < .01$).

An additional benefit of simulations is alignment between the decision making environment and real-world applications. A concern in applied educational settings, such as the undergraduate business disciplines and MBA programs, is that the learning environment differs greatly from the application environment (Lainema & Lainema, 2007). While alternative active approaches such as case studies can emulate situational aspects, simulations have two key advantages. First, regardless of the decision that the learner makes, the decision must be translated into investments being made or withheld. This is highly similar to the actual decisions that upper managers make which typically entail two dimensions: To invest in an action or not and, if so, how much and when to invest. Second, unlike case studies which are static, the student can see and experience the results of their decisions. Similar to real decisions, an initiative either pays off or does not. While in actual organizations the outcome of decisions make take months or even years to realize, in a simulation this is commonly compressed to one or two decision rounds. Both the feedback and its immediacy are vital to learning. Trim (2004) succinctly notes, "simulation exercises provide potential managers with an opportunity to understand the complexity of the marketplace before they are given the freedom to exercise their own judgment in a position of authority" (p. 405).

In the context of strategic management, both students and instructors rate simulations as more effective than traditional instructional methods, such as lectures and textbooks, as well as other active approaches such as case analysis and consulting projects. In a review of prior studies comparing simulations with other instructional approaches, instructors, using a 1−10 scale, rated business simulations (rating = 7.9) above cases (6.8), lectures (5.9), and textbooks (5.5) in terms of perceived effectiveness

(Wolfe & Roge, 1997). Jennings (2002) compared student reports of learning effectiveness under three methods: simulation, case analysis, and consulting project. Across ten learning areas including knowledge, problem solving and decision making, planning and implementation, and realism, simulations were rated as superior to the alternative approaches. Wolfe and Roberts (1993) report an association between student involvement in simulation decision making, esteem, and value to a team with five-year career success. High-performing individuals within simulation teams were more likely to be high performers in later professional environments, suggesting external validity of the method. Those who use simulations are committed to continued use: Ninety-one percent of faculty currently using a simulation indicate it unlikely they would discontinue usage (Faria & Wellington, 2004).

Simulations encourage involvement consistent with the characteristics of engaging learning environments. Bowen (1987) describes three aspects, emotional arousal, relative safety, and learning-based sense making, as key elements in such environments. Simulations create healthy competition between individuals managing different teams. A student's identity quickly becomes interconnected with the performance of their company in the simulation, the success or failure of their company is an extension of the self. For the student, the self can be difficult to separate from the performance of their simulated team due to high identification (Ashforth & Mael, 1989). Not lost on the students is the primary objective of a simulation to learn. This learning can occur through success or, sometimes more dramatically, through failure. The nature of failure within a simulation is rather benign. The highest cost is perhaps a slightly lower grade and a slightly bruised ego. Actual investments are not lost nor are jobs terminated.

The individual and team processes in simulations yield high levels of engagement. Unlike many active learning methods, much of the engagement occurs outside the classroom. Students commonly work individually to interpret and diagnose annual reports and earning statements and understand the competitive environment. These students then bring their insights together in team strategy sessions where individual interpretations and suggested actions are shared, dissected, contrasted, and used as the basis of team-level integrated actions.

The author's own experience is that student response to simulations is bi-modal: Half of the students in a course greatly enjoy the simulation and see how it illustrates course concepts while the other half see the simulation as requiring considerable time, being overly complex, and having seemingly arbitrary results. Informal analysis suggests some causality to the relationship consistent with game engagement theory (Whitton, 2011). Students who make significant time investments during early simulation rounds appear to benefit from an upward spiral of positive engagement experience. Higher levels of performance lead to greater interest and confidence and continued improvement. Individuals with lower level of course content knowledge make poor simulation decisions, entering into a downward cycle which results in negative engagement (Whitton, 2011). These students have the lowest levels of performance in later rounds and indicate the lowest levels of satisfaction. Without understanding and mastery of content knowledge, students have difficulty overcoming complexity to make sound decisions and report dissatisfaction with the simulation. These students often view the performance of the simulated firms as arbitrary.

Importantly, there appears to be differences in who responds favorably to simulations. A select group of students who are not attracted to the case study approach seem especially motivated by the competitive and interactive nature of the simulation. They become actively engaged in learning, seeking content solutions as they encounter situations for which they have limited knowledge. Simulations, therefore, engage a group of students who otherwise are not actively engaged in the course.

In sum, simulations offer instructors a proven, active learning technique that results in high levels of student engagement. Instructors who use simulations indicate high satisfaction and rank it as one of the most effective approaches. The student experience in a simulation parallels future role expectations, offering an opportunity and incentive to participate.

Peer Assessment

Peer assessment is a process wherein students are involved in the evaluation of another student's work. It occurs when "learners consider and specify the level, value, or quality of a product or performance of other equal status learners" (Topping, 2009, p. 20). By reviewing the work of others, students develop their own abilities. Peer assessment supports student engagement as additional time is expended on assignments and students apply higher order learning skills such as critical evaluation of another's work. The approach, like simulations, is not new. Gaillet (1992, as reported in Topping, 2009) traces use of the technique to 1774 for the assessment of writing by students at the University of Glasgow.

The benefits of peer assessment accrue to all parties involved: Instructors selecting the method, ratees whose work is reviewed, and raters who assess and provide feedback. For instructors, the benefits may be practical. Peer assessment may mean less time is needed for assessment activities by the instructor. It also may be instructional, such as the creation of more actively engaged students. For the student who is rated, the benefits are greater feedback frequency and volume of timely feedback (Topping, 2009). Raters may be recipients of the greatest benefits as peer assessment provides both direct and indirect benefits. Directly, raters may benefit equally as students "assess each other's work using relevant criteria, and give feedback, not only for the benefits of the receiver but also for the purpose of their own development" (van den Berg, Admiraal & Pilot, 2006, p. 342). Assessment directly improves both individual skills through reinforcement, the quality of work (Cestone, Levine & Lane, 2008) and one's ability to evaluate one's own work (Luparelli, Wei Pang & Kalia, 2008). The use of peer assessment increases raters time spent on specific assignments from a perspective that complements assignment completion. Assessment requires subject area knowledge, which is reinforced through repeated exposure during assessment, as well as critical evaluation of the application of that knowledge. Indirectly, raters may benefit from peer assessment through increased motivation, increased confidence in abilities, greater ownership and sense of control over assignments, and greater future self-evaluation (Cestone et al., 2008). Collectively, peer assessment facilitates student engagement, providing rewards that are "plentiful and beneficial to both" raters and ratees (Topping, 2009, p. 20).

The validity and reliability of peer assessment across a range of educational settings and course environments is well established. In the context of peer assessment, validity is the degree to which the appraisal of a work is consistent with a true standard. In the case of simple arithmetic, an objective standard is known (e.g., $1 + 1 = 2$). Reliability is agreement between raters: If two students mark as correct $1 + 1 = 2$ then reliability is high. However, high reliability also exists if both record $1 + 1 = 3$ as correct. In this case, only the former has validity as it corresponds to a known objective standard. In the context of a subjective standard, which is common in competitive analysis, the solution of the expert is considered the standard for comparison. For example, in Porter's (1980) widely used 5-forces framework for assessing industry structure, the assessment of an industry as attractive or unattractive is based on weighting each of five structural forces which are based on multiple, often contradictory, determinants. If a student's evaluation of a peer's conclusion of industry attractiveness corresponds to the instructor's, it is valid. Reliability assesses the comparison across multiple peer raters in relationship to one another.

Evidence suggests peer assessment techniques possess sufficient reliability and validity for use in performance evaluation. Topping (2009), for example, reports that over 70% of studies show adequate reliability (i.e., the level of agreement between multiple raters) and validity (i.e., the degree of correspondence between an external standard or teacher score and peer rater scores). In a comprehensive meta-analysis, Falchikov and Goldfinch (2000) report minimal differences in the validity of peer assessment across disciplines. Not surprisingly, the lowest validity is in the social sciences ($r = .66$) where subjectivity is more common than objectivity. In the social sciences, the difference between peer ratings of a work and instructor's ratings are the greatest. The average agreement between student and instructor scores is higher in the physical sciences ($r = .76$) and engineering ($r = .74$). There is little difference across business disciplines and business does not differ significantly from nonbusiness disciplines. Nor does the validity of peer assessment significantly differ ($p > .05$) between lower and upper division college courses (Cestone et al., 2008). Overall, the literature suggests that across disciplines and course-levels, the peer-approach is a valid approach to assessment. A complete review of the approach is well beyond the scope of this chapter. For more thorough coverage of reliability and validity, the reader should consider excellent review such as those by Dochy, Segers, and Slujismans (1999), Topping (1998), and a meta-analysis by Falchikov and Goldfinch (2000).

A number of peer assessment aspects can be altered to influence the level of learner engagement through the peer assessment process. Decisions regarding these aspects can be used by the instructor to increase engagement through time on task, repetition, supervision by instructor, use in grading, and other aspects. Topping (1998) identifies 17 distinct facets to studies of peer assessment to consider. While several are specific to assessment research, the majority are best considered as controllable, constituting considerations pertinent to the customization of assessment within a course design (Table 1). Manipulation of these aspects can inspire or dissuade student engagement through the peer assessment process and influence student acceptance. In the second section, how these dimensions were structured within a course to facilitate learner engagement is detailed.

Skepticism over student acceptance is a primary concern of those considering adoption of the peer assessment approach. Acceptance by students can be influenced by structure and facilitation (Topping, 1998). Peer assessment acceptance and satisfaction are positively related to the perceived fairness, usefulness, and tone of feedback (Kaufman & Schunn, 2011). Ratees report concern over fairness as their single greatest area of

Table 1.   Instructor Controllable Peer Assessment Design Considerations.

Peer Assessment Aspect	Structural Decisions
Form	Quantitative/summative versus qualitative/formative)
Output	Physical deliverable versus presentation or activity
Grading	Relative weight of peer and instructor evaluations, allocation in course
Directionality	One-way, reciprocal, or mutual
Anonymity	Anonymous, confidential, or public
Form	Written, verbal, or combined
Ability of peers	Same or cross level
Relationship of raters to ratees	One to one, one to many, many to one, many to many
Place and timing	Within class or out of class
Voluntary versus compulsory	
Motivation for rater	Incentives versus no incentives, form of incentives

Source: Adapted from Topping (1998).

concern (Kaufman & Schunn, 2011). Course structures that incorporate instructor monitoring to ensure fairness are better able to encourage engagement than those that do not. Assessments that are considered positive in tone and useful are met with the greatest satisfaction. Positive impressions of peer assessment result from perceptions of self-improvement which creates trust in the process (Cestone et al., 2008).

Thus far, this chapter has summarized how simulations, and in particular whole-enterprise strategic management simulations, and peer assessment can increase student engagement. Both are well-established teaching techniques which are valid for increasing engagement and promoting direct and indirect learning outcomes. Next, this chapter will examine how these techniques can be used together in an integrated manner to further increase engagement, both within and beyond in-class meeting times.

WHOLE-ENTERPRISE SIMULATIONS AND PEER ASSESSMENT TO LEARN COMPETITIVE ANALYSIS

In this section, the use and extension of whole-enterprise simulations and peer assessment are reviewed in the context of a graduate elective course on competitive analysis taught at a private mid-western university. The course was designed around learning objectives with interconnected simulations and peer assessment as central components. For illustration, the innovative use and extension of whole-enterprise simulations and a variant of peer assessment in the context of the MBA elective course on competitive analysis will be presented. These approaches are readily transferable to undergraduate and graduate strategic management, strategic marketing, and other courses that use a simulation or could use peer assessment.

Competitive Analysis

Competitive analysis is a subsystem of comprehensive competitive intelligence systems which involve identification of informational needs; system planning; creation and monitoring of information; information storage and processing; data collection, analysis and reporting; and ensuring information availability to decision makers. Competitive analysis consists of a broad set of analytical techniques and organizational processes for scanning the general and industry environment in which a firm operates, assessing the firm's existing direct, indirect, and potential competitors, and evaluating existing and potential effects that these will have on the firm's competitive position in the marketplace. As these are critical roles performed by top managers, a whole-enterprise computer-based simulation has the essential information necessary to create a valid context for applying competitive analysis principles.

It should be noted that competitive analysis is distinct from data warehousing and mining techniques centered around information systems and data management. While competitive analysis may utilize these data and systems, it specifically seeks to develop usable information from the data to aid managerial decision making. Key competitive analysis activities identify needed information, including analysis and reporting, and disseminate the analysis to key decision makers. The focus, therefore, is on identifying the information needs of the decision makers and the use of tools and analytical techniques to inform them.

The competitive analysis course introduces the essential analytical tools for identifying and understanding competing firms. Competitive analysis encompasses more than 100 analytical techniques (Myburgh, 2004). The course focuses on 32 specific tools organized around seven common areas of analysis (Table 2) including issue identification, the general business environment, industry, subindustry and cross-industry analysis, internal analysis, competition between diversified multi-business firms, and

Table 2.   Competitive Analysis Techniques Examined and Applied to the
Simulation.

Issues, constituents and outcomes
  Stakeholder analysis[1]
  Competitor analysis[1]
  Strategic issue analysis

Environments, industries and firms
  Macroenvironmental (STEEP/PEST-D) analysis[2]
  Industry analysis[2]
  Business-level strategy[3]
  Functional capability and resource analysis[3]
  Value chain analysis[3]
  Business models

Industries and Interactions
  Competitive dynamics and rivalry[4]
  Product life cycle analysis[4]
  Technology life cycle (S-curve) analysis[4]
  Experience curve analysis[4]

One industry or many? groups and segments
  Customer value analysis[5]
  Customer segmentation analysis[5]
  Strategic group analysis[5]

Resources and capabilities of competing firms
  Patent analysis
  Financial ratio and statement analysis[6]
  Management profiling

SWOT as shorthand
  From SWOT to TOWS

Competitors in a corporate context
  Corporate-level strategy
  BCG growth/share portfolio matrix
  GE business screen matrix
  Growth vector analysis[7]
  Strategic funds programming[7]
  Sustainable growth rate analysis[7]

Competitor decisions and alignment
  Scenario analysis[8]
  Blindspot analysis[8]
  Game theory and decision making[8]

Analyzing configuration and implementation
  Organizational structure, decision and span of control
  Galbraith Model
  McKinsey's 7S analysis

Note: Superscripts (1–8) indicate tools eligible for application for analyst reports by analyst
report assignments.

organizational configuration and strategy implementation. The content comes from the primary textbook, Fleisher and Bensoussan's (2003) *Strategic and Competitive Analysis: Methods and Techniques for Analyzing Business Competition.* Each week, several tools are introduced and their history, utility, applicability, and application detailed.

Simulations: Incorporating and Extending

Whole-enterprise simulations are used in strategic management courses primarily for the purpose of providing the perspective of top managers tasked with ensuring organizational success and survival. In the competitive analysis course, the purpose differs. The simulation is used to create a *common context* among all student in the course for learning about the needs and value of competitive analysis from the perspective of both users and producers of it. The course incorporates the Capstone™ Business Simulation (Capsim Management Simulations, 2012). This is the most widely used whole-enterprise business simulation in strategic management, adopted by 17.7% of faculty using a simulation (Faria & Wellington, 2004).

Each simulated "industry" consists of up to six teams engaged in direct competition. Consistent with the use of simulations in common strategic management courses, students take on the role managers within one simulated firm. They are tasked with assessing the firms operating situation, setting strategy, and responding to changing events in a manner that maximizes company performance. Each decision round in the simulation represents one fiscal and calendar year in the life of an organization and the simulation can run up to eight rounds.

A Microsoft Excel-based interface is used for entry of all managerial spending and investment decisions in four areas: research and development (R&D), production, financing, and marketing (Figs. 1–4). Collectively, these decision areas are sufficient to control the performance of the organization. The simulation is interactive on a decision-cycle basis, with the effect of each round of decisions dependent on the decisions, prior conditions, and the decisions made by competing teams.

After each round, the simulation produces a report called "The Capstone Courier" which presents all product-level, company-level, and industry-level information needed for competitive analysis. Thus, all firms competing within a simulated industry face different aspects of a common situation. Overall industry conditions, such as excess inventory, are common to all firms while specific firm-level factors vary across teams. One

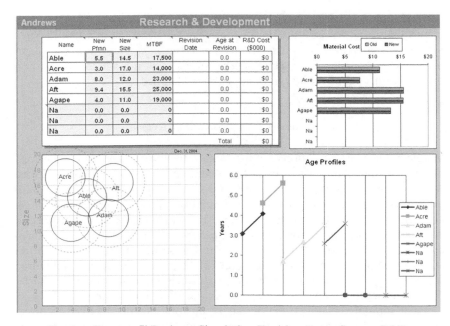

Fig. 1. Capstone™ Business Simulation Decision Entry Screen: R&D.

Andrews — Production

Schedule	Able	Acre	Adam	Aft	Agape	Na	Na	Na	TOTAL
Unit Sales Forecast	919	1,424	348	388	394	-	-	-	3,474
Inventory On Hand	141	8	37	54	69	-	-	-	309
Production Schedule	1,188	1,802	406	436	376	-	-	-	4,208
Production After Adj	1,176	1,784	402	432	372	-	-	-	4,167
Margins									
2nd shift/Overtime%	0.0%	28.7%	0.0%	0.0%	0.0%	0.0%	0.0%	0.0%	
Labor Cost/Unit	$7.85	$7.44	$8.97	$8.97	$8.97	$0.00	$0.00	$0.00	
Material Cost/Unit	$11.28	$7.63	$15.53	$15.45	$13.23	$0.00	$0.00	$0.00	
Total Unit Cost	$19.13	$15.07	$24.50	$24.42	$22.20	$0.00	$0.00	$0.00	
Contribution Margin	31.7%	28.3%	35.5%	26.0%	32.7%	0.0%	0.0%	0.0%	
Physical Plant									TOTAL
1st Shift Capacity	1,800	1,400	900	600	600	-	-	-	5,300
Buy/Sell Capacity	0	0	0	0	0	0	0	0	-
Automation Rating	4.0	5.0	3.0	3.0	3.0	-	-	-	
New Autom. Rating	4.0	5.0	3.0	3.0	3.0	0.0	0.0	0.0	
Investment ($000)	$0	$0	$0	$0	$0	$0	$0	$0	$0
Workforce	Last Year	Needed	This Year	1st Shift	2nd Shift	Overtime			
Complement	700	694	694	636	58	0.0%			

Fig. 2. Capstone™ Business Simulation Decision Entry Screen: Production.

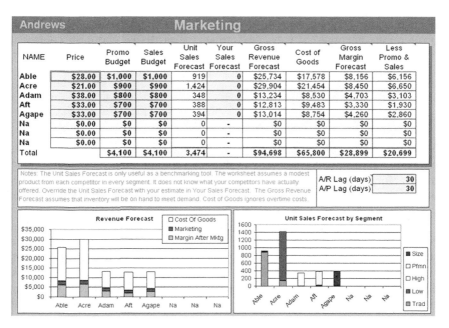

Andrews   **Finance**

Plant Improvements	
Total Investments ($000)	$0
Sales of Plant & Equipment	$0
Common Stock	
Shares Outstanding (000)	2,000
Price Per Share	$40.37
Earnings Per Share	$2.19
Max Issue ($000)	$16,148
Issue Stock ($000)	$0
Max Retire ($000)	$4,037
Retire Stock ($000)	$0
Dividend Per Share	$0.00
Current Debt	
Interest Rate	11.4%
Due This Year	$0
Borrow ($000)	$0
Cash Positions	
December 31, 2003	$5,352
December 31, 2004	$3,851

Outstanding Bonds

Series Number	Face ($000)	Current Yield	2003 Close
12.5S105	$6,917	12.4%	$101.19
14.5S107	$13,833	13.4%	$108.24
15.5S109	$20,750	13.4%	$115.30

Long Term Debt

Retire Long Term Debt ($000)	$0
Issue Long Term Debt ($000)	$0
Long term interest rate	12.8%
Maximum issue this year	$24,228

Fig. 3. Capstone™ Business Simulation Decision Entry Screen: Finance.

Andrews   **Marketing**

NAME	Price	Promo Budget	Sales Budget	Unit Sales Forecast	Your Sales Forecast	Gross Revenue Forecast	Cost of Goods	Gross Margin Forecast	Less Promo & Sales
Able	$28.00	$1,000	$1,000	919	0	$25,734	$17,578	$8,156	$6,156
Acre	$21.00	$900	$900	1,424	0	$29,904	$21,454	$8,450	$6,650
Adam	$38.00	$800	$800	348	0	$13,234	$8,530	$4,703	$3,103
Aft	$33.00	$700	$700	388	0	$12,813	$9,483	$3,330	$1,930
Agape	$33.00	$700	$700	394	0	$13,014	$8,754	$4,260	$2,860
Na	$0.00	$0	$0	0	-	$0	$0	$0	$0
Na	$0.00	$0	$0	0	-	$0	$0	$0	$0
Na	$0.00	$0	$0	0	-	$0	$0	$0	$0
Total		$4,100	$4,100	3,474	-	$94,698	$65,800	$28,899	$20,699

Notes: The Unit Sales Forecast is only useful as a benchmarking tool. The worksheet assumes a modest product from each competitor in every segment. It does not know what your competitors have actually offered. Override the Unit Sales Forecast with your estimate in Your Sales Forecast. The Gross Revenue Forecast assumes that inventory will be on hand to meet demand. Cost of Goods ignores overtime costs.

A/R Lag (days)	30
A/P Lag (days)	30

Revenue Forecast — ☐ Cost Of Goods, ■ Marketing, ☐ Margin After Mktg

$35,000
$30,000
$25,000
$20,000
$15,000
$10,000
$5,000
$0

Able Acre Adam Aft Agape Na Na Na

Unit Sales Forecast by Segment

1600
1400
1200
1000
800
600
400
200
0

Able Acre Adam Aft Agape Na Na Na

■ Size ☐ Pfmn ☐ High ■ Low ☐ Trad

Fig. 4. Capstone™ Business Simulation Decision Entry Screen: Marketing.

Financial Summary	CAPSTONE. COURIER				Round: 3 December 31, 2014	
Cash Flow Statement Survey	Andrews	Baldwin	Chester	Digby	Erie	Ferris
Cash flows from operating activities						
Net Income (Loss)	$16,654	$11,910	$8,618	$11,236	$12,510	($5,696)
Adjustment for non-cash items:						
Depreciation	$12,407	$8,333	$10,867	$10,647	$5,525	$11,313
Extraordinary gains/losses/writeoffs	($24)	($316)	$0	($340)	($1,825)	$0
Changes in current assets and liabilities:						
Accounts payable	$807	$4,069	$778	$2,338	($2,321)	($6,813)
Inventory	($15,260)	($6,660)	($11,917)	($8,284)	$8,150	$25,250
Accounts receivable	($1,108)	($4,402)	$24	($2,074)	$391	($265)
Net cash from operations	$13,476	$12,934	$8,369	$13,523	$22,431	$23,790
Cash flows from investing activities						
Plant improvements (net)	($20,977)	($6,020)	($38,700)	($30,820)	$10,518	$0
Cash flows from financing activities						
Dividends paid	($240)	($9,164)	$0	($1,242)	($523)	$0
Sales of common stock	$0	$0	$2,619	$0	$0	$0
Purchase of common stock	($5,002)	$0	$0	$0	($3,257)	$0
Cash from long term debt issued	$10,000	$0	$12,706	$8,167	$0	$0
Early retirement of long term debt	$0	($2,402)	$0	$0	($2,000)	$0
Retirement of current debt	($15,950)	($22,689)	($19,857)	($21,834)	($3,087)	($41,066)
Cash from current debt borrowing	$0	$22,031	$23,502	$28,954	$0	$0
Cash from emergency loan	$7,635	$0	$0	$0	$0	$17,276
Net cash from financing activities	($3,557)	($12,223)	$18,970	$14,045	($8,868)	($23,790)
Net change in cash position	($11,057)	($5,310)	($11,361)	($3,251)	$24,082	$0

Fig. 5. Firm and Competitor Financial Summary Capstone™ Simulation.

team may hold a large quantity of unsold inventory while another faces production shortages. It is at the industry level that a common context is created (Figs. 5–7).

Competitive Analysis Using Simulations

Thus far the use of the simulation largely mirrors its usage in the typical strategic management context. The student's role of *manager* is the primary means for involvement in a whole-enterprise simulation. To further increase engagement and illustrate course concepts, the additional role of *competitive analyst* is added to the traditional managerial role.

Consistent with the course content and professional expectations, the role of the competitive analyst is presenting to a company's management the status of competitors, their planned actions, and how they will potentially impact the firm. Analysts aid decision making, they do not suggest courses of action. Analysts are not responsible for managing the organization, but for providing sound, independent, objective insight into the actions of the firm's competitors and the task environment so that managers can make effective decisions.

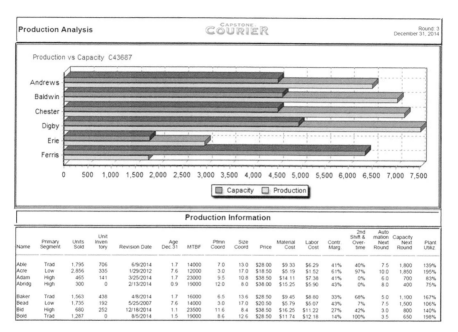

Name	Primary Segment	Units Sold	Unit Inventory	Revision Date	Age Dec 31	MTBF	Pfmn Coord	Size Coord	Price	Material Cost	Labor Cost	Contr. Marg.	2nd Shift & Over-time	Auto mation Next Round	Capacity Next Round	Plant Utiliz
Able	Trad	1,795	706	6/9/2014	1.7	14000	7.0	13.0	$28.00	$9.33	$6.29	41%	40%	7.5	1,800	139%
Acre	Low	2,856	335	1/29/2012	7.6	12000	3.0	17.0	$18.50	$5.19	$1.52	61%	97%	10.0	1,850	195%
Adam	High	465	141	3/25/2014	1.7	23000	9.5	10.8	$38.50	$14.11	$7.38	41%	0%	6.0	700	83%
Abridg	High	300	0	2/13/2014	0.9	19000	12.0	8.0	$38.00	$15.25	$5.90	43%	0%	8.0	400	75%
Baker	Trad	1,563	438	4/8/2014	1.7	16000	6.5	13.6	$28.50	$9.45	$8.80	33%	68%	5.0	1,100	167%
Bead	Low	1,735	192	5/25/2007	7.6	14000	3.0	17.0	$20.50	$5.79	$5.07	43%	7%	7.5	1,500	106%
Bid	High	680	252	12/18/2014	1.1	23500	11.6	8.4	$38.50	$16.25	$11.22	27%	42%	3.0	800	140%
Bold	Trad	1,287	0	8/5/2014	1.5	19000	8.6	12.6	$28.50	$11.74	$12.18	14%	100%	3.5	650	198%

Fig. 6. Portion of Firm and Competitor Production Summary Capstone™ Simulation.

Within the course, analysts report to managers in a company operating in a different simulation. These two roles are:

1. *Manager* — responsible for running a technology company aided, in part, by insights provided by competitive analysts. Additional role under competitive analysis approach: The manager is also the client who uses, provides feedback, and grades analyses based on quality, technical accuracy, use of appropriate tools, and usefulness for managing the company.
2. *Competitive Analyst* — responsible for applying the tools of competitive analysis to capture critical issues in the task environment to managers who will use the information.

Assignment of a manager to the additional role of competitive analyst within the same industry is problematic for several reasons. First, while the emphasis of the course is on competitive analysis, it should be noted that the managers strongly identify with their simulated firms. It is clear that

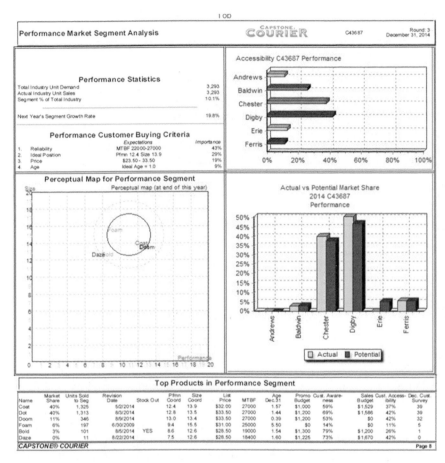

Fig. 7. Firm and Competitor Market Segment Report Capstone™ Simulation.

the individual's identity becomes intertwined with that of the firm they manage. Successful performance of their firm becomes their success; firm failure becomes their personal failure. As the role of the analyst is to provide insights to aid performance, an individual serving as an analyst to a competing firm would face a clear conflict of interest. Second, while a simulation can provide context for analysis, application of the tools to a variety of contexts is beneficial. The greater the application of the tools to multiple environments the greater the opportunity to see the contextual benefits and limitations of the tools.

To overcome these limitations, a second Capstone™ simulation industry is used. These two industries share some common user controls and many characteristics, such as the product categories and common reporting structures. They can, however, differ dramatically through instructor control over factors such as the number of firms in the industry (range of 2–6), the strategy utilized by computer teams, the manipulation of other factors such as growth rates, level of difficulty, and the use of advanced simulation modules such as labor disputes and total quality management (TQM) initiatives. The two industries will also become increasingly unique over the course of multiple rounds due to the differences in strategies and participant decisions.

These roles and the multiple simulations are presented (Fig. 8). Two independent simulation section or "industries" are created − simulation "A" and "B." One half of the class assumes the traditional managerial role in simulation "A" while also assuming the role of analysts reporting to manager "clients" in simulation "B." For the other half of the class, the roles are reversed − students are analysts in simulation "A" and managers in simulation "B." In this simulation, sufficient variability is introduced within each industry so that, across the two industries, the task environments constitute unique competitive situations.

This is a pioneering approach in which students take on multiple roles in two separate simulations. In the first simulation, they take on the role of a manager. In the second simulation, they take on the role of analyst reporting to managers. These dual roles mutually reinforce learning about the content area. Being a manager provides insights into what competitor information is needed for effective decision making. Being a competitive analyst, alternately, provides insights from an important but different perspective in great depth of detail. Removed from the need to make decisions and the responsibility for organizational performance, the analyst is commonly more objective and impartial, providing a more realistic assessment of conditions and options.

Creation of the analyst role and written reports results in a higher level of student engagement than the role of manager alone for three reasons. First, time on task is increased. Students must prepare a written analysis which requires greater scrutiny of the competitive situation than might be expected without a written component. Second, by analyzing the second simulation, the student spends time learning about a different competitive environment. Comparisons between the industry in which they are managers and the industry in which they are analysts create a richer learning experience. Third, students select the analysis tools that are of interest to

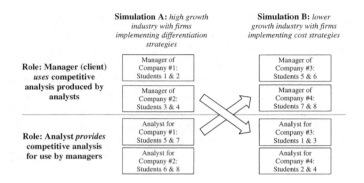

Example: Shown are student roles for a single course section with eight students; each is assigned to both managerial and analyst roles. Student #1 shares responsibility for managing company #1 in Simulation A with student #2. Their task is aided by analysis of the competitive environment produced by students # 5 and 7. Student #1 uses and assesses (grades) these analyses. Additionally, student #1, along with student #3, is an analyst for Company #3 in simulation B, providing analysis of the competitive situation that firm operates within. Those analyses are graded by students #5 and 6.

Fig. 8. Dual Manager (Client) and Analyst Roles in Whole-Enterprise Simulation.

them. Feedback from students indicates the process of selection is equal parts educational consumerism and pragmatic selection. Their first task is to select a tool they foresee as having potential use of in their work lives. Thus, the selection achieves an active learning element consistent with the tenets of andragogy. Students cannot apply what they do not understand (Whetten, 2007) and the students are driven to understand the tool so that it can be applied immediately in the context at hand as well as in future professional settings. Students also seek to please their client evaluators through selection of the most applicable and beneficial tool given situational factors. Collectively, these aspects yield an environment with a high level of engagement.

The level of learning needed to effectively complete a competitive analysis is comparable to that needed as a manager in a simulation. Effective application of the content to a situation requires progression along stages within Bloom's (1956) learning taxonomy. To complete any analysis, the student must move beyond knowledge (Bloom's level 1) and comprehend the tool (level 2). A true analysis (level 4) requires at a minimum the use of the tools to bundle and interpret facts in different manners to create new knowledge (i.e., level 3 application) while understanding the underlying cause and effect relationships. While the insights from multiple tools may be synthesized (level 5) to provide a more comprehensive solution, the students must select one tool for application, explaining why that tool was selected over others. This evaluation component (Bloom's level 6) represents the highest level of engrained knowledge: The ability to compare and contrast the available options and make a selection based on which is most appropriate. This is both the highest level of learning and is directly comparable to decisions that students will make when applying the techniques in their careers. As an analyst, the student needs to understand the tools available and which fits the particulars of a problem. As a user of analyses, much can be elicited about the nature of a situation simply from understanding which analysis tools was used. This, of course, requires a certain level of analyst quality. The astute user of information must place considerable trust in the abilities of the analyst or be able to assess this independently.

The result of the double simulation is a high level of learner engagement due to involvement in both the manager and analyst roles. Students in both actively seek to understand cause and affect relationships in a constantly evolving competitive situation, provide solutions to increase performance, and evaluate potential courses of action. This approach appears to be novel: Discussions with the simulation provider indicates this is the only course to integrate the role of competitive analyst or use multiple simulations to increase engagement.

From Peer Assessment to Client-Based Assessment

Two objectives of the course are (1) the development of skills to serve as a competitive analysts and (2) the development of skills needed to be an effective user of decision aids developed within competitive analyst systems. Both are facilitated through completion of peer assessments, a form of student engagement (Willey & Gardner, 2010). The product of competitive analysis is commonly a report which highlights important factors facing the firm, changes in those factors, and how they will impact the firm. From a pragmatic perspective, the key measure of learning success in a business school is not the teacher's evaluation of the student's work, but the ability of the student to create value for their post-graduation employing organization. Assessment of the quality of an analysis may not be best provided by the instructor, but by the users of the analysis. While instructors are perhaps the best judge of the technical merits of the analysis, they may not the best judges of their accuracy and usefulness.

Peer assessment increases student engagement in learning the process (Cestone et al., 2008; Falchikov & Goldfinch, 2000; Kaufman & Schunn, 2011; van den Berg, Admiraal & Pilot, 2006). In general, peer assessment involves the review of student work by peers — individuals at the same hierarchical level of the student. Learning takes place both by exposure to the work and perspective of fellow students, but also by the application of critical evaluation of the work. This critical evaluation is embedded in memory and becomes part of the development of students' future work.

The incorporation of the second role as an analyst reporting to a manager in another industry presents an opportunity and a dilemma for grading. While the instructor can evaluate technical validity of a tools application, its value and usefulness is best evaluated by those who rely on it for insights. That individual is the manager. The incorporation of a second role of analyst represents a change from peer assessment (i.e., at equal hierarchical levels) to individuals at holding positions at different levels within a hierarchy. As the analyst relationship is most typically structured with managers as the recipient or clients of analyst output, this is labeled "client-based" assessment.

In typical peer assessments, the equality of peers standing is emphasized, specifically to increase the receptivity of the ratee to the rater's insights. In a client-based approach, the *divergence* in status is emphasized — differences in hierarchical standing are desired and emphasized. This divergent status difference best represents the real-world environment within which competitive analysis is created and utilized. As students using the simulation enact the role of managers, this is extended to the assessment. The managers have "hired" the analyst to provide specialized insights on particular aspects of a competitive environment. The status difference mirrors the work environment of competitive analysts within firms. It is more than role play — the managers actually use and find value in the analyses, relying on them to provide unique insights on the situation. These insights aid performance on the simulation which in turn influences student course grades. It is truly isomorphic — realistically representing the real-world relationship between analysts and clients. The peer is truly a "client" — a fellow student in the course, but one who relies on the analysis to make decisions which directly influence actual course grades. The client approach introduces an added sense of realism to the assignment. Paraphrasing student comments on the technique: "Assignments did not seem to be 'assignments.' You had to take each seriously. They guided and were graded by your client who needs the insights." The rating form used by managers to complete the assessment of their analysts' report is presented in Fig. 9.

The engagement offered by client-based assessment is accomplished largely outside of the classroom where active learning approaches commonly do not reach. In this course, analyst reports were collected and distributed electronically per a predetermined schedule as were assessments of the reports by managers. This is facilitated by the nature of the simulation. Each student was provided access codes to both simulations. The information needed for the analysis assignments was readily available and the analysis could be completed at any time over a multi-day period. Similarly, the analyst reports were collected electronically and, once all received, were distributed electronically to managers to facilitate their decision making. Managers then completed their evaluations of those analyses.

In this course, several steps increase the acceptance and benefits of the assessments with positive results. First, research suggests that raters should be motivated to do a good job and that there should be some type of incentive to complete good work or some disincentive to complete poor or improper evaluations (Cestone et al., 2008). Given the nature of the MBA students, an informal mechanism was incorporated. The instructor reserved the right to reduce the scores on analyst assignments if the grading deviated significantly from the instructor's and if the assignment was of unacceptable quality or generally unprofessional.

Second, the use of an average score from multiple raters is advised over the use of a single rater. Cestone et al. (2008) review of studies suggests two or three evaluators are ideal. Too few or too many raters decreased validity. Too few rates increase random error and rater biases. Too many raters increase fatigue from completing assessment of a large number of works. Each team manager, there are typically two, rates the work of each analyst.

Third, while anonymous assessments may yield greater honesty, they can also be harsher. A negative or critical tone in assessments reduces the acceptance of the assessment. This is hedged by having all analysts present their analyses face-to-face to their managers during class time, while refraining from providing complete breakdown of managers' evaluations of their reports. This increases engagement and the ability to convey nuanced insights from the analyses. Managers are not required to provide complete feedback to their analysts, but these face-to-face debriefings allow managers to ask follow-up questions. Anecdotally, it seems the analysts leave these debriefings with a sense of how their analyses compare to those produced by other analysts and how it is received by their client. To

Peer Assessment Form

To complete the peer review, first read the paper. Then provide the following:
1. Written Assessment.
   a. Two to three aspects of the analysis that were done well.
   b. Two to three aspects of the analysis which could be improved.
   c. Overall comments.

2. Quantitative Assessment.
   Using the Likert-type scale below, please indicate your level of agreement with each of the following statements. Note that all scores except a 1 are considered passing.
   1. Insufficient − did not meet expectations. Would not contract with this analyst in the future.
   2. Sufficient − met the minimum contractual expectations
   3. Average − met contractual expectations
   4. Strong − exceeded contractual expectations
   5. Excellent − Wow! Would sole source this analysts in the future.

	Insufficient/ Strongly Disagree			Excellent/ Strongly Agree
1. Of the tool(s) available for use, the tool(s) the analyst selected was the most appropriate choice(s).	1	2	3	4	5
2. The tool(s) were used in an appropriate manner and with emphasis on competitors.	1	2	3	4	5
3. The level of detail is appropriate.	1	2	3	4	5
4. Data − the appropriate level of data used and it is accurate.	1	2	3	4	5
5. Data − the data presented is the most appropriate for the tool; is free from errors.	1	2	3	4	5
6. The analysis will aid your decision making.	1	2	3	4	5
7. The analysis highlights important issues for you as the client and these are the major issues facing the client.	1	2	3	4	5
8. Overall, this analysis is of professional quality.	1	2	3	4	5
9. Overall, this analysis is of better quality than that from other analysts.	1	2	3	4	5
10. Overall, this analysis is of better quality than that which you submitted to your client.	1	2	3	4	5

Fig. 9.   Peer Assessment Form.

balance the need for feedback with the need for objective evaluation, analysts are provided with the instructor's score and the average scores from all managers. Instructor and client scores are equally weighted in grade calculations.

The combination of these approaches results in few concerns of fairness being expressed by the students. The overall response is positive. The manager and client roles appear to result in the enactment of the student's professional persona and the completion all roles in a similar manner.

CONCLUSION AND LIMITATIONS

Thus far, two instructional techniques to increase student engagement — simulations and peer assessment — have been detailed. While these approaches can be utilized independently, integrating them results is a highly interactive and engaging course where the simulation and peer assessments achieve symbiotic benefits. Performance in the simulation is enhanced by the application of competitive analyst reports which are used by peer "clients." Assessment of analyst reports leads to greater insights on the simulation, and subsequently higher levels of performance on both the simulation and future analysis work. Despite the benefits examined, these approaches are not without several important limitations and costs that should be considered before adoption.

Limitations

Educators should incorporate pedagogies based on what best facilitates the student's learning process (Diamond, 1998). If simulations and peer evaluation are valuable components, what limits their adoption? While each of these methods has been outlined and their efficacy illustrated, their adoption is not without complications that may legitimately hinder their usage.

In the case of simulations, three factors appear most prohibitive: learning curves, recurring time commitments, and concerns about technology. Simulations require substantial up-front investments of time for both instructors and learners. Each simulation has unique interface and operating parameters. Most simulations are accompanied by lengthy user manuals explaining environmental factors, decisions to be made, decision parameters, and other operating rules. While necessary, this results in a considerable up-front learning curve for instructors and students. Based on a survey of non-adopters, Faria and Wellington (2004) report preparation time as the leading cause of non-usage. If a simulation is to be adopted, the use of a simulation in a class must be balanced in regard to the learning curve required.

Ongoing time is also a factor in simulation usage. While the benefits of learning from complex, whole-enterprise simulations are substantial, so are the demands of interactions between student and instructor. It is not uncommon for a strategic management course, for example, to include three or four practice rounds for students to learn the basics of the simulation, a reset of the simulation, followed by six to eight rounds of graded performance. It is not uncommon for strong teams to seek out instructor advice on advanced and complicated plans. Nor is it uncommon for the instructor to meet with poorly performing teams for learning from the simulation to occur. On average, instructors should expect to commit to two or three one-hour sessions with each team involved in a simulation over a semester. This level of involvement is necessary to ensure continued engagement of high performers as well as present disengagement by those disenfranchised with their performance.

A third concern about simulation adoption comes from dissatisfaction with the technology based on prior use. Simulations have used several levels of technology, all of which have greatly advanced recent years. Most whole-enterprise simulations are based on a Microsoft Excel or web platform, facilitated via Internet-hosted sites. From a logistics standpoint, instructors can largely schedule the simulation and forget it. The need for actively processing rounds and handling decision files has long passed. Administrative demands have declined. However, the need for interaction with student teams has not.

While this chapter focuses on a course that utilizes simulations in a traditional in-class setting, the approach is readily adaptable to distance learning environments. The weekly presentation of analytical tools by the instructor can be adapted to synchronous and asynchronous settings. The submission of analyst reports can be easily conducted via standard classroom management software such as Sakai or Blackboard. The face-to-face interactions between analysts and their client managers can be accomplished using video chat software. Lastly, instructor collection of managers rating of their analyst's reports could be streamlined through the use of built-in grading and/or survey tools.

Faculty may also have concerns about the adoption of peer assessment. While a large literature on the technique supports its acceptance, reliability, and validity, instructors may still be fearful. The peer assessment process, in the use context of this advanced and integrated course, appears to be both valid and reliable. Student acceptance is both manageable and high, as is engagement in the process. It should be cautioned that the implementation of the approach increases rather than decreases instructor time on grading. This is due to combining both instructor and peer assessment techniques. The beneficial aspects in terms of learning and engagement, however, exceed the time demands in this setting.

CONCLUSION

This chapter has detailed two instructional techniques, simulations and peer assessment, which can be used to increase student engagement. Student engagement has been defined consistent with Kuh (2009) as the level of involvement and the quality of effort. An overview of these methods as active learning approaches and how each influences student engagement has been presented. Each of the approaches can be utilized independently to increase learner engagement.

In a whole-enterprise simulation, students take on the role of top managers responsible for setting strategy, analyzing competitive environments, and making decisions for their virtual organizations. Whole-enterprise simulations have a long history of use and are immersive, requiring a high level of active engagement. Simulations elicit complexity through the integration of interrelated functional decisions that is difficult to achieve using other instructional techniques. This complexity creates the need for students to expend considerable time and effort to assess and understand causal associations. Students actively engage in simulations because the context of the simulation parallels what they are seeking to hold upon degree completion. Simulations are competitive, creating intrinsic motivation to outperform fellow students. This requires active participation, providing intrinsic motivation to spend time on tasks.

Next, peer assessment techniques in which students take partial responsibility for the evaluation of work created by fellow students are reviewed. Peer assessment benefits all students involved in the process. For the student whose work is evaluated, benefits include greater feedback frequency and volume in a timely fashion (Topping, 2009). Those completing assessment of other students work benefit as the process increases their skills through direct and indirect benefits. Completing peer assessments directly increases the quality of an individual's subsequent work (Cestone et al., 2008) and improves one's ability to evaluate their own work (Luparelli et al., 2008). Indirectly, peer assessment results in increased motivation, increase confidence in abilities, greater ownership and sense of control over assignments, and greater future self-evaluation (Cestone et al., 2008).

Next an elective graduate-level course on competitive analysis that incorporates simulations and peer assessments as core structural course elements to encourage and facilitate engagement is detailed. The basic forms of whole-enterprise computer simulations and peer assessment can be adapted, expanded and integrated within a course structure to further enhance engagement is illustrated. The extensions include the multiple simulations and assessment of competitive analyst work by fellow students in the position of client. Learning and performance in the simulation is enhanced by the application of competitive analyst reports which are evaluated and assessed via peer assessment. This assessment in turn leads to greater insights on the simulation and subsequently higher levels of performance on both the simulation and the analyst reports.

Each of the techniques detailed may be incorporated independently. Collectively, the chapter provides the insights needed for adoption and of these methods with the hopes of additional extension and combination with other active learning methods that will advance efforts to increase student engagement.

REFERENCES

Ashforth, B. E., & Mael, F. (1989). Social identity theory and the organization. *Academy of Management Review, 14*(1), 20–39.

Bandura, A. (1997). *Self-efficacy: The exercise of control.* New York, NY: W.H. Freeman.

Bloom, B. S. (1956). *Taxonomy of educational objectives: The classification of educational goals.* London: Longmans, Green and Company.

Bowen, D. (1987). Developing a personal theory of experiential learning. *Simulation & Games, 18*, 192–206.

Cannon-Bowers, J., & Bowers, C. (2010). Synthetic learning environments: On developing a science of simulations, games, and virtual worlds for training. In S. W. J. Kozlowski & E. Salas (Eds.), *Learning, training, and development in organizations* (pp. 229–262). New York, NY: Routledge.

Capsim Management Simulations. (2012). Capstone™ Business Simulation. Retrieved from http://www.capsim.com

Cestone, C. M., Levine, R. E., & Lane, D. R. (2008). Peer assessment and evaluation in team-based learning. *New Directions for Teaching and Learning, 116*, 69–78.

Diamond, R. M. (1998). *Designing and assessing courses and curricula: A practical guide.* San Francisco, CA: Jossey-Bass.

Dochy, F., Segers, M., & Slujismans, D. (1999). The use of self-, peer and co-assessment in higher education: A review. *Studies in Higher Education, 24,* 331–350.

Falchikov, N., & Goldfinch, J. (2000). Student peer assessment in higher education: A meta-analysis comparing peer and teacher marks. *Review of Educational Research, 70*(3), 287–322.

Faria, A. J. (1986). A survey on the use of business games in academia and business. *Simulation & Games, 18,* 207–224.

Faria, A. J., & Nulsen, R. (1996). Business simulation games: Current usage levels a ten year update. In A. L. Patz & J. K. Butler (Eds.), *Developments in business simulation and experiential exercises* (pp. 22–28). Madison, WI: Omnipress.

Faria, A. J., & Wellington, W. J. (2004). A survey of simulation game users, former-users, and never-users. *Simulation & Gaming, 35*(2), 178–207.

Fink, L. D. (2003). *Creating significant learning experiences: An integrated approach to designing college courses.* San Francisco, CA: Jossey-Bass.

Fleischer, C. S., & Bensoussan, B. E. (2003). *Strategic and competitive analysis: Methods and techniques for analyzing business competition.* Upper Saddle River, NJ: Prentice Hall.

Gaillet, L. I. (1992, March). *A foreshadowing of modern theories in higher education: The work of the Scottish rhetorician George Jardine.* Paper presented at the 43rd Annual Meeting of the Conference on College Composition and Communication, Cincinnati, OH.

Harrington, C. F., & Schibik, T. J. (2004). Methods for maximizing student engagement in the introductory business statistics course: A review. *Journal of American Academy of Business, 4*(1&2), 360–364.

Jennings, D. (2002). Strategic management: An evaluation of the use of three learning methods. *Journal of Management Development, 21*(9), 655.

Kaufman, J. H., & Schunn, C. D. (2011). Students' perceptions about peer assessment for writing: Their origin and impact on revision work. *Instructional Science: An International Journal of the Learning Sciences, 39*(3), 387–406.

Knotts, U. S., Jr., & Keys, J. B. (1997). Teaching strategic management with a business game. *Simulation & Gaming, 28*(4), 377–394.

Knowles, M. S. (1990). *The adult learner: A neglected species* (4th ed.). Houston, MA: Gulf Pub. Co.

Kuh, G. D. (2009). The national survey of student engagement: Conceptual and empirical foundations. *New Directions for Institutional Research, 141,* 5–20.

Lainema, T., & Lainema, K. (2007). Advancing acquisition of business know-how: Critical learning elements. *Journal of Research on Technology in Education, 40*(2), 183–198.

Luparelli, G. N., Wei Pang, L., & Kalia, T. (2008). The use of peer assessment grading forms and case studies in undergraduate business administration classes. *Proceedings of the Northeast Business & Economics Association,* 207–209.

Myburgh, S. (2004). Competitive intelligence: Bridging organizational boundaries. *Information, Management Journal, 38*(2), 46–55.

Porter, M. E. (1980). *Competitive strategy: Techniques for analyzing industries and competitors.* New York, NY: Free Press.

Tompson, G. H., & Dass, P. (2000). Improving students' self-efficacy in strategic management: The relative impact of cases and simulations. *Simulation & Gaming, 31*(1), 22–41.

Topping, K. J. (1998). Peer assessment between students in colleges and universities. *Review of Educational Research, 68,* 249–276.

Topping, K. J. (2009). Peer assessment. *Theory Into Practice, 48*(1), 20–27.

Trim, P. R. J. (2004). Human resource management development and strategic management enhanced by simulation exercises. *Journal of Management Development, 23*(4), 399–413.

van den Berg, I., Admiraal, W., & Pilot, A. (2006). Design principles and outcomes of peer assessment in higher education. *Studies in Higher Education, 31*(3), 341–356.

Whetten, D. A. (2007). Principles of effective course design: What I wish I had known about learning-centered teaching 30 years ago. *Journal of Management Education, 31*(3), 339–357.

Whitton, N. (2011). Game engagement theory and adult learning. *Simulation & Gaming, 42* (5), 596–609.

Willey, K., & Gardner, A. (2010). Investigating the capacity of self and peer assessment activities to engage students and promote learning. *European Journal of Engineering Education, 35*(4), 429–443.

Wolfe, J. (1976). The effects and effectiveness of simulations in business policy teaching applications. *Academy of Management Review, 1,* 47–56.

Wolfe, J. (1993). A history of business teaching games in English-speaking and post-socialist countries. *Simulation & Gaming, 24,* 446–463.

Wolfe, J. (1997). The effectiveness of business games in strategic management course work. *Simulation & Gaming, 28*(4), 360–376.

Wolfe, J., & Roberts, C. R. (1993). A further study of the external validity of business games: Five-year peer group indicators. *Simulation & Gaming, 24*(1), 21–33.

Wolfe, J., & Roge, J. N. (1997). Computerized general management games as strategic. *Simulation & Gaming, 28*(4), 423–441.

BRINGING THE CLASSROOM TO LIFE: USING VIRTUAL WORLDS TO DEVELOP TEACHER CANDIDATE SKILLS

Danielle Mirliss, Grace May and Mary Zedeck

ABSTRACT

Preparing future teachers requires teacher educators to share both theory and its translation to best practice. Traditional approaches to this learning process include textbooks, case studies, role-play, observation, and eventually fieldwork in a classroom. Understanding what their future students need or appropriately responding to situations in the classroom is far different than the reality of teaching in schools. Although case studies provide an opportunity for perspective taking, collaboration, and developing problem solving skills in a safe environment, it is still a relatively passive experience. The use of virtual worlds to create engaging simulations offers a possibility in bridging this gap between theory and practice. The School of Education and Human Services at Seton Hall University has designed a virtual world simulation to provide college students with the opportunity to be immersed in a virtual classroom setting in which they take on the roles of avatar teachers and grade school

Increasing Student Engagement and Retention using Immersive Interfaces: Virtual
Worlds, Gaming, and Simulation
Cutting-edge Technologies in Higher Education, Volume 18, 129–160
ISSN: 2044-9968/doi:10.1108/S2044-9968(2012)000006C008

students who may require various modifications/accommodations. This chapter will discuss the design and implementation of this project. Data were collected on the students' experiences in order to assess possible learning gains, affordances of the technology, and lessons learned for future educators who are considering the implementation of virtual world technologies.

INTRODUCTION

Seton Hall University is committed to providing its learning community with access to technologies needed to support academic work. In response to the University's 1996 strategic plan, a mobile computing program was designed and implemented to ensure all members of the learning community have access to learning resources which are increasingly online. It includes three interdependent components: (1) Access — the University provides students the use of a laptop as part of their tuition fees, (2) Curricular Integration — the University provides support and incentives to faculty to facilitate the integration of technology into the curriculum, and (3) Services and Support — includes wireless Network access, Support Service Desk, laptop repairs, insurance, training, etc. The University has also been investigating alternative form factors. In 2005, convertible tablet PCs were provided to Math and Science majors and faculty were given the choice between this model and a standard laptop (Weitz, Wachsmuth, & Mirliss, 2005). Recently, the potential of mobile devices has been investigated, beginning with a Nokia smartphone pilot in 2009. Pilots were launched in 2011 for Education faculty using iPads and Math and Science majors using Android tablets.

With its commitment to investigating emerging trends and adopting new technologies that support teaching and learning, it was a natural progression for Seton Hall to explore the potential of virtual worlds. The first virtual world simulation was implemented in 2006 in an undergraduate Industrial/Organization Psychology course taught by one of the authors. The goal of this simulation was to provide students with the experience of completing a collaborative activity using a virtual technology that could prepare them for the dispersed nature of work in a global economy (Mirliss & Trotta, 2006).

Since that initial simulation activity, faculty members at Seton Hall have explored the potential of virtual worlds in various disciplines. Projects include the House of 7, a reproduction of the House of the Seven Gables to support literature courses (Balkun, Zedeck, & Trotta, 2009), Emergency Preparedness Training (Hewitt, Spencer, Mirliss, & Twal, 2010), Environmental Studies (Trotta & Glenn, 2012), and Business Law. These projects currently reside on Pirate Island, Seton Hall's virtual land located in Second Life™.

The inspiration for many of these projects originated from workshops and faculty showcases that are hosted by Seton Hall's Teaching, Learning and Technology Center (TLTC). It was within the context of one of these faculty workshops that Dr. Grace May, Associate Professor of Educational Studies, learned about the potential of virtual worlds and the educational impact made by the previously mentioned projects. Reflecting on the challenge of teaching future teachers how to handle behavior issues in the classroom, she realized that virtual worlds like Second Life™ could provide an essential intermediate step between theory and real life application. The creation of a classroom where students could bring traditional case studies to life through avatars might broaden their understanding of what behavior represents to a pupil, how it affects others, and different approaches to classroom management.

PREPARING FUTURE EDUCATORS

Shulman (2004) once described classroom teaching as "perhaps the most complex, most challenging, and most demanding, subtle, nuanced, and frightening activity that our species has ever invented" (p. 504). Preparing teachers for that role requires the development of a rich knowledge base translated to application in a dynamic environment. There is often a chasm between teacher preparation programs, which focus on having students understand the role and content associated with teaching, and K-12 schools that focus on student teachers' ability to perform teaching (Calderhead & Shorrock, 1997).

One of the most challenging areas for teacher preparation programs to fully prepare their students in is classroom organization and management. A teacher's ability to exercise effective classroom organization and behavior management skills is critical to the success of a wide range of students. This is true for both general education and special education settings. For students with emotional and behavioral disorders (EBD), the lack of successful teaching and management strategies can exclude them from participating in the learning environment of a classroom. "Children who perform low academically are at a greater risk for behavioral problems because inappropriate behavior typically results in escape from difficult academic tasks" (Oliver & Reschly, 2010, p. 188). This can result in removal from the classroom, which reinforces that student's behavior as well as the teacher's; that student no longer has to participate in the task and the teacher no longer has the disruption. In addition, if behavioral problems are allowed to manifest and progress in the early school years, then these behaviors will most likely stay with the student in later grades. The ability of a teacher to handle these situations is critical to the later success of these students.

In their analysis of 26 course syllabi from teacher education programs, Oliver and Reschly (2010) provide evidence that teacher education programs may be inadequately preparing teachers to effectively educate diverse learners. Their findings suggest that very few universities offer a dedicated course on classroom management and even if the content is taught in sections through the curriculum, there is no consensus, based on research, as to what topics should be covered. Westling's (2010) review of general and special education teachers' knowledge and experience with students with behavioral problems reveals that both groups report feeling inadequately prepared by their teacher preparation programs for these issues. The findings suggest that general education teachers are at a greater disadvantage because they possess fewer classroom management strategies and cannot identify sources for support.

The challenge for teacher preparation programs is to develop more meaningful practice before and during clinical experiences to enhance pedagogical content knowledge and classroom management and discipline skills. In the Educating School Teachers report, Levine (2006) stresses the need for educators to "refocus work on the world of practice" (p. 9). Knowledge acquisition should go beyond providing learners with a set of tools but also provide them with opportunities to use those tools (Brown, Collins, & Duguid, 1989). Enculturation of learners into a community of practice is vital to their understating of how to apply knowledge. The use of educational technology to provide ill-structured, authentic learning opportunities can support preparation of future teachers for the challenges of managing a classroom. Specifically, simulations and games may provide engaging opportunities for teacher candidates to practice skills that can be transferred to a real classroom setting.

Simulations and Games

The power of simulations and games as educational tools lies in their ability to provide learners with safe venues to practice important skills. The Society for the Advancement of Games and Simulations in Education and Training (SAGSET) defines simulations and games as:

> teaching and learning methods in which participants are directly involved in making decisions and learning from the outcomes of these. Their active, student centered nature means that they are memorable and highly motivating. They enable the exploration of the complex nature of the real world and interdisciplinary, interacting subjects as well as the more basic needs of understanding, doing and skills practice. (Society for the Advancement of Games and Simulations in Education and Training, 2002 as cited in Conrad & Donaldson, 2011, p. 101)

A distinction can be been made between the terms games and simulations. Games are described as competitive and entertaining activities in which users apply knowledge inherent to the game to advance in levels to win. In contrast, simulations are more structured experiences designed with interacting variables which requires the user to assume a particular role, make real world decisions, and experience the effects of those decisions in a safe environment (Aldrich, 2009; Gredler, 2004). Both activities support experiential learning in which learners are active recipients of knowledge and become negotiators of their experiences. They can also provide authentic learning experiences that mirror the complexity encountered in the real world including failure and contradictions that challenge learners to question their assumptions (Lindsey & Berger, 2009, p. 121).

Pedagogical praxis proposes that technology can be the vehicle in which students are able to participate in communities of practice (Shaffer, 2004), and the creation of games/simulations can facilitate this goal. Gee (2005) states that instructional games can support *authentic professionalism* by providing learners with a simulated opportunity to experience the behavior and problem solving skills of various professionals. Similarly, Shaffer (2005) uses the term *epistemic games* to refer to simulations in which learners develop the knowledge, skills, and abilities of a practitioner in a professional domain (e.g., doctor, lawyer, or journalist) during game play.

The adoption of an alternative identity is facilitated through the use of role-play which allows for the exploration of complex social issues and situations. Technology mediated role-play has the ability to transcend the possibility of face-to-face role-play scenarios by allowing players to assume new digital identities and be transported to various computer generated

locations. This allows individuals to assume roles that are drastically different from their real-world identities in terms of age, race, ethnicity, and
physical descriptors. It has also been suggested that lengthy exposure to
realistic simulations can facilitate the development of new moral and ethical choices (Prensky, 2009). In addition, possible gains in performance
through increased self-awareness have been reported (Fletcher & Bailey,
2003), as well as the idea that speaking and assessing from different role
perspectives may help us think about the basis of our own and others'
views and prejudices, potentially revealing valuable insights (Morse,
Littleton, Macleod, & Ewins, 2009).

Ip and Naidu (2001) explored the importance of role-play to increase
student engagement and discover new possibilities in alternative worlds.
The incorporation of role-playing into the design of simulations, categorized by the authors as first-hand-experience-based designs, provides students with a realistic environment in which they can safely make decisions,
reflect on mistakes, and become active in the learning process. Authenticity
and complexity is achieved by creating a cover story that gives context to
the learners who must assume the roles of the various characters to work
through ill-structured challenges.

POTENTIAL OF VIRTUAL WORLDS

The unique attributes of virtual worlds support the development of active
learning experiences for students, including role-play simulations. In an
educational context, virtual worlds have been described as a sub-category
of Virtual Learning Environments (VLEs) (Dalgarno & Lee, 2010). VLEs
also include technologies such as learning management systems (i.e., Blackboard and Moodle), but it is the unique affordances of virtual worlds that
expands their educational potential. In addition, virtual worlds allow faculty to inexpensively explore the use of 3D VLEs and possibly "co-opt"
(Buchanan, 2003) technologies that students are already familiar with from
their leisure activities (e.g., online gaming).

Virtual worlds can be defined as online, 3D environments in which users
can communicate with others and construct their virtual surroundings.
Schroeder (2011) distinguishes between immersive virtual reality (VR)
systems that require single-user head mounted display (HMD) systems that
were widely researched in the 1990s and present day networked virtual
worlds that can run on standard desktops and laptops. The advantage
of being networked is that virtual worlds become persistent spaces that

allow many users to interact with one another and customize their virtual space by interacting with objects (i.e., building, scripting, and acquiring objects).

Even though there are similarities, online games and virtual worlds differ in important ways that are pivotal to the development of role-play simulations. As previously mentioned, virtual worlds do not contain a built-in script with goals for users to achieve. They are open-ended spaces that exist as social places for users to interact with one another using avatars. Users can actually live another life inside of a virtual world, developing relationships and even securing employment. Finally, virtual worlds are completely customizable and can support the use of scripting languages to support interactivity with the digital surroundings, creating a unique canvas for the creation of educational experiences.

Another unique aspect of virtual worlds when compared to other VLEs is the representation of oneself as an avatar. An avatar can be defined as an online, graphical representation of oneself that can interact with objects and other users (through their avatars) in a virtual world (Peterson, 2005; Taylor, 2002). Avatars are customizable and can take on many forms from idealized selves, animals, furries (cross between an animal and person), inanimate objects, and fantasy characters.

Avatars enhance the role-playing experience in simulations. They allow users to engage in experiences that transcend their day-to-day real life (Deuchar & Nodder, 2003). Users no longer exist solely in the mind; instead they can assume digital identities that allow them to engage in various interactions. Taylor (2002) adds that the combination of being embodied and the ability to interact with the environment through this embodiment creates a feeling of realism for the user (p. 41). Assuming an alternate identity challenges students to think outside of their comfort zones and learn how to view problems through the perspectives of that role (Lee & Hoadley, 2007).

In addition to transcending reality and assuming new identities, role-play and learning in virtual worlds is supported by their ability to make users feel as if they are in another location (presence) with other people (co-presence). This can have a powerful impact on learning through simulations since low fidelity 3D technologies (i.e., virtual worlds) can create environments and experiences that are perceived as real to users. There is the potential for higher transfer of knowledge from the simulation environment to real life if the learning environments (identical-elements theory) and tasks (transfer-through-principle theory) used in each are considered similar (Goldstein, 1993, pp. 124–128).

Presence is linked to how immersed a person feels within an environment. Immersion has been defined as the sensory modalities and their fidelity (i.e., realism) provided by the technology (Slater, 2003), a psychological state in which one perceives a constant stream of stimuli that is enveloping (Witmer & Singer, 1998) and the ability of a game to draw people in (Jennett et al., 2008). Different people can experience various levels of presence within the same immersive system. Conversely, different systems with various levels of immersion can result in similar levels of presence for different people. While highly fidelity systems can come close to being indistinguishable from real life, finding out what is perceptually important for users to experience presence in low fidelity systems can benefit educational research.

Presence has also been linked with the embodiment provided by the use of avatars in virtual worlds. Taylor (2002) defines presence through the actions of an *embodied activity*. It is through interacting with others in a shared place that users find themselves *there*. A user's presence is grounded in a virtual space through his/her avatar's interactions as well as the ability of one to be self-mirrored as well as mirror back (Taylor, 2002, p. 44).

This notion of *embodiedpresence* is similar to the concepts of *teleproximity* and *sociability*. Teleproximity is defined as the proximity that is experienced through the use of computers and through the awareness of others in the mediated environment. This group awareness allows others to be perceived and for a communication exchange to begin. Sociability describes the mediated environment and its ability to support social interactions (Kreijins, Kirschner, & Jochems, 2002, p. 14). An environment high in sociability is more likely to result in a sound social space and the establishment of a community of learning.

Teleproximity and sociability are both supported by the social affordances of virtual worlds. Gibson (1977) first introduced the term *affordances* to describe the interactions that can occur between an object and user based on the attributes of each. Kirschner, Martens, and Strijbos (2004) define *social affordances* as the properties of a learning environment that act as "social-contextual facilitators" (p. 13) facilitating the social interactions of a learner. Many VLEs are designed to focus on cognitive process (e.g., assessment tools found in course management systems) but lack tools necessary for social interactions (synchronous tools such as instant message, use of avatars, voice over IP, or webinar functionality). Social functionality, as well as usability and attractiveness of the learning environment, is critical for learners to develop the social cohesiveness and trust required to participate in an online community (Kreijins & Kirschner, 2004, p. 221).

EXISTING SIMULATIONS FOR TEACHER CANDIDATE TRAINING

Several examples of virtual world simulations and games have been developed to support teacher candidate training. In 2003, a team from the University of Wollongong, Australia created their first prototype of a kindergarten classroom simulation using Stella™ as the programming tool. They scripted four key *teaching episodes* where participants read about a teacher, students, and classroom space and were asked to make decisions based on the script. Feedback from the pilot participants was positive, suggesting that teacher candidates "engaged in processes of connecting experiences, problem solving, critiquing the simulation teacher, and reflective practice" (Ferry & Kervin, 2007, p. 200).

Alternatively, the simSchool project simulates the experience of teaching a 7–12th grade classroom and focuses on the complexities of managing students who possess a variety of different learning characteristics and personalities (Zibit & Gibson, 2005). SimSchool was funded by the Preparing Tomorrow's Teachers to Teach with Technology program of the U.S. Department of Education and was recently awarded a Next Generation Learning Challenges grant. It is a first person, single player game in which the user assumes the role of a teacher. Teachers interact with programmed students who respond to the tasks assigned and the teacher's interactions. Complexity is added by the fact that the students also exhibit emotional states that are tied to their diverse personalities and learning preferences. The success of these students hinges on the choices made by the teacher, providing players with the experience of working with diverse learners.

Another example of a single player simulation is the University of Central Florida's TeachME (Teaching in Mixed-Reality Environments) project (Andreasen & Haciomeroglu, 2009). In this example, a mixed-reality simulation was constructed to allow teacher candidates to practice classroom management skills in front of a large screen in which digital students appear. Each imaginary student has a detailed background and is operated by a human "interactor." This interactor operates all five of the students and challenges the teacher candidate to interact with classroom distractions appropriately by escalating or deescalating student behaviors. The teacher candidate can lean in closer to a specific digital student to address individual needs or stand in front of screen to manage the entire group.

Finally, a team from the University of Nevada, Reno created a classroom management simulation in Second Life™ (Mahon, Bryany,

Brown, & Kim, 2010). A virtual middle school classroom was created and included a virtual teacher, virtual students, and student "bots," virtual entities that are not operated by humans but are instead programmed to respond to the teacher avatars. Teacher candidates rotated through the role of operating virtual teachers while challenged to manage a classroom that was a mix of programmed bots and avatars operated by fellow class-mates. The bots were programmed to systematically display uncontrolled behaviors and could be returned to a state of normalcy by the intervention of the teacher avatar. Bots searched for keywords that would indicate that the teacher avatar was implementing the correct intervention such as using the name of the student bot when he raised his hand. Data collected to assess the simulation suggest that students had a positive experience but that the simulation needed to be more structured.

The previous examples show the broad spectrum of computer-mediated experiences that have been created for teacher education simulations that focus on classroom management and/or classroom organization. Of the technologies highlighted in these examples, virtual worlds provide the flexibility for the creation of cost-effective simulations that can address any grade level and learning goals (i.e., classroom management, organization, needs of diverse learners). In addition, teacher candidates can role-play any member of the classroom, from teachers to learners with special needs, providing them with multiple perspectives.

CREATION OF SETON HALL'S SIMULATION

During the Fall 2010 semester, Dr. May partnered with instructional designers from the TLTC to create a simulation that would provide teacher candidates with the opportunity to practice working with, and assuming the roles of, diverse grade school students in a classroom setting. These virtual students may present behavioral challenges and require various instructional accommodations or modifications. The simulation, which included both virtual teacher and student roles, was embedded within Diverse Learners and Their Families Part I, a Freshman level course offered through the College of Education and Human Services at Seton Hall University. The purpose of this course is to introduce teacher candidates to the profession of special education, the laws and legislation associated with the field, including concepts covered under IDEA (Individuals with Disabilities Education Act) and Section 504 (of the Rehabilitation Act of 1973).

Virtual Classroom Design

The first step in constructing the virtual classroom space was to develop a floor plan. The result was a blueprint of a classroom that replicated elements typically found in a third-grade classroom. These elements include the following:

- Teacher's desk and chair
- Kidney shaped table for small group work with the teacher (four chairs)
- Small group table (three or four chairs)
- eight children's desks and chairs
- three low books shelves (pencil sharpener on top of one shelf)
- three windows
- one classroom door opening to the hallway
- Whiteboard in the front of the room
- Computer station

In addition, it was important that the various items found in the virtual classroom were moveable so that teacher avatars could make changes to the environment for students with special needs (Fig. 1).

Once the floor plan was developed, the actual construction of the virtual classroom began. A one room classroom was constructed on Pirate Island,

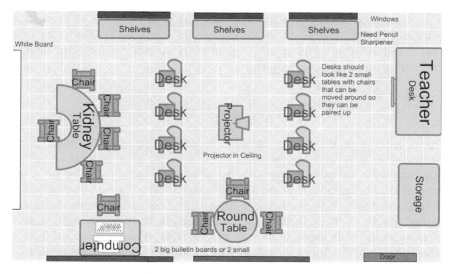

Fig. 1. Blueprint for Virtual Classroom Design.

the Seton Hall owned virtual island in Second Life™. In order to meet the specifications of the floor plan, items for the classroom were built using the 3D modeling tools available in Second Life™ or purchased from Second Life™ community members. One of the challenges faced during construction was replicating the complexity of a real classroom while keeping the virtual classroom easy for avatars to navigate. This required the virtual classroom space to be larger in scale than a real classroom and contain less classroom-specific items (e.g., boxes, crafts, storage). Images in Fig. 2 compare the level of detail found in a real classroom versus the virtual constructed classroom.

In addition to the details found within the interior of the virtual classroom, outside items included a fence, playground, and bus. The transparent windows of the classroom allowed these items to be viewable by teacher candidates while they worked within the virtual classroom space, possibly increasing the authenticity of the experience (Fig. 3).

Avatar Creation

Eight avatars were created and modified to resemble the descriptions provided in the simulation scenario. Avatars were created for JoAnne Somersley and Aimee Woodside, General Education and Special Education Teacher avatars, as well as for six third-grade students. Two of the students were characterized as having special needs; Mick Roth has low vision and requires glasses, and Johnathan Lisa has mild cerebral palsy and uses a pronged cane (Fig. 4).

Student Training and Simulation

One week before the actual simulation, during normally scheduled class time, all teacher candidates received hands-on training in Second Life™. Students were assigned a premade avatar created specifically for the purpose of training and were given a brief explanation of virtual worlds, what they are and how they are being used in education and industry. Students gained practice in basic avatar functions including walking, flying, communicating with other avatars, and interacting with objects in Second Life™. The purpose of the training was to give all teacher candidates exposure to virtual world technologies and to allow those participating as actors in the simulation an opportunity to learn essential skills.

Multi-colored rug   Virtual multi-colored rug available for purchase

Classroom easel   Interactive virtual easel available for purchase

Semi-Circle Table   Semi-Circle Virtual Table

Classroom Bins and Storage   Virtual Classroom Bins and Storage

Fig. 2. Real Life Items Replicated for Virtual Classroom.

Fig. 3. Outside View of Classroom.

Simulation Scenario

The simulation was conducted as part of a class exercise one week after the initial training was completed. Eight teacher candidates volunteered to operate the avatars and play out the simulation on desktop computers while the remainder of the class (simulation audience) watched on a large wall-mounted monitor. The objectives of the simulation were to provide teacher candidates with an opportunity to apply essential concepts previously discussed in class: (1) the development of classroom rules to promote a positive climate, and (2) designing a classroom space that works for all learners.

Prior to the start of class, teacher candidates were given the virtual student and teacher descriptions as well as background information and action items for the simulation. Teacher candidates were told the following:

> The setting is a third-grade classroom in which an experienced general education teacher, Mrs. Somersley is partnered with Aimee Woodside, a newly graduated special education teacher. Since Mrs. Somersley taught second grade last year she is familiar with some of the children in the class and shared this information with Ms. Woodside (see Fig. 4).
>
> Ms. Woodside does not know any of the children or their family members. However, she has attended the workshop by the TVI specialist about accommodations and modifications to support low vision students. In addition, Ms. Woodside has completed a field experience in another school where a blind child was a member of the class so she has experiential knowledge to draw on in support of Mick.

Teacher candidates operating the avatars (further referred to as simulation actors) began the activity with the virtual students arriving to class,

Mrs. Somersley – Virtual General Education Teacher
Mrs. Somersley has been teaching for 15 years. She has co-taught with faculty over the years and this year she has a new partner, Aimee Woodside.

Aimee Woodside – Virtual Special Education Teacher
Ms. Woodside just graduated from a nearby university and completed her senior teaching in the Jefferson School. She did well during that experience and the staff was happy to welcome her back as a full time special education teacher.

Mick Roth – Virtual Student with Low Vision
Mick is a new student to Mrs. Somersley, but many teachers know him because he has low vision. He is able to read 12 point font with a magnifier. A TVI (Teacher of Students with Visual Impairments) has provided trainings to faculty about various strategies for including Mick into the general classroom curriculum and activities.

Johnathan Lisa – Virtual Student with Mild Cerebral Palsy
Johnathan has a mild case of cerebral palsy which affects his right leg and his gait. He is very bright, sociable, and helpful to others. Johnathan attends physical therapy within the school and is able to walk on his own with the use of a pronged cane.

Fig. 4. Avatar Descriptions.

greeting the virtual teachers (further referred to as Mrs. Somersley and Ms. Woodside), and finding their desks. Once everyone was seated, Mrs. Somersley and Ms. Woodside welcomed everyone and explained that they are going to start the year by establishing some rules for the classroom that would help everyone learn and enjoy their time together. Ms. Woodside took the lead on this discussion with the virtual students, asking them to think about some simple rules that would help their classroom run smoothly.

Fig. 5. Simulation in Progress.

Using the chat function in Second Life™, the simulation actors discussed and decided on a set of rules to use which was recorded on an interactive write board in the virtual classroom. Once the rules are established, Mrs. Somersley asked the group to offer suggestions on the layout of the classroom. She noted that when everyone entered they sat down at any desk, but now they need to consider if moving or rearranging items would potentially benefit learning for the virtual students. Again, the simulation actors discussed the learning needs and preferences of the virtual students and an accommodating layout of the classroom (Fig. 5).

METHODOLOGY

In other to assess the impact of the simulation the following research questions were asked: (1) Are there differences in self-reported learning between simulation actors and the simulation audience? (2) Does participation in the virtual world simulation affect teacher candidates' feeling of being *present* during the activity? (3) Would teacher candidates perceive the virtual classroom and avatars to be realistic? (4) Would teacher candidates be satisfied with the virtual world simulation? (5) Would teacher candidates be satisfied with the virtual world technology? (6) Would exposure to a virtual world simulation change teacher candidates' preferences in the use of technology to support learning?

Surveys

There were four survey instruments utilized to access this activity. One week prior to the simulation activity, teacher candidates completed a pre-survey which consisted of questions regarding technology usage and preferences originally developed for the 2009 ECAR Study of Undergraduate Students and Information Technology (Smith, Salaway, & Caruso, 2009). EDUCAUSE has conducted a national survey aimed at investigating how information technology affects the college experience since 2004. Each year institutions of higher education are invited by EDUCAUSE to recruit their students to participate in the survey which consists of questions that ask them to assess their technology skills, preference for IT in their courses, and their perception of how IT affects their learning experience.

Just prior to the starting the simulation, teacher candidates completed the Immersive Tendencies Questionnaire (ITQ). Witmer and Singer (1998) developed the ITQ "to measure differences in the tendencies of individuals to experience presence" (Witmer & Singer, 1998, p. 225). This survey was designed to "measure involvement in common activities" (p. 233). As described by the authors, "Increased involvement can result in more immersion in an immersive environment. We expect individuals who tend to become more involved will also have greater immersive tendencies" (Witmer & Singer, 1998, p. 233). It consists of 29 questions in which subjects are asked to rate statement on a scale of 1 (never) to 7 (often) in order to rate their immersive tendencies. Sample questions include: "Do you ever become so involved in a movie that you are not aware of things happening around you," or "Do you ever become so involved in doing something that you lose all track of time." This data were used to determine if an individual's tendency to feel or not feel immersed would affect the simulation experience.

Following completion of the simulation the teacher candidates were given the post surveys. The first survey was the ITC-Sense of Presence Inventory (SOPI, Lessiter, Freeman, Keogh, & Davidoff, 2001). This survey measures the subjects' level of presence while observing or participating in the scenario. This survey was designed to measure presence across various media (movie or virtual world) which is why it was chosen for this study. It consists of 44 questions in which subjects are asked to rate each statement on a scale of 1 (strongly disagree) to 5 (strongly agree) to determine if presence was experienced. Example questions include: "I had a sense of being in the scenes displayed," or "I enjoyed myself." This measure was used to compare the level of presence experienced by the simulation actors and the simulation audience in the simulation in order to determine if there were differences between groups or if there was a relationship to other measures such as self-reported learning and satisfaction.

The second post survey, created by the researchers, included the following question categories: self-reported learning, perceived realism, satisfaction with the simulation, satisfaction with the virtual world (VW) technology, and a series of open-ended questions (see Table 1). These measures were included to identify relationships with other measures and to determine if there were differences between groups. In order to identify any possible shifts as a result of using the simulation, this survey also included several duplicate questions related to technology preferences from the pre-survey.

Demographics

The class consisted of 23 teacher candidates with many more females ($n = 20$) than males ($n = 3$). The age range was 18–29 years with a mode of 18 ($n = 23$). Nineteen teacher candidates selected Freshman as their class standing. The age range in the class was representative of a typical Freshman level introductory course (Table 2).

Additional demographic data were collected to establish the teacher candidates' use of and comfort level with technology, as well as their preference for its use in their academic lives. Analysis of the data reveals that, although teacher candidates engage in technology for school and personal activities, they are conservative in their preference for its use in education. In addition, contrary to the *digital immigrants* vs. *digital natives* debate (Prensky, 2001) or the increased interest in gamification of education (Lee & Hammer, 2011), teacher candidates did not report possessing expert technology skills, nor did they characterize themselves as gamers. These facts are important to note since the use of a 3D virtual world was a new experience for many in this group.

Teacher candidates reported that the most popular tools used for educational work included text messaging (71%), use of college/university web site (71%), use of presentation software (67%), use of spreadsheets (54%), social networking web sites (54%) and downloading music and videos (50%). The least used were participation in 3D online games (6%) and participation in virtual worlds (0%). When asked about recreational use, the most utilized tools were text messaging (75%), video chat (70%), downloading music or video (67%), instant messaging (63%), social networking sites (63%), graphics software (54%), and college/university library web site (50%). Although there was an increase in the frequency of

Table 1. Question and Categories.

Topic	Items Included on Post Survey
Self-reported learning	I was able to develop an understanding as to how the room should be arranged based on the needs of the students.[a]
	I was able to link the specific needs and characteristics of the students with the proposed arrangement of classroom[a] space.
	I considered the student characteristics within the class when creating rules that would benefit the whole.
	I was able to provide specific reasons for the creation of rules.
	I was able to explain positive phrasing of rules.
	I was able to consider the combination of students needs and physical space when creating rules.
	The simulation helped me make the link between the needs and characteristics of the students the classroom space, and the development of an accurate classroom arrangement.
	The simulation helped me learn about characteristics of the students in the classroom.
	The simulation helped me to create rules based on the needs of the whole.
	The simulation allowed me to apply my knowledge of the subject.
Perceived Realism	The virtual students looked like their physical descriptions described in the profiles provided.
	The virtual classroom represents a real third-grade classroom.
	Specific needs of the virtual students were apparent by their physical appearance.
Satisfaction	I would like to participate in additional virtual world simulations in future courses.
	It is a good idea to use virtual world simulations to conduct case studies.
	I enjoyed the simulation.
Technology	In general, Second Life™ is easy to use.
	Moving my avatar around in Second Life™ is easy.
	Communicating with others in Second Life™ by Chat is easy.
	I like being in virtual worlds such as Second Life™.
Open ended questions	What did you like the most about working through the scenario Education Classroom "Start of the School Year"?
	What did you like the least about working through the scenario Education Classroom "Start of the School Year"?
	Did this scenario give you tools/ideas that you would apply as a future teacher?
	Other comments
	All participants answered the above questions

Table 1. (*Continued*)

Topic	Items Included on Post Survey
Only participants that actively participated in the simulation answered the following:	How did you feel about your avatar?
	Do you remember feeling anxious during the role-play/simulation? If so please explain.
	How engaged did you feel in the role? Please explain.
	Did you feel that your inexperience with the technology affected your ability to participate in the role-play/simulation? How much more comfortable with the technology did you feel after some time in the simulation?
	Other Comments

Strongly agree (5); Agree (4); Neutral (3); Disagree (2); Strongly disagree (1)
[a]"Students" and "classroom" refer to virtual students and virtual classroom as references in the narrative regarding this study.

Table 2.   Demographics of Teacher Candidates.

Variable		Frequency	Percentage	Mean Age	Std. Dev.
Condition	Simulation actor	8	35%	19.63	3.815
	Simulation audience	15	65%	18.53	1.125
Gender	Male	3	14%	18.33	.577
	Female	20	87%	19	2.555
Class standing	Freshman	19	83%	18.16	.375
	Sophomore	2	9%	19.5	7.7
	Junior	2	9%	25.5	4.95

using 3D online games (21%) and 3D virtual worlds (13%), these percentages were much lower than for other tools (Table 3).

The data suggest that these teacher candidates were conservative in their preference for the use of technology in their courses and their belief that technology supports their learning. When asked about their preference for the use of technology in their courses, less than half (46%) responded that they prefer taking courses that use a moderate level of technology. Even less (25%) agreed that they get more actively involved in courses that use technology or that the use of technology in their courses improves their learning (25%). Less than half (42%) described themselves as using new technologies after they have been adopted by their peers. Finally, when asked how they like to learn, only a few (21%) selected "Programs I can control such as video games, simulations, etc."

Table 3. Current Technology Used in Courses.

Technology Tool	Percentage Used	Number
Text message	71	17
University web site	71	17
Presentation software	67	16
Spreadsheets	54	13
Social networking web sites	54	13
Downloading music and videos	50	12
Graphics software	50	12
Audio-creation software	21	5
Video chat	33	6
Instant messages	42	10
Video-creation software	21	5
3D online games	6	1
Virtual worlds	0	0

Note: $N = 18$ for the pre-survey data.

When asked "By the time I graduate, the technology I have used in my courses will have adequately prepared me for the workplace" less than half agreed (46%), which could indicate that teacher candidates do not recognize the applicability of the technology that they are using for their course work in their future employment. It should be noted that the majority of these teacher candidates were Freshman and their perceptions regarding technology use may change over time. The utilization of emerging technologies that promote active participation in higher education courses could serve as a model for the use of educational technology by future teachers in an actual classroom setting. While this project does not directly investigate this question, the lack of effective modeling of instructional technologies has been a criticism of teacher preparation programs (Levine, 2006).

Research Questions

Research Question 1: Are there differences in self-reported learning between the simulation actors and the simulation audience?

A series of questions was developed, in partnership with the faculty member, to address the learning objectives for the activity (see Table 1). The 5-point Likert scale was collapsed into 3 points, Positive, Neutral, and Negative. In response to many of the survey questions, both simulation actors and audience reported learning benefits. "I was able to explain the positive phrasing of rules" was the only item in which the average rating was higher for the simulation audience (73%) than for actors (57%).

An independent samples t-test revealed a significant difference for the item "The simulation helped me to create rules based on the needs of the whole" between the simulation actors ($M = 4.0$, SD = .756) and audience ($M = 3.0$, SD = 1.195) with a 1.0 difference in means: $t(21) = 2.137$, $p = .045$. In addition, a mean difference of .983 was found between actors ($M = 4.25$, SD = .707) and audience ($M = 3.27$, SD = 1.1) for the item "The simulation allowed me to apply my knowledge of the subject"; $t(21) = 2.277$, $p = .033$. Finally, the survey item "The simulation helped me learn about the characteristics of the students in the classroom" was close to showing significant difference between simulation actors ($M = 3.75$, SD = .463) and audience ($M = 3.0$, SD = 1.0) with a .75 difference in means: $t(21) = 1.994$, $p = .045$.

In the open-ended question responses, simulation actors also mentioned being active contributors to the learning experience; "*I was very engaged because I had to lead the classroom discussion and ask the students questions.*" In addition, they identified tools and ideas that they would apply as future teachers as a result of this experience. The concept of taking a different perspective and appreciating the diversity of a classroom was a prevalent theme:

- "*Seeing differences in partners made me realize how you need to take everyone into consideration for all changes.*"
- "*It will make me think like a student when planning for a classroom which will benefit the students.*"

Simulation audience members also mentioned concepts that were learned that can be applied in their future teaching. These included the importance of understanding the dynamics of the classroom and receiving input from students when creating rules and considering the arrangement of the classroom. Comments included:

- "*It gave me ideas of how to handle children and make a good classroom.*"
- "*It shows to get your students' opinions and ideas into the classroom.*"

Research Question 2: Does participation in the virtual world simulation affect teacher candidates' feeling of being *present* during the activity?

Presence was measured post simulation using the ITC-SOIP presence survey (Table 4). Significant differences were found for the following factors:

Table 4. Presence *t*-Test Measures

	Condition						*t*	*df*	Sig *(two-tailed)*
	Actors			Audience					
	N	*M*	SD	*N*	*M*	SD			
Spatial	8	3.04	.46	14	1.98	.68	3.941	20	.001
Engage	8	3.21	.42	14	2.63	.62	2.374	20	.028
Naturalness	9	3.50	.78	14	2.64	.55	3.025	20	.007
Negative	9	1.83	.61	14	2.19	.60	− 1.337	20	.196

Engagement (tendency to feel psychologically involved and to enjoy the content), Ecological Validity (tendency to perceive the mediated environment as lifelike and real), and Sense of Physical Space (a sense of being there). No significant difference was found for the fourth factor, Negative Effects (adverse physiological reactions). Simulation actors experienced a sense of presence and perceived the simulation environment as being lifelike without experiencing negative side effects (e.g., dizzy feeling or nausea).

Responses to the open-ended questions suggest that the simulation actors were able to *get into character* and focus enough attention on the simulation activities to feel as if they were actually happening. Comments included:

- *"I was able to comment in the conversation the same way that my avatar's character would have in real life."*
- *"I like the fact that it seemed real, and that we got the chance to put ourselves in the shoes of the individuals."*
- *"I liked thinking about the situation through the eyes of a student. It makes it more realistic rather than just looking at something on paper."*
- *"...I began imagining if these were happening in real life and how I would react."*

The ITQ was used to investigate whether there was a relationship between levels of perceived presence and innate characteristics of the respondents. The relationship between the ITQ factors and items measuring self-reported learning was investigated using Spearman *rho* correlation coefficient. There was a strong, positive correlation between ITQ Games (tendency to play video games) and "The simulation allowed me to apply my knowledge of the subject," $rho = .601$, $n = 23$, $p < .002$. A moderate, positive correlation was also found between ITQ Games and "The simulation helped me learn about the characteristics of the classroom;" $rho = .420$, $n = 23$, $p < .046$. Further research should investigate if participants who have familiarity with gaming perceive (or actually achieve) greater increases in learning from simulations.

Research Question 3: Would teacher candidates perceive the virtual classroom and avatars to be realistic?

Simulation actors reported higher percentages of agreement that the virtual classroom represented a real third-grade classroom and the virtual students looked like their physical descriptions described in their profiles. The 5-point Likert scale was again collapsed into 3 points. A larger percentage of simulation actors (75%) than audience (33%) positively agreed that the virtual classroom represented a real third-grade classroom. Similarly, a larger percentage of simulation actors (88%) than audience (50%) positively agreed that the virtual students looked like their physical descriptions described in the profiles provided. Finally, there was a smaller difference found between simulation actors (75%) and audience members (67%) in their positive agreement that the specific needs of the students were apparent by their physical appearance.

A significant difference was found for the item "The virtual classroom represents a real third-grade classroom" between simulation actors ($M = 4.24$, SD $= 1.165$) and audience ($M = 3.00$, SD $= 1.069$) with a mean difference of 1.25: $t(21) = 2.591$, $p = .017$. In addition, a significant difference was also found for the item "The virtual students looked like their physical descriptions described in the profiles provided" with a mean difference of 1.214: $t(20) = 3.417$, $p = .003$. The results suggest that actors in the simulation experienced more "realism" in the representation of the classroom and student avatars than the simulation audience.

Even though significant differences were found between the two groups, the simulation audience described the simulation as realistic in the open-ended responses, although not as frequently as the simulation actors; "*It is more realistic than a written case study. Watching the classroom interact was something that cannot come from a written case.*" The simulation audience also noted that they wanted to be able to actively participate in the simulation.

The realism of the avatars was repeatedly mentioned in the open-ended responses by both simulation actors and audience. Comments included reference to how the child avatars (virtual students) resembled their profile descriptions:

- "*My avatar was extremely realistic. The description on the case study and the physical appearance of my avatar were almost completely the same.*"
- "*My character was very realistic. Made perfect.*"
- "*I liked how the avatars looked like children.*"

The simulation audience also mentioned that they liked being able to see the virtual students during the simulation; *"The graphics were geared to the physical traits of each character, which was interesting."*

Research Question 4: Would teacher candidates be satisfied with the virtual world simulation?

More actors (36%) than audience (0%) strongly agreed that it was a good idea to use virtual world simulations to conduct case studies. Similarly, more actors (36%) than audience (0%) strongly agreed that the simulation allowed them to apply their knowledge about the subject, while more than half of all respondents (57%) agreed with the same statement. In addition, more than half of all respondents (57%) agreed/strongly agreed that they would like to participate in additional virtual world simulations in future courses.

Independent Samples t-tests showed significant differences between the simulation actors and audience on two items related to satisfaction with the simulation. A significant difference was found for the item, "I enjoyed the simulation" between actors ($M = 4.38$, $SD = .518$) and audience ($M = 3.33$, $SD = .816$) with a mean difference of 1.042: $t(21) = 3.257$, $p = .004$. A significant difference was also found between actors ($M = 4.13$, $SD = .835$) and audience ($M = 3.33$, $SD = .724$) for the item, "It is a good idea to use virtual world simulations to conduct case studies" with a mean difference of .792: $t(21) = 2.372$, $p = .027$. There was no significant difference found between the two groups for the item, "I would like to participate in additional virtual world simulations in future courses," possibly indicating that both actors and audience would like to use this technology for simulation training in the future.

The relationship between satisfaction with the simulation (either as actors or audience) and self-reported learning was investigated using Spearman's *rho* correlation coefficient. There were moderate, positive relationships between enjoyment of the simulation and three of the self-reported learning items. The results suggest that the enjoyment experienced by either acting in or being in the audience during the simulation may facilitate the ability to focus on the activity and therefore perceive learning gains (Table 5).

Responses to the open-ended questions further reinforced that the actors enjoyed the simulation. Comments included:

- *"I wish we had more time to use it because it was fun."*
- *"I really enjoyed my role in the classroom."*
- *"Great Idea — Great Program."*

Table 5. Correlations: Satisfaction with Simulation and Self-Reported
Learning Items.

I enjoyed the simulation	*rho*
The simulation helped me to create rules based on the needs of the whole.	.647**
The simulation allowed me to apply my knowledge of the subject.	.563**
The simulation helped me learn about the characteristics of the students in the room.	.521*
The simulation allowed me to apply my knowledge of the subject.	.451*

*p < .05 (two-tailed).
**p < .01 (two-tailed).

Even though the results suggest that the simulation was enjoyable, some obstacles were reported in the open-ended responses. The simulation was designed so that the actors would take on the roles of either a virtual student or virtual teacher and work through the scenario to meet the learning goals. The simulation was loosely structured, resulting in the conversation among virtual characters to become chaotic. Actors mentioned that the experience seemed disorganized:

- *"No order in the classroom. Certain characters talked the whole time and got somewhat annoying."*
- *"It was a tad disorganized."*
- *"I thought the flow of the conversation could have been less random. It seems like nothing was accomplished. I think a class discussion would have been better."*

One simulation actor suggested that more interactivity rather than chatting would have made the experience even more engaging.

Research Question 5: Would teacher candidates be satisfied with the virtual world technology?

Both groups had experience using the software (Second Life™) during the training session. Again, the 5-point Likert scale used for these survey items was collapsed into 3 points. When asked specifically about Second Life™, less than half (48%) of the total number of respondents agreed that Second Life™ was easy to use. More than half (57%) of the respondents also agreed that moving their avatar in Second Life™ as well as using the chat function (81%) was easy. Finally, less than half (41%) agreed that they like being in virtual worlds such as Second Life™.

Even though there were some technical drawbacks, actors in the simulation responded in the open-ended questions that they were comfortable using

Second Life™ to complete the simulation. Two simulation actors noted initial nervousness in using the software but after the training session seemed comfortable with operating the avatar. One expressed her fear of making typing mistakes while using the chat feature; it should be noted that synchronous forms of computer-mediated communication can be difficult for individuals who have poor typing skills or those who are not native speakers of the language being used (Park & Bonk, 2007).

Despite reports of feeling comfortable, respondents described a variety of challenges related to the technology. Several of the simulation actors revealed that the chat feature in Second Life™, the main vehicle for communication between avatars during the simulation, was an impediment to the experience. It was described as being chaotic and hard to follow:

- *"The chatbox was hard to keep up with so the teacher would have a hard time listening and seeing everyone's responses."*
- *"The chaos of all the avatars IMing. If they could have raised their hand they could have been more productive. They all IMed over each other that it was hard to keep track."*

Simulation actors suggested the use of sound, gestures, and highlighted chat for the virtual teachers as a way to enhance the experience. Some also mentioned that the movements of the avatars were awkward and that one of the virtual teachers was dressed inappropriately. Finally, one simulation audience member commented that *"I do not learn off computers like that so I did not find it very educating."* Another stated that watching the monitor made him/her dizzy.

Research Question 6: Would exposure to a virtual world simulation change teacher candidates' preferences for the use of technology to support learning?

The demographic data suggest that these teacher candidates were conservative in their preference for and use of technology to support course work. The question of whether exposure to a virtual world simulation would change their opinions was investigated through the use of common technology preference questions included in both the pre-survey and post survey. An Independent Samples t-test did not indicate significant differences for technology preferences pre and post simulation.

DISCUSSION

Both simulation actors and audience reported learning benefits after the completion of the simulation. Even though learning gains were reported by both groups, the data suggest that simulation actors felt a greater sense of presence during the activity. Analysis of responses to the ITC-SOIP presence survey revealed significant differences for the following three factors; Engagement, Ecological Validity, and Sense of Physical Space (see Table 4). Simulation actors felt more psychologically involved and enjoyed the content, had higher perceptions of the environment as being lifelike and real, and had a greater sense of *being there*. No significant difference was found between groups for Negative Effects (adverse physiological reactions). Even though one audience member noted feeling dizzy, the findings suggest that there was no adverse impact for either the actors or audience.

Responses to the open-ended questions suggest that the simulation actors also felt more immersed in the experience. Comments included, "I began imaging if these were happening in real life and how I would react" and "I like the fact that it seemed real, and that we got the chance to put ourselves in the shoes of the individuals." Part of this experienced immersion could be attributed to simulation actors' perception that the virtual classroom and virtual students were realistic. Actors noted that the child avatars resembled their profile descriptions and closely matched the profiles provided in the case study. One member of the audience also commented on the benefits of seeing the virtual students and the classroom, noting that it was more realistic than a paper case study. The data suggest that being able to visualize and role-play the virtual students enabled teacher candidates to consider the needs of their future students.

Subjects reported that Second Life™ was easy to use, but some technical drawbacks were reported. Both groups felt that the chat conversations were chaotic and sometimes hard to follow. Suggestions included incorporating sound and gestures, as well as highlighting the virtual teachers' comments in the chat box. In addition, it was suggested that more interaction would have made the experience more engaging.

NEXT STEPS

Even though the subjects did not characterize themselves as technology experts or gamers, they enjoyed the virtual world simulation experience and reported learning benefits. The ability to role-play a virtual student had a strong impact on the actors and the relationship to many of the self-reported learning items. In addition, actors were able to focus on the simulation activities and feel present in the virtual environment. Visualizing a classroom with realistic diverse learners has the potential to shape a future teacher's mental model of a classroom in a way that a paper case study cannot. Simulations can facilitate the ability of teacher candidates to develop respect for diversity, consider multiple perspectives, and increase their empathy for students in their future classrooms.

The Department of Educational Studies at Seton Hall is planning to incorporate additional virtual world simulations into the curriculum. Future plans include the use of simulations to support the online Certificate of Advanced Standing (CEAS). The CEAS program is a fully online, intensive eighteen credit program intended for professionals seeking teacher certification. The purpose of the certificate is to provide skills and competencies needed to fulfill certification requirements and to prepare teacher candidates with the knowledge, skills, and dispositions to meet the changing landscape of today's classrooms. Since many of these candidates have not been in a classroom for several years or not at all, the virtual classroom exercise can play a vital role in their ability to gain practice.

In addition, recent legislation and need for anti-bullying training in K-12 school communities has educators searching for effective instructional methods. Seton Hall faculty are considering the creation of an anti-bullying virtual world simulation to provide users with an immersive role-playing experience. Based on the results from this classroom management simulation, participants would benefit by taking on different perspectives and put themselves in the shoes of *all* the individuals.

Since both actors and audience of the simulation reported learning gains, the data suggest that the creation of movies (or machinima) created in virtual worlds could be effective tools for creating educational training videos. Educational video production is an expensive process that requires a large time commitment as well as access to people and locations. Conkey (2010) compared instructional videos that used real actors versus avatars on several dimensions. He found no difference between groups except for skills that require attention to body language and facial expressions. In addition, the process of creating a machinima (scripting, storyboarding, and executing) may also prove to be a powerful learning exercise for teacher candidates as they explore the creation of their own teaching vignettes.

SECOND LIFE RESOURCES

Seton Hall University's Pirate Island: http://maps.secondlife.com/second life/Seton%20Hall%20University/127/132/25.

ACKNOWLEDGMENTS

We would like to acknowledge Wendiann Sethi and Stewart Warner for their hard work in supporting this simulation. Their expert knowledge of building and customizing the Second Life™ environment contributed to the success of this project. We would also like to thank Allison Barbag from Mount Pleasant Elementary School in Livingston, NJ for providing pictures of her classroom.

REFERENCES

Aldrich, C. (2009). Virtual worlds, simulations, and games for education: A unifying view. *Innovate: Journal of Online Education, 5*(5).
Andreasen, J. B., & Haciomeroglu, E. S. (2009). Teacher training in virtual environments. Paper presented at the Annual Meeting of the North American Chapter of the International Group for the Psychology of Mathematics Education, OMNI Hotel, Atlanta, GA. Retrieved from http://www.allacademic.com/meta/p369936_index.html
Balkun, M., Zedeck, M., & Trotta, H. (2009). Literary analysis as serious play in second life. In C. Wankel & J. Kingsley (Eds.), *Higher education in virtual worlds teaching and learning in Second Life* (1st ed., pp. 141–157). Bingley, UK: Emerald Group Publishing Limited.
Brown, J. S., Collins, A., & Duguid, P. (1989). Situated cognition and the culture of learning. *Educational Researcher, 18*(1), 32–42.
Buchanan, K. (2003). Opportunity knocking: Co-opting and games. *ALT-N, 43*, 10–11.
Calderhead, J., & Shorrock, S. B. (1997). *Understanding teacher education: Case studies in the professional development of beginning teachers.* London: The Falmer Press.
Conkey, C. A. (2010). *Machinima and video-based soft skills training.* Doctoral dissertation. Retrieved from ProQuest Dissertations & Theses (PQDT). Accession Order No. UMI 3415061.
Conrad, R., & Donaldson, A. (2011). *Engaging the online learner: Activities and resources for creative instruction.* San Francisco, CA: Jossey-Bass.
Dalgarno, B., & Lee, M. J. (2010). What are the learning affordances of 3-D virtual environments? *British Journal of Educational Technology, 41*(1), 10–32.
Deuchar, S., & Nodder, C. (2003). The impact of avatars and 3D virtual world creation on learning. *16th Annual NACCQ Conference*, Palmerston North.
Ferry, B., & Kervin, L. (2007). Developing an online classroom simulation to support a pre-service teacher education program. In D. Gibson, C. Aldrich & M. Prensky (Eds.), *Games and simulations in online learning* (pp. 189–205). Hershey, PA: Information Sciences Publishing.
Fletcher, C., & Bailey, C. (2003). Assessing self-awareness: Some issues and methods. *Journal of Managerial Psychology, 18*(5), 395–404.
Gee, J. P. (2005). What would a state of the art instructional video game look like? *Innovate: Journal of Online Education, 1*(6).

Gibson, J. (1977). The theory of affordances. In R. Shaw & J. Bransford (Eds.), *Perceiving, acting, and knowing: Toward an ecological psychology* (pp. 67–82). Hillsdale, NJ: Lawrence Erlbaum.

Goldstein, I. L. (1993). *Training in organizations*. Pacific Grove, CA: Brook/Cole Publishing Company.

Gredler, M. E. (2004). Games and simulations and their relationships to learning. In D. Jonassen (Ed.), *Handbook of research for educational communications and technology* (2nd ed., pp. 571–581). Mahwah, NJ: Lawrence Erlbaum Associates.

Hewitt, A., Spencer, S., Mirliss, D., & Twal, R. (2010). Incident and disaster management training: Collaborative learning opportunities using virtual world scenarios. In E. Asimakoloulou & N. Bessis (Eds.), *Advanced ICTs for disaster management and threat detection: Collaborative frameworks* (pp. 179–199). Hersey, PA: IGI Global.

Ip, A., & Naidu, S. (2001). Experienced-based pedagogical designs for eLearning. *Education Technology*, *XLI*(53), 58.

Jennett, C., Cox, A. L., Cairns, P., Dhoparee, S., Epps, A., Tijs, T., & Walton, A. (2008). Measuring and defining the experience of immersion in games. *International Journal of Human-Computer Studies*, *66*(9), 641–661.

Kirschner, P. A., Martens, R. L., & Strijbos, J. W. (2004). CSCL in higher education? A framework for designing multiple collaborative environments. In J. Strijbos, P.A. Kirschner & R. L. Martens (Eds.), *What we know about CSCL: And implementing it in higher education* (1st ed., pp. 3–30). Boston, MA: Kluwer Academic Publishers.

Kreijins, K., & Kirschner, P. A. (2004). Designing sociable CSCL environments. In J. Strijbos, P. A. Kirschner & R. L. Martens (Eds.), *What we know about CSCL: And implementing it in higher education* (1st ed., pp. 221–244). Boston, MA: Kluwer Academic Publishers.

Kreijins, K., Kirschner, P. A., & Jochems, W. (2002). The sociability of computer-supported collaborative learning environments. *Educational Technology & Society*, *5*(1), 8–22.

Lee, J. J., & Hammer, J. (2011). Gamification in education: What, how, why bother? *Academic Quarterly*, *15*(2), 1–5.

Lee, J. J., & Hoadley, C. M. (2007). Leveraging identity to make learning fun: Possible selves and experiential learning in massively multiplayer online games (MMOGs). *Innovate: Journal of Online Education*, *3*(6).

Lessiter, J., Freeman, J., Keogh, E., & Davidoff, J. (2001). A cross-media presence questionnaire: The ITC-sense of presence inventory. *Presence: Teleoperators & Virtual Environments*, *10*(3), 282–297.

Levine, A. (2006). *Educating school teachers*. The Educating Schools Project.

Lindsey, L., & Berger, N. (2009). Experiential approach to instruction. In C. M. Reigeluth & A. A. Carr-Chellman (Eds.), *Instructional-design theories and models: Building a community knowledge base* (Vol. 3, pp. 117–142). New York, NY: Routledge.

Mahon, J., Bryant, B., Brown, B., & Miran, K. (2010). Using second life to enhance classroom management practice in teacher education. *Educational Media International*, *47*(2), 121–134.

Mirliss, D., & Trotta.H. (2006). Supporting virtual teams in Second Life™: A case study. Paper presented at the New Media Consortium (NMC) Regional Conference, San Antonio, TX. Retrieved from http://www.slideshare.net/dmirliss/supporting-virtual-teams-using-second-life

160   DANIELLE MIRLISS ET AL.

Morse, S., Littleton, F., Macleod, H., & Ewins, R. (2009). The theatre of performance appraisal: Role-play in second life. In C. Wankel & J. Kingsley (Eds.), *Higher education in virtual worlds: Teaching and learning in Second Life* (1st ed., pp. 181–201). Bingley, UK: Emerald Group Publishing Limited.
Oliver, R. M., & Reschly, D. J. (2010). Special education teacher preparation in classroom management: Implications for students with emotional and behavioral disorders. *Behavioral Disorders, 35*(3), 188–199.
Park, Y. J., & Bonk, C. J. (2007). Synchronous learning experiences: Distance and residential learners' perspectives in a blended graduate course. *Journal of Interactive Online Learning, 6*(3), 245–264.
Peterson, M. (2005). Learning interaction in an avatar-based virtual environment: A preliminary study. *PacCall Journal, 1*(1), 29–40.
Prensky, M. (2001). Digital natives, digital immigrants. *On the Horizon, 9*(5), 1–6.
Prensky, M. (2009). H. sapiens digital: From digital immigrants and digital natives to digital wisdom. *Innovate: Journal of Online Education, 5*(3).
Schroeder, R. (2011). *Being there together. Social interaction in shared virtual environments.* Oxford: Oxford University Press.
Shaffer, D. W. (2004). Pedagogical praxis: The professions as models for postindustrial education. *Teachers College Record, 106*(7), 1401–1421.
Shaffer, D. W. (2005). Epistemic games. *Innovate: Journal of Online Education, 1*(6).
Shulman, L. S. (2004). *The wisdom of practice: Essays on teaching, learning, and learning to teach.* San Francisco, CA: Jossey-Bass.
Slater, M. (2003). A note on presence terminology. *Presence Connect, 3*(3).
Smith, S. D., Salaway, G., & Caruso, J. B. (2009). The ECAR study of undergraduate students and information technology. *Educause Center for Applied Research, 6.* Retrieved from http://net.educause.edu/ir/library/pdf/ers0906/rs/ers0906w.pdf
Taylor, T. L. (2002). Living digitally: Embodiment in virtual worlds. In R. Schroeder (Ed.), *The social life of avatars: Presence and interaction in shared virtual environments* (pp. 40–62). London: Springer.
Trotta, H., & Glenn, M. (2012). Salt marsh dynamics: A problem-based learning scenario. In R. Hinrichs and C. Wankel (Eds.), *Engaging the avatar: New frontiers in immersive education.* Charlotte, NC: Information Age Publishing Inc.
Weitz, R., Wachsmuth, B., & Mirliss, D. (2005). The tablet PC goes to college: Evaluating the utility of tablet PCs for faculty in the classroom. In P. Kommers & G. Richards (Eds.), *Proceedings of World Conference on Educational Multimedia, Hypermedia and Telecommunications 2005,* pp. 2565–2570. Retrieved from http://www.editlib.org/p/20463
Westling, D. L. (2010). Teachers and challenging behavior: Knowledge, views, and practices. *Remedial and Special Education, 31*(1), 48–63.
Witmer, B. G., & Singer, M. J. (1998). Measuring presence in virtual environments: A presence questionnaire. *Presence, 7*(3), 225–240.
Zibit, M., & Gibson, D. (2005). simSchool: The game of teaching. *Innovate: Journal of Online Education, 1*(6).

ENGAGING CHINESE STUDENTS AND ENHANCING LEADERSHIP DEVELOPMENT THROUGH VIRTUAL SIMULATION: A CROSS-CULTURAL PERSPECTIVE

Scott A. Johnson and Jing Luo

ABSTRACT

Engaging students in an active, self-directed approach to learning about leadership is best accomplished through personalized self-awareness, reflection, and connection to real-time, practical applications/examples through experiential learning. This is especially challenging for students whose cultural backgrounds, language, and/or educational preparation/ training predispose them to more passively "receive knowledge" in an unquestioning, unexamined manner, without critical thinking. At the University of Greenwich Business School, a final year course has been re-imagined as personalized leadership development integrated with learning technology. Our teaching team is taking advantage of an inter-active virtual simulation (vLeader) to engage Chinese students who

Increasing Student Engagement and Retention using Immersive Interfaces: Virtual Worlds, Gaming, and Simulation
Cutting-edge Technologies in Higher Education, Volume 6C, 161–202
ISSN: 2044-9968/doi:10.1108/S2044-9968(2012)000006C009

otherwise might not participate fully in the expected manner of a West-
ernized learning environment. This chapter outlines our integrated
approach to support and engage these students in learning outcomes for
continuing success in their lives, careers, and leadership opportunities.

INTRODUCTION

Over the last decade, nearly 1 million Chinese students have come to the
United Kingdom to pursue higher education, an upward trend that is
expected to continue. In 2010, over 90,000 Chinese students were engaged
in some kind of learning experiences in the United Kingdom, concentrated
in business/management, finance/accounting, computing science, and engineering (an increase of 27% when compared to 2009) (Chen, 2011). The
growth of Chinese students studying in the United Kingdom produces new
demands and challenges for universities, for academic staff, and for the
students themselves. Strategies for improving these students' educational
and social outcomes have become increasingly important and even crucial
to the success of their experiences, in terms of learning outcomes, adjustment, and well-being for the student population as a whole. Although
some of the barriers to the engagement of Chinese students in the United
Kingdom are rooted in cultural customs going back millennia, modern
technology and innovative pedagogy hold the promise for resolving many
cross-cultural challenges.

The increasing use of emergent technology in teaching has been shaping
learning with a significant impact on modern higher education. However,
technology alone does not necessarily enhance learning without well-
designed integration into learning environments, experiential curriculum,
and interactive, student-centered pedagogy. One subject area in which integrated technological learning is both relevant and appropriate is leadership. As a dynamic systems skill, instead of a linear process skill (Aldrich,
2003), it is difficult to teach leadership through standardized curriculum
using traditional classroom techniques. However, students can effectively
learn about leadership through the right combination and balance of personalized pedagogy and innovative, cutting-edge tools to engage the students in self-directed transformation.

Recent papers tend to support the effectiveness in using a simulation
approach to develop leadership skills (Gurley & Wilson, 2010; Knode &
Knode, 2011). These and other studies serve as a general background to

the chapter. This chapter will focus on exploring the integration of a virtual simulation (vLeader) into an experiential learning framework as an innovative pedagogical approach to a course in leadership development that positively impacts direct entry Chinese student engagement and improvement in confidence, self-awareness, and communications skills. Background research in cross-cultural barriers will be examined and linked to clarify factors other than financial pressures hindering Chinese students' study (as 93% self-fund their studies in the United Kingdom) and learning styles. Our investigation shows that language and cultural differences are major barriers which impact Chinese students' engagement. The role of universities and local learning communities in developing strategies to improve Chinese students' social outcomes while studying in the United Kingdom is addressed.

LOCAL LEARNING CONTEXT: THE UNIVERSITY OF GREENWICH BUSINESS SCHOOL

The University of Greenwich was established in the late nineteenth century as a polytechnic institute, infusing traditional vocational skills-oriented organizational culture over a century of supporting wider access to students who may not otherwise go on to higher education. The community-partner presence in Greenwich attracts many first-generation university attendees from the surrounding urban areas, along with a focus on closer personal connections among faculty and students, pastoral care, and historical emphasis on teaching over research. However, the reach of Greenwich is extended from its largest campus on the River Thames to a wider global market, based on its prominence as a London university, its rising standings in the league tables (particularly the ascension of the Business School), and its widely known nature of accessibility (lower entry tariffs, lower costs, a worldwide network of recruiters and alumni). The result is a student demographic representing 140 countries. Diversity is even higher in the Business School, where more than 60% of the students are from underserved demographic groups (designated in the United Kingdom as Black and Ethnic Minority, or BEM), and based on national origin, more than 60% are from a country outside the United Kingdom on the management studies programs (the most popular destination for overseas students). Of the approximately 500 students in the final year of degree programs in Business Management (BABM), Human Resource Management

(BAHRM), and Business Studies (BABS, with some combined subjects), more than 125 (25%) of these students arrive directly from China for their third and final year only.

Another stunning feature that attracts students is the physical learning space at University of Greenwich, situated on a world-heritage site of historic significance, and housed in buildings designed by Christopher Wren in the seventeenth century. However, with more than 3,000 students in the Business School, this means that pedagogy is bounded to a large extent by resource constraints – timing (one 50 minute "tutorial" and one 50 minute lecture each week, for 12 weeks), room capacity (20 students maximum in half of the rooms, creating tutorial groups of that size), one course leader to design and coordinate, and 8 tutors to staff the tutorial sessions.

All degree programs in the Greenwich Business School take 3 years to complete, with courses focused only on business and related topics (i.e., there is no requirement for "general education" or non-business topics such as liberal arts disciplines, and it is extremely rare for any students to take a course outside the Business School; many business students do not take courses outside their own departments). All business students do take a departmentally controlled sequence of Personal and Professional Development (PPD) in years 1, 2, and 3, emphasizing learning activities that instill self-awareness, critical thinking, continuous learning, and transferrable skills applied toward career success and employability. In the final term, the 500 BABM/BAHRM/BABS students take a course in Organizational Behavior 3 (OB3), building on OB1 (Managing Individual Performance in Organizations) and OB2 (Managing Groups and Teams). However, a large number of the overseas students – especially the direct entry Chinese – come to Greenwich for their final year only, so they do not receive the same foundation of OB1 and OB2 before taking OB3. OB3 was first proposed (and approved) as a traditional leadership course, but through deliberate design and delivery has evolved into Leadership Development to reinforce the PPD themes.

OB3 is in many ways the final year culmination of these 500 students' degree programs, along with a dissertation and PPD3 (employability/career preparation), creating a de facto capstone experience (officially, there is no school wide capstone that integrates learning from all courses). For the past 3 years, the final year OB3/PPD3 sequence has been directed by the same course leader and a consistent team of supporting tutors. The aim of OB3 is to engage students through a combination of self-directed and interactive activities that provide experiential learning beyond classroom-bound, teacher-centric, lecture-driven passive knowledge reception.

Can Leadership be Taught, Learned, Developed?

The topic of leadership education itself is a source of disagreement but also an opportunity to explore new ways of learning, connecting, and applying lessons through experience. On the one hand, there is some popular sentiment among academics and employers that students cannot be taught to be leaders (indeed, as this view holds, courses that purport to "teach leadership" may present unrealistic expectations for graduates, which are not validated by employers). This is consistent with Adair's (1983) initial premise that leadership cannot be taught, it can only be (or must be) learned. Adair (1983) further maintains that learners are responsible for their own self-development. There is mixed support from academic researchers and teachers on whether leadership can be taught to everyone, or whether some aspects of leadership skills can be taught more effectively than others, as well as differences in views about developing skills through formal courses and coaching (Capowski, 1994). Regardless of the differences in semantics and specifics, there is a consensus that learning about one's own capacity for developing as an effective leader is a highly personal process that can be best understood by students through individual application, intuition, and self-awareness.

To accomplish effective learning processes and outcomes, then, a course on leadership development must present student opportunities for increased awareness of self and others, understanding of situations and contexts, and application of internal models and theories to external opportunities for continuing learning/development. A highly formatted/formulaic curriculum following a more externalized approach often leaves many students "detached" from the impersonal concept of leadership. This is especially true for students from foreign cultures, who cannot identify with frequently touted exemplars from the business world (UK magnates Richard Branson, Sir Alan Sugar) or Western governments (David Cameron, Barack Obama), or even more multicultural historical figures (Mahatma Gandhi, Martin Luther King, Nelson Mandela). Students may find the surface-level characteristics and media friendly staged-behaviors/sound bites easier to digest through such an externalized approach, but it requires students to infer a leader's internal states (attitudes—values—motivation) to explain their behavior; that can be very confusing when the things leaders do (theory-in-use) do not match things they say (espoused theory), as explained by Argyris and Schon (1978). Such generic template curricula can become exercises in stereotypical symbolism — often reinforcing the "worst" of Western ideals (perhaps ascribed to and reinforced by instructors) rather than increasing understanding of multiple perspectives. Such perspectives are influenced by national backgrounds, ethnic origins, gender differences, belief systems, practical experiences, and contemporary global issues that impact students on a personal level. In externalized leadership courses, students can achieve the assessment criteria (e.g., profiling external leaders) through descriptive analysis but not reflective critical thinking.

For students coming from educational cultures emphasizing externalized and impersonal methods of learning — such as memorization and rote learning that records the words and structure of leadership theories without meaning and application — an externalized approach to leadership study can increase tendencies for plagiarism. As defined by Western standards, such plagiarism is often unintended, as many students from other cultures and educational training do not see a problem using existing ideas to describe external theories and leaders — reasoning that "experts" (researchers, authors) know more about these theories and leaders than the students do. Thus, the students are still "learning" and acquiring/transmitting knowledge by copying the ideas and words of noted authors.

The OB3 curriculum was intentionally redesigned to focus more on personalized leadership development. The possibility of plagiarism was immediately reduced, as it is nearly impossible to lift the ideas and written words of others in creating a personal model, theory, and development plan. Instead of distant leadership archetypes, students are introduced to more immediately identifiable and relevant role models presented as "virtual guest speakers" (using video clips from www.TED.com in lecture sessions). Students can relate to many of the TED speakers along cultural and ethnic dimensions (as well as age and gender); these are not the famous or traditionally powerful, but unknown individuals tackling real social problems and conflicts in familiar parts of students' worlds. One example that encapsulates the OB3 concept is TED speaker Devdutt Pattanaik, a Chief Belief Officer from Mumbai, India, who emphasizes the need to understand "my world" and "your world," in terms of subjective reality.

OB3 is focused on students making their own connections through a triangulation of self-assessment, personal model/theory, and simulated leadership practice. We ask students to explore their inner drives, values, and personal characteristics to prioritize their goals and create an explicit set of action steps for implementation. From this, they create a personal model of leadership incorporating multiple inputs, and explicate their personal theory-in-use and espoused theory of what effective leadership means to them. Throughout this "inside-out" approach to leadership development, student engagement can be increased by practicing and testing theoretical concepts of leadership on a personal level, and using the results to align their own models and understanding. This allows them to progress beyond single-loop to double-loop learning (Argyris & Schon, 1978) to explicitly detail their individualized plan for ongoing development as an effective leader. We emphasize that students make meaningful connections and applications to the external real world by asking them to identify, think beyond, and challenge their own preexisting underlying assumptions. Further, students are required to investigate and apply an existing, validated, widely accepted "emergent perspective" on leadership (e.g., authentic, distributed, complexity theory) to support their own personal understanding. This ensures substantial rigor beyond a hazy "circular reasoning" or ad hominem criticism.

Although some students do comment on the "relentless" pace of the course, these ongoing, formative activities are designed to keep students busily engaged — that is, they are continuously linking concepts to applications in real-time, without the kind of lags often found in the lecture/revision/exam format of British university curriculum. (In a peculiar practice of traditional UK higher education, many courses assess student "learning" through one or two pieces of summative assessment at the end of term — such as an essay and an exam — which can skew instrumental learning most heavily toward a single "revision" lecture preceding final exams.)

The Integrated IT-Based Pedagogical Model of OB3

OB3's personalized, continuously engaged "inside-out" approach is important for students learning about their capacity to develop as globally competent, culturally intelligent leaders, especially during the process of interacting with students from so many different (foreign) cultures and educational backgrounds. In addition to "quiet time" in self-directed learning activities, OB3 students are assigned to computer labs where they complete an interactive virtual simulation called vLeader, with the hands-on guidance and support of a trained lab tutor. This approach is consistent with Mendenhall's (2007) effective type of global leadership development programs using instructive coaching in "real-time" training, so that learners from multicultural backgrounds can take advantage of expert assistance to learn and deploy new competencies as they happen. Mendenhall (2007, p. 429) notes three distinct advantages of real-time training/personal coaching over more traditional management development approaches that may be found in externalized generic template leadership courses:

1. High individualization – allowing for self-assessment and evaluation of an individual learner's competencies.
2. Focus on the present – developing within the learner competencies and personal strategies to deal with challenges that exist in the present, immediately practiced, with subsequent, ongoing evaluation of the learner's effectiveness in implementing newly learned competencies.
3. Confidentiality and inner freedom to learn – providing learners with the inner freedom to experiment without fear of retribution (failure on an assessment), which will suppress the willingness to try out a new competency.

In addition to positive impact on active, self-directed learning, pedagogically integrated technology is reported to have a positive impact on student engagement and learning in general. Findings from a 2011 survey by Cengage/Eduventures reveal that a majority (58%) of instructors believe that technology in courses positively impacts student engagement and highly benefits learning; nearly half (45%) also agree/strongly agree that technologies help students who cannot perform well in the traditional classroom environment. A much higher percentage of students (86%) report improved academic engagement from increasing use of digital tools in their coursework, which also improved their overall learning (94%) and further helped them to overcome personal challenges (94%). The gap in perceptions between instructors and students is intriguing, and may be telling – as younger generations of learners tend to be more technologically aware (to the point where it is "unconscious competence" for them to use learning technologies, when it may be "conscious incompetence" for some instructors who do not know how to use them).

This same survey suggests that the current state of incorporating simulations in the classroom is not as effective as it could be: only 11% of instructors and 12% of students identify simulations as having the potential to improve engagement and learning (although this is a larger percentage than supported digital tools such as e-readers, handheld polling devices/"classroom clickers," social networks, learning management systems, podcasts, text messaging, online news aggregators, or blogs). However, nearly half (46%) of students believe simulations have had significant impact on their overall learning – so the promise is there, as evidenced by the fact that more than two-thirds of students want more technology-based learning tools in the classroom. What could account for the low percentage of respondents perceiving simulations as improving engagement and learning outcomes?

It may be that some simulations are decidedly non-interactive and, in fact, could even be defined as "passive" and disconnected from real-time (asynchronous, e.g.). For example, in one business simulation where students start a new company in the microcomputer industry (with results measured based on profitability, customer satisfaction, market share, human resource management, asset management, and preparation for the future), students were required to make group decisions on their business in each quarter (as opposed to continuous, interactively input action and reaction). Students playing this simulation did not perceive that it significantly improved their transferable skills (with the exception of three specific self-reliance skills, all related to the team-based decisions made with other students: giving constructive feedback to other team members, dealing with criticism of your work, and having a proactive approach to new situations or tasks). Overall, students perceived that their leadership and interpersonal skills remained comparatively low (Begum & Newman, 2009). Thus, when students are involved in an essentially "externalized" simulation — one that is not individually personalized and presented as interactive experience, lacking reflection on the experiences, without integration with seminar discussion and strong alignment with course topics/sequence — they might perceive the technology as more about punching numbers than working with people (beyond the immediate members of their student team).

On the other hand, students who undertook a more interactive, real-time role-playing simulation — one where they could immediately measure their personal impact on the outcomes — reported higher levels of engagement and deeper learning (Johnson, Graham, & Hsueh, 2006). These students found that in at least some ways use of the simulation improved their ability to visualize procedures and concepts, the quality and quantity of practice, the level and authenticity of their engagement and learning, the interaction and collaboration among students and the students with the instructor, and the opportunities for reflection in-practice and on-practice (Johnson et al., 2006).

FACILITATING ENGAGEMENT AND ENHANCING LEADERSHIP DEVELOPMENT THROUGH SIMULATION

Student engagement is essential to achieving successful learning outcomes, psychological and emotional adjustment, and multicultural awareness and understanding. Simulations can engage learners in ways other approaches do not, by creating more opportunities for students to become self-aware and self-developmental — matched to learning outcomes to be collaborative, to challenge themselves and their perceptions, and to apply their knowledge to set situations (Morton et al., 2009). This can generate students' creative problem solving and innovative thinking, engaging more learners in the excitement and discovery of the learning process itself. Morton et al. (2009) recommend that, as more sophisticated role-plays engage the players in virtual worlds, the activity should be about the process of engagement rather than an end solution; as such, the students should be able to determine pace and pattern of activity (within broadly imposed guidelines and schedules), which helps them to create an individualized experience by applying their own knowledge and understanding. At the same time, there is still a focus on the development of transferable skills suitable for a professional environment, which fits with the nature and purpose of OB3 (Morton et al., 2009).

Cross-cultural learners attempt to make sense of a new environment through their existing "mental maps," or set of specific beliefs, attitudes, and emotional reactions about situations. The most effective way to help them challenge these preexisting underlying assumptions is by presenting opportunities to increase their self-awareness toward a more discerning and integrated understanding, in effect, expanding and reorienting their frame of reference (Mezirow, 1991). Mezirow describes this as the process of transformative learning, whereby engagement in critical reflection leads to "perspective transformation" (p. 167).

Mezirow's (1990) notion of task-oriented problem solving is similar to the concept of single-loop learning articulated by Argyris and Schon (1978); in the vLeader simulation, students experience this kind of instrumental learning as they grasp the "rules" governing each scenario, technical methods of communicating toward people and ideas (tasks), and the effects of power and tension on the relationship (leadership) outcomes. Primarily, students tend to attempt attaining tangible business results using their initial, instinctive style and logic. However, through guided reflection and interactive discussion after each scenario, students are encouraged to progress beyond single-loop to double-loop learning, becoming aware of "their presuppositions through challenging established and habitual patterns of expectation" (Mezirow, 1990. p.4). In vLeader, this can mean trying new "styles" of leadership that may be out of the student's comfort zones, or explaining why personal issues can affect organizational results. For the Chinese students in particular, there are profound implications when "anomalies and dilemmas occur from the inability of old ways of knowing cannot make sense become catalysts or 'trigger events' that precipitate critical reflection and transformations" (Mezirow, 1990, p. 5).

Johnson et al. (2006) argue that classroom technology can help to actively and authentically engage students in the learning process if the experiences and opportunities are authentic (similar to real-life), offer high-quality practice and feedback, promote interaction and collaboration with instructors and peers, and support meaningful student reflection. vLeader provides a realistic, interactive "business oriented" practice experience, wherein students interact and collaborate with virtual colleagues during the simulation − and also discuss their experiences and interpretations of results with classmates and instructors in focused seminars.

Consistent with Johnson et al.'s (2006) recommendations, vLeader's authentic cases are likely to contribute more to the students' understanding of the underlying concepts, enabling students to visualize procedures and concepts. In other areas, vLeader is integrated in the leadership development curriculum to support experiential learning through the quality and quantity of practice and the opportunities for reflection and connection. Building on this platform for successful deployment of a simulation, we present the integration of vLeader into the OB3 curriculum.

Implementing the vLeader Simulation in OB3

vLeader, developed by SimuLearn Inc., is an award-winning training simulation used by more than 130 universities and Fortune 500 corporations worldwide, as well as military and government organizations. As shown in Fig. 1, through completing a progressive sequence of five increasingly complex meeting-based scenarios, users interact with "live" characters to recognize communication cues and person/task-based issues while providing feedback and suggesting ideas to achieve outcomes that reflect effective leadership and business results.

vLeader can be readily deployed and integrated into existing academic courses as a "off the shelf" turnkey solution, or through curriculum design and pedagogical adjustment it can be customized in a combination of self-paced delivery and classroom instructions, with or without SimuLearn Certified Mentor (e.g., instructors trained by SimuLearn). In the Greenwich Business School, two of the OB3 lab tutors are Certified Mentors (the first in the United Kingdom), as the Business School is the

Scenario One: One-to-One Meeting with Oli

Scenario Two: Team Building

Fig. 1.   The Five Scenarios in vLeader.

Scenario Three: "Managing Up" to Challenge the Status Quo

Scenario Four: Merger of Two Cultures

Fig. 1.   (Continued).

Scenario Five: Crisis and Opportunity

Fig. 1.   (Continued).

first British academic institution to use vLeader (as well as one of the largest single user-based in the world, with more than 500 students each year).

vLeader is presented in three parts when the students launch the simulation, as shown in Fig. 2:

1. Leadership Fundamentals: The first part provides an introduction to
   the simulation and the underlying framework of 3-to-1 Leadership (as
   shown in Fig. 3, based on the model of Power, Tension, and Ideas
   developed by Clark Aldrich, 2003, and SimuLearn). This takes the students through a series of guided practice steps in using the navigation
   tools and the controls to interact with the characters and concepts.
2. Learning the Principles: The second part consists of five exercises to
   help students learn the principles that reinforce 3-to-1 Leadership. (a)
   Try Doing Work: How to get the right work done and prevent the
   wrong work as a successful leader by supporting good ideas and oppos-
   ing bad ones. (b) *Try Lowering Tension*: In this exercise, students work
   on tactics to reduce tension levels, understanding that sometimes leaders
   should relax or excite people temporarily to stimulate their creativity.
   (c) *Try Moderating Tension*: Students have to adjust the tension in a

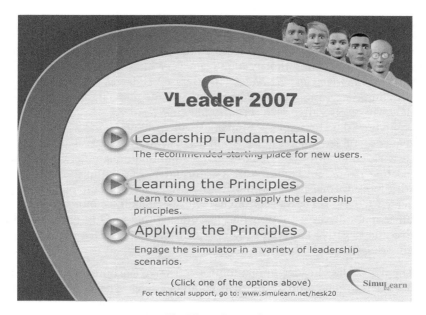

Fig. 2. The Three Parts of vLeader.

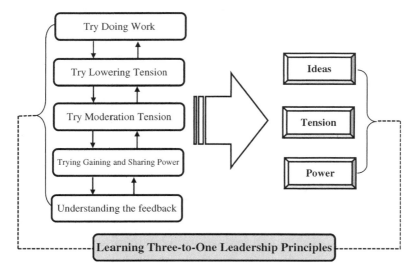

Fig. 3. The vLeader Framework (Aldrich, 2003, and SimuLearn).

group in order to make it productive in this exercise session. (d) *Try Gaining and Sharing Power*: Power is the keyword in this exercise, from which students should realize the components of the power and that reliance on formal authority alone is a very limited view of leadership. (e) *Understanding the Feedback*: It offers 62 slides of scenario analysis with audio narration, designed to help students understand the feedback they will receive after each scenario play in vLeader.

3. Applying the Principles: Students will role-play in a progressive sequence of five increasingly complex meeting-based scenarios. From scenario one through scenario five, additional characters join each meeting (some colleagues with less formal power/authority, and some with more formal power/authority than the students' role-playing character, "Corey"). The variety of character personalities, motivations, and other inner drives – along with ideas (tasks) that vary in terms of positive and negative impact to the organization, makes each scenario progressively more challenging.

The use of the vLeader simulation for reflective learning is supported by dedicated tutorial group sessions in computer labs. The lab tutors begin each session with a briefing on the relevant part of the simulation (helping students to connect the "mouse clicks" to the concepts), after which tutors wander the lab unobtrusively observing students playing the simulation, offering coaching and help when needed (or asked). Ultimately, however, tutors reinforce the message that students must take initiative and responsibility for understanding the results and explaining their meaning – that is, simply achieving a certain numerical score is not sufficient. Student's vLeader activities are tracked through a centralized database containing all user log-in dates/times, and results achieved – so that the teaching team can see whether students are functionally engaging (although we cannot track mental or emotional engagement, the kind of reflection that supports experiential learning). In this way we can see whether students are experimenting by attempting different styles of leadership – using a proxy of their dialogue (percentage of interactive conversation taken by the student in each attempt). According to the vLeader guidelines, a directive style is approximated by the student taking at least 60% of dialogue turns (up to 70% in some scenarios), with shorter overall length of "meetings" (less than 100 turns); a participative style by taking between 30% and 60% of the dialogue turns (with meeting length between 100 and 150 turns); and a delegative or "hands-off" style by taking less than 30% of the dialogue turns. Students are required to play each scenario a minimum of three times (using each leadership style once), up to a recommended number of eight times to achieve "mastery" — being able to replicate excellent results, building on learning from previous experiments. This helps to ensure that results are not simply from random clicks. At the same time, students are encouraged to strive for the target overall "score" of 90 or above, which reflects a set of relationally oriented leadership results. This score is derived from algorithms representing the process of the meeting itself, interacting with other characters in terms of power (personal influence, group opinion), tension (productive or unproductive), and ideas (uncovering all ideas for discussion — including "hidden agenda" ideas that other characters must introduce — to increase consideration of available possibilities), as well as a set of task-oriented business results (the effects of the meeting outcomes at the organizational level on financial performance, customer satisfaction, and employee morale). The open systems notion of equifinality is also reinforced — there are multiple paths to achieve excellent outcomes, and no single best way — which ensures continuous awareness and conscious double-loop learning by students.

Reviewing students' results indicates whether they appear to be stuck in a closed feedback cycle, continuing to play a scenario in essentially the same style/approach on multiple attempts yet not progressing in their overall numerical scores. This is equivalent to single-loop learning (getting very good at one approach, or at least achieving consistent and predictable outcomes). The goal is for students to display double-loop learning, by using the different leadership styles to determine which approach is most effective for the particular scenario (or possibly a combination of styles), ideally while recording their learning and feelings. Students also display resilience by experimenting with the different styles of leadership and playing the scenario up to another five times to progress toward the desired target score of 90.

OB3 seminar sessions follow lab sessions. That is, students complete the required part of the simulation in lab (and continue to play outside of lab) and return the following week in seminars to discuss what they have learned. OB3 tutors adapt the seminars to their own professional experiences, knowledge, and teaching strengths, using group-based questions relating the simulation to leadership concepts. Students and tutors use supporting written materials such as a custom-designed lab/seminar workbook (drawing from SimuLearn guides and the Leadership Experience Instructors Compendium by Dunning, 2007), which integrates the concepts from core textbook (Daft, 2008) with the students' experiences learned from vLeader.

The evolution of OB3 over the last 3 years is a prime example of experiential learning on the part of the course leader and team of tutors. When vLeader was first deployed in the 2009 term of OB3, not all students engaged as effectively in the self-directed completion of the online scenarios, nor participated as fully in the seminar discussions; this was most apparent with more than 100 students from China, who came to the OB3 course their final year of study. Tutors (who had not expected to teach any direct-entry students from outside the United Kingdom) reported encounters with Chinese students who would not contribute to discussion in the expected "Western" method – for example, they would not share during small group exercises, would not volunteer to share with the larger class, and would not respond to direct questioning, even for simple questions (such as "what is the difference between autocratic and democratic styles of leadership?"). From their UK teaching orientation, the OB3 tutors tend to suspect that students who "turn up" to class but refuse to participate most likely are not prepared, lack the background knowledge, and, in the case of this OB3 course, have not completed the required part of the simulation in advance.

However, as the OB3 teaching team continues to become more culturally conscious – continuously taking a step outside our frames of reference, examining our own underlying assumptions and "functional fixedness" – we are more aware of multiple learning styles, cross-cultural barriers, and blind spots. This increased awareness drives our exploration of two fundamental questions: How can we generally ensure that the use of the vLeader simulation improves student engagement and related experiential learning in the OB3 course? And, in particular, how can we more effectively support the learning styles/needs of Chinese students while maintaining the rigor and integrity of the course curriculum and consistent teaching quality through innovative pedagogy?

CHALLENGES OF ENGAGING CHINESE STUDENTS IN THE UNITED KINGDOM

Many researchers have recently acknowledged the considerable challenges faced by Chinese students in the United Kingdom, and by the teaching and administrative staff supporting these students' engaged learning (e.g., Gao, Arnulf, & Henning, 2011; Gu & Brooks, 2008; Gu & Maley, 2008;

Wang, L., 2010; Wang, Y., 2010; Wan, 2001; Warring, 2007; Weber, 2011). The challenges are largely influenced by the students' background in China's education system based on teacher-centered repetition and deference to professors rather than critical thinking in individual study and deep, interactive discussions in seminars. As one overseas student notes, "With Chinese universities, you've got a more rigid education system, where it is really hard to challenge the professors and to challenge the academic staff" (Mackie, 2005).

Based on our own teaching/administrative experiences and student feedback at the University of Greenwich, we have identified key issues for which technology applications may help to overcome barriers experienced by teachers. In addition to tutor frustration with non-participating Chinese students in mixed groups, one "unspoken" challenge tutors informally mentioned in the faculty lounge (but not officially raised) is that many of the direct entry Chinese students seem to possess oral communication skills in English language at levels below those expected/required for functioning in a UK university undergraduate degree program. Tutors who mention this challenge note that the language barrier may not be evident if Chinese students choose not to speak up in group settings, but it becomes apparent during tutor attempts at interpersonal conversation. Several tutors shared anecdotes where Chinese students appeared unable to comprehend the tutor's questions and statements of instruction (e.g., responding with blank stares, or continuing to use incorrect procedures when playing the simulation), or exhibited difficulty in making themselves understood in English. At times, these students "double up" with a second Chinese student serving as a type of translator/observer/recorder (or second set of ears), even in cases where neither student individually appeared to be proficient in English. Unfortunately, most tutors are not as aware of their own language and comprehension barriers — for example, when they speak in Western (and British) colloquialisms, academic code, acronymic shortcuts, or outdated jargon. As a side note on firsthand experience, neither author of this chapter (one American, one Chinese) speaks "British" English or UK academic code as a first language, and we have each experienced our share of resultant confusion and misunderstanding with students and with colleagues.

In the following section, we will explore the pressures and obstacles hindering Chinese student success, and share our integrated approach with the vLeader simulation that has helped improve Chinese student engagement at the University of Greenwich.

LANGUAGE BARRIER

According to the 2011 academic survey by Cengage Learning and Eduventures, the major distractive factors to student engagement are external responsibilities like caring for and raising families, or financial pressure (e.g., paying for school or debt). Despite the fact that international students face significant costs associated with university study in the United Kingdom (considering course fees, accommodation costs, and living expenses), nearly all Chinese students receive substantial financial support from their families. Hence, they do not typically face this degree of external financial pressure. For Chinese students, the most common difficulty is associated with language ability, especially for the direct entry students, coming straight into final-year study at a foreign institution after finishing studies of 2 or 3 years in Chinese partner institutions.

International students who wish to enroll in any undergraduate program at the University of Greenwich are required to take the IELTS (International English Language Testing System) and achieve a score 6.0 or above. For the majority of direct entry Chinese students who are not able to meet these standards a short-term course of English language study will be provided to help them improve to the minimum level. However, despite using IELTS band 5.5/6.0 as an entry criterion, Chinese students' relatively weak English proficiency remains one of the key obstacles in learning and teaching activities.

The focus of English language learning in China has consistently been on reading and writing, rather than listening and speaking (Wan, 2001). For this reason, a good score in IELTS cannot warrant sufficient English capability for successful university study in the United Kingdom (Yen & Kuzma, 2009). The restrictions of international students' language abilities, mixed with emotional and situational difficulties, often limit their academic performance (Cross, 2006).

CULTURAL BARRIER

In addition to language-specific factors, Ho, Holmes, and Cooper (2004) note how cultural attitudes and values influence Chinese students' learning engagement and academic achievement. The distinctive characteristics of Confucian Heritage Culture (CHC) are particularly relevant to Chinese students' challenges of successfully adapting to an unfamiliar academic context. In the following sections, relevant cultural barriers influencing Chinese student learning engagement will be discussed.

CONFUCIAN TEACHER-CENTERED PARADIGM

One of the most fundamental values of the CHC tradition is respect for authority. Confucius' teachings hold that learners maintain respect for age and rank, and obey authority figures. Chinese students usually respect their teacher as an authority without preconditions, which means that should obey and listen to teachers. In CHC, hierarchy is seen to be natural and there is a sense of the complementarity of relationships (Bond, 1986, cited by Marx, 2001). Also, according to Hofstede and Hofstede (2005), China is one of the CHC nations scoring highest on the Power Distance Index. It is generally asserted that nations with high scores on power distance place greater emphasis on hierarchical relationships.

Therefore, the educational paradigm in China is more "teacher centered." Only students are viewed as learners. Knowledge is transmitted from teacher to students, who passively receive information. In addition, many students are only taught with lectures in front of a large class without smaller breakout sessions (tutorial arrangements), so that Chinese students coming to UK universities are accustomed to a very formally structured classroom situation where active interaction with one another or with the teacher in the classroom is rarely allowed.

When Chinese students start their studies in UK universities where the education paradigm is more "student-centered" on active learning, they frequently find difficulties engaging in group presentations and tutorial discussions, as these are not a part of classroom interaction in China (Ho et al., 2004). The lack of English language proficiency can exacerbate feelings of discomfort if they are forced to answer questions or speak up in class. Often, Chinese students are afraid of "losing face" if they share the "wrong" idea or give a less than perfect answer. They have an overriding concern with asking the "right" questions and not sounding "silly". They are also extremely sensitive to saving face for others. For example, they will try to avoid direct disagreement with their teacher (which would lead to the teacher's loss of face). It is also extremely difficult for Chinese students to ask for more clarification in the classroom, because it would suggest that the teacher did not fully explain the questions in a systematic way.

In student-centered educational environments where discussion-based interaction is highly encouraged, these differences in cultural influence greatly affect Chinese students' academic performances. Therefore, it has become increasingly important and even crucial that we employ strategies to help Chinese students more seamlessly facilitate the transformation from a teacher-centered approach to the student-centered approach used at the University of Greenwich.

CONFUCIAN MEMORY-BASED ROTE LEARNING

Although some researchers (intriguingly, not always from CHC) have challenged the long-term impression of East Asian learners as passive rote learners (Beaver & Tuck, 1998; Watkins & Biggs, 1996, 2001), Chinese students are predominantly perceived as using a surface approach to learning (Horwitz, 1999; Wu, 2008). CHC tradition highly values expenditures of necessary effort and perseverance in order to succeed, but this does not necessarily equate with individualistic creativity and critical thinking. Chinese students generally regard repetition and memory-based rote learning strategies as the best approaches to increase their level of understanding necessary to pass examinations.

Memory-based learning could act as a major obstacle to critical thinking. Due to a lack of cultivation in critical thinking skills, Chinese students are frequently characterized as hardworking and diligent but lacking in creativity and originality (as perceived by Western culture teachers and fellow students).

ENGAGING CHINESE STUDENTS WITH VLEADER

Infiltrative Bilingual Teaching Support: More Than Just Language

Despite relatively inadequate English-language proficiency among Chinese students, their potential academic interest is strong and can be enhanced through engagement with transformative, experiential learning. Ninnes (1999) affirmed that university and lecturer awareness of international students' special needs could facilitate their adaptation to academic environment to build up their academic and social experiences. The Chinese students' English-language levels and teaching models are two major factors that influence bilingual teaching (He, Xu, & Zhu, 2011), which frequently results in higher student satisfaction with learning based on general course components (Li & Wang, 2010). However, the main limitations of traditional bilingual teaching are over-translation and cramming (He et al., 2011), which inhibit deeper learning.

The provision of academic supervision, additional personal support, and mentoring for direct entry Chinese students is time consuming and sometimes ineffectively implemented when academic staff do not have awareness of the CHC influences and prior Chinese educational values. McClure (2001) suggests that institutions look for ways to help international students develop their language skills and provide applicable pedagogical strategies; at the University of Greenwich, this extends to helping them quickly adapt to the UK education system to better understand the theoretical knowledge and master the practical skills to build their confidence in multinational communication.

In the 2011 term of OB3, we first offered the option of non-mandatory tutorial groups designed specifically for direct entry Chinese students, staffed by two tutors: one from Europe (for whom English is a second language, common among University of Greenwich faculty), and one from China (whose first language is Mandarin). Consistent with university and UK higher education regulations, all teaching is in English, and students must speak English to participate fully in larger class discussions (and receive contribution marks); however, small group discussion may be in Mandarin. The Chinese-language tutor also helps to translate difficult words, phrases, or concepts into Mandarin – alongside the English-language delivery. All written assignments also must be submitted in English. Although we designed these tutorial groups for direct entry Chinese students, any students are welcome to join; for example, there are several "continuing" Chinese students who started in the Greenwich Business School degree programs in year 1 or year 2 and who feel more comfortable in these Chinese support groups. At the same time, Chinese students are not required to join the Chinese language/culture support groups – and in fact, several have chosen to return to mixed groups. Potential downsides to the Chinese-only groups are that Western students lose the multicultural contribution/challenge of working with Chinese students, and the Chinese students lose the same exposure to their multicultural peers. However, for the immediate – and lasting – positive impacts of experiential learning and sharing of knowledge with and by the Chinese students (and effective teaching and learning by the Greenwich faculty), the demonstrated upsides outweigh the possible downsides.

The more Chinese students improve their English language ability, the more they will enjoy their classes in an open and interactive way (Sun, 2005). In the current OB3 course, 15 direct entry Chinese students submitted voluntary feedback with some interesting and honest personal reflections about their own key takeaways and insights gained from the course. All 15 respondents (more than 50% of those invited to participate) mentioned that bilingual support offers great help and support to them. Here are some sample comments from these students.

Quotes from direct-entry Chinese students enrolled in OB3 2012

"I really like the bilingual teaching, which could help me catch the points in a more efficient and effective way."

"It is not bilingual teaching indeed. Explanation in Mandarin only is provided only when we felt confused or the whole class is in silence, but it is always working for us."

"For me, the best part of learning vLeader is confidence gained from bilingual support; the experience of deeply understanding the core concepts encourages me to go through and analyse meeting dynamics."

From Rote Learning to Meaningful Deep learning

Compared with surface learning, deep learning is more long-term learning and comes from "real" understanding. The cutting-edge technology of vLeader uses avatars and intelligent agents to build a supportive environment that actively engages students in Kolb's (1984) four stages of experiential learning (experience, reflect, conceptualize, experiment), which Ng et al. (2009) relate to improved global leadership self-efficacy, accurate mental models of leadership across cultures, and flexibility of leadership styles. Fig. 4 depicts the cyclical nature of Kolb's model.

- Concrete Experience: Students play each scenario, trying to achieve balanced relationship and business results in each of the three styles, in a very extreme and not necessarily realistic fashion: directive, telling people what to do consistently; participative, ensuring input and discussion from other people in the meeting, allowing them to support or prevent certain ideas, focusing on the process/interaction more than the outcomes; and delegative, allowing the others to take control.
- Reflective Observation: Students record their thoughts in online journal, connecting the learning to wider concepts and future experiences. Guiding questions ask them to take a "step back" and see the way in which

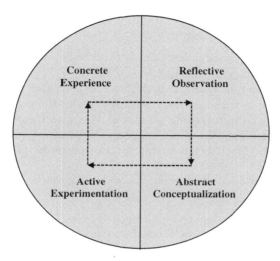

Fig. 4. Experiential Learning Model. Adapted from Kolb's (1984).

they have different influences on the people and ideas (e.g., can you explain why you attain different results using different styles?).

• Abstract Conceptualization: Students apply and extend the results and lessons to create new ideas for better approaches, determining their own "best" style to play vLeader, explaining why that approach would work (or would not), why results were attained, and recognizing their "functional fixedness" or tendency to approach a situation in the same way (predisposed mental map/mindset).

• Active Experimentation: Based on their previous learning, asking students to try a new approach or adjust and practice their "best" style to achieve even higher results.

The Role of Reflective Observation

According to the Kolb (1984) model, at stage two (reflective observation) students could turn their own experience into meaningful deep learning by observing their actual learning experience, analyzing what happened and reflecting on their own experience. Rather than passive rote learning, Chinese students could build up their own record of the experience in different scenarios and answer corresponding questions based on their own "story."

Here is an example of personal reflection questions based on the vLeader experience after playing scenario two:

1. What challenging or negative behaviors did you notice in the simulator and how did you deal with them?
2. Describe a situation where it is difficult to prioritize yourself or other people, and/or a scenario where a conflict stifles the productivity of the team. Consider the following questions: Who are the people involved? What are the ideas? What is the group's opinion of you? What is the group's tension level? What is your level of personal influence? What is the right work?
3. What have you discovered about the style of leadership you most often use?

Chinese students are highly encouraged to reflect on what they learned, how they learned it, why they learned it, whether the learning experience could have been more effective, and so on. They could endeavor to share some honest and interesting reflections about their own learning experience, or any worries and insights during the whole course. Moreover, they could go into more reflective detail to discuss their own strengths and weaknesses, helping to demonstrate clarity of thought about the insights they have gained from the simulation, providing a good overview of the key points from the scenarios and clearly relating them back to the real world. An emphasis on meaningful learning is consistent with the view of learning as knowledge construction in which students seek to make sense of their experiences. Reflecting on those actions, evaluating the significance of the actions and finally experimenting with new strategies are the essential variables provided to students by business simulations.

'Safe' Feature: Positive Face-Keeping

Students also engage through psychological and emotional adjustment, using what Narvaez (2010) terms an "Ethic of Engagement" oriented to face-to-face emotional affiliation with others. vLeader enables students to interact with virtual characters to build relational as well as professional bonds (or, choose not to do so); the key feature is that students can replay a given scenario by taking an extremely relational and interpersonal approach one time, and a more aloof and professionally distant approach the next. Narvaez (2010) argues that the ability to build relational bonds engenders values of compassion and openness toward others, so that providing environments such as those in vLeader that foster "social relations and cultural narratives for the ethics of engagement and imagination" can help students to realize and achieve "peaceful coexistence" (p. 174).

Increased awareness of multiple perspectives and cross-cultural understanding improves students' engagement on both an immediate level with fellow students and teachers, and on a global societal level. Rhee and Sagaria (2004) indicate that international students who voluntarily engage with foreign cultural, political, and socioeconomic elements as "consenting participants" neutralize power differentials (p. 91), although students for whom English is not the first language still experience power differentials and language and cultural barriers in English-speaking learning environments. Weber (2011) notes that multiculturalism in an impersonal, externalized, universally applied "one size fits all" fashion can inhibit the examination of broader social relations, and produce silences that disengage students from the ability to apply their global knowledge in a creative and useful manner. In Weber's (2011) view, oppression and power differences that exist within intercultural relationships need to be acknowledged so all students can remain engaged in productive learning. Because students bring their past experiences to their new learning environments, Weber maintains, students who are more able to understand the multiple cultures of contexts which form their identities can more successfully and critically engage with their learning and with others. Engaging multicultural identities requires that students explore, balance, and even attempt to reconcile their internal self-perceptions (connectedness) with awareness of external perceptions and categorizations made by others (Gu, 2009; Jenkins, 2004). Gu (2009, p. 14) shares useful insights from a Chinese student who may be juggling, rather than engaging, multicultural identities: "I've got two sets of values: one is for here and one is for China, because I don't want to be treated as a foreigner in either context."

The artificial intelligence underlying the vLeader simulation "assumes" that effective leaders know how to recognize, adjust, and optimize three elements (power, ideas, and tension) to mobilize teams and individuals to be productive — get the right work done. Students are provided an excellent opportunity to observe theory in practice, to develop new skills and attitudes. Throughout the process, the message is reinforced that it is safe for Chinese students to take risks, try approaches that may be unnatural or uncomfortable for them at first, and even to "fail"; because vLeader is an individual, interactive experience (no one else can see or hear how the students interact with the other characters), there is no loss of face if the highest possible results are not attained. The intention is that Chinese students will come to realize the benefit of experiential learning as a process, and not simply focus on the outcomes as indicated of success. As Li (2009) also advises, Chinese students should actively experiment with some risk taking to enact acceptable behaviors that improve communication in cross-cultural environments.

Mandarin-speaking language support was only given to clarify and explain the "Cues" and "Clues." For example, the most important learning objective in vLeader scenario one (one-on-one meeting) is that students recognize autocratic, democratic, and laissez faire leadership behavior and the impact of each style. If they were in a purely English-taught class, many of the Chinese would have achieved nothing even if they had played scenario one many times. When they misunderstand one concept or even part of the terminology (they found the terms autocratic, democratic, and laissez faire confusing and difficult to immediately translate), then they found themselves completely lost in the class. But with the necessary Chinese translation/explanation and familiar examples for application, they can quickly understand and catch up with the learning progression. In addition, almost every direct-entry Chinese student finds it extremely difficult to understand the dialogue among different virtual characters in the vLeader simulation, even with English-language captions provided along with "live" audio narration in each scenario. So it is very crucial to outline the contextually embedded instructions, elaborate a clearer portrait of the characters' "personality," and briefly analyze and explain the personal and professional relationships among the students (playing the role of Corey, the new middle manager) and the characters.

Due to the tendency of face-saving and concerns about exam-centered impact, Chinese students at the beginning of the simulation typically fall into two categories: (1) those expecting different results without taking different approaches; or (2) those repeating the same style and approach which could consistently produce the same approximate score (which may be low, in the 60s–70s, or high, in the 90s). In the OB3 bilingual support labs and seminars, Chinese students are highly encouraged to try different approaches for dealing with different situations without pressure of achieving high scores. The most important things will be that the students understand that an important leadership perspective is to balance power, ideas, and tension to accomplish effective relationship-oriented processes as well as outcome-focused business results (rather than figuring out a method or skill to simply score the highest numerical score in every play).

The risk-free environment in vLeader can help Chinese students overcome the pressure of face-saving, and at the same time, strengthen understanding of different leadership styles.

Table 1 shows three distributions of results achieved in scenario two. This information helps students understand how they approached the meeting, through detailing how often and where they "clicked" on people and on ideas (tasks).

As students explore the different scenarios, they should initially look for ways to make this results very "different" (experimenting with new styles to understand the difference in results). As is shown in Table 1, Student A had successfully made progress toward a score in the 90s more than once in scenario two. The dialogue percentage (turns of conversation taken by the student, playing the role of "Corey") in three plays was 49.46%, 50.00%, and 48.75%, respectively, which is designated by vLeader as a "participative" style (falling into a range between 30% and 65%). From this example, it appears the student tried to figure out ways to stay in a comfort zone, continually achieving higher scores by using the same leadership style and without considering alternative possibilities to approach the meeting (i.e., a case of single-loop learning).

In contrast, as shown in Table 2, Student B tried to use different leadership styles in different plays of scenario two, instead of a single style.

In B1, the student uses a directive style (mostly task-focused), indicated by a dialogue percentage above 65%. In B2, the student uses a delegative ("hands off," or laissez faire) style focused mostly on people (but at the extreme of letting the other characters dominate the conversation and thus make most of the decisions), indicated by a dialogue percentage below 30%. In B3, the student uses a participative style that considers both the people and the tasks in a more balanced perspective, indicated by a dialogue percentage between 30% and 65%.

Students often achieve the best overall results ("high scores" for relational aspects of power, tension, and ideas, along with business results of financial performance, customer satisfaction, and employee morale) using the participative style. However, the requirement is that students try each leadership style at least once – to assess (and interpret) the results as well as their own feelings – and there are many instances where several different styles may be combined within a given scenario (i.e., different styles may work best with different characters, or when faced with tasks that have crucial impact compared with those that are more routine).

Table 1. Three Completions of Scenario Two by Student A, Achieving "High" Scores Using the Same Leadership Style Repeatedly (i.e., Single-Loop Learning).

Student A, Attempt 1			Student A, Attempt 2			Student A, Attempt 3		
Total Score: **92.17**			Total Score: **92.13**			Total Score: **90.61**		
Leadership	Business Results		Leadership	Business Results		Leadership	Business Results	
89.67	94.67		89.58	94.67		86.56	94.67	
Dialogue: **49.46%**			Dialogue: **50.00%**			Dialogue: **48.75%**		
People-Focused	20	43%	People-Focused	10	25%	People-Focused	14	36%
Ideas-Focused	26	57%	Ideas-Focused	30	75%	Ideas-Focused	25	64%
Participative	46	100%	*Participative*	40	100%	*Participative*	39	100%

Table 2. Three Completions of Scenario Two by Student B, Showing All Three Leadership Styles[a] and Progress Toward a High Score (i.e., Double-Loop Learning).

Student B, Attempt 1		
Total Score: **88.29**		
Leadership		Business Results
81.90		94.67
Dialogue: **77.27%**		
People-Focused	7	10%
Ideas-Focused	61	90%
Directive	68	100%

Student B, Attempt 2		
Total Score: **76.48**		
Leadership		Business Results
74.30		78.67
Dialogue: **27.94%**		
People-Focused	18	95%
Ideas-Focused	1	5%
Delegative	19	100%

Student B, Attempt 3		
Total Score: **95.70**		
Leadership		Business Results
96.73		94.67
Dialogue: **52.50%**		
People-Focused	40	36%
Ideas-Focused	44	64%
Participative	84	100%

[a] Achieving 60% or higher of dialogue turns for a Directive style; less than 30% for a Delegative style; and between 30% and 60% of dialogue turns for a Participative style.

"Realistic" Feature: Facilitating Leadership Skill

As we have previously noted, compared with the United Kingdom, Chinese culture measures high on the "power distance" scale, which means greater emphasis on hierarchical relationships. Thus, Chinese students learning in the United Kingdom are highly influenced by a relative sense of how perceived formal power and influence are hierarchically distributed. On one hand, Chinese students believe the teacher has the ultimate authority to decide everything, so they seldom ask questions or challenge teachers even when that is the teacher's aim through provocative pedagogy (such as the Socratic Method for debate and inquiry). On the other hand, Chinese students are educated to accept that people in lower positions are expected to obey those in higher position and subordinates must maintain a distance from their superiors with respect and awe. This leads to Chinese students regarding "power" as based on formal power and hierarchical positions and not understanding (or not accepting) notions of informal power and influence. The awareness of "imbalanced power" hinders Chinese students improving leadership skills. According to the analysis of results in vLeader and our ongoing observation and feedback from Chinese students, power has become the "short board" effect for many of them (derived from the popular Chinese metaphor of wooden barrel theory, where the capacity of the barrel is determined by the shortest board, not the longest; the Western equivalent is a chain only as strong as its weakest link). In other words, many Chinese students cannot readily envision how people in subordinate roles influence decisions through informal power. Thus, even if these students could achieve high total scores (above 90) in vLeader, they are still encouraged to practice listening to characters without formal power and increase their awareness of self and others in team situations.

In the following example of a vLeader scenario results screen the total score in Fig. 5 is 88%, which is made up of the average of Leadership and Business Results (totals of 81% and 96%, respectively).

In vLeader, an important principle is that "Business Results" are only affected by the ideas that are completed during the meeting. The "Leadership" percentage (more accurately, the interpersonal/relational dynamics during the meeting) shows the maximum leadership potential in the scenario, broken out into the average of power, productive tension, and how many ideas introduced/discussed in the meeting.

Because of a low score on Leadership, especially on power, many Chinese students are prevented from achieving high overall results, even if they have supported/completed the right set of ideas and scored high in Business Results. The goal is for students to realize that effective leaders

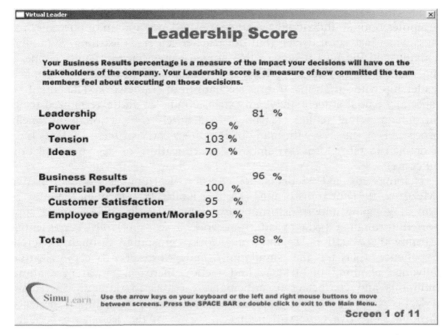

Fig. 5. Results Screen Shown to Students After Playing a Scenario in vLeader.

value and optimize the use of informal power to influence people, rather than relying only on formal power. The power score in vLeader is derived from (1) informal power: how much the group is aligned with you, based partly on the other people's opinion of you and how much they trust you (achieved by choosing the right times to listen to, and speak to, other characters) and (2) personal influence: the ability to direct the conversation at any point of time. If students have no influence when playing vLeader, they will find it difficult to buy-in and engage people. If they have a lot of personal influence, during the meeting, they will realize that it is much easier to get other characters to focus on discussing and supporting the right ideas (tasks).

Self-Paced Environment: Developing Student-Centered and Deep Learning

In the vLeader simulation, Chinese students are put in a self-paced learning environment that allows the user to role-play interactively with intelligent avatars to learn and practice leadership skills. This technology promotes both an individualized student experience and an opportunity for class wide, instructor-driven (but not teacher-centered) learning. Standifer, Thiault, and Pin (2010) suggest that students may have difficulty connecting their technological experiences to concepts of practical and applied leadership without an integrating mechanism or framework. This might be especially true if students have an extrinsic mindset and externalized focus on outcomes that reduce "learning" to a purely transactional and linear process, as is the case with many of the direct entry Chinese students (i.e., if defined in terms of a "commodity" of education, or degree completion outcome).

Helping engaged students to envision learning as transformative (Mezirow, 1991) or transforming (Kolb & Kolb, 2009) through the integration of grasping and transforming experiences (Kolb, 1984) can be supported through a pedagogical framework based on Kolb's experiential learning theory (ELT). In this framework, "grasping" through Concrete Experience (playing the simulation) and Abstract Conceptualization (advance planning of strategy and tactics, increasing awareness about situations and characters to anticipate reactions to different leadership styles) is part of a cyclical process integrated with transforming experience through Reflective Observation (making sense of the scenario experience and results) and Active Experimentation (trying different leadership styles, deliberately going beyond one's natural "comfort zone"). Kolb and Kolb (2009) explain that experiential learning results from the creative tension among the four stages of the cycle, through a constant dynamism and iterative feedback/feedforward process rather than a static, passive lock-step sequence or a non-retentive "data dump."

All OB3 students are encouraged to take time for "connecting the dots" (experiencing, reflecting, thinking, and acting), to take responsibility for not only creating their own knowledge but also their self- and situational awareness of how and when to apply it. Kolb and Kolb (2009) expand the concept of experiential learning to encompass simulations that involve students in the learning process in different ways. Learners may expend effort to make sense of an experiential exercise − abstracting the concrete − while their individual reflection can also involve the transformation of abstract thoughts and feelings into an intensely emotional concrete experience.

In discussing experiential learning that is particularly relevant to Chinese students, Ng, Van Dyne, and Ang (2009) propose that learners' level of cultural intelligence enhances the likelihood that they will actively engage in the four stages of experiential learning in cross-cultural settings, which in turn can help them to develop and externally apply global leadership self-efficacy, accurate mental models of leadership across cultures, and flexibility of leadership styles. Thus, Chinese students with higher levels of cultural intelligence should be better at balancing and integrating the dual dialectics of the ELT process: grasping and transforming experience. Further, Chen and Ching (2012) found that students' who contributed to, and helped to create, a cross-cultural environment of acceptance and understanding greatly enhanced their own cross-cultural sensitivity and flexibility.

FROM TEACHER-CENTERED TO STUDENT-CENTERED

In the OB3 environment and vLeader lab sessions, the student is the center of attention, not the teacher. This is reinforced by pedagogical and curriculum design (requiring students to complete the scenarios at their own pace, by themselves − but also allowing them the flexibility of working ahead and practicing/experimenting as many times as they wish) and also by structural realities. vLeader is completed on individual personal computers, either in the scheduled and supported lab sessions − with the student "isolated" front and center from the instructor through headphones and the inability to share a computer monitor − or at home or any place of the student's choosing. Rather than teacher-centered learning experiences that follow a standardized pace dictated by traditional resources and philosophy, the time allotted for the class and the instructor's preferred approach, vLeader allows the freedom and flexibility for student-centered experiential learning. vLeader's mobility integrated with self-paced learning and collaborative seminar discussion give students the opportunity to learn through a specific task (or the cumulative, gestalt process) as often as they want to until they are confident they have reached their self-determined learning goals (as well as some specific course requirements).

The balance among students' self-determination, collaboration with teams in small tutorial groups, and higher-level course assessment achieves the significant elements of mutual interdependency, reflective learning, and required student engagement that Morrison, Rha, and Helfman (2003) acknowledge in their learner centered model. The kind of real-life leadership scenarios that students encounter in vLeader promote self-discovery as an effective way to connect simulation activities with leadership theory, principles, and practices (Morrison et al., 2003), so that changes in learning style and leadership styles indicate that "being aware of what one is learning is a likely outcome for students who are actively engaged in their own learning" (p. 16).

In transforming their learning from teacher-centered to student-centered, Chinese students on the OB3 course suggest they feel more comfortable and engaged in a self-paced learning environment, in conjunction with the conventional classroom learning providing bilingual/bicultural support, thereby improving their academic performance in a UK university setting. There is generalized support for our findings from Soyemi, Ogunyinka, and Soyemi (2012), who find that the integration of self-paced e-learning together with traditional classroom learning can have profound positive impact on students' academic performance.

FINAL REMARKS

In this chapter, we have thoroughly discussed the use of a virtual leadership simulation (vLeader) integrated within the OB3 course at the University of Greenwich Business School to engage Chinese students through experiential learning. Our experience in dealing with unexpected large numbers of direct entry students who seemingly were disengaged from traditional educational practices forced us to expand our own global mindsets and increase our cultural intelligence − challenging our existing assumptions that non-participating students are either not prepared or are uninterested in learning and sharing their understanding from alternative perspectives. We have explored and explained the challenges Chinese students bring with them from previous educational and cultural influences, and how these can present barriers to effective teaching and learning in Westernized academic settings, from the perspectives of instructors and students themselves.

It is appropriate to note that the focus of this chapter is explicitly confined to devising a solution for an existing and novel problem, relative to current constraints: how can we most effectively engage direct-entry Chinese students arriving unexpectedly to study at Greenwich, given the limitations imposed by our staffing, regulations, budget, rooming/timing availability, and other resources? The underlying premise is that all overseas students come to Greenwich fully aware they will be undertaking a

British university learning experience, delivered in English; indeed, an oft-stated objective is receiving a degree from the United Kingdom (which connotes a distinction in many other countries). Nearly 100% of the Chinese students will be returning to work and live in China, but it is increasingly likely that this new generation of managers will need to interact effectively with non-Chinese colleagues, customers, competitors, etc. Thus, although we take care to be sensitive to language and cultural barriers that impact Chinese students' engagement, we have no provision to go beyond our current arrangement as one helpful anonymous reviewer of this chapter suggested ("to restructure OB3 into different tracks which will encourage students to develop notions of leadership relevant to their own cultures, rather than Western culture"). It is also important to note the pressures on teaching and learning that come from outside the classroom, and how these can impact our best efforts.

Given the turmoil of the global economy and uncertainty of the graduate job market, there is increasing push in the UK higher education sector to promote employability as the most significant "learning" outcome of a university degree program. This short-term focus is exacerbated by public anxiety over rising costs of a university education, and government-encouraged rhetoric about "value for money," equating learning with a monetized commodity. According to Rothwell, Jewell, and Hardie (2009), UK university students relate their employability potential mostly to university brand strength, subject popularity, and labor market forces, and least of all to study engagement and individual ambition. This suggests an extrinsic perspective wherein students are at the "mercy" of the elements (subject to forces beyond their individual, immediate control) — which discourages them from taking individual initiative and responsibility, driving them away from intrinsic motivation and self-direction. Unfortunately, such an emphasis on external locus of control is at odds with contemporary theories of effective leadership, which advocate internal locus of control. In many ways, this undermines the core concepts of personalized leadership development, provoking more a short-term, instrumental approach to learning focused solely on outcomes, rather than a longer-term perspective wherein the outcomes are balanced (and integrated) with the processes through cycles of experiential learning and reflection.

So, what to do when caught between students' needs for personalization and cultural sensitivity, government and university pressures to demonstrate extrinsic value, and teachers who must satisfy both sides with resources at hand? We find insightful direction from writings in critical pedagogy described by Giroux (2010) as "guided by passion and principle, to help students develop consciousness of freedom, recognize authoritarian tendencies, and connect knowledge to power and the ability to take constructive action." Simultaneously, we recognize the reality in Hicks' (2004) argument that modern higher education (especially when publicly funded and business-related) is geared toward training "cognitive capacity for reason in order to produce an adult capable of functioning independently in the world" (p. 17) rather than to instill a social identity. While further discussion of critical pedagogy and postmodernism is beyond the scope (and word limit) of this chapter, we feel that we have achieved a promising first step in balancing stakeholder needs and demands through OB3. We look forward to future exploration of cross-cultural learning and global leadership issues (such as the questions of hegemony versus cultural relativism).

The vLeader simulation is not presented here as a universal solution, but as an example of one technology tool that addresses the unique needs of Chinese students through an integrated pedagogical delivery and curriculum design. Our success at Greenwich comes from supporting the Chinese students on the simulation with specially trained, multicultural and bilingual tutorial teachers. This chapter draws from the lessons of successfully engaging Chinese students on the OB3 course, to present new insights into ways in which interactive simulations can foster the kind of deep reflection and double-loop learning that are so essential to learning experientially. Feedback from students and tutors, and interactive discussion and observation with students as "co-generators" taking responsibility for their learning, validates and reinforces our beliefs that this approach helps students from multicultural perspectives to "grasp" and "transform" various elements in their personalized understanding of leadership.

As the world's First Professor of Leadership Studies (at the University of Surrey in the United Kingdom), John Adair (1989) related action-centered leadership to an ancient Chinese proverb: "Not the cry but the flight of the wild duck leads the flock to fly and follow." In terms of learning and leading, actions indeed can speak louder than words (including perceived inaction, or lack of words from students such as those from China, who face internal and external barriers to engagement in foreign academic environments). The most engaged and effective learning leaders/leading learners will be aware of how to integrate their implicit action "theory-in use" with their articulated "espoused theory," through engagement in experiential learning and reflection. The incorporation of the vLeader simulation into the "inside-out" curriculum and pedagogy of OB3 is one way in which all students are encouraged to personally engage. In particular, this approach enables Chinese students to overcome cross-cultural barriers to participation, understanding, and sharing (making themselves understood) − going beyond the superficial, surface level to deeper meaning and clarity, which can then be applied to the external world. The wild duck is an apt analogy, as waterfowl are known for an appearance of serenity above the water while paddling furiously below the surface, maintaining flexibility to change direction quickly, dive deep, or ascend in flight as needed. In this case, "duck" does not suggest shirking or avoiding responsibility, as in the harm avoidance advice to "duck and cover" − rather it is more appropriately a sense of being like the wild duck who can *discover*.

REFERENCES

Adair, J. (1983). *Effective leadership*. Aldershot, UK: Gower.

Adair, J. (1989). *Great leaders*. Guilford, UK: The Talbot Adair Press.

Aldrich, C. (2003). The new core of leadership. *Training & Development, 57*(3), 32–37.

Argyris, C., & Schon, D. (1978). *Organizational learning: A theory of action perspective*. Reading, MA: Addison-Wesley.

Beaver, B., & Tuck, B. (1998). The adjustment of overseas students at a tertiary institution in New Zealand. *New Zealand Journal of Educational Studies, 32*(2), 167–179.

Begum, M., & Newman, R. (2009). Evaluation of students' experiences of developing transferable skills and business skills using a business simulation game. In *Proceedings of the 39th ASEE/IEEE frontiers in education conference*, October 2008. San Antonio, TX.

Bond, M. H. (1986). Mutual stereotypes and the facilitation of interaction across cultural lines. *International Journal of Intercultural Relations, 10*, 259–276.

Capowski, G. (1994). Anatomy of a leader: Where are the leaders of tomorrow? *Management Review, 83*, 10–17.

Chen, S. (2011, April 18). Chinese overseas students "hit record high". *BBC News Asia-Pacific*. Retrieved from http://www.bbc.co.uk/news/world-asia-pacific-13114577

Chen, Y. L., & Ching, G. S. (2012). A case study on the effects of campus climate to the cross-cultural norms of Taiwanese students. *International Journal of Research Studies in Psychology, 1*(1), 3–16.

Cross, J. M. (2006). Engaging diversity at an Australian university: Chinese international students' perceptions of their social experience while studying in Australia. In *Proceedings of the EDU-COM 2006 international conference*, November 2006. Perth, Australia.

Daft, R. L. (2008). *The leadership experience*. Mason, OH: South-Western.

Dunning, J. E. (2007). *A guide to integrating vLeader 2007 with the leadership experience*. Retrieved from http://www.simulearn.net/Daft_Dunning/Guide-Dick_Daft_Leadership_Experience.pdf

Gao, J., Arnulf, J. K., & Henning, K. (2011). Western leadership development and Chinese managers: Exploring the need for contextualization. *Scandinavian Journal of Management, 27*(1), 55–65.

Giroux, H. (2010, October 27). Lessons from Paulo Freire. *Chronicle of Higher Education*. Retrieved from http://chronicle.com/article/Lessons-From-Paulo-Freire/124910/

Gu, Q. (2009). Maturity and interculturality: Chinese students' experiences in UK higher education. *European Journal of Education, 44*(1), 37–52.

Gu, Q., & Brooks, J. (2008). Beyond the accusation of plagiarism. *System, 36*(3), 337–352.

Gu, Q., & Maley, A. (2008). Changing places: A study of Chinese students in the UK. *Language and Intercultural Communication, 8*(4), 224–245.

Gurley, K., & Wilson, D. (2010). Developing leadership skills in a virtual simulation: Coaching the affiliative style leader. *Journal of Instructional Pedagogies, 5*, 46–59.

He, W., Xu, Y., & Zhu, J. (2011). Bilingual teaching in nursing education in China: Evolution, status, and future directions. *Nursing & Health Sciences, 13*(3), 371–377.

Hicks, S. R. C. (2004). *Explaining postmodernism: Skepticism and socialism from Rousseau to Foucault*. Tempe, AZ: Scholargy Press.

Ho, E. S., Holmes, P., & Cooper, J. (2004). *Review and evaluation of international literature on managing cultural diversity in the classroom*. University of Waikato.

Hofstede, G., & Hofstede, G. J. (2005). *Cultures and organizations: Software of the mind* (2nd ed.). New York, NY: McGraw-Hill.

Horwitz, E. K. (1999). Cultural and situational influences on foreign language learners' beliefs about language learning: A review of BALLI studies. *System, 27*(4), 557–576.

Jenkins, R. (2004). *Social identity*. Abingdon, UK: Routledge.

Johnson, M. C., Graham, C. R., & Hsueh, S. L. (2006). The effects of instructional simulation use on teaching and learning: A case study. *Current Developments in Technology-Assisted Education, 2006*, 1843–1847.

Knode, C. S., & Knode, J. (2011). Simulations and teaching leadership. In *Proceedings of the ASCUE*, June 2011. Myrtle Beach, SC.

Kolb, A. Y., & Kolb, D. A. (2009). The learning way: Meta-cognitive aspects of experiential learning. *Simulation & Gaming, 40*(3), 297–327.

Kolb, D. A. (1984). *Experiential learning: Experience as the source of learning and development*. Englewood Cliffs, NJ: Prentice-Hall.

Li, M. (2009). An examination of the role of experiential learning in the development of cultural intelligence in global leaders. *Advances in Global Leadership, 5*, 251–271.

Li, Y., & Wang, L. (2010). A survey on bilingual teaching in higher education institute in the northeast of China. *Journal of Language Teaching and Research, 1*(4), 353–357.

Mackie, N. (2005, September 7). Chinese students drawn to Britain. *BBC News*. Retrieved from http://news.bbc.co.uk/1/hi/education/4219026.stm

Marx, E. (2001). *Breaking through culture shock: What you need to succeed in international business*. London, UK: Nicholas Brealey.

McClure, J. (2001). Developing language skills and learner autonomy in international postgraduates. *ELT Journal, 55*(2), 142–148.

Mendenhall. (2007). The elusive, yet critical challenge of developing global leaders. *European Management Journal, 24*(6), 422–429.

Mezirow, J. (1990). *Fostering critical reflection in adulthood: A guide to transformative and emancipatory learning*. San Francisco, CA: Jossey-Bass.

Mezirow, J. (1991). *Transformative dimensions of adult learning*. San Francisco, CA: Jossey-Bass.

Morrison, J. L., Rha, J., & Helfman, A. (2003). Learning awareness, student engagement, and change: A transformation in leadership development. *Journal of Education for Business, 79*(1), 11–17.

Morton, N., Hill, A., Curzon, R., Tomas, C., Eland, J., Lawton, R., & Popovic, C. (2009). The creative dynamic: Innovative solutions to teaching transferable skills in the classroom. In *Proceedings of the 3rd international technology, education and development conference*, March 2009. Valencia, Spain.

Narvaez, D. (2010). The emotional foundations of high moral intelligence. *New Directions for Child and Adolescent Development, 129*, 77–94.

Ninnes, P. (1999). Acculturation of international students in higher education: Australia. *Education and Society, 17*(1), 73–101.

Ng, K. Y., Van Dyne, L., & Ang, S. (2009). From experience to experiential learning: Cultural intelligence as a learning capability for global leader development. *Academy of Management of Management Learning and Education, 8*(4), 511–526.

Rhee, J. E., & Sagaria, M. A. D. (2004). International students: Constructions of imperialism in the chronicle of higher education. *Review of Higher Education, 28*(1), 77–96.

Rothwell, A., Jewell, S., & Hardie, M. (2009). Self-perceived employability: Investigating the responses of post-graduate students. *Journal of Vocational Behavior, 75*(2), 152–161.

Soyemi, J., Ogunyinka, O. I., & Soyemi, O. B. (2012). Integrating self-paced e-learning with conventional classroom learning in Nigeria educational system. *Mediterranean Journal of Social Sciences, 3*(4), 127–133.

Standifer, R., Thiault, P., & Pin, R. (2010). Leadership development in an electronic frontier: Connecting theory to experiential software through supplemental materials. *Journal of Leadership & Organizational Studies, 17*(2), 167–176.

Sun, Y. C. (2005). Listening to the voices of Chinese immigrant girls. In L. D. Soto & B.B. Swadener (Eds.), *Power and voice in research with children* (pp. 89–105). New York, NY: Peter Lang Publishing.

Wan, G. F. (2001). The leaning experience of Chinese students in American universities: A cross-cultural perspective. *College Student Journal, 35*(1), 25–44.

Wang, L. (2010). *Chinese postgraduate students in a British university: Their learning experiences and learning beliefs*. Doctoral thesis. Durham University. Retrieved from http://etheses.dur.ac.uk/196/

Wang, Y. (2010). *Young Chinese students' teamwork experiences in a UK business school: From a cultural perspective*. Doctoral thesis, University of Westminster. Retrieved from http://isls-eprints-31.wmin.ac.uk/8586/1/Yi_Wang_ADDED.pdf

Warring, S. (2007). *Facilitating independent learning amongst Chinese international students*. Business Studies Conference Papers, Paper 1. Retrieved from http://repository.digitalnz.org/system/uploads/record/attachment/180/facilitating_independent_learning_amongst_chinese_international_students.pdf

Watkins, D. A., & Biggs, J. B. (Eds.). (1996). *The Chinese learner: Cultural, psychological, and contextual influences*. Hong Kong and Victoria, Australia: Comparative Education Research Centre, The University of Hong Kong, and The Australian Council for Educational Research.

Watkins, D. A., & Biggs, J. B. (Eds.). (2001). *Teaching the Chinese learner: Psychological and pedagogical perspectives*. Hong Kong and Victoria, Australia: Comparative Education Research Centre, The University of Hong Kong and The Australian Council for Educational Research.

Weber, L. J. (2011). *International Chinese and Canadian students' experiences of internationalization at a Canadian university*. Doctoral dissertation, University of Western Ontario. Retrieved from http://ir.lib.uwo.ca/cgi/viewcontent.cgi?article = 1083&context = cie-eci

Wu, M. M. F. (2008). Language learning strategy use of Chinese ESL learners of Hong Kong: Findings from a qualitative study. *Electronic Journal of Foreign Language Teaching*, *5*(1), 68–83.

Yen, D., & Kuzma, J. (2009). Higher IELTS score, higher academic performance? The validity of IELTS in predicting the academic performance of Chinese students. *Worcester Journal of Learning and Teaching*, *3*, 1–7.

ENGAGEMENT IN AN ONLINE VIDEO SIMULATION IN EDUCATIONAL LEADERSHIP

R. Martin Reardon, Dale Mann, Jonathan Becker, Charol Shakeshaft and Michael R. Reich

ABSTRACT

Against the backdrop of digital gaming, this chapter presents a cutting-edge, immersive, online video simulation of events that follow the calendar of a year in a chronically low-performing middle school in the United States. The traditional approach to preparing educational leaders has been harshly criticized by those who have, at times, shared in sustaining the traditional approach. The time is right for innovation. The intention of this simulation is to engage potential educational leaders in the professional development of their leadership skills. These skills are designated in a range of standards-based documents generated by the individual states in the United States, as well as at the national level by the Educational Leadership Policy Standards: 2008 *document issued by the Council of Chief State School Officers. A highly sophisticated back-end to this simulation gathers evidence of both engagement and learning.*

Increasing Student Engagement and Retention using Immersive Interfaces: Virtual Worlds, Gaming, and Simulation
Cutting-edge Technologies in Higher Education, Volume 6C, 203–224
ISSN: 2044-9968/doi:10.1108/S2044-9968(2012)000006C010

The online format empowers anytime/anywhere learning in a mistake-tolerant educational setting at minimal incremental cost.

Tobias and Fletcher (2011) described the research on the instructional role of simulations as "massive both in absolute terms and relative to the research literature on computer-based games" (p. 6). Their description raises the distinction between simulations and games — a distinction they addressed in generic terms by contrasting simulations and games on the dimensions of focus (reality versus entertainment), context, interactivity, and the role of rules. As Table 1 shows, Tobias and Fletcher dichotomized simulations and games on these dimensions, providing a useful, if simplistic, way of distinguishing between them. Tobias and Fletcher's concluding generalization was that all games are simulations, but not all simulations are games.

The online video simulation that is the topic of this chapter matches all of the properties of a simulation that Tobias and Fletcher (2011) designated, except one: It is like a game in that interactivity is essential. According to Whitton (2011), specific types of digital games have the potential to engage and motivate adult learners. Whitton focused on the conditions under which "well-designed and appropriate computer games" (p. 597) enhanced the engagement of adult learners, and how such games potentially constituted effective learning environments for adults. Whitton's research is particularly relevant to this chapter in which we explore the engagement of prospective educational leaders with an online video simulation. This simulation encompasses a full year in a middle school, and was designed specifically as a learning tool to enhance participants' learning in

Table 1. Contrasting Properties of Simulations and Games.

Simulations	Games
Focus is reality; entertainment is secondary	Focus is entertainment; reality is secondary
Scenario or task based	Storyline or quest based
Task completion is paramount	Competition in context of task is paramount
Interactivity optional	Interaction essential
Focus is on rule-defined accuracy; attention to detail	Focus is on rule-defined clarity; stylized

Source: Adapted from "Introduction" by Tobias and Fletcher (2011).

a graduate degree course in educational leadership. We believe that our online video simulation is the first of its kind in the field of educational leadership.

TOWARD THE CREATION OF EFFECTIVE SETTINGS

In contrast to direct instruction, the creation of effective learning environments has long been understood to lie at the heart of the teaching endeavor. For example, Dewey (1932) asserted that "we practically never teach anything by direct instruction but rather, by the creation of settings" (p. 1032). Mann, Reardon, Becker, Shakeshaft, and Bacon (2011) quoted Dewey in discussing the potential for online video simulations to create settings that engage participants not as spectators but as agents who determine their own destiny in the context of the simulation by the choices they make. Mann et al. (2011) proposed that online video simulations designed to engage learners in virtual settings modeled on professional realities have the potential to enliven and enlighten the educational process for prospective educational leaders.

This chapter expands the discussion in Mann et al. (2011) by exploring the concept of learner engagement in the educational leadership-oriented online video simulation described previously against the background of digital gaming. We will focus initially on the characteristics of digital gaming — especially engagement — that pertain to the more specifically educational digital learning settings. An engaging online simulation of a principal's interactions during the course of a full year in a middle school will have to consist of more than video clips — important though they are for engaging the learner. Having discussed how digital games interface with learning, we will move on to focus specifically on simulation and learning. Digital simulations will be positioned as effective learning tools that are well-established in a number of fields — for example, in military settings, organizational leadership, and health care — but have been hitherto unknown in educational leadership. We will then discuss the structure of this simulation, focusing on the way in which the technological infrastructure supports the educational setting. We acknowledge that the long-term effects of learning through simulations are clearly paramount, but we assert that proximate indicators, particularly engagement, provide compelling short-term evidence of effectiveness. Consequently, we will focus on the engagement metrics of the initial group of users. We will conclude this chapter by proposing clear advantages of online video simulations that off-set and reward the investment of funds and expertise required to develop them.

DIGITAL GAMES AND LEARNING

Digital games constitute settings in which players learn what they need in order to play the game, but also, at least potentially, in some games, real-life lessons. As Owston (2012) commented, "many have sought to harness for instructional purposes the entertainment value, engagement, task persistence, and motivational power" (p. 105) of digital games. For example, Dickey (2005) highlighted the educational potential of "gameplay" (p. 67) by observing that "players may be required to analyze, synthesize, and use critical thinking skills in order to play and execute moves" (p. 67). Engagement in the context of instructional design, Dickey suggested, involves providing learners "with both authentic activities and opportunities for interacting with other learners" (p. 70). Authentic activities in the context of this chapter would closely align with the activities with which an educational leader would engage as a part of his or her job description.

The Fit of the Digital Learning Environment

Prospective educational leaders typically would be required to have 3 or more years of successful teaching experience prior to being admitted to an educational leadership program through a university. Consequently, the age of such participants might be thought to place them at a disadvantage in a digital game-like environment. However, the digital milieu appeals to a widely diverse clientele. Owston (2012) referred to trade data to correct any potential misconception in this regard. According to the Entertainment Software Association (ESA, 2011), the average player of computer and video games in 2011 in the United States was 37 years old. In 2011, only 18% of computer and video game players were under 18 years of age, and fully 29% were 50 years of age or older. Furthermore, while such players were predominantly male, the predominance was slight in that 42% of game players were female. Hence, there appears to be no inherent conceptual challenge from either an age or a gender perspective to engagement with an online video simulation by participants in an educational leadership program.

Engagement

From a cognitive perspective, Schlechty (2001, 2002) regarded engagement as a continuum, and proposed five levels of engagement in the compulsory schooling context, ranging from, at the high engagement end, (a) authentic engagement — defined as "associated with a result or outcome that has clear meaning and relatively immediate value to the student" (Schlechty, 2002, p. 3) — down through (b) ritual engagement, (c) passive compliance, (d) retreatism, to (e) rebellion — defined as refusing to do assigned tasks and actively performing non-assigned tasks. In a licensure-oriented graduate educational leadership program focused on increasing the competency of participants to fill educational leadership positions, authentic engagement is the baseline expectation.

Benyon, Turner, and Turner (2005) took the concept of engagement a step further than Schlechty (2002) when they associated engagement with a reader's immersion in a good book, the challenge of playing a good game, and the fascination of a radio drama. The fascination of a radio drama — where a listener is engaged with the interactions among the characters — is analogous to an online video simulation. In a radio drama, the dramatist is striving to engage a listener who is only virtually present. Orson Welles's expert direction of the simulation of a fictitious *War of the Worlds* encounter in New Jersey on October 30, 1931, was a compelling example of how engaging virtual presence can become — some listeners made preparations to evacuate their homes.

The higher levels of personal relevancy referred to by Benyon et al. (2005) on the part of the participants in our online video simulation may be problematic. However, it is anticipated that participants will identify with the principal whose perspective is always the perspective captured by the video segments, as Fig. 1 shows.

Engagement as Optimal Experience

Many games researchers (for example, Cowley, Charles, Black, & Hickey, 2008; Dickey, 2005; Moreno-Ger, Burgos, & Torrente, 2009; Whitton, 2011) reference Csikszentmihalyi's concept of flow in the context of engagement (for example, Csikszentmihalyi & Csikszentmihalyi, 1988; Csikszentmihalyi, 1990). Csikszentmihalyi (1990) described optimal experience (to describe which, Csikszentmihalyi chose the word "flow") as "a sense that one's skills are adequate to cope with the challenges at hand, in a goal-directed, rule-bound action system that provides clear clues as to how well one is performing" (p. 71). Csikszentmihalyi suggested that

Fig. 1.   The Superintendent Directly Addresses the Participant and Welcomes Him or Her as Principal of C.T. Jones Middle School, Before Being Distracted by a Phone Call.

games are "*designed* to make optimal experience easier to achieve. They have rules that require the learning of skills, they set up goals, they provide feedback, (and) they make control possible" (p. 72).

The aspects of games highlighted by Csikszentmihalyi (1990) conceptually align with the properties listed by Tobias and Fletcher (2011). However, beyond these empirically verifiable characteristics of games, the engagement of players, Csikszentmihalyi proposed, relates to the way in which they are removed from reality for the duration of the game. For athletes, removal from reality may involve the wearing special clothing and occupying a dedicated space – in the way that is characteristic of many high-profile sports events (for example, on Center Court at the U.S. Open Tennis Competition). For virtual game players, Csikszentmihalyi conjectured, removal from reality enables them to exist for the duration of the game in the "peculiar reality" (p. 72) defined by the gameplay context.

Simulation and Reality

The ability of players to enter into Csikszentmihalyi's (1990) "peculiar reality" may well be a factor in the popularity of action and sport video games, which were the top two sellers in the video game genre in 2010, accounting for 21.7% and 16.3% of sales respectively (ESA, 2011). While Tobias and Fletcher (2011) suggested that simulations are open to preferring reality to entertainment, this online video simulation draws on the necessity of interaction as a way of engaging the participant. By having to make choices and enjoy the game-like outcome of making a "good" choice our online video simulation approximates the creation of a peculiar reality that invites the participants' entry. Of course, sometimes participants will make "bad" choices, and will suffer loss of credibility. A good example is shown in Fig. 2 in which an administrative assistant indicates with "the look" her perspective on a participant's decision.

The particular characteristic of games that this online video simulation incorporates is the necessity for interaction. Interaction in this context goes beyond simply clicking a button to continue. For example, participants frequently have to prioritize among a number of alternatives, as Fig. 3 illustrates. In this instance, over a sound track of keyboard use from the main office, the principal is faced with a view of his or her office with an overlay of blinking icons (mouse, memo, and visitor flag), and informed that he or she cannot leave his or her office because of a number of pending tasks. The participant's responses to these tasks will determine the subsequent path of the simulation. An impatient participant may be tempted to deal with the tasks without giving too much thought to his or her responses, in which case his or her responses will return to haunt him/her.

Fig. 2. An Administrative Assistant Indicates That, from Her Perspective, a Sub-optimal Choice Has Been Made by "The Principal."

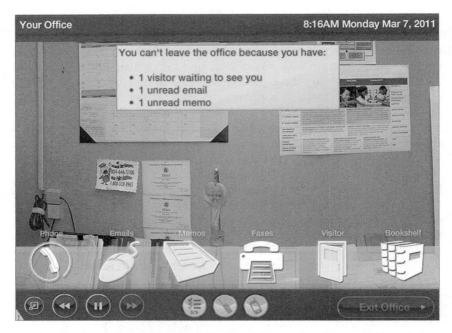

Fig. 3. Against a Sound Track of Keyboard Use, a Participant Is Barred from Leaving the Office (the "Exit Office" Button is Grayed-Out) While There Are Pending Tasks Requiring Attention.

Interaction is one of the keys to enhancing participants' engagement with the simulation. In addition, as shown in Figs. 1–3, the video camera's point of view is the principal's (and, hence, the participant's) point of view. The intention is that the participant will become immersed in the peculiar reality into which he or she is invited, potentially attaining the engagement level of flow. The scenarios with which the participant is confronted are derived from current best-practice standards of educational leadership (for example, CCSSO, 2008) to ensure their authenticity.

CREATING SETTINGS FOR EFFECTIVE LEARNING

Simulations and games have long been valued as effective learning settings. For example, prior to the digital age, Abt (1968) first used the term "serious games" to refer board and card games designed primarily for educational purposes. According to Kirkley, Duffy, Kirkley, and Kremer (2011), this term re-emerged in the late 1990s, when the focus was on utilizing entertainment game technologies for educational purposes. Tobias and Fletcher (2011) provided their perspective on the success of serious games in asserting that "there are few instructional methods used in either the educational or training communities that engage similar intense interest among learners, or induce students to persist on a task as long as games do" (p. 6).

Digital simulations, which Tobias and Fletcher (2011) conceptualize as a superset of digital games, and allow learners to develop their ability to operate effectively in and understand the ramifications of complex scenarios without dire consequences for their mistakes. For example, the use of flight simulators allows pilots to learn to fly in difficult conditions that, if encountered by an untrained pilot in reality, might be life-threatening. In flight simulators and similar implementations, the engagement of the learner is propelled by the strong motivation of self-preservation. The same instinct may propel the participant in the "war games" that have been used in military training (Games & Squire, 2011; Squire, 2008).

The field of health care has seen the development of a number of digital simulations. Nehring and Lashley (2009) noted that computer-assisted simulation in nursing education emerged in the 1980s. They cited support from the American Nurses Association for the claim that such simulations allow nursing students to learn more efficiently than they do in a classroom. They referenced a landmark Web-based simulation of a family in a virtual neighborhood developed by Giddens (2007) that incorporated 30 characters from varying ethnicities and socioeconomic backgrounds and that "is used throughout the nursing curriculum" (p. 533). Broom (2009) described a virtual pediatric ward in which nurses could refine their clinical reaction to fever. More recently, Kilmon, Brown, Ghosh, and Mikitiuk (2010) described the simulation they were developing to train nurses in using a "crash cart" for use in emergency situations. Kilmon et al. took the earlier claims of efficiency a step further and declared that "the use of simulation technology to supplement clinical instruction is becoming necessary as health care agencies reach their capacity to handle an increased number of students" (p. 314). Cannon-Bowers, Bowers, and Procci (2011) pointed out that the diverse digital learning environments in health care are "expected to yield outcomes that have serious – sometimes life and death – consequences" (pp. 64, 65).

Although the consequences of inept practice may emerge only in the long term, no less than nurses are expected to know how to deal with medical emergencies, graduates from educational leadership programs are expected to know how to lead schools. Educational leadership programs have traditionally relied on face-to-face learning environments, and have focused on ensuring graduates' proficiency in knowing important information. However, the graduates of such programs have been seen as unable to effectively lead schools (for example, Levine, 2005; Murphy, Moorman, & McCarthy, 2008).

Schools are complex environments in which leaders are required to make multiple decisions quickly — often with only partial data. Bransford, Brown, and Cocking (2000) referenced and supported Simon's (1996) assertion that knowing has shifted in current understanding from referring to the learner's ability to remember and reproduce information, to the learner's ability to retrieve and use information. A particular educational leader may remember the textbook details of how to deal with a particular situation and be quite capable of reproducing those details, yet be quite inept at retrieving those details in real time, and using them appropriately. Learning in the context of a simulation strongly implicates a constructivist theoretical lens, and an inquiry-based approach to learning (Kirkley et al., 2011). Mann et al. (2011) referenced problem-based learning as the particular inquiry-based approach most applicable to this online video simulation.

Key aspects of problem-based learning include the ill-defined context of the learning — which conforms closely to the reality faced by educational leaders — along with the engagement of the learner as an active participant in the learning environment. Bransford et al. (2000) asserted that the ability to act professionally in high-stakes, complex environments in which only partial data may be available and time is short requires a redefinition of what constitutes a knowledgeable learner. Bransford et al. went on to point out that a wide variety of approaches guide and enrich contemporary endeavors to developing such knowledgeable learners. These new approaches, Bransford et al. asserted, highlight the role of active learning by emphasizing "the importance of helping people to take control of their own learning" (p. 12). Active learners, Bransford et al. suggested, seek to understand complex subject matter and, subsequently, they are better prepared to apply what they know; active learners exhibit transfer of training by appropriately applying what they have learned in one setting in analogous settings.

Going one step further, Bransford et al. associated metacognition with active learning. They described metacognition as referring to "people's abilities to predict their performances on various tasks (for example, how well they will be able to remember various stimuli) and to monitor their current levels of mastery and understanding" (p. 12). Active learning and metacognition – understood as "sense-making, self-assessment, and reflection on what worked and what needs improving" (p. 12) – are aspects of knowledge acquisition that are particularly amenable to implementation in the context of simulations. If graduates of educational leadership possessed a refined ability to make sense of the complex environments in which they lead, the ability to bring a metacognitive approach to their practice, and the habit of mind to reflect effectively on their leadership practice, perhaps they would lead their schools more effectively. To develop this kind of educational leader, a different concept of effective learning is implicated. The critiques of current educational leaders by those closely associated with their legacy approaches to leadership stand as testaments to the need for change.

STRUCTURE OF THIS SIMULATION: ENGAGEMENT AND EFFECTIVE LEARNING

Oblinger (2004) referred to digital games as informal learning environments. Oblinger compared the projected 60 hours it might take to read *War and Peace* to the 60 hours or more students might spend in a virtual world – the difference being that, in the virtual world, students would be present in body (or, as least as an avatar) as well as in spirit. Oblinger proposed that this greater engagement would lead to the enhancement of their memory.

In a less enthusiastic declaration, as mentioned above, Whitton (2011) proposed that certain types of digital games facilitate the engagement of certain types of learners. This conditional declaration makes a minimalist claim to efficacy that runs counter to the claims of those who wholeheartedly invoke the intrinsic motivational power of digital media. For example, Marinelli (2005) described today's students as "enamored of all digital technology," and enthused about the "whole social dynamic of interactive video games as a pinnacle expression of individual personality and social intercourse in young people of the twenty-first century" (p. 17).

As noted above, Whitton (2011), coming from the perspective of adult learners, expressed some reservation about the extent to which digital games universally motivated learners in higher education, while conceding that there may be some basis for the intrinsic motivation ascribed to digital games designed for younger players. In particular, Whitton found that the two factors that contributed positively to engagement were (a) perceiving swift and steady improvement, along with (b) being good at playing the game. There were four factors that detracted from engagement (a) difficulty starting the game, (b) reaching an impasse, (c) distrust in the simulation environment, and (d) boredom with either the subject matter or the activity itself (pp. 601, 602).

The Big Picture

In this simulation, the potential educational leader *is* the principal of a middle-school; he or she sees and hears through a video camera. The various actors in the simulation talk to the video camera when they are talking to the principal.

From the outset, the simulation avoids the first two of the factors that Whitton portrayed as detracting from engagement (difficulty starting and reaching an impasse). As Fig. 1 showed, the simulation opens with an interview with the superintendent of the school district in which the fictional C. T. Jones Middle School (CTJ) is located. The superintendent addresses the participant directly and welcomes him/her to the principalship. The superintendent begins to explain the special circumstances of CTJ briefly, but barely gets started when she is distracted by an important phone call, directing the principal to choose from a set of documents to guide his or her planning. Not all the documents offered are equally significant for a new principal. As soon as the principal makes his or her choice, the superintendent interrupts the phone conversation just long enough to editorialize on the wisdom or otherwise of the choice, and directs the principal what to do next. From the outset, this simulation immerses the participant in an authentic, continually evaluative simulation that provides many opportunities for perceiving swift and steady improvement and interacting positively with the actors.

The simulation continues along the path to engagement by utilizing an authentic, self-explanatory interface. As Fig. 2 showed, the blank wall of the office space is what the principal would see if he or she looked straight ahead from behind his or her desk. The large icons across the bottom of the screen – highlighted in Fig. 4 – represent some of the broad categories of "interruptions" that a principal encounters on a daily basis. This "analogue" interface uses icons that need little explanation, and they are programmed to blink when the participant is required to click on them to respond (the mouse, the inbox memo tray, and the office door – which refers to the presence of a visitor).

While the input from such sources may impinge on the tasks the principal has set for himself or herself on a particular day, they also constitute vital data for his or her practice of leadership. In case the principal is tempted to put off dealing with the interruptions indicated by the blinking icons, as Fig. 5 shows, a large "sticky note" informs him or her that specific items must be dealt with before leaving the office.

A final authentic connection to running a school situates this particular part of the simulation in the context of the school year by showing the date of this particular screen in the year-long simulation panorama. Fig. 3 shows that screen corresponds to Monday, March 7, 2011 in "simulation time."

The simulation environment preserves the integrity of the medium of the interactions. For example, when the principal opens the e-mail (see Fig. 6), he or she finds a dismissive comment from the assistant principal regarding community involvement in a planning project. The assistant

Fig. 4.   The Icons Used in the Simulation Interface Are Analogous to the Corresponding Real Item, Aiding Engagement.

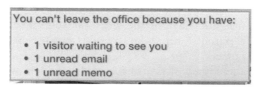

Fig. 5.   The "Sticky Note" Makes it Clear That There Is No Escaping the Demands of Leadership.

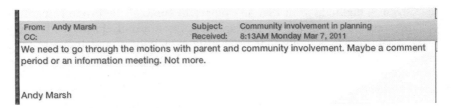

Fig. 6. Text of an E-mail That Under-values the Importance of Community Involvement in Planning.

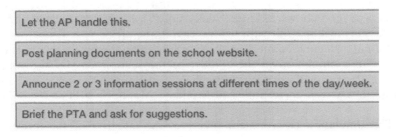

Fig. 7. Four Options for Inviting Community Involvement in Planning.

principal (Andy Marsh) is prompting the principal for a quick decision that will indicate little interest in involving the community in planning.

As shown in Fig. 7, the principal is then offered a choice of actions to take. In the first response, the principal delegates the process to Andy Marsh. This may make life easier for the principal in the short term, but, given Andy Marsh's email, it appears that there will be little good will generated if he is in charge of involving the community with the planning process. The second option distances the CTJ administration from the community involvement by sending a message that close engagement of the community with the planning exercise is not welcome. The third option shows that the CTJ leadership is open to talking about planning, but it retains control of the process by presuming that the CTJ leadership knows the best times and days of the week for such meetings. The fourth option invites the parents' representatives to engage in the consultative process from the outset.

As in real life, the course of future events depends on what the principal does today (on March 7). Depending on the option the principal takes here, in conjunction with his or her subsequent actions, the situation becomes either more combative, or more conducive to good relations.

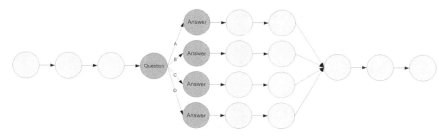

Fig. 8.   Hidden Decision Trees Guide Presentation of Subsequent Material Based on Prior Decisions.

Technical Details

The building blocks of this turn-based simulation are 35,000 + lines of ActionScript 3 and 13,000+ lines of YAML content. The content is stored in a MySQL database with 150+ tables. All of which is coordinated by a Symfony application consisting of over 10,000 lines of PHP code. All of this is used to display 120 video segments as determined by the principal's prior decisions. To provide a sense of how this infrastructure plays out, the segment discussed here may be viewed at the online simulation playable demonstration site at http://projectall.vcu.edu/play.

Fig. 8 is a schematic representation of one sequence out of 100 that branches based on the principal's decision. After a decision is made, the scenario can branch (without the participant principal's knowledge) based on his or her answer.

PROXIMATE INDICATORS OF SUCCESS

Engagement Metrics

A sophisticated back-end tracks the principal's decisions and overall inter-action with the simulation, and provides the quantitative metrics for deter-mining engagement. The most basic metric recorded is the principal's score. This is determined by matching the principal's choices to the value assigned by a set of experienced principals to those choices. This reference group takes into account their own experience as well as the stipulations of current best-practice standards in educational leadership (for example,

Council of Chief State School Officers, 2008). The amount of time players spend on each turn is also recorded.

Impact of Engagement Data on Ongoing Development

As discussed above, the aim of using an analogical interface is to increase the immersion factor — to make the interface as transparent as possible so that the principal can feel as challenged by the simulation as he or she might be challenged by a good book or fascinated by a radio drama. By tracking button clicks we are able to determine the extent to which it appears that the interface is intuitive for players. On this basis, some of the graphical elements in earlier versions of the simulation appeared to be confusing to the principals and they were either removed or modified.

We propose that the quantitative engagement of participants provides strong support for the effectiveness of this simulation in the context of educational leadership. As mentioned above, in its current advanced beta version, first person, point-of-view videography appears to motivate engagement by placing the participant in the forefront of decision-making in the myriad situations that are typical of the complex fast-paced life of a middle school.

Growth in Performance

The initial group of participants in this simulation consisted of nine teacher leaders from an urban school district who were selected to participate in a collaborative school/university partnership process on the basis of their perceived potential for promotion to school leadership positions. In the first trimester, their average correct score was 53% (range from 44% to 64%). In the second trimester, the average correct score was 63% (range from 54% to 71%).

It is worth noting that CTJ was designed as a chronically low-performing school with prominent dysfunctions (from the point of view of the simulation creators). One of the more interesting outcomes of this venture has been the extent to which prominent dysfunctions are not adverted to by some of the participants. This came to light in the course of the interaction opportunities (Dickey, 2005) that were provided to participants by the blended format in which the initial trial of the simulation was conducted. Some of the participants were uncomfortable with the constant feedback regarding their decisions. This was a little off-putting as it seemed to imply that they thought that their actions, should they become principals, would be free of critique. Some questioned the scoring rubric, but the concerns on this front were allayed by the input and careful oversight of the advisory panel of principals. At the end of the simulation, two of the nine declined to pursue the option to apply for a leadership position, but the simulation played an indeterminate role in their decisions.

ADVANTAGES OF THE ONLINE FORMAT

The implementation of this simulation in the online environment facilitated access at times that suited the participants' schedules, and a sophisticated "back end" provided the scoring outcome and the in-depth analysis of the path taken by each participant. These characteristics strongly connote the context of digital games.

Paper-based simulations have long been part of the instructional tool kit utilized in educational leadership programs. Through legacy simulations, prospective educational leaders were provided with a virtual school, and invited to engage in active learning in the course of making decisions in a range of real-world situations. The legacy simulation approach to active learning allows budding educational leaders to hone their leadership skills in an environment where dealing effectively with everyday issues is acknowledged, and no-cost missteps become learning opportunities under the guidance of a skilled facilitator.

However, in the pre-digital era, simulations were limited by a number of factors associated with a necessarily print-based environment. For example, at the conceptual level, designers of print-based simulations had to keep in mind the practical limitations on the number of alternative decision paths. The participant had to be presented with consequences pertinent to his or her individual decision, but the sheer volume of paper involved in extensive multiple branching could quickly become unmanageable if too many choices were presented too often. This constrained the simulation of fast-paced, complex environments like schools. At the implementation level, a paper-based simulation customarily relied on the mediation of a facilitator who distributed materials and perhaps acted as a gatekeeper to inhibit precipitous rushing to closure by the participants. Finally, when it came to debriefing the participants, feedback was typically limited by the effectiveness of the participants' record-keeping, their reflection on their progress, and/or the ability of the facilitator to keep track of the participants' choices.

All of the above drawbacks are obviated when simulations are implemented on digital platforms. In addition, the digital environment offers the potential for enhanced participant engagement — that lies at the heart of the notable success of first-person digital entertainment.

However, while the digital environment obviates the paper-chase associated with print-based simulations, it presents its own set of challenges. A straightforward approach simply replaces the print-based artifacts with digital artifacts and simulated Web pages. While a significant step forward, such static simulations, we assert, do not engender participant ownership and engagement to the same degree as dynamic first-person interactions in a fast-paced environment.

CONCLUSION

Simulations have been noted as being less costly than the situations they mimic (for example, Raser, 1969), although Fletcher (2011) cautions against any such blanket assumption. It is our contention that simulations that enhance the competence of educational leaders, even though they require considerable capital investment during the development phase, are less costly in the long term than inept school leadership. Furthermore, as Raser (1969) pointed out, simulations are repeatable (allowing for comparison among participants in terms of competence), and adaptable (scenarios can be modulated, refined, or replaced), and detailed feedback and decision-path analysis can facilitate the interaction and learning of participants as they construct their own meaning.

Csikszentmihalyi (1990) described the state of flow as an activity that "is so gratifying that people are willing to do it for its own sake, with little concern for what they get out of it, even when it is difficult or dangerous" (p. 71). Intrinsic motivation underpins flow. Christensen, Horn, and Johnson (2008) looked to online learning to make "school intrinsically motivating" (p. 10) by means of customizing each student's learning experience. Christensen et al. did not object to learning prompted by extrinsic motivation, but their explanation of declining educational standards in the United States had to do with a prosperity-fueled decline in students' extrinsic motivation. Consequently, they pinned their anticipation of an improved learning experience through customization to their anticipation of increased levels of intrinsic motivation.

At a considerably less ambitious level than complete customization, Jones (2011) found that middle school students expressed appreciation for an adaptive online credit-recovery program that took account of what they recalled from the corresponding course that they failed in the conventional classroom setting. Jones reported that the online credit-recovery program did not present instruction on topics that students addressed correctly on a pre-test, thus perceptibly lessening the time the extrinsically motivated students needed to take to recover their course credit and be promoted to rejoin their age-peers.

The educational leadership simulation that is reported here represents a major leap forward to the ideal of individually customized path to proficiency for educational leaders. Through a sophisticated technological framework it facilitates authentic responses to participants' (potential future principals') attempts to lead in ways that align with best practice. Now that the infrastructure is established, our attention can turn to explore the qualitative aspects of participants' engagement with and learning from the simulation. Some features of this online simulation are clear: (a) participants are removed from reality to the extent that the consequences of any missteps will be less painful than they would be in real life, (b) participants' poor choices are followed by authentic consequences which constitute feedback, sometimes in terms of approval or disapproval, but more often in terms of a downward spiral of unfortunate events, and (c) participants are challenged by the dramatic impact of the issues that confront them, but they learn new skills as they learn to control – at least to some extent – the environment of the school they are running. In a very real sense, it would be rare to have two participants with exactly the same path through this simulation.

Now that the simulation has been created in the online environment, its delivery cost is minimal. It will need to be maintained and kept current, but, for example, there are no printing costs associated with any changes. We believe that the engagement engendered by this format greatly accelerated participants' learning. The participants were able to engage with the simulation at any time that fit their schedule, and for some of them it really was a case of burning the midnight oil. This online format is easily taken to scale, and is free of the message degradation issues that plague traditional programs that are taken to scale. Once the details of the simulation are built-in, they are there until they are modified centrally.

Even with the many advantages that this simulation offers it is still in development. Christenson et al. (2008) made the point that, at the outset, an innovation can establish itself against an established procedure if it offers a viable alternative to those who cannot avail of the established procedure. In this case, the established procedure (graduate school classes) has been harshly critiqued as being ineffective. This simulation potentially offers access to the core beliefs of educational leadership to anyone at any-time and anywhere in a format which engenders engagement. Against the background of digital gaming, this simulation utilizes a number of the aspects of a genre that depends on engagement to generate a setting that is conducive to the professional development of potential educational leaders.

ACKNOWLEDGMENT

The development of this simulation was made possible by a grant from the U.S. Department of Education to Virginia Commonwealth University (U363A80045, 2008).

REFERENCES

Abt, C. (1968). Games for learning. In S. Boococ & E. Schild (Eds.), *Simulation games in learning* (pp. 65–84). London: Sage.
Benyon, D., Turner, P., & Turner, S. (2005). *Designing interactive systems.* Harlow, England: Addison-Wesley.
Bransford, J. D., Brown, A. L., & Cocking, R. R. (Eds.). (2000). *How people learn: Brian, mind, experience, and school.* Washington, DC: National Academy Press.
Broom, M. (2009). Using online simulation in child health nurse education. *Pediatric Nursing, 21*(8), 32–37.
Cannon-Bowers, J. A., Bowers, C., & Procci, K. (2011). Using video games as educational tools in health care. In S. Tobias & J. D. Fletcher (Eds.), *Computer games and instruction* (pp. 47–72). Charlotte, NC: Information Age Publishing.
Christensen, C. M., Horn, M. B., & Johnson, C. W. (2008). *Disrupting class: How disruptive innovation will change the way the world learns.* New York, NY: McGraw-Hill.
Council of Chief State School Officers. (2008). *Educational leadership policy standards: 2008.* Washington, DC: Council of Chief State School Officers.
Csikszentmihalyi, M. (1990). *Flow: The psychology of optimal experience.* New York, NY: Harper Perennial.
Csikszentmihalyi, M., & Csikszentmihalyi, I. S. (Eds.). (1988). *Optimal experience: Psychological studies of flow in consciousness.* Cambridge, UK: Cambridge University Press.
Cowley, B., Charles, D., Black, M., & Hickey, R. (2008). Toward an understanding of flow in video games. *ACM Computers in Entertainment, 6*(2), Article 20, 1–26. Retrieved from http://www.idemployee.id.tue.nl/g.w.m.rauterberg/amme/cowley-et-al-2008.pdf
Dewey, J. (1932). *How we learn.* Boston, MA: Houghton-Mifflin.

Dickey, M. (2005). Engaging by design: How engagement strategies in popular computer and video games can inform instructional design. *Educational Technology Research and Development, 53*(2), 67–83.

Software Association. (2011). *Essential facts about the computer and video game industry.* Retrieved from http://www.theesa.com/facts/pdfs/ESA_EF_2011.pdf

Fletcher, J. D. (2011). Cost analysis in assessing games for learning. In S. Tobias & J. D. Fletcher (Eds.), *Computer games and instruction* (pp. 417–434). Charlotte, NC: Information Age Publishing.

Games, A., & Squire, K. D. (2011). Searching for the fun in learning: A historical perspective on the evolution of educational video games. In S. Tobias & J. D. Fletcher (Eds.), *Computer games and instruction* (pp. 17–46). Charlotte, NC: Information Age Publishing.

Giddens, J. F. (2007). The neighborhood: A web-based platform to support conceptual teaching and learning. *Nursing Education Perspectives, 28*, 251–256.

Jones, E. L. (2011). *A second chance to graduate on-time: High school students' perceptions on participating in an online credit-recovery program.* Unpublished doctoral dissertation. Virginia Commonwealth University, Richmond, VA.

Kilmon, C. A., Brown, L., Ghosh, S., & Mikitiuk, A. (2010). Immersive virtual reality simulations in nursing education. *Nursing Education Perspectives, 31*(5), 314–317.

Kirkley, J. R., Duffy, T. M., Kirkley, S. E., & Kremer, D. L. H. (2011). Implications of constructivism for the design and use of serious games. In S. Tobias & J. D. Fletcher (Eds.), *Computer games and instruction* (pp. 371–394). Charlotte, NC: Information Age Publishing.

Levine, A. (2005). *Educating school leaders.* New York, NY: Education Schools Project.

Mann, D., Reardon, R. M., Becker, J. D., Shakeshaft, C., & Bacon, N. (2011). Immersive, interactive, Web-enabled computer simulation as a trigger for learning: The next generation of problem-based learning in educational leadership. *Journal of Research on Leadership Education, 6*(5), 272–287.

Marinelli, D. (2005). I still don't quite get it: Video games and new realities. *Phi Kappa Phi, 85*(2), 16–19.

Moreno-Ger, P., Burgos, D., & Torrente, J. (2009). Digital games in eLearning environments: Current uses and emerging trends. *Simulation & Gaming: An Interdisciplinary Journal of Theory, Practice and Research, 40*, 669–687. doi: 10.1177/1046878109340294

Murphy, J., Moorman, H. N., & McCarthy, M. (2008). A framework for rebuilding initial certification and preparation programs in educational leadership: Lessons learned from whole-state reform initiatives. *Teachers College Record, 110*(10), 2172–2203.

Nehring, W. M., & Lashley, F. R. (2009). Nursing simulation: A review of the past 40 years. *Simulation Gaming, 40*(4), 528–552. doi: 10.1177/1046878109332282

Oblinger, D. (2004). The next generation of educational engagement. *Journal of Interactive Media in Education*, 8. Special issue on the Educational Semantic Web. Retrieved from http://www-jime.open.ac.uk/2004/8/oblinger-2004-8-disc-paper.html

Owston, R. D. (2012). Computer games and the quest to find their affordances for learning. *Educational Researcher, 41*(3), 105–106.

Raser, J. R. (1969). *Simulation and society: An exploration of scientific gaming.* Boston, MA: Allyn and Bacon.

Schlechty, P. C. (2001). *Shaking up the schoolhouse: How to support and sustain educational innovation.* San Francisco, CA: Jossey-Bass.

Schlechty, P. C. (2002). *Working on the work: An action plan for teachers, principals, and superintendents.* San Fransisco, CA: Jossey-Bass.

Simon, H. A. (1996). Observations on the sciences of science learning. *Journal of Applied Developmental Psychology, 21*(1), 115–121.

Squire, K. D. (2008). Video game-based learning: An emerging paradigm for instruction. *Performance Improvement Quarterly, 21*(7), 7–36.

Tobias, S., & Fletcher, J. D. (Eds.). (2011). *Computer games and instruction.* Charlotte, NC: Information Age Publishing.

Whitton, N. (2011). Game engagement theory and adult learning. *Simulation & Gaming: An Interdisciplinary Journal of Theory, Practice and Research, 42*(5), 596–609. doi: 10.1177/1046878110378587

AUGMENTING ENGAGEMENT: AUGMENTED REALITY IN EDUCATION

Jon Cabiria

ABSTRACT

Education and new technologies travel parallel pathways, with each often informing development of the other. In recent decades, educators have utilized technologies, such as television and the Internet, to develop and deliver course content. More recently, another technology has emerged that might possibly change education as it is currently practiced. Augmented reality merges manipulable digital imagery into real-world spaces and in real time. The technologies used to create augmented environments already exist in the mass market and have already begun to show up in a wide variety of fields, including education. This chapter will provide an overview of augmented reality and explore current and potential uses in higher education.

Increasing Student Engagement and Retention using Immersive Interfaces: Virtual Worlds, Gaming, and Simulation
Cutting-edge Technologies in Higher Education, Volume 6C, 225–251
ISSN: 2044-9968/doi:10.1108/S2044-9968(2012)000006C011

INTRODUCTION

The transfer of information, as a process of education, occurs through many different media. If we go back in time, there is no dearth of media methods used to communicate to others for the purposes of skills building, history sharing, and increased self-efficacy. Ancient cave drawings showed hunting, primitive calendars, and daily life. Rock carvings, or petroglyphs, did the same. Throughout communication history, the use of symbols played an key role in educating others about the world they lived in. Prior to the development of language and the written word, these symbols, along with pictures, conveyed significant information and meaning. Eventually, groups of pictures and symbols formed more complex stories, such as ideograms (Diringer, 1982).

Beyond representative symbols placed on rock, clay, or paper, societies developed their own standardized alphabets, eventually leading to new educational practices, including learning the alphabet and its related writing rules (Diringer & Freeman, 1983). In a relatively brief amount of time, even newer processes, improvements, and discoveries were integrated into the information delivery process: printing presses, electricity, radio, and telephone all altered the education paradigm. Television soon joined the ranks. Students of all ages began to have access to more and more learning opportunities when educational options by mail, radio, and television broke through the traditional classroom walls. Even more recently, the advent of the Internet created a whole new approach to information storage and retrieval, leading to distance education. The rise of distance education has been nothing short of spectacular over the past few decades.

The pace of integration of new technologies with education continues unabated. In the past decade alone, there have been important initiatives that included the use of avatars in virtual world spaces (Michels, 2008), class content delivery and student interaction over social networks (aka educational networking) (Schneider, Ford, & Perez-Felkner, 2010), Massive Open Online Courses (Siemens, 2009), and cell phones (Moura & Caravalho, 2009). We are now on the cusp of the next generation of technological marvels that will further enhance the learning process and possibly forever change how we view the means and methods of education.

This chapter focuses on the next generation of technologies that will have an impact on education: augmented reality (AR). The technology has been in existence, in one form or another, for several decades. A basic description is that Augmented Reality layers digital effects on top of real life spaces, in real time. Some of these digital effects (i.e., digital objects) can be physically manipulable by the person viewing them. The ramifications of this ability have far-reaching implications for education. The effect of this merger of real and digital brings a new level of human-computer interaction to the educational experience. The augmentation process allows teachers and students to engage in an infinite number of settings, using a variety of devices to achieve deeper exploration of content. It is clear to the initial developers of educational augmented reality products that the scope of how they can be used for educational purposes is limited only by the human imagination.

Augmented reality, though familiar to people closely associated with digital technologies and to early-technology adopters in education, is not well known outside these circles. The vast majority of educators and students are still unaware of this major force just on the horizon. For some, it heralds an exciting turning point in the evolution of educational practices; for others, there is concern that the "bells and whistles" might overshadow more meaningful intellectual stimulation.

The next section will provide a more detailed look at the evolution of augmented reality by first describing and revising the continuum on which reality and virtuality reside, followed by a brief timeline of its development and how it operates. Succeeding sections will explore the use of augmented reality in education, briefly touching on some early research results regarding learning outcomes. They will also address some concerns about augmented reality in education, and will predict how augmented reality might evolve education. Because augmented reality is a visual effect that is not always easily explained in text, these sections will provide helpful images to support the explanations.

OVERVIEW OF AUGMENTED REALITY

It would be useful to think of reality and virtuality as part of the same continuum. The simplest depiction of this would be the Milgram–Kishino Reality Virtuality Continuum, designed by Paul Milgram & Fumio Kishino (1994). In the below chart, noted on the left of the continuum is "reality," as experienced by the senses without mediation from digital sources. Moving to the right along the continuum, there is an assumption of increasing levels of integration of digital stimuli with the real environment, which influence the senses in some way. At some point, the major sensory stimuli still come from real environmental factors, but the load of digital influence is higher. This region is referred to as augmented reality (a primarily real environment with digital enhancements). Moving further to the right, more digital information increases and the balance shifts between what is real and what is digital. When the overall environment is primarily digital rather than real, the region is referred to as augmented virtuality (primarily digital with some real world artifacts). Finally, at the far right of the continuum is pure virtuality, in which there are no traces of real-world artifacts (Fig. 1). Upon further reflection, it seems that the chart is not fully explanatory, in that it does not address the more precise concepts of virtuality and mixed realities, which can help further delineate under-standing of the various categories. Using the Milgram chart as a founda-tion, a clearer understanding can be arrived at by incorporating virtual reality and mixed reality into the environment (Fig. 2).

In the above two figures, the real environment is isolated in its pure state. Moving left, the realm of virtual reality is immediately entered. This

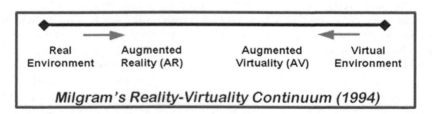

Fig. 1. Milgram Continuum.

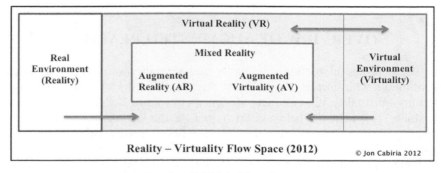

Fig. 2. Cabiria's Flow Space.

makes up the bulk of the remaining environment. In the center, mixed reality indicates that the exact balance of real and virtual is not clearly distinguishable. A more precise definition of augmented reality can state that it is primarily a real environment enhanced by digital effects, and that it lies within the realm of virtual reality. Conversely, augmented virtuality is primarily a digital environment enhanced by real-world effects, which also lies within the realm of virtual reality. Anything other than pure reality could be considered part of the virtual environment.

Augmented Reality Timeline

Augmented reality has existed prior to its current name. While there can be claims that augmented reality arrived when the first computers were being developed in the 1930s, it is more accurate to place it on a timeline in the 1950s–1970s, when direct sensory alteration devices were being explored. These devices were primarily large, stationary, box-like devices developed in the 1950s to present multisensory (multimodal) stimulation (Heilig, 1992[1955]). In the 1960s and beyond, instead of using a stationary display device, people wore display apparati, such as head-mounted displays and sensory gloves, making the augmented reality device, more-or-less, mobile, but impractical for mass-marketing.

Below is an abbreviated timeline of key augmented reality milestones. It is not conclusive and is meant only to illustrate a few interesting developments over the past six decades (Augmented Reality Timeline, 2012):

- 1957–1962: Morton Heilig creates and patents a sensory simulator called Sensorama.
- 1966: Ivan Sutherland invents the head-mounted display.
- 1975: Myron Krueger creates Videoplace to allow users to interact with virtual objects for the first time.
- 1989: Jaron Lanier coins the phrase Virtual Reality.
- 1990: Tom Caudell coins the phrase Augmented Reality.
- 1992: L.B. Rosenberg develops one of the first functioning Augmented Reality systems.
- 1992: Steven Feiner, Blair MacIntyre, and Doree Seligmann present the first major paper on an Augmented Reality system prototype, KARMA.
- 1993: First demonstration combining live Augmented Reality-equipped vehicles and manned simulators.
- 1998: Spatial augmented reality introduced at University of North Carolina at Chapel Hill.

- 2000: Bruce H. Thomas develops ARQuake, the first outdoor mobile Augmented Reality game.
- 2008: Wikitude Augmented Reality Travel Guide launches on October 20, 2008 with the G1 Android phone.
- 2009: Augmented reality comes to the web browser.
- 2010: Augmented reality apps developed for multiple uses and readily available for public download.
- 2011: Major developers of augmented reality software and hardware explore the boundaries, including work on augmented reality contact lenses.
- 2012: Development of augmented reality touch screen for common surfaces continue to make inroads in the public spheres.

How Augmented Reality Works

Before getting to the heart of a discussion on augmented reality in education, it is helpful to first understand the basic mechanics of how it works. This overview will not explore the technical aspects such as coding, architecture, and other engineering processes. Instead, it will look at operation from the user perspective.

Basically, augmented reality needs four things to operate: a computing device (e.g., laptop, desktop, smartphone), a web camera, a display device (a computer or phone screen), and software to read the environment and to project images onto the screen. An additional technology to enhance augmented reality functioning is the incorporation of a global positioning system (GPS), which provides the coordinates of where the user is located, and which delivers digital imagery to those coordinates. The GPS system, in concert with the augmented reality software, also allows that imagery to move as the user moves, or to bring up new images as the user's perspective and position changes.

In short, the camera sends an image of the environment to the software in the computer, which may include the global position of the computing device and/or the real world object. The software generates the preprogrammed digital imagery for that location or image and projects it onto the screen, overlaying it upon the existing real image or environment. It might also generate text, audio, or video files as part of the augmented experience. The images can be interactive. This interactivity allows the user to view the digital object in 3D, with potential 360 degree rotation, which can be manually repositioned by the user.

The capture devices used for augmented reality can be any basic web camera attached to a laptop, desktop, or smartphone that have access to an augmented reality program. Additionally, cameras can be located in headsets or special-made goggles. Of great interest are augmented reality-enabled contact lenses currently in various stages of testing.

The computing power needed to engage in common augmented reality activities can be handled by any consumer computing device that is currently on the market. It is the accessible processing power and relatively low cost of everyday communications devices that have finally allowed augmented reality to emerge into the mainstream.

Obviously, augmented reality environments are created as the result of programming, which determines when, where, and how digital information is displayed. Pointing a web camera at real-world objects and spaces, or viewing them through special augmented reality enabled headwear, triggers software to retrieve the coding for that object or space and delivers a digital image to the screen along with the real object image. Common software triggers include marker codes or QR codes. A marker/QR code is a unique printed pattern placed in the environment (see below). When the camera viewfinder frames the marker code, it matches that image to the marker-recognition feature of the software and triggers the projection of a digital image along with the original real object image.

Some augmented reality programs rely on GPS technology and marker-less object recognition. GPS technology tells the software program exactly where the camera is and, possibly, where the object is in relation to the camera. It can then use mapping information, such as that provided by Google Earth, and display the real-time landscape onto the screen, with accompanying digital imagery as the viewer moves around in the environment. Markerless object recognition can occur if the device is coded for specific objects. When the camera frames an object, it matches the qualities of that object, which are similar to object images in the program. It then displays digital information about the object. The resulting images will often be observable in three dimensions. As previously noted, some digital information responds to human movement and is manipulable, as would be a real-world object.

It is helpful to understand that while augmented reality capability has been available in some form or another for several decades, it wasn't until the mass marketing of personal computers, the decline in components prices, and the rise in processing power that encouraged augmented reality applications developers to create products with broad appeal. However, the real accelerator that is driving augmented reality into the public realm, including education, is the widespread use of smartphones (Cabiria, 2011a). The relatively low expense of smartphones, large user-base, broad user demographics, and portability make them the perfect vehicle for augmented reality applications. No matter where a person is, she or he can access an augmented reality environment.

How Augmented Reality is Used

Although the specific purpose of this chapter is to discuss augmented reality in education, it is helpful to also understand other areas in which augmented reality is useful — especially when considering that educational methods are becoming more broadly explored. Additionally, given that introduction of new technologies in other fields is an ongoing process, educators who prepare students for those fields will have to help students understand how to use them. An area of augmented reality utility that has already occurred is in marketing and advertising. Major brands have included QR codes in their print and promotional collateral, allowing people to engage in interactive experiences with the product. Another area in which Augmented Reality is making in-roads is the medical professional, where surgical students are learning new surgical techniques using augmented surgical scenarios. In the field of architecture, architects, architect students, and others involved in visual display are creating easily configurable and manipulable 3D representations of building plans and space designs for their clients. In mental health, psychologists are replicating scenarios in the treatment of phobias and post-traumatic stress disorder (PTSD). In leisure industries, the travel industry is identifying and describing key points-of-interest for sightseers, including digital overlays of how an environment looked in the past. The list of current applications in all fields grows everyday.

Of special consideration is the application of augmented reality to gaming. This is relevant to education in that gaming principles are seen as an important learning adjunct (Campos, Pessanha, & Jorge, 2011). Video game producers are in the forefront in developing augmented reality products and experimenting with advanced augmented reality applications. The development of the ability to play live games in real spaces is of interest, in which the user is surrounded by digital imagery when viewed through AR goggles. The gamification of education will be discussed later in this chapter.

Interactivity is a key attribute in many augmented reality environments (De Sa, Churchill, & Isbister, 2011). As described earlier, some virtual

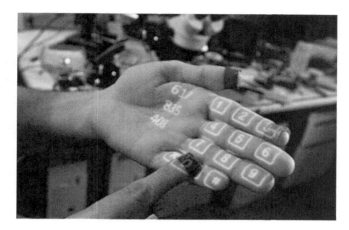

Fig. 3. Operational Cellphone Keypad Projection Onto a Hand.

objects can be manipulated as if in real space. For example, a digital image of a computer keyboard that is projected on a surface can actually function like a real keyboard. Taping on the projected keys is the same as tapping on a real keyboard, causing letters to appear in whatever application is visible on the computer screen or in the augmented environment. Similarly, when a number is tapped out on a digital projection of a cell phone keypad, it will activate the cellphone provider and connect the caller to the number through a small headset (Fig. 3).

AUGMENTED REALITY EDUCATION

The 2012 Emerging Technologies Hype Cycle report by respected technology analysts, Gartner (2012), projected that augmented reality applications can expect mainstream acceptance within the next 5–10 years. Additionally, the 2011 Horizon Report, an annual joint publication by the New Media Consortium (Johnson, Levine, Smith, & Stone, 2011) and Educause, both leading organizations in the study and advancement of new technologies in education, stated that augmented reality will have widespread use in the classroom over the next few years (2011). While a timeline cannot be precisely predicted with any assurance, it is safe to say that augmented reality will become a part of our consciousness in the very near future.

A reason for the expected embrace of augmented reality into the learning environment, if the Horizon Report is accurate, can be partly explained by expansion of online learning, the younger generation's use of and demand for technologies in their daily lives, and the need for more engaging and immersive learning tools. To further elaborate on this last point, psychologist Jerome Bruner, respected professor in the study of cognitive learning theory, furthered the concept of "Discovery Learning" decades earlier (1960). Discovery Learning proposes that students learn best when they engage in the process of acquiring information to solve a problem — in essence, they learn through lived experiences that are relevant to the issue at hand. Students are expected to learn by doing. Although discovery learning, in its purist form (unassisted learning), has received some criticism for its lack of real learning efficacy (Mayer, 2004; Tuovinen & Sweller, 1999), a modified form of it, enhanced discovery learning, includes some level of a instructor guidance until the student is competent enough to engage in self-directed study (Alfieri, Brooks, Aldrich, & Tenenbaum, 2011; Mayer, 2004). The role of augmented reality in discovery learning is still being studied but shows promise. Some research demonstrated increased engagement and discovery by students when using inquiry-based instruction with augmented reality tools (Ketelhut, Nelson, Clarke, & Dede, 2010; Leonard & Penick, 2009).

Continuing with the theme of using augmented reality as a discovery tool for learning, we can now expand its value to include student-controlled learning. Student-controlled learning is an important concept found frequently in online education (Castronova, 2002; Dunleavy, Dede, & Mitchell, 2009). In student-controlled learning, the student determines what and how to learn within the objectives of the course. This constructivist approach to learning theorizes the notion that students actively generate meaning and knowledge as a result of their prior experiences interacting with the current course content. In a constructivist-learning environment, students are viewed as being unique individuals who have specific, individual learning needs that are best addressed through their own learning choices. As with many learning theories and philosophies, constructivism in education is controversial (Kirschner, Sweller, & Clarke, 2006) because of the minimal guidance provided during the learning process.

Augmented reality tools can easily be integrated into a constructivist design. Because the digital imagery projected into real space can be manipulated, the student has the potential for exploring objects and locations according to her or his learning needs, rather than through a pedagogy that assumes what those needs are. An obvious benefit is that, if errors occur as a result of learning choices made, no real-world harm can occur. For example, in medical training, a medical student can manipulate body organs exactly as they appear within the body, without the need for the actual human body and, of course, without compromise to a human volunteer.

Another example would be courses dealing with science. A student can learn about chemical properties by manually combining various digital objects representing elements, and seeing the resulting molecule name and appearance. She or he can assemble and disassemble chains of molecules as needed to learn their structures and interactions. This process of physical and sensory activity increases levels of student presence and engagement and, depending on the scope of the augmented reality environment, might even create total immersion (to be discussed in upcoming sections of this chapter) (Fig. 4).

Regardless of the learning method, what seems clear is that students in the online learning environment, as well as in traditional settings, need

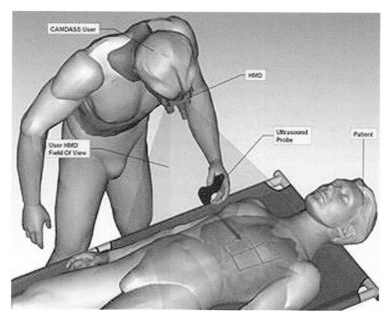

Fig. 4. Augmented Reality in Surgical Training.

learning tools that match their twenty-first century lives (Castronova, 2002; Trilling & Fadel, 2009). Learning by rote has limited appeal and, in an information-laden society, becomes impractical. Of greater importance seems to be the need for enhanced critical thinking and problem-solving skills that are germane to the individual. The delivery methods in which these skills are acquired are best developed with the students' and instructors' real-world lives in mind. What we know is that increased sense of attention, presence, and engagement are hallmark requirements for students in the new millennium (Dunleavy, Dede, & Mitchell, 2009).

COGNITIONS AND LEARNING

This section explores some of the cognitive processes that come into play during learning, and how augmented reality stimulates these cognitions to enhance the learning environment. Of special focus will be deeper explorations of effects already touched upon, including presence and engagement.

Cognition

An attraction of augmented reality in education is its ability to capture and hold attention. This speaks directly to cognition and the role of the senses in perceiving and making meaning out of the blended real and digital stimuli received by the brain. Cognition is simply how people perceive and respond to the world around them through their external senses and internal memories and reflexes. Although cognitive processing is quite complex and beyond the scope of this chapter, it is worth discussing some of the brain structures involved in certain types of cognition and how they apply to augmented reality environments in general, and learning in those environments specifically.

The Cognitive Brain

The human brain is a masterful product of evolution that still retains some very ancient yet powerful features. The earliest brain structure is referred to as the reptilian brain. The next evolutionary structure is called the mammalian brain. The most recently evolved structure is called the neocortex.

Each structure has specific functions, but each is also part of a matrix of interconnections. With all three structures working collaboratively, we are able to consciously and subconsciously experience the world around us and within us.

The reptilian brain, aka the R-Brain or Triune Brain (MacLean, 1990), controls many of our reflexes, including life-sustaining functions such as breathing, organ functioning, and basic survival responses. It does not analyze stimuli in terms of right or wrong, but simply responds to meet the needs for survival. The mammalian brain is one of the locations for learning new things and for memory storage, as well as a source of our basic emotional responses, especially survival responses such as fear and aggression. It makes people keenly aware of their environments. Many external stimuli past through the reptilian structures first before an end-response is filtered by the neocortex. The neocortex is often described as the part of the brain that makes people "human." It is here that they experience the sophistication of the stimuli-response mechanisms, which includes the ability to override more primitive emotions and needs in order to make other choices of behavior. All together, these three structures include the ability to process sensations, connect them to memories, and respond to them in an infinite number of ways. This is particularly important, as will soon be seen, in the ability to perceive and respond to digital information as real world information. In essence, the more primitive brain structures do not always do a good job distinguishing between real and artifice (MacLean, 1990) but it can be surmised that so long as the augmented objects contain basic characteristics of "realness," they will be accepted as such and responded to accordingly.

There is active research on how the brain cognitively reacts to augmented reality environments as part of the learning process. For example, Shelton and Hedley (2003) found that certain augmented reality approaches to education, especially those related to spatial relationships, have cognitive advantages over traditional settings. They noted how the Augmented Reality interface, due to the creation of a familiar spatial and visual context, can provide cognitive relationships between the learner visual spaces beyond traditional learning interfaces (Shelton and Hedley, 2003). Similarly, Furmanski, Azuma, and Daily (2002) found that digital objects were perceived as having a real location in a mixed environment situation, and that real objects placed in front of or behind the digital image enhanced perception of the location of the digital object. In their experiment, they found that study participants were unable to separate perceptions of position of digital objects in relation to real objects once position had been accepted. In essence, depth perception of the digital object in the real space had been achieved (Furmanski et al., 2002). It is interesting to note that how a student views the relationship of digital objects with real world objects is a key indicator of the effectiveness of the overall display in terms of holding attention, creating a sense of presence, and producing engagement (Neal, Cabiria, Hogg, & Pase, 2011).

Attention

It is helpful to recognize at this point that the great appeal of augmented reality, no matter the field in which it is being used, is its ability to capture one's attention (Schnier, Pitsch, Dierker, & Hermann, 2011). Certainly, from a cognitive perspective, attention is a prerequisite to effective learning (Canal-Bruland, Zhu, van der Kamp, & Masters 2011). How this process of converting attention into learning is described in the adaptive resonance theory. This theory describes how, when attention is directed toward something, the information coming into the brain from the source of attention (bottom-up pathways) triggers activation of a series of expectations (based in memories) about the object of attention (top-down pathways). When the incoming sensory stimuli meet expectations, the brain "matches-up" expectations with reality, but sidelines what it perceives as irrelevant information. The stronger the match, the greater the information will be retained rather than forgotten. Essentially, the more attention one pays to something, the stronger the excitation responses will be, creating stronger connections between the object and the cognitions about that object (Carpenter & Grossberg, 2003), Any technology that can draw and hold attention would seem to have an edge in creating valuable learning opportunities. For younger generations raised with digital gaming, and in control of the digital environment, the creation of learning activities that incorporate digital control and virtual simulation can provide attention-stimulating learning experiences.

In order to effectively learn, students must direct some level of attention to what they perceive through one or more of their senses. Attention can be thought of as focused awareness, in which something stands out from the constant mix of sensory stimulations and is recorded in memory. In its most simplistic description, the more attention given to something, and the more exposure provided to this attention-drawing event, the more likely students are to recall that attention-drawing activity or event and be able to utilize it as a basis for related stimuli in the future. Often, the more unique something is, the more likely it will command attention (Cabiria, 2011b). As well, events that are related to survival will also stimulate basic reptilian and mammalian brain structures, drawing immediate attention (MacLean, 1990). A parallel can be draw to how an audience responds to a scene in a horror movie. Although the viewers know that they are in the safety of a movie theater, and that the movie is just an image on a screen, they will still experience emotional reactions, including hiding their eyes, gasping, screaming, or nervously laughing – all the results of the activation of primitive brain survival mechanisms mixed with memories. The audience members have, in essence, suspended disbelief of the artifice of the situation, having given it their full attention. In fact, they have reached a level of attention that has passed through engagement and achieved presence – they have become immersed in the mediated environment.

It is not a stretch to claim that an augmented reality learning environment, due to its uniqueness, has attention-drawing capabilities, and that it has the ability to stimulate basic reflexive responses in a way that lecture and book reading may not. It would seem, then, that uniqueness and stimulation of basic emotions are key to attention formation, and that acceptable cognitive load levels occur when attention is given to the activity or event where the brain can easily perceive what is in the environment and relate to it on, at least, a very basic level (Cabiria, 2012).

Presence

When discussing the use of virtual or augmented environments for various educational endeavors, successful outcomes depend upon the creation of a scenario in which sense of "presence" within the mediated environment is achieved (Cabiria, 2011b; Nagy, 2011; Witmer & Singer, 1998). Presence can be defined as awareness, in which attention is directed toward the created environment and in which one's senses become engaged as a result of that environment, to the increased exclusion of external factors. Presence can refer to a subjective degree of realism that is experienced by the individual (Parsons & Rizzo, 2007). A key feature in achieving presence in an augmented learning environment is the ability of the technology to create a context that is natural, or is not so disruptively unnatural as to draw attention to its unnaturalness. It requires that the mediated environment appears to be unmediated. But beyond that, it can also require awareness of the social environment in which the other people and objects exist, and of awareness of the interactions within that social cultural web (Cabiria, 2008, 2011a; Mantovani & Riva, 1999; Riva, 2009).

An augmented 3D presentation of an object provides students with a sense of "presence," as proposed by Mantovani (1999, 2001, 2003), in which the interaction with the learning environment is recalled on a similar level as a real world experience would be. In fact, as levels of interaction increase, there appears to be a positive correlation to strength of sense of presence. This sense of presence is often enhanced through the integration of gaming into the learning process. Kaplan-Leiserson (2004) argues that augmented reality gaming woven into the learning method, with its high propensity for engaging visuals and audio, ability to recall and replay scenarios, provision of escalating rewards for achievement, and collaborative options with other students promotes a high level of engagement, leading to immersive learning opportunities.

In a well-designed augmented reality learning environment, students quickly enter a state of suspended disbelief, accept the blended real and digital environment, give their attention over to it, and engage in the variety of options available to them to access content related to the topic being addressed. In short, the students develop a sense of presence within the augmented environment (Furmanski, Azuma, & Daily, 2002).

Engagement

A recent meta-analysis of 20 years of research on undergraduate education revealed that students were more likely to learn, were more likely to continue their studies, and were more likely to attain their academic goals when they were able to become actively engaged with the course content (McClenney, Marti, & Askins, 2012). Engagement is when students become fully focused on the content, applying existing knowledge with new information in a way that is stimulating and attention-grabbing. Engaged students, in finding that learning is pleasurable and meaningful, will be more motivated to continue the learning process, especially if there is a level of self-regulation allowable in the process (Sun & Rueda, 2012). In fact, according to the researchers, this self-regulation, along with situational interest, correlated significantly with behavioral, emotional, and cognitive engagement (Sun & Rueda, 2012).

Drawing from studies previously noted, augmented reality learning approaches should provide enough sensory stimulation, through various video, sound, content choices, and student control of features so that attention is directed, and the levels of engagement become negotiable according to the needs of the student. Augmented reality education, whether it be in the form of fully immersive environments, through digital "pop-up" books, or as viewed through various cameras, screens, or headsets, should allow students be able to engage in some level of suspense of disbelief, even if only at the primitive brain levels, to accept the digital as 'realistic enough' (Cabiria, 2011a), thus promoting engagement.

In the next section, we will explore, more specifically, how augmented reality can be used in education. Because formal education can occur anywhere due to Internet and mobile technologies, we will look at applications of augmented reality that encompass both real and virtual spaces, and that utilize real and virtual objects, persons, and places.

Using Augmented Reality in Education

At the beginning of this chapter, it was stated that basic augmented reality applications would be in widespread use in education in the next few years (Johnson, Levine, Smith, & Stone, 2011). Certainly, given the increasing technological footprint on everything in society, students would be expected to utilize various applications that comprise their working and social lives. In many respects, it can be surmised that students drive the evolution of new educational modalities by virtue of the expectation that educational tools should model real-world experiences.

When using the word "students," it will be defined broadly in this discussion. In addition to students who attend institutions of higher learning, it will also include K-12 students, corporate training program students, military training students, and a host of other activities in which learning something is an objective. The application of augmented reality technologies to education, therefore, can encompass many different types of learners in many different fields. The types of educational objectives to be discussed in this section fall into five main categories, which have overlapping qualities: skills training, discovery learning, educational gaming, object modeling, and interactive learning.

Skills-Based Training
Skills-based training provides opportunities to practice and refine one's ability to perform a task. Augmented reality, with its 3D aspects, geolocation, and geotagging options (based on GPS functionality), and gesture-based potential (using hands to activate and manipulate digital environments), allows students to manipulate objects in real time and

space to practice certain exercises, whether it be working on a car engine, a human heart, or a golf swing, to name a few.

Discovery Learning

Discovery learning allows students to explore topics and solutions to problems in a manner that is most appropriate for them. Students can delve into topics to fill in unique gaps in knowledge while still fulfilling overall learning objectives for the course. An augmented reality-based discovery learning process provides a practical alternative to consolidating information in one platform that would be difficult to do in the real world. Semi-transparent touchscreens, for example, can be built into any object, allowing the user to interact with what is being viewed through the screen using digital menus and controls.

Gamification

Gamification is the application of gaming principles to non-gaming contexts. For education, this can mean using various gaming strategies and skill-sets to enhance learning. It provides a familiar process now that digital gaming has saturated many areas of industrialize societies. Increasingly, children and adults alike are likely to engage in some level of gaming (Squire & Jenkins, 2003) The gamification of education offers students incredible learning opportunities for critical thinking skill development, kinesthetic development, social development (for collaborative interactions), and topic-specific development (Gee, 2003). Augmented reality can enhance gaming and thus increase the potential for presence, attention, and engagement.

Object Modeling

Object modeling, used by artists, architects, and various fields in engineering requires the ability to draw, build, and/or manipulate objects as part of a larger process of building them. In the real world, object modeling often occurs on paper or on the computer screen with specialized software. However, the sense of scale can be lost for large items, and changes can take quite a bit of time. In an augmented environment, objects appear to be in real space, on any scale, and can be modified quickly through the use of gesturing in which boundaries of the object respond to finger and hand commands to be reconfigured (Fig. 5).

Fig. 5.   Object Modeling Goes Here.

Course Topic Examples

Interactive textbooks are currently in various stages of development. Essentially, textbook pages will be embedded with markers. These markers will trigger activation of an image, textbox, video, or link to web pages that will enhance the content of the textbook page. The augmented information will either appear above the page, as if floating in real space, or will open a window in the page to view media or live websites.

There is no limit to the course topics that can be "augmented" in textbook form. A few of many examples include the following:

Chemistry: Students can manipulate chemical elements in 3D space to create compounds and molecules.

Geography: Students can explore various surface and below-surface aspects of the Earth. They can manipulate layers of the Earth's surface, visit unique geographical formations, and view additional media.

History: Students can view various locations as they appeared throughout history, based on paintings, pictures, drawings, and original illustrations overlaid on a real space. Students can also view reenactments of historical events in real space.

Art: Students can view major and obscure works of art regardless of their current location and trigger programs that provide additional information. Some museums have already begun leading the way in augmenting their galleries.

Business (marketing and advertising): Students can learn how to enhance product and brand awareness, provide greater levels of information to consumers, and more effectively utilize social communities. For example, smartphone cameras pointed at a product can display product information, company information, offer a discount code, or bring up the company website. Pointing a camera at a building can inform the consumer about which companies are in the building, what they do, how to contact them, and whatever other information the companies want to provide.

Languages: Using text language translators, students can point their smartphone camera to any text and see its translation to the language of their choice. They could then play an audio file of its sound and a video file of its use in an interaction. This is currently in limited use as a downloadable app for some smartphones.

The implications for learning are obvious — students will have greater flexibility in accessing a wider variety of content and will be able to utilize that content in a manner that best suits their learning needs. One of the challenges of the current models of learning is the limitation of the 2D space. For topics requiring object-oriented learning, the student must translate the 2D representation of the object into a mental model of its actual 3D state in order step from the abstract to the real. This requires strong cognition abilities, which are not common to everyone.

RESEARCH AND ISSUES

Research is limited but growing on the subject of the effectiveness of augmented reality in education, although it seems obvious at this point that the attention-drawing potential of augmented reality is an excellent match for educational applications. Its scalability alone creates infinite, flexible uses: A student can view a small 3D pop-up feature in a textbook or be surrounded in a massive 3D environment among other students. Of interest to educators is if the Augmented Reality textbook, the large-scale Augmented Reality environment, or any other varied and unique uses for augmented reality show any substantive benefit in information retention and recall. Preliminary research results in selected fields seem to indicate that there is positive benefit. For example, the sense of presence of experienced augmented environments can allow for greater application of content (Hughes & Moshell, 1997). Similarly, Kalawsky, Hill, Stedmon, Cook, and Young (2000) found that Augmented Reality systems can be an effective educational option when it comes to multitasking tasks. Of special interest would be those learning activities requiring development of special skills, in which Augmented Reality environments proved beneficial (Marin-Gutierrez, Contero, & Alcaniz, 2010). Massachusetts Institute of Technology is one of several leading research centers exploring augmented reality technologies and uses. Of special consideration is the integration of augmented reality, gaming, and educational themes. Researchers there have been designing augmented learning games over the past few years that focus on a variety of topics in math, languages, the humanities, and science. It was determined that the context of the real world, imbued with digital enhancements, provide students with the skills needed in modern industrialized societies (Schrier, 2005). Harvard's Graduate School of Education produced research showing the immersive power of the realistic experience found in the augmented environment, which students found to be highly motivating (Dede, 2009). These studies found that augmented reality, by allowing multiple perspectives, situated learning, and (knowledge) transfer, greatly enhanced the learning experience (Dede, 2009; Schrier, 2005). Researchers at the Helsinki Institute for Information Technology hypothesized that in comparative studies of similar 2D and 3D (augmented reality) games, there was an increase in collaboration and problem-solving when using the augmented gaming platforms (Morrison et al., 2009).

Issues

Certainly, the benefits of augmented education are far from comprehensive and are meant to provide just a glimpse of the ongoing research going on throughout the world. It is worth noting that using augmented reality, as part of a learning approach, is not without flaws and criticism. For example, many of the augmented reality effects rely upon GPS. GPS, as has been shown, is a satellite-based navigation system that connects people (actually, their GPS-enabled device) to their location. Although GPS has the capability of extremely precise location of objects in a coordinate, the U.S. government (which owns the technology and transmission paths) limits civilian use as a matter of national security (Arms Control Association, 2012). As a result, exact placement of digital imagery on existing real space can be somewhat inaccurate unless the GPS system is used in concert with image recognition software.

Viewing augmented landscapes is also limited, currently. Most applications depend upon using a smartphone screen or computer camera. The former requires constant holding of the phone and a steady hand, which is impractical for any duration of time. However, recent advances in augmented reality goggles and contact lens development will greatly open up viewing options.

There are some ethical and safety issues involved in the use of augmented reality as well. Developers of augmented reality educational games that are played in real spaces and require participant movement need to be alert to the possibility of participant injury resulting from lack of attention, or diminished attention to real world objects while interacting with virtual ones. This is an area of concern that is currently under-researched.

Another major concern for educators is the distraction that augmented reality educational applications might cause. People are experiencing cognitive overload as information confronts them at every opportunity throughout their waking moments (Squire & Jenkins, 2003). Children, already engrossed with digital technologies, will have yet another technology to add to their toy boxes. Parents and educators wonder at what point it becomes too much − if it is not already. While the benefit of immersion, which greatly aids in information retention and recall, is desirable, is there a harmful trade-off? This speaks directly to the quality of the educational design of the augmented reality program. Educators are concerned that the "flash" and entertainment functions of the augmented reality design will falsely be perceived as educational (Squire & Jenkins, 2003).

Clearly, augmented reality in education has its pros and cons. Looking at how it is trending in all fields, including education, indications are that growth of augmented reality development and implementation appears to be mostly positive thus far (Johnson, Levine, Smith, & Stone, 2011). However, given the dearth of research in some of these key areas, it cannot be assumed that there will not be significant drawbacks with poorly designed and implemented Augmented Reality educational approaches.

THE FUTURE

Imagine sitting anywhere, opening up a computing tablet and initiating a program that transmits an image of the professor in front of the student, in real time and in 3D, presenting a lecture on that day's topic. Imagine again sitting in a classroom, surrounded by classmates, except none of them are actually in a classroom. In fact, each of them is sitting in some other location apart from each other, anywhere else in the world; yet, they can be seen, heard, and interacted with along with the digital professor, in real time. Taking this further, imagine, instead, a class field trip to the African savannahs, where students view wildlife passing by just a few feet in front of them. Students can click in the direction of each animal or plant to view its information. The reality may actually be that the students are actually all in a field on the school grounds and the African savannah is a digital overlay. New applications for the uses of augmented reality in education are being proposed, developed, and/or implemented everyday.

CONCLUSION

Educators have always looked to technology for ways to enhance the learning experience. In many cases, educators have been at the forefront in the development of these technologies. From the well-endowed research departments of major universities to the proselytization of the individual teacher who introduces interesting technological tools to her or his classroom, some of these technologies make their way into the standard norm of everyday learning. It wasn't too long ago that television sets were introduced into some classrooms, with custom-made programming used to accentuate course topics. Other television programs were broadcast into the home, with students learning, and earning credit, in the comfort of their homes. A few decades later, the Internet, aside from providing a staging ground for learning, brought a vast repository of information of public and subscription-based databases to the classroom, becoming the latest iteration of a library. Along the way, cellular technologies and virtual worlds found their way into the educational realm. Now, it is the dawn of another major step forward in education with the emergence of augmented learning through augmented reality.

What makes augmented reality more likely to now become a fast-track application is the fact that it utilizes a lot of existing technology, reducing development and testing time and costs. The core hardware needed to operate the software already exists in any home or facility with a camera-enabled smart device, such as a computer, netbook, or phone. It has virtually no learning curve for anyone who wants to understand how to use it.

In its simplest form, it is point and view. On the development side, a lag can be expected as companies create and test new applications, determine content priority, ramp up production, and bring products to market. It is not hard to find examples of leadership in many segments of industry. An Internet search for almost any industry along with "augmented reality" will likely bring up information, as will many searches for similar queries in video databases. While some technologies enter the marketplace with great hype and widespread acknowledgement, often before their time, it is expected that augmented reality will mostly weave itself quietly through the fabric of people's lives, as is already occurring. The virtuality that already exists in many entertainment options has desensitized people, to some extent, to the specialness of augmented reality. It is not a giant leap from one paradigm to another, as some technological advances are, but a logical progression of a series of smaller innovations over time. In some ways, it is expected.

Educators and students interested in keeping abreast of advances in augmented reality in general, and in education specifically, can find a variety of support sites, forums, and social networks to keep them informed (see Resources following this section). Expect new augmented reality resources, including research articles, books, and websites to continue to appear with increasing frequency over the next five-to-ten years. Expect, too, that the augmented reality of tomorrow will be vastly different than the augmented reality of today, as innovation continues to mold its potential.

REFERENCES

Alfieri, L., Brooks, P. J., Aldrich, N. J., & Tenenbaum, H. R. (2011). Does discovery-based instruction enhance learning? *Journal of Educational Psychology*, *103*(1), 1–18.

Arms Control Association. (2012). *Missile technology control regime (MTCR)*. Retrieved form http://www.armscontrol.org/documents/mtcr

Augmented reality timeline (2012). In *Wikipedia*. Retrieved from http://www.en.wikipedia. org/wiki/augmented_reality. Accessed on January 30, 2012.

Bruner, J. (1960). *The process of education*. Cambridge, MA: Harvard University Press.

Cabiria, J. (2008). Benefits of virtual world engagement. *Media Psychology Review*, *1*(1). Retrieved from http://mprcenter.org/mpr/index.php?option = com_content&view = article&id = 167&Itemid = 126

Cabiria, J. (2011a). *AR and the human factor: Designing for the mind*. Presentation at the Augmented Reality Event, May 18, 2011. Santa Clara, CA.

Cabiria, J. (2011b). The Internet and interaction. In G. Brewer (Ed.), *Media psychology*. London: Palgrave-Macmillan.

Cabiria, J. (2012). Quality augmented reality: Cognitive task design. In *Proceedings of the 2012 international conference on e-learning, e-business, enterprise information systems, & e-government, EEE 2012*, July 16–19, Las Vegas, NV: CSREA Press.

Campos, P., Pessanha, S., & Jorge, J. (2011). Fostering collaboration in kindergarten through an augmented reality game. *International Journal of Augmented Reality, 10*(3), 33–39.

Canal-Bruland, R., Zhu, F . F., van der Kamp, J., & Masters, R. S. W. (2011). Target-directed visual attention is a prerequisite for action-specific perception. *Acta Psychologica, 136*(3), 285–289.

Carpenter, G. A., & Grossberg, S. (2003). Adaptive resonance theory. In M. A. Arbib (Ed.), *The handbook of brain theory and neural networks* (2nd ed., pp. 87–89). Cambridge, MA: MIT Press.

Castronova, J. A. (2002). Discovery learning for the 21st century: What is it and how does it compare to traditional learning in effectiveness in the 21st century? *Action Research Exchange, 1*(1), 1–12.

De Sa, M., Churchill, E. F., & Isbister, K. (2011). Mobile augmented reality: Design issues and opportunities. *MobileHCI '11, proceedings of the 13th international conference on human computer interaction with mobile devices and services*. ACM, New York, NY.

Dede, C. (2009). Immersive interfaces for engagement and learning. *Science, 323*(5910), 66–69.

Diringer, D. (1982). *The book before printing: Ancient, medieval and oriental*. New York City, NY: Courier Dover Publications.

Diringer, D., & Freeman, H. (1983). *History of the alphabet* (4th ed.). Headley-on-Thames, UK: Gresham Books.

Dunleavy, M., Dede, C., & Mitchell, R. (2009). Affordances and limitations of immersive participatory augmented reality simulations for teaching and learning. *Journal of Science Education & Technology, 18*(1), 7–22. doi: 10.1007/s10956-008-9119-1

Furmanski, C., Azuma, R., & Daily, M. (2002). Augmented-reality visualizations guided by cognition: Perceptual heuristics for combining visible and invisible information. In *Proceedings of the international symposium on mixed and augmented reality* (pp. 215–224). Los Alamitos, CA: IEEE Computer Society Press.

Gartner. (2012). *Hype cycle emerging technologies report*. Retrieved from http://www.gartner.com/it/page.jsp?id = 1763814

Gee, J. P. (2003). *What video games have to teach us about learning and literacy*. New York City: Palgrave Macmillan.

Heilig, M. (1992[1955]). Cinema of the future. *Presence, 1*(3), 279–294.

Hughes, C., & Moshell, J. M. (1997). Shared virtual worlds for education: The explorenet experiment. *ACM Multimedia, 5*(2), 145–154.

Johnson, L., Levine, A., Smith, R., & Stone, S. (2011). *The 2011 Horizon report*. Austin, TX: The New Media Consortium.

Kalawsky, R. S., Hill, K., Stedmon, A. W., Cook, C. A., & Young, A. L. (2000). Experimental research into human cognitive processing in an augmented reality environment for embedded training systems. *Virtual Reality, 5*(1), 39–46.

Kaplan-Leiserson, E. (2004). *Trend: Augmented reality check*. Alexandria, VA: Learning Circuits. Retrieved from http://www.neiu.edu/~sdundis/textresources/New%20Technology_Programs/Augmented%20Reality.pdf

Ketelhut, D. J., Nelson, B. C., Clarke, J., & Dede, C. (2010). A multi-user virtual environment for building and assessing higher order inquiry skills in science. *British Journal of Educational Technology, 41*(1), 56–68. doi: 10.1111/j.1467-8535.2009.01036.x

Kirschner, P. A., Sweller, J., & Clark, R. E. (2006). Why minimal guidance during instruction does not work: An analysis of the failure of constructivist, discovery, problem-based, experiential, and inquiry-based teaching. *Educational Psychologist, 41*(2), 75–86. doi: 10.1207/s15326985ep41021

Leonard, W. H., & Penick, J. E. (2009). Is the inquiry real? Working definitions of inquiry in the science classroom. *Science Teacher, 76*(5), 40–43.

MacLean, P. D. (1990). *The triune brain in evolution: Role of paleocerebral functions*. New York: Plenum Press.

Mantovani, G. (2001). The psychological construction of the Internet: From information foraging to social gathering to cultural mediation. *CyberPsychology Behavior, 4*(1), 47–56.

Mantovani, G. (2003). VR learning: Potential and challenges for the use of 3D. In R. Riva & C. Galimberti (Eds.), *Towards cyberpsychology: Mind, cognitions, and society in the Internet age* (pp. 208–225). Amsterdam: IOS Press.

Mantovani, G., & Riva, R. (1999). 'Real' presence: How different ontologies generate different criteria for presence, telepresence, and virtual presence. *Presence, 8*(5), 540–550.

Marin-Gutierrez, J., Contero, M., & Alcaniz, V. (2010). Evaluating the usability of an augmented reality-based educational application. In J. Kay & J. Mostow (Eds.), *Intelligent tutoring systems: 10th International conference* (pp. 296–306). Berlin, Germany: Springer.

Mayer, R. E. (2004). Should there be a three-strikes rule against pure discovery learning? *American Psychologist, 59*(1), 14–19. doi: 10.1037/0003-066X.59.1.14

MacLean, P. D. (1990). *The triune brain in evolution: Role in paleocerebral functions*. New York: Plenum Press.

McClenney, K., Marti, C. N., & Adkins, C. (2012). *Student engagement and student outcomes: Key findings from the CCSSE validation research*. Austin, TX: Community College Survey of Student Engagement. Retrieved from http://www.ccsse.org/aboutsurvey/docs/CCSSE%20Validation%20Summary.pdf

Michels, P. (2008, February 25). Universities use Second Life to teach complex concepts. *Government Technology*. Retrieved from http://www.govtech.com/education/Universities-Use-Second-Life-to-Teach.html

Milgram, P., & Koshino, F. (1994). A taxonomy of mixed reality visual displays. *IEICE Transactions on Information Systems, E77-D, 12*. Retrieved from http://www.eecs.ucf.edu/~cwingrav/teaching/ids6713_sprg2010/assets/Milgram_IEICE_1994.pdf

Morrison, A., Oulasvirta, A., Peltonen, P., Lemmela, S., Jacucci, G., Reitmayr, G., & Juustila, A. (2009). Like bees around a hive: A comparative study of a mobile augmented reality map. In *Proceedings of the 27th international conference on human factors in computing systems*. New York City, NY.

Moura, A., & Carvalho, A. A. (2009). Mobile learning: Two experiments on teaching and learning with mobile phones. In R. Hijon-Neira (Ed.), *Advanced Learning* (pp. 89–103). Vukovar, Croatia: InTech. Retrieved from http://www.intechopen.com/articles/show/title/mobile-learning-two-experiments-on-teaching-and-learning-with-mobile-phones

Nagy, I. K. (2011). *Cognitive aspects of augmented reality applications. Cognitive Infocommunications.* Presented at the 2nd International Conference on Cognitive Infocommunications, Budapest, July, 2011.

Neal, M., Cabiria, J., Hogg, J. L., & Pase, S. (2011). *Psychological keys to success in MAR systems. Proceedings of the 10th annual international symposium on mixed and augmented reality.* Los Alamitos, CA: IEEE Computer Society Press. doi: 10.1109/ISMAR-AMH.2011.6093642.

Parsons, T. D., & Rizzo, A. A. (2007). Affective outcomes of virtual reality exposure therapy for anxiety and specific phobias: A meta-analysis. *Journal of Behavior Therapy and Experimental Psychology, 39,* 250–261. doi: 10.1016/j.jbtep.2007.07.007

Riva, G. (2009). Is presence a technology issue? Some insights from cognitive sciences. *Virtual Reality, 13*(3), 159–169.

Schneider, B., Ford, T. G., & Perez-Felkner, L. (2010). *Social networks and the education of children and youth.* Chicago, IL: University of Chicago Press.

Schnier, C., Pitsch, K., Dierker, A., & Hermann, T. (2011). Collaboration in augmented reality: How to establish coordination and joint attention? In *ECSCW 2011: proceedings of the 12th European conference on computer supported cooperative work* (pp. 405–416), September 24–28, 2011, Aarhus, Denmark.

Schrier, K. L. (2005). *Revolutionizing history education using augmented reality games to teach histories.* Master's thesis. Massachusetts Institute of Technology. Retrieved from http://cms.mit.edu/research/theses/KarenSchrier2005.pdf

Shelton, B. E., & Hedley, N. R. (2003). Exploring a cognitive basis for learning spatial relationships with augmented reality. *Cognition and Learning, 1,* 323–357.

Siemens, G. (2009). *Socialization as information objects.* Retrieved from http://www.connectivism.ca/?p=127

Squire, K., & Jenkins, H. (2003). Harnessing the power of games in education. *Insight, 3*(1), 5–33.

Sun, J. C.-Y., & Rueda, R. (2012). Situational interest, computer self-efficacy and self-regulation: Their impact on student engagement in distance education. *British Journal of Educational Technology, 43,* 191–204. doi: 10.1111/j.1467-8535.2010.01157.x

Trilling, B., & Fadel, C. (2009). *21st century skills: Learning for life in our times.* New York City, NY: Wiley.

Tuovinen, J. E., & Sweller, J. (1999). A comparison of cognitive load associated with discovery learning and worked examples. *Journal of Educational Psychology, 91*(2), 334–341.

Witmer, B. G., & Singer, M. J. (1998). Measuring presence in virtual environments: A presence questionnaire. *Presence: Teleoperators and Virtual Environments, 7*(3), 225–240.

BOLSTERING STUDENT HANDS-ON EXPERIENCE THROUGH THE USE OF VIRTUALIZATION

Denise M. Pheils

ABSTRACT

Virtualization is the simulation or emulation of computer resources to the user (Grauer, n.d.; Simpson, 2008). This chapter discusses virtualization as a viable classroom methodology for providing students with course relevant hands-on experience (Simpson, 2008) while synchronizing course specific content in traditional on-ground and online courses (Pheils, 2010). More specifically, this chapter provides an overview of virtualization, detailing several open source tools, and offering possible applications for incorporation into other courses including free resources for sample content. Proof-of-concept is established through examples of successful usage at two colleges. The adoption of virtualization within course development may provide a solution that spans disciplines and offers students the ability to practice and further their studies beyond the classroom.

Increasing Student Engagement and Retention using Immersive Interfaces: Virtual Worlds, Gaming, and Simulation
Cutting-edge Technologies in Higher Education, Volume 6C, 253–282
ISSN: 2044-9968/doi:10.1108/S2044-9968(2012)000006C012

INTRODUCTION

Most school computer labs have policies against downloading applications and content to lab computers. It is also not feasible to have students download or install a separate Operating System (OS) for use in a class as it would significantly alter the computer and may prevent use by others. Institutions are also faced with the dilemma of how to address courses that are offered a variety of ways including at different locations and those offering on ground, online, and hybrid models. Should each offering be unique? Or should there be consistency across the various sections and platforms so students have similar exposure to the content and the activities in each course? Institutions must still answer these questions, but virtualization provides the means through which courses offered on ground, online, hybrid, and in other ways, can all provide students with similar hands-on experiences and learning opportunities.

In many states school funding is shifting from enrollment numbers to retention successes (Indiana Commission for Higher Education, 2008). Providing a means for students to have more hands-on interaction with the content could foster higher retention and increased student satisfaction. A move to more complex and relevant course content created a need within the computer courses detailed within this study to find a way to support student learning. The challenge to provide relevant hands-on experiences and practice to students, both on-ground and online, and allow for further application of content outside the classroom, drove the search for a viable solution.

This chapter discusses virtualization as a viable classroom methodology for providing students with course relevant hands-on experience (Simpson, 2008) while synthesizing course-specific content among all delivery systems. More specifically, this chapter provides an overview of virtualization while detailing several open source tools for virtualization, OSs, and building content and their many possible applications. This chapter does not delve into the concepts or applications of virtual reality, such as Second Life, but does detail the use of a virtual platform that may host a variety of applications, utilities, and OSs for student use.

Before embarking on a plan to build virtualization into the course content and lab infrastructure, several alternatives were investigated. Practice of skills using the school's computer network was not possible due to the need for security, the unwanted increase in network traffic testing would cause, the desire for job security of the faculty, and the need to remove the school and students from any vulnerability. Several options were considered and tried including removable hard drives to allow each course to contain the applications and programs necessary without impacting the ability of other courses to function while using the same computer resources. The shared drives posed numerous problems and disadvantages. This lab setup requires multiple drives: a general classroom drive for any class to use allowing access to the school network and to the Internet, separate drives for each specialized computer class. The drives were costly, prone to breakage and issues, and took up a large amount of space to store. If a drive failed to function, became corrupt, or went missing, the student assigned to the drive would have to begin progressive labs at the beginning once the instructor built a new drive, if a new drive could be secured for use. Several times there were more problems than spare drives resulting in several students having to share a drive to complete activities. Each term the implementation required that all the removable drives were erased, reinstalled, labelled, and repaired if needed, and stored in the stacks for each class. This was a time-consuming process that required many hours of faculty work beyond the normal classroom preparation.

The option pursued after abandoning the removable drives was a segregated classroom environment. The content was not separated by placement on select hard drives but by installation on separate computers at various locations within the classroom. Initial configuration physically divided a small classroom into two discrete lab sections. One side included 16 production computer systems and an instructor station to allow for a variety of computer courses and topics to utilize the space and have an unobstructed view of the overhead projector and whiteboard. The back half of the classroom consisted of 16 non-production computer systems that were offline from the school's network and provided no access to the Internet. This configuration was very costly as separate computers were used instead of changing only the hard drive. This option also suffered from an inability to support students' use of the computers outside of class time if the classroom was in use. Additionally, the physical classroom solution did not address the need to support the online student in any manner as there is not and cannot be a requirement for online students to come on campus to complete coursework.

The quest for a solution that cost less, had fewer limitations, and took less time and maintenance began. In researching the possible options, several authors indicated similar experiences to the ones described above when constructing separate laboratories, the unresolved need for content portability, and the need for faculty training (Dobrilovic & Odadzic, 2006;

Fuertes, López de Vergara, & Meneses, 2009; Lehrfeld, 2009). The similarities provided hope that a solution could be found (Padman & Memon, 2002).

On-ground and Online Classrooms

Online courses are free from geographic and time constraints, and are growing at a significant rate with online learners estimated to have exceeded 3 million in 2007 (Ternus, Palmer, & Faulk, 2007). Half of all colleges are providing online education making the market for solutions that translate to the online environment great (Pheils, 2010; U.S. Department of Education, 2007). Online courses are not without challenges; faculty must find ways to replicate or improve upon the experiences students would traditionally have within the classroom (Chang & Smith, 2008). Failure to provide those experiences diminishes the learning opportunities for the student, and in some cases minimizes the effectiveness of online education to that of an independent study course (Pheils, 2010). "Distance education causes us to embrace change and creatively design new modes of delivery to respond to the needs of the learners" (Dooley, 2005, p. 12). The use of virtualization empowers educators to design the new modes of delivery Dooley (2005) spoke of. The choice of which technology to include, and how to implement and support that technology, can enhance or hinder student engagement, understanding, and success within the online course (Chang & Smith, 2008).

Lessons can be learned from unsuccessful attempts to offer online courses including the need to equate the experience in traditional courses by providing access to the content and to application of the content (Ternus et al., 2007). Student success within an online class has been linked to gender, age, and identification as a first-generation college student (Chang & Smith, 2008). The ability for anonymity in remediation is one of the greatest features of the online environment (Pheils, 2010). Some experts believe a strong link between self-confidence and self-efficacy, the basic view of oneself, are tied to student success (DeWitz, Woolsey, and Walsh, 2009). A student's self-confidence can be nurtured through success in hands-on exercises and labs and in the ability to perform the learned functions outside of a lab. The use of virtualization and snapshots can aid in that learning and confidence, and provide as many attempts for success as is needed by the student. An area lacking in most courses is the ability to immerse the students in the course's content with detailed hands-on activities while empowering the student to solve problem within the content themselves (Pheils, 2010). Customizing the learning experience is the new face of online education (Ternus et al., 2007) and virtualization may provide the customized approach for active learning and student success.

The Schools

This chapter presents virtualization as a viable option for improving the hands-on student experience. The two schools discussed herein needed low-cost, flexible options to support student learning. The specific successes experienced at each school, including faculty and student comments, occur later in the chapter.

Owens Community College (OCC) is a low-cost, open-entry, community college serving a commuter and online student population of approximately 24,000 students with a main campus in a suburb of Toledo, OH. The System Security and Information Assurance (SSIA) Associate of Applied Business (AAB) degree at OCC provided the challenge to deliver quality hands-on lab experience to students at several college locations and online. The concepts in the SSIA degree include a variety of computer activities that could impact the performance of the college's network. Providing a delivery system for such potentially dangerous and contentious topics while maintaining quality, consistency, and integrity posed a unique challenge. OCC became a National Security Agency (NSA) Center of Academic Excellence for 2 Year Schools (CAE2Y) in June, 2011, largely due to the ability to offer the NSA-required curriculum content through virtualization to the students in the SSIA courses.

In developing the SSIA degree, the focus on innovation and high-quality hands-on experience for the diverse student population required a new medium for presenting content. Training students in technical concepts and techniques requires instruction and guidance in ethical behavior and professionalism. Respecting security and privacy while supporting classroom technology can be accomplished within the boundaries of virtualization. The solution was implementation of virtualization using open source software. Implementing virtualization provided students with the necessary hands-on lab experience while maintaining consistency for students regardless of the course delivery selected.

Indiana Institute of Technology, commonly known as Indiana Tech, is a private, independent college providing various associate, bachelor, master, and doctorate degree opportunities for a growing student population presently under 3,000 students. With a main campus in Fort Wayne, IN, Indiana Tech offers students several different alternatives for degree completion including a traditional day school, online courses, accelerated courses, and independent study courses. The School of Engineering and Computer Science (SECS) is forward-thinking, student-focused, and incorporates realistic hands-on opportunities for students to practice skills, expand knowledge, and extend learning beyond the classroom. Indiana Tech's (n.d.) SECS has the luxury of small class sizes affording personalized instruction with a faculty that works diligently to continue that commitment while the school grows in student population and course offerings. With a large resident population it became important to find a solution students could access from anywhere within the college campus including dorms. Virtualization provided the solution for creating student learning opportunities while keeping costs low, and providing the level of safety and security desired.

The desire to provide relevant, hands-on experience for the students in Indiana Tech's two Linux courses was the impetus for expanding the use of virtualization at the college. The Cisco and networking courses already relied heavily on virtualization. The flexibility of virtualization allowed for students in the introductory course to have ample practice and exposure without requiring that they reconfigure their personal computers. For the advanced Linux Networking course it allowed for a 'Proof of Concept' approach that challenged students and faculty to build the necessary network infrastructure to support a conceptual business and all the services and communication the business would require if it were real. Inherent tools within the virtual environment allowed for troubleshooting exercises and significant modification when presented with a scaling challenge.

The programs at each college focus on different content and outcomes and serve different populations, thus providing broader examples of the use of virtualization. What is not unique about these schools is the impetus to remain fiscally vigilant and responsible in an ever tightening economy while maintaining a quality of education that will enable students to secure gainful employment. What follows is an overview of virtualization and how success was achieved at each college. Course-specific information is included at the end of the chapter.

Open Source

Open source OSs and applications are software that has been licensed under the GNU Not UNIX (GNU) license authored by the Free Software Foundation. "The GNU General Public License is a free, copyleft license for software and other kinds of works" (General Public License (GPL),

2007, p. 1). Users of the GNU license may "copy and distribute verbatim copies of this license document, but changing it is not allowed" (GPL, 2007, p. 1). Any software author distributing software under this license agrees to adhere to the terms of the license. Generally, Open Source software is free for use and in the public domain. Often, support is available through communities, such as for many Linux OSs which have support from the Linux community. "The availability of open source and free virtualization software coupled with open source OSs and academic licensing allows this technology to be deployed at a minimal cost to the students and the institution" (Lehrfeld, 2009, p. 9). Open Source software is free and available, but not usually provided with assistance or support outside of the aforementioned communities, which can make integrating the software difficult if the teacher is not experienced with the programs. Support resources have been provided at the end of the chapter.

There are several options for virtualization software. The options range from those offered free for use with no warranty or support to fully appointed versions requiring licensing and that may provide customer support services. VirtualBox (n.d.), provided by Oracle under the GNU license, is one of many virtualization options available. Success has been achieved at OCC and Indiana Tech as described herein using this particular virtualization software. Other virtualization packages may be used; VirtualBox is specified and mentioned here simply for adherence to the methods successfully employed and for its free acquisition. For classroom use, OCC uses VMware. Additionally, several of the implementations described herein were successfully constructed and deployed using Microsoft Virtual PC to compare use and effectiveness, but Microsoft Virtual PC is not open source software.

Open Source software options for academic uses include applications, OSs, virtualization products, and online learning management systems (LMS). Linux is the primary Open Source OS used in the examples below. Specific distributions have included Ubuntu 6-11.04 Server and Client; Fedora 5–12; Helix 3; Cent OS 4-6; and FreeBSD Unix 7.4-9. The Open Source LMS used is Moodle and applications include the Open Office Suite, LibreOffice, andnumerous software development kits (SDK) (Fig. 1).

Introduction to Virtualization

To begin, a working definition of virtualization is needed to aid in understanding. Virtualization refers to anything that has been made to resemble reality. According to Simpson (2008), "[v]irtualization software works by

VirtualBox

Download VirtualBox

About

Here, you will find links to VirtualBox binaries and its source code.

Screenshots

VirtualBox binaries

Downloads

By downloading, you agree to the terms and conditions of the respective license.

Documentation

End-user docs

Technical docs

Contribute

Community

- **VirtualBox platform packages.** The binaries are released under the terms of the GPL version 2.
  - ○ **VirtualBox 4.1.8 for Windows hosts** ⇒x86/amd64
  - ○ **VirtualBox 4.1.8 for OS X hosts** ⇒x86/amd64
  - ○ **VirtualBox 4.1.8 for Linux hosts**
  - ○ **VirtualBox 4.1.8 for Solaris hosts** ⇒x86/amd64

- **VirtualBox 4.1.8 Oracle VM VirtualBox Extension Pack** ⇒All platforms
  Support for USB 2.0 devices, VirtualBox RDP and PXE boot for Intel cards. See this chapter from the User Ma
  Extension Pack binaries are released under the VirtualBox Personal Use and Evaluation License (PUEL).
  Please install the extension pack with the same version as your installed version of VirtualBox!
  If you are using VirtualBox 4.0.16, please download the extension pack ⇒here.

Fig. 1.   Virtual Box Download Screen retrieved from https://www.virtualbox.org/
wiki/Downloads.

emulating a separate hardware environment, including the hard drive, memory, network interface card (NIC), and peripheral devices ... in an existing OS environment" (p. 3). Some virtualization software is installed on a computer system and acts like an application while other virtualization packages are installed and run directly on the computer system and hardware without any middleware to facilitate the process (Luce, 2007). Basically, virtualization works by providing a contained environment that supports software programs independent of the OSs and application software programs running on and available to the host computer. Because the virtual container is running on the host computer the capabilities of the software within the virtual container is limited by the physical capabilities of the host computer (Simpson, 2008). "[Virtualization] can be used to partition physical equipment to support multiple virtual machines, interconnect them, and to share hardware resources" (Fuertes & López deVergara, 2009, p. 2). Multiple virtual containers running on a single host computer will share the capabilities of that host computer when each container is running (Simpson, 2008). The physical limits of the host computer can directly impact performance of the virtual container and any application software utilized (Simpson, 2008).

The two main categories of virtualization software are server type software and a version that is more suited for a workstation, desktop, or single user (Dobrilovic & Odadzic, 2006). "[V]irtualization is the representation (to the user) of a hardware resource (storage, memory, network) in a different format than it actually is" (Grauer, n.d., p. 1). Grauer (n.d.) further delineates the type of virtualization as to emulation/simulation, full/native virtualization, para virtualization, and OS level virtualization. This chapter focuses on virtualization from the stand point of general definitions and applications and leaves the more specific nuances and applications for later research.

Benefits of virtualization include "server consolidation; energy conservation, simpler IT resource management; less time required to back up data; and space savings" (McCrea, 2010, p. 1). In addition, the portability of individual virtual builds, access outside the class, the potential increased self-sufficiency, and the ability to implement progressive course assignments are all valid reasons to consider incorporating virtualization (McCrea, 2010). While virtualization can have a significant cost savings it does not fit every situation. Virtualization should only be attempted on computers that exceed the minimum requirements of every application planned for use at the same time within the virtual container, and for all virtual containers planned for concurrent operation within a single host. The system requirements for each virtual package vary but key areas to identify are hard drive storage space, working memory (RAM), and the speed of the central processing unit (CPU) (McCrea, 2010).

Virtualization is not a new concept having been developed in the computer hardware and OS environment in the 1960s (Dobrilovic & Odadzic, 2006) and continues to support the traditional network environment with use focused on computer hardware, networking OSs, and network administration. Business, industry, and government have been using virtualization for many years (Lehrfeld, 2009). Examples include the need to test software programs and changes in a sandbox setting prior to moving the changes to the company's production environment (Lehrfeld, 2009). "A sandbox is an isolated environment that can be used to safely run programs that might pose a threat to the operating system, other applications and for the network" (Shinder, D., 2008, p. 1). If resources do not allow for a separate sandbox environment to test the software, a company may utilize virtualization in order to adequately simulate the production environment and the impact the software changes have on it, while not actually disturbing the production environment (Shinder, D., 2008). Once satisfied with testing of the changes, the software can be moved into production. Another example is for hardware and software testing purposes. A new server may be tested through virtual emulation to ensure that the OS has been installed properly and all necessary safeguards, including patching and other hardening measures, have been employed. Upon successful penetration tests, where the virtual system passes all tests and shows no unknown vulnerabilities, the server would be made accessible to the rest of the network.

With virtualization the OS running on a computer can be different than the one the course requires as students can use a virtual build of the different OS to perform tasks while not interfering with the operation of the host computer (Shinder, D., 2008). Students and faculty should be careful to select the appropriate virtual host for the platform that is on the computer they will be using to support the virtual build and not focused on the OS that will be included in their virtual build as the native or host OS determines which package they should select to begin the building process (Lehrfeld, 2009). When used to host single-purpose applications such as cryptography concepts or to host, a small Linux distribution virtualization success has been achieved on a computer installed with an older OS such as Microsoft Windows XP SP3 without costly equipment. The more system intensive the application(s) planned for use within the virtual container, the newer and better appointed the computer system needs to be. Virtualization is not limited to a computer platform and OS, but can be used to simulate or emulate other network devices (Fuertes & López de Vergara, 2009).

As Lehrfeld noted "[virtual machines] simplify any troubleshooting problems that can arise with the students or translations issues that occur between students using different operating systems" (2009, p. 125). A feature that strongly benefits educational environments is the snapshot concept. In addition to providing the platform for hosting various applications, OSs, and hardware, most virtualization provides additional benefits with options such as presenting a "roll back" position through the use of saving versions of the platform as snapshots for possible later reference or use within the virtual system. A snapshot is a picture, or snapshot, of how the virtual system "looked" at that time and can be used as a backup, safeguard, and rewind/undo for exercises to make learning less stressful and safe. Many problems encountered while using the virtual environment can be quickly solved or eliminated if the tools are properly employed to revert to a snapshot. Problems in one virtual build do not adversely affect other the builds used by other students (Lehrfeld, 2009). Students will not need to seek assistance from technical support or the faculty, but will be empowered to solve simple problems through the use of snapshots.

Another virtualization product that may be of value in support of academic uses of virtualization is a hypervisor, a product that supports both container virtualization, described above, and full virtualization

(Xen, n.d.). A hypervisor uses Kernel Virtual Machine (KVM) virtualization of the host computer and uses virtualized hardware to support a virtual OS (Hess, 2011). KVM, OpenVZ, Xen, and Proxmox are Open Source hypervisors, and Proxmox has a commercial, for-cost, version that is offered with full support (Hess, 2011). Examples of how virtualization technology can benefit students and faculty are included within the course list. There are multiple uses for virtualization in non-computer courses which will be discussed later in a virtualized content breakdown example.

Virtualization as a Versatile Teaching Aid

There are many good resources available for instruction on incorporating virtualization into the classroom experience. The bulk of the materials identify how to build virtual labs and racks and support the various activities through specifications of hardware and software. The paucity in the literature is, once the lab specifications are understood or built, what is to be done next. The remainder of this chapter details specific ways in which virtualization can be used to create and support classroom and online learning. Specific open source tools and techniques will be provided. The tools described are open source, and when not, that change is noted. Resources for the tools are provided at the end of this chapter. This will aid in assessing if the move to virtualization is logical for your college or university, providing specific examples of activities supported through virtualization.

Virtualization provides additional benefits not yet described, including the ability to enhance and support group work, both in and outside of class; provide a platform for courses that have a flexible content structure such as capstone courses built as culminating events; and, as such, require the use of many of the tools and techniques learned through the curriculum, but as the students often proceed through the coursework at varying paces, and as college requirements change, the content available must span several college catalogues. Research and development activities can be supported through virtualization.

Some schools, such as the United States Military Academy, have been using virtualization in an on-ground only setting to support courses since 2001 (Nance, Hay, Dodge, Wrubel, Burd, & Seazzu, 2009). The Software Engineering Institute (SEI) at Carnegie Mellon University moved to a virtualized remote server model to support courses, while others including the University of Alaska Fairbanks support a local and remote lab experience through virtualization (Nance et al., 2009). Providing a remote, virtualized solution for students has additional benefits outside of the classroom including additional time for hands-on experience, platform for assigning homework similar to the concepts taught in class, and the ability for faculty and students to access the computer lab resources from outside a static lab environment, such as from the office, at home, or with a mobile device.

Schools in several states including Ohio have pilot programs providing laptop computers to students for their use in accessing course resources from home. Providing access to all of the coursework including content which can be successfully virtualized may aid in student understanding, free class time from multiple attempts at the same work to allow for exposure to additional content. In a recent study comparing traditional homework to computer aided homework assignments showed a key factor in student success was the access to assistance and access to replicate the content or experience for reinforcement of concepts (Mendicino, Razzaq, & Heffernan, 2009). Lehrfeld (2009) noted, "[p]roviding students with productive hands on lab time is vital to the learners' progress and mastery of the course material" (p. 124).

Providing a computer-supported platform for learning through the use of virtualization may have additional benefits including aiding the support of diversity through the ability to translate the content into the native language of the learner and aiding in support of students with disabilities. The U.S. Department of Education determined that in 2007 as many as 6.5 million school children suffered from learning disabilities. Those school-aged children may become the college-bound students we serve. Worthy of note are the many adult learners who were never diagnosed as having a learning disability due to lack of knowledge and testing at the time they were in primary and secondary school. Adding virtualization may not be a solution for every course but may aid in measuring of outcomes and in achieving the stated outcomes through providing an opportunity and platform for practicing the course objectives (Partnership for 21st Century Skills, 2006).

Academic Licensing

Several academic programs offer support and low-cost versions of specific applications to students if subscribed to through the school to support classroom learning. To assist faculty in identifying some of the academic options available, several academic academies are identified and noted herein. This listing is not exhaustive and the products selected for inclusion were only done so as the author has experience with these programs. The various academies and their potential offerings to students, faculty, and schools are listed by alphabetical order and do not denote or infer any ranking of the academy or its offering.

The Citrix Academic Network "The Citrix IT Academy Program allows Citrix approved higher-education institutions to deliver the latest Citrix virtualization administration courses during an academic term using Citrix academic instructors" (Citrix Academic Network, 2010, p. 1). An added benefit of academic membership is the potential for students to obtain Citrix certifications. Of benefit to faculty is the Citrix academic instructor and the relief from creating coursework in platforms the teacher may not know well. The Center for System Security and Information Assurance (CSSIA) offered a faculty Citrix XenApp, XenDesktop, XenServer Bootcamp over the summer break in 2011. The training provided was entirely hands-on and provided faculty the ability to receive instruction from seasoned trainers able to answer all questions and provide real-world examples that can be used in the classroom.

Microsoft provides access to full versions of OSs, the .Net development platform, and several applications to students through its DreamSpark academic licensing program, formerly known as the Microsoft Developer Network Academic Alliance (MSDNAA). The computer and engineering students and faculty at OCC and Indiana Tech have access to this resource. Several of the courses' implementations described below use the Microsoft OSs and the .Net development framework. Students appreciate the ability to receive full versions of the OSs that do not expire in comparison with some of the student version OSs bundled with various textbooks. The classic desktop virtualization product offered is Virtual PC. A significant limitation of Microsoft Virtual PC for the classroom use described below is the inability to host the virtualization product on any OS other than Microsoft OSs or to run virtualized OSs other than Microsoft OSs.

VMware provides a virtualization platform that can accomplish all of the things described within this chapter as using VirtualBox. VMware is an industry-recognized virtualization product and may be the platform students encounter once employed. A free trial of the desktop virtualization client is available on the VMware website. "The VMware IT Academy Program is designed to introduce students to VMware technologies and equip them with VMware technical skills to complement their chosen fields of study. VMware will provide selected academic institutions with course materials developed by VMware for this purpose" (VMWare Academy, 2012, p. 1). An added benefit of academic membership is the potential for students to obtain VMware certifications.

Content Sources

In addition to the virtualization platforms available there is also support for identifying and creating course content. There are several curriculum projects that may benefit faculty researching options for their respective classes. Virtualization may provide the necessary containment and support and these projects address the content a teacher may place within the virtual container. Many of the authors make themselves available to answer questions, offer suggestions, and brainstorm solutions with faculty.

CSSIA has spent years developing quality curriculum for use by consortium member schools. Content available includes networking concepts, many security topics, disaster recovery, forensic accounting, IP telephony, and content on how to support college recruitment activities such as Girl Camp and We Are IT! Functions. CSSIA is the contact for the Citrix Academy training mentioned in the previous section.

The Open Web Application Security Project (OWASP) built several applications with detailed exercises to teach difficult concepts. OWASP's "WebGoat is a deliberately insecure J2EE web application maintained by OWASP designed to teach web application security lessons. In each lesson, users must demonstrate their understanding of a security issue by exploiting a real vulnerability in the WebGoat application" (OWASP, n.d., p. 1). Another OWASP project is WebScarab. "WebScarab is a framework for analyzing applications that communicate using the HTTP and HTTPS protocols. It is written in Java, and is thus portable to many platforms" (OWASP, n.d., p. 1). OWASP offers many additional projects in addition to the two noted here.

The Secure WEb dEvelopment Teaching (SWEET) project "is a set of portable teaching modules for secure web development. SWEET features eight teaching modules, six project modules and a virtualized web platform that allows instructors to conduct hands-on laboratory exercises" (SWEET, 2012, p. 1). The projects mentioned above have open licensing or licensing that is similar to open licensing to allow faculty to freely incorporate the material into their courses (Fig. 2).

Specific Course Applications in Virtualization

A brief breakdown of how virtualization is or can be incorporated into each course at OCC and Indiana Tech is provided here. Basic computer courses that train students to use various OSs and networking techniques

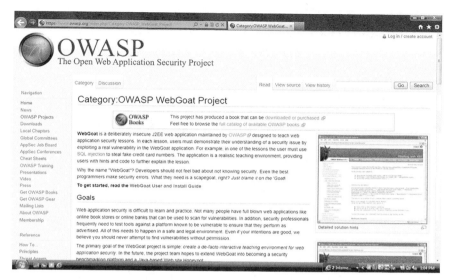

Fig. 2. OWASP WebGoat Project Page retrieved from https://www.owasp.org/
index.php/Category:OWASP_WebGoat_Project.

are a logic use of virtualization. Inclusion of virtualization in application and other courses may not be as apparent as in networking type courses, but should not be discounted as a viable platform for presenting content and applications and in making the content portable for the students to continue working and learning.

At OCC, the use of virtualization in courses covering computer hardware, network hardware, and various OSs is a natural application of virtualization. A standard feature of several Information System Technology degrees at OCC is a foundation in CompTIA A+ concepts. IST133 (*Troubleshooting Apps and Hardware*) and IST225 (*Operating Systems*) provide the introduction concepts for students using hands-on exercises incorporating virtualization for basic troubleshooting and OS use. Building on the basic foundation, IST125 (*Network Technologies*) expands the concepts from standalone computer hardware and OSs to the idea of networked hardware and network OSs. The Microsoft OSs are not free. OCC subscribed to the MSDNAA, now DreamSpark. This affords students the opportunity to install the Microsoft OSs within the virtual builds for class use using the specific license assigned to the student via the product code in the student's Microsoft DreamSpark account and use the fully featured product (Microsoft DreamSpark, n.d.). The students work with virtual builds of several OSs including Microsoft DOS to introduce them to the Command Line Interface (CLI), Microsoft Vista, Microsoft 7, a Linux desktop distribution (usually Ubuntu) and the Linux Graphical User Interfaces (GUI) of Gnome and KDE, the MAC OS X, and identification of other platforms including the Mainframe, AS400's OS400, the iSeries, and Unix OSs, without using them specifically. At this time the later OSs mentioned have not been virtualized (except Unix) to be usable in class.

IST241 (*Linux Essentials*) is one of the most logical uses of virtualization as most Linux distributions are free and open source and when paired with VirtualBox, provide the student with the ability to practice and experiment with the Linux OSs in both GUI and CLI modes. Specific use includes the ability to construct a Virtual Private Network (VPN) through virtualization. VPNs require more hardware and resources as each piece of equipment within the network is virtualized. Benefits include the ability to quickly reset problems, stage troubleshooting scenarios for students to complete, allow for practice certification exams using the virtualized hardware (Fig. 3).

The Indiana Tech courses that rely heavily on virtualization include CS1500 (*Server Operating Systems*) and NET2500 (*Linux Networking*). The

Fig. 3.   VirtualBox Hosting Linux.

students in CS1500 are introduced to Linux and the Microsoft Server environments, relying heavily on command line and scripting. Shell scripting is a form of programming that relies on the pre-built commands and functions within the platform to allow the user to specify and configure operations to accomplish specific tasks. The OS distributions and versions change so the content must be flexible enough to change as the platforms do. The more hands-on activities, the more satisfied students are with the course. For the Microsoft Server OS the students use their DreamSpark license to allow for installation in the virtual environment.

A new concept spring semester 2012 for the NET2500 course is the selection of a business or industry by the students. Then, the students will develop a plan, with faculty guidance, to develop every part of a Linux network to support the business activities of the selected industry. This includes developing a naming convention, IP addressing plan, determining which business activities to support (email, file server, DNS, web host, IDS, etc.), which application or protocol to use in support of the previous (Samba, Apache, Snort, various email packages), how to divide the activities among the least number of servers, and provide a detailed topology of the network. All applications and services use Open Source products and the students' research and identify the best option for their planned network.

Excitement for the concept and freedom of the course has exceeded expectations. The students are enthusiastic and freely contribute their ideas. When a decision is needed, each factor is presented to the students by students who have completed the research and identified a solution. The benefit beyond computer concepts is the heavy reliance on developing the students' research abilities, and soft skills through the need for constant research and communication inside and outside of class.

Three courses at OCC guide the student through the Administration of Microsoft Server 2008: IST240 (*Microsoft Net Admin I*), IST242 (*Microsoft Net Admin II*), and IST243 (*Microsoft Net Admin III*). Once the courses are completed, the student may delete the virtual build and install the full, licensed version of the Microsoft OS as native to a computer. Using virtualization with the Microsoft DreamSpark also eliminates the issues associated with 90-day and 180-day use versions of the OSs including the need to reinstall the OS midway through the course, thus eliminating the previous work of the student when the OS is reinstalled.

Many courses at Indiana Tech incorporate virtualization into the support of exercises including the Cisco curriculum courses, the Microsoft Server courses, and the Linux OS courses mentioned above. Specific networking and OS courses included in the various concentrations and in the networking degree are listed in the appendix.

Most schools offer courses in programming and web development. Both types of courses are treated the same for demonstration purposes. Programming and web development courses can benefit through the use of virtualization to prevent security issues, allow for secure coding, minimizing the possibility of program creep when testing student programs, and safeguard production systems and programs by providing a virtual sandbox for testing (Shinder, 2008). The courses focused on fully functional programming languages and concepts are listed in the appendix. The benefit of using a virtual container such as VirtualBox in courses for programming and web development is the isolation of executable code from the production computer. For teachers, the ability to correct assignments in a safe, isolated environment provides protection from any error, intentional malware inclusion, or accidental file compromise. Some languages have multiple development platforms available to users, such as Java which can use the Java Development Kit (JDK), NetBeans, Java BlackBerry Development Kit (BlackBerry JDE), JCreator, among others, and potentially causes issues in grading and testing of student work when the same platform is not installed on the faculty system. Through the use of virtual builds, the faculty can have all development environments accessible on their computer at the same time without harm or conflict to the code or the computer system. The wide variety of programming and web development courses at Indiana Tech that could and do benefit from virtualization are listed in the appendix.

The uses for virtualization in basic application courses includes hosting various applications including Microsoft Office and industry standard accounting software packages. This preserves the host system including any version of the application currently installed. If the student has an older version of QuickBooks installed on a personal computer, and then must take a course using a newer version of the application, the course-required version could be installed on a virtual platform within the software so as not to interfere with the installed versions of the application. Several courses were proposed for virtualization and for using open source tools. There are Open Source options available for the current Microsoft Office courses including the use of Apache Open Office Suite (Apache Open Office, n.d.) or LibreOffice Suite (LibreOffice, n.d.). A solution incorporating either Open Source product would provide a platform-free, license-free solution to application courses. Referencing the dangers of programming noted above, it is important to remember that the Microsoft Applications mentioned herein have the built-in ability to create macros with Visual Basic for Applications (VBA), and therefore hold the potential to unleash harm upon launching or opening student work submissions.

A popular use for virtualization includes courses in Security & Information Assurance (IA) concepts. To maintain a secure environment and manage student hands-on experiences in an ethical manner, virtualization can be used to limit application creep and the consequences of using various tools. There are many resources for teaching these concepts, and when installed in a virtualized environment, the student can practice concepts without fear of unleashing the tools on the school's computer network, a personal computer system, and the Internet. Resources for these courses include virus simulators, penetration testing tools, and hacking tools. This allows for teachers to demonstrate and provide hands-on opportunities for proof of concept activities while not compromising the school's network.

The course introducing students to cryptography, steganography, and hashing from concept to creation, IST266 (*Web Security/Secure Transactions*), provides a wonderful opportunity to utilize virtualization. Managing session keys, developing hashing schemes, and creating cryptography schemes requires an element of coding and working with the computer and processes outside of typical application use. By building the system in a virtual environment the computer environment of the host system is protected and removed from the immediate interactions with the code the user develops.

IST281 (*Cyber Crime and Info Security*) covers the complex area of legal compliance. Students have the ability to mimic real-world situations including E-Discovery demands. The virtual environment provides access to the test environment so that document retrieval, database copies, and log management do not interfere with the production environment and do not alter the actual logs on the computer system.

Three courses delve into the tools, techniques, and concepts used for securing networks, determining network hardening levels, penetration testing, and use of various hacking tools to identify system vulnerabilities: IST282 (*Network Security*), IST283 (*Advanced Network Security*), and IST284 (*Internet Security Administration*). Performance of even basic network communication tests, such as PINGing a specific host, can have negative consequences to network speed. Creating a virtual system or network allows for the use of the tools and techniques without affecting other network users. Some of the specific tools used include NetStumbler, Nessus, BackTrack, Metasploit, and various virus simulators.

The snap shot tool in most virtualization products provide great benefit to courses in Design, Project Management, and Capstone Courses. The ability for students to interact and brainstorm using a common platform, even if that platform is not native to the users' computer, simplifies sharing and collaboration. The freedom to create projects spanning multiple disciplines, applications, and OS, makes this type of course a wonderful candidate for virtualization.

IST111 (*Introduction to E-Business*) uses a virtual network build to allow for work with existing encryption schemes, unlike IST266 which develops a scheme, so that the encryption keys and management of the keys do not interfere with any keys used on the actual computer. The creation of a Certificate Authority (CA) is also simplified when completed within a virtual environment instead of on the production system. IST230 (*Systems Analysis and Design*) utilizes a mimic technique whereby students are paired with a character in a video scenario and as the character is assigned work and required to make presentations to the department, so is the student, and presentations are made to the class.

The technologically sensitive security courses at Indiana Tech that could benefit from virtualization include IS 3100 (*Information Security*), IS 4600 (*Disaster Recovery*), and NET 3300 (*Network Security*). While IS 3200 (*Computer Forensics*) could benefit by providing the students with their own virtual build, the Forensic Recovery Evidence Device (FRED) used it, the course does offer students an excellent hands-on experience.

Teaching students how to knowledgeably and tactfully provide information technology (IT) support to internal or external customers is the purpose of IST268 (*Web-Based Tech Support*). Using various applications and tools to gain remote access to a customer's computer, with permission, of course, the student is expected to identify, diagnose, and correct a variety of common computer issues. The IT concepts progress to difficult troubleshooting scenarios that require the student to make configuration changes to the customer's computer system. Simulation of these activities is difficult. Providing the student with virtual environments allows for effective practice and exposure to the concepts without the potential harm if the student makes a mistake while working through the hands-on exercises.

Additional courses that can use virtualization to provide a hands-on element to the course include IST289 (*Project Management*), IST293 (*Cooperative Work Experience*), and the Capstone Course (not yet numbered) allow the faculty to expand the hands-on experiences and exercises beyond the learned applications and techniques from other courses, to try and apply new techniques and innovations. When working with anything new that may inadvertently alter or compromise the student's computer, the encapsulation of a virtual environment is welcomed.

Virtualization Beyond the Classroom

Virtualization opportunities beyond course content include collaboration and competition, providing valuable skills and learning opportunities to aid in students securing jobs and support of the lifelong learning concept. To compete with the loss of research and design jobs going overseas, employers today desire employees with hands-on experience and an understanding of concepts beyond simple term memorization (Atkinson & Wial, 2008). "It has been suggested in the literature (Chu, 1999; Leitner and Cane, 2005) that simply attending class will not provide enough practice for mastery of a given material" (Lehrfeld, 2009, p. 125). The concept in training and education of developing information workers who can adapt skills to meet challenges requires a teaching methodology that trains students in flexibility, resourcefulness, and experience (Partnership for 21st Century Skills, 2006).

There are several projects focused on building sharable labs to support virtualized instruction at geographically diverse institutions. Several of these projects have National Science Foundation (NSF) funding. These labs include the United States Military Academy, the University of New Mexico, Carnegie Mellon University, and the University of Alaska, Fairbanks (Nance et al., 2009). Other labs include the Alliance for Secure Computing Education (ASCENT) which is composed of the University of North Texas (UNT), the University of Texas at Arlington (UTA), and the University of North Carolina at Greensboro (UNCG) (Ho, Mallesh, & Wright, 2009). The CSSIA constructed a virtual laboratory, known as the CSSIA Virtualized Data Center (CVD) as a NSF-funded Advanced Technological Center (ATE) for class use and hosts the Midwest Collegiate Cyber Defense Competition (CCDC) at the state and regional levels each year (CSSIA, n.d.; CSSIA ATE Centers, n.d.).

A use of virtual labs beyond the traditional classroom in Capture the Flag competitions (Nance et al., 2009). The Collegiate Cyber Defense Competition (CCDC) sponsored in the Midwest by the CSSIA has used virtualization to support the competition for the last three years. The use of virtualization greatly reduces expenses, travel, and logistics problems. The past three years CCDC has been hosted via the CSSIA virtual lab, including the interaction with a Red Team from industry that seeks to find and use vulnerabilities intentionally left in the virtual systems against the teams competing (CSSIA ATE Centers, n.d.). The simulated competitions provide students with exposure to content and topics not available in a traditional classroom. Exposure to skilled experts on the Red Team in the CCDC competition offers a challenge beyond the exercises developed by the instructor and provides a complicated situational environment where student teams must maintain many dissimilar OSs and applications within one network in support of internal and external customers.

In 2010, CSSIA provided a virtual network for the CCDC competition with participating student teams traveling to a designated host school within the competing state(s). For the 2011 and 2012 CCDC competitions, the competitions were fully deployed using remote virtualization and saving transportation costs, hotel costs, and inconvenience, potentially opening the competition to any school with an Internet connection and eight well-equipped PCs to host the virtual station. Virtualization has broadened opportunities when used in situations such as those described herein. In 2011, the OCC team participated from the SSIA lab on the OCC campus in supervision of industry partners located on site and with a Skype connection to the competition judges.

The 2012 Indiana CCDC, held Saturday, February 18, at Ivy Tech Community College in Fort Wayne, Indiana brought together students from five schools: three four-year colleges, and two of the many locations of Ivy Tech Community College. The networks the student teams of up to eight participants were responsible for maintaining consisted of various OSs and applications. Points are awarded based on maintaining connectivity to the network, securing each system, completing assignments referred to as "Business Injects," and warding off attacks from a remote "Red Team" as they attempt to attack and take control of each schools' systems. The benefit to students in showing them what to expect in the workplace is unparalleled. Stressed within the day of activities is the need for teamwork, professionalism, and recognizing issues within each network.

Honeypots, or honeynets, are networks or computers that simulate a real production system and pose as a target for hackers and exploits on the Internet (Project Honeypot, n.d.). Researchers can learn about potential attacks and vulnerabilities through the data collected from a honeypot including log files, traffic analysis, and packet analysis. The information learned may aid in securing computers and networks from similar attacks in the future. Shinder (2008) contends that virtualization can be used to build and support a honeypot to lure attackers at a much lower cost.

Determining potentially dangerous attack behaviors and vulnerabilities before they are launched or exploited offers the ability to become more proactive in teaching and industry and less reactive.

Several of the colleges and institutions mentioned herein noted plans for future remote access to virtualization resources (Nance et al., 2009; OCC, n.d.; Indiana Tech, n.d.). Such plans are in discussion at OCC. Remote access for students is already possible through Indiana Tech andCSSIA. If an entire virtualized lab environment is not needed, a single virtualized host installation may be a viable solution.

Problem Areas

Virtualization is not without potential drawbacks. Issues involved with virtualization deployment include a need to train students in how to use the virtual equipment and environment. Depending on the host system and virtualized host used, the use of the three keys [ctrl] + [alt] + [del] may not have the desired effect depending on which virtual host is used. Likewise, the action of leaving the virtual interface with the mouse or keyboard, or attempting to leave the virtual host may prove problematic as there are different ways to leave the virtual machine and for activating the mouse in applications outside the virtual host. Suspending the virtual build or shutting the virtual host software or the host computer down may also cause problems if not properly demonstrated and understood. Last semester, after several iterations of in class instructions on accessing the virtual machine through VSphere, and the navigation and use of the machine, the students encountered several problems. The initial use in the Linux courses at Indiana Tech had students in one class sharing the virtual server within the class. Students were expected to use Secure SHell (SSH) and not access the system from the desktop. When one student suspended or shut down the virtual build accessed from the desktop, it kicked the other students off and made the server unavailable until reset. Teaching faculty and students to use SSH or PuTTY, a Telnet and SSH client, adds complexity and an added layer of necessary knowledge to access content.

Opportunities exist outside geographic boundaries to include a very diverse population for enhanced learning and to move ideas beyond the course material (Ternus, Palmer, & Faulk, 2007).If the student is remote the difficulty in instructing students may be more difficult given the potential number of host OSs the students may employ (Ho et al., 2009). Although time-consuming, the creation and maintenance of instructions is essential to provide the information necessary for the student to use the content beyond the end of a course for further practice and troubleshooting.

Cooperative agreements between schools and institutions may require fees, the creation of labs exercises, or equipment monitoring and support. If no faculty or staff member has the expertise, the integrity of the system may be compromised, leaving faculty and students without a working system. Traditional technical support issues become more complicated with the array of possible OS and platform host machines. It may be simple to state that the issue is with the host system, but such decisions may leave students without assistance in completing the tasks assigned.

Information technology implementations always have a maintenance cost associated with the project. Several of the shared lab settings mentioned above were supported in part by NSF grants. If future funding is not continued the longevity of such projects may be cut short, again leaving students and faculty without a viable option for hands-on lab experiences. Control of the labs and the decisions for upgrading and maintenance may cause conflicts among partner schools.

As partnerships or consortium grow, if resources do not scale in complement, the new school may not have the benefit of equal use of the existing system resources. Likewise, established partners may not be able to continue with their system usage at a level they have become accustomed to. Determining who makes and keeps the schedule and how each school is accommodated in access to the system may cause conflict within the partnership. Scheduling time for classes and student practice on a shared system may also be problematic. Participants in the CCDC affords student teams the ability to practice on a test build of the planned network configuration for the competition. The scheduling is on a first-come, first-served basis and when teams are not organized or prepared to request time within the system they are not afforded the time desired.

Ethical considerations in teaching some topics, including computer security, can benefit from uniting contact on defensive practices and behaviors with attack sequences to show the benefit of proper care and due diligence and to deemphasize the thrill of attack scenarios (Ho et al., 2009, Livermore, 2007). Suggested for security courses, but applicable to all courses, is the concept of having students sign a lab agreement (Ho et al., 2009) or an applicable code of ethics for the degree discipline. Most industries have standards of conduct or codes of ethics. Making students aware of the applicable standards and using those within the classroom prepares students for the workplace in those disciplines.

Shinder (2008) warns of the danger of sharing content between virtual OSs and with hard disks as it could invalidate the separation and isolation of the OSs and become exploitable. Extreme care and due diligence when constructing the lab or server host, implementation deployment, and instruction of the students are essential to a successful lab experience. Maintaining current knowledge of advances within the area of virtualization, maintaining patches and updates, and security implementations around the virtual system are essential to a secure lab environment.

Feedback from students has been very encouraging. At OCC and Indiana Tech, students are appreciative of the opportunity and eager to apply more concepts to a virtual lab experience but do notice a need for concise instruction for using the new technology. Witnessed at Indiana Tech, for example, is the need to retrain students each term on the naming and addressing scheme used within the virtual server and on the steps to access the system, both from class and remotely. A survey of faculty and students, resulting in 50 participants, was noted by Fuertes et al. (2009) and included positive feedback, but some areas for improvement. Among the areas noted, the drain on computer resources and the slowness of the virtualized system were significant problems for students and faculty. Additionally, many observed that the need for, or current lack thereof, for technical support was a problem that had not been addressed.

Martin and Klein (2008) acknowledge the need for constant reevaluation of a course by the designer and faculty to ensure applicability. Essentially, a course should never be considered completely developed, but is, instead, a work in progress. Virtualization does not eliminate the need for review and maintenance of a course.

A consequence of application use is the licensing requirement of each application. For most license agreements, installation in a virtual build will constitute installation for licensing purposes, so usage of virtualization in this manner preserves the installation of the host computer, but may require additional expense to manage licenses.

CONCLUSION

Virtualization is a low-cost solution for many educational applications, not a panacea for all schools, but rather an effective means of providing quality hands-on experience to students so that they may practice and master skills. When supported through a host of servers and appropriate network bandwidth, entire virtualized networks can be available to the student. Access to such complex and relevant teaching tools paired with quality instruction and examples exposes students to the most realistic business settings and situations possible. Troubleshooting techniques can be practiced which before virtualization could only be discussed. As wonderful and flexible as virtualization is for many educational situations, it is not without problems or issues. In addition to the course content knowledge the faculty and student must know, there is the additional element of understanding the virtual environment. Troubleshooting problems is more complex given the layers of OSs and applications, and it may be difficult to impossible to provide appropriate tech support with the variety of platforms and application combinations the students and faculty can use.

Building the server or laboratory infrastructure is only part of the foundational requirements for teaching content using the virtualized platform. Designing, testing, and implementing the content takes time and effort that is not normally expected for classroom preparation and usually falls to the faculty member to create. Fortunately, faculty at a variety of institutions and organizations have created content to support the use of virtualization and are willing to share their knowledge and assist in helping faculty decide if a virtual solution is the correct one for their students and courses. To begin, schools may subscribe to several existing virtualized networks to sample the possibilities without the expense of creating such a network for their school. The web addresses for the virtualization projects mentioned in this chapter are located in the references section.

Classroom and course use does not require a school to build an entire network infrastructure to support the lab activities. Much of the course use described above can be accomplished with a virtual host loaded with the application or OS to be used and launched from the student's desktop, a USB drive, or external hard drive plugged into the student's computer. Providing a low-cost solution that supports in-class and homework activities and allows the student as much time on task as the student desires may lead to an increase in student learning, comprehension, and satisfaction within the courses.

ACKNOWLEDGMENTS

The author would like to recognize the work of several individuals who provided insight, effort, and specific knowledge on how to construct the virtual environments described in this chapter: Colonel Ronald Dodge, U. S. Military Academy, for your expertise in defining the specifications for the System Security & Information Assurance lab classroom during the 2008 CISSE; Erich Spengler, Director of CSSIA, for all of your support, insight, and wisdom on what to do and how to best support the students and the curriculum; Professor Julie Mansfield and Associate Dean Gary Messick, Indiana Tech, for letting me teach the CS1500 and NET2500 courses and to experiment with the "Proof of Concept" approach – I believe it is a hit!; to my students for humoring me as I tried new things that did not always work as planned; and finally, Nathan Whetstone, Networking Lab Supervisor, for his support of the Indiana Tech virtual servers and continued good natured support of the students.

REFERENCES

Apache Open Office. (n.d.). *The free and open productivity suite.* Retrieved from http://www. openoffice.org/product/index.html. Acessed on February 2, 2012.

Atkinson, R., & Wial, H. (2008, September 21). *Creating a national innovation foundation. Issues in Science and Technology.* Dallas, TX: University of Texas at Dallas.

Chang, S. H., & Smith, R. A. (2008, Summer). Effectiveness of personal interaction in a learner-centered paradigm distance education class based on student satisfaction. *Journal of Research on Technology in Education, 40*(4), 407–426.

Chu, K. C. (1999). What are the benefits of a virtual laboratory for student learning? HERD-SA annual international conference. Melbourne.

Citrix Academic Network. (2010). *Building desktop transformation expertise.* Retrieved from http://www.citrixtraining.com/campaigns/cpn/1/ilfp2e/. Accessed on January 11, 2012.

CSSIA. (n.d.). Retrieved from http://www.cssia.org/. Accessed on January 11, 2012.

CSSIA ATE Centers. (n.d.). Retrieved from http://atecenters.org/cssia/. Accessed on January 11, 2012.

DeWitz, S. J., Woolsey, M. L., & Walsh, W. B. (2009). College student retention: An exploration of the relationship between self-efficacy beliefs and purpose in life among college students. *Journal of College Student Development, 50*(1), 19–34.

Dobrilovic, D., & Odadzic, B. (2006). Virtualization technology as a tool for teaching computer networks. *World Academy of Science, Engineering & Technology, 13*, 126–127.

Dooley, K. E. (2005). *Advanced methods in distance education: Applications and practices for educators, administrators and learners.* Hershey, PA: Information Science Publishing.

Fuertes, W., & López de Vergara, J. E. (2009). An emulation of VoD services using virtual network environments, Workshops der Wissenschaftlichen Konferenz Kommunikation in Verteilten Systemen 2009.

Fuertes, W., López de Vergara, J. E., & Meneses, F. (2009). Educational platform using virtualization technologies: Teaching-learning applications and research uses cases, In *Proceedings of II ACE seminar: Knowledge construction in online collaborative communities.* Albuquerque, NM, USA.

General Public License. (2007). *Free Software Foundation*. Retrieved from http://www.gnu. org/copyleft/gpl.html

Grauer, Z. (n.d.). *Using virtualization*. Peer1 Hosting. Retrieved from http://www.peer1.com/ resources/questions/63/_print. Accessed on December 11, 2011.

Hess, K. (2011). *Proxmox: The ultimate hypervisor*. ZDNet. Retrieved from http://www.zdnet. com/blog/virtualization/proxmox-the-ultimate-hypervisor/3482. Accessed on April 2, 2012.

Ho, J., Mallesh, N., & Wright, M. (2009). The design and lessons of the ASCNT security teaching lab. In *Proceedings of the colloquium for information system security education (CISSE)*.

Indiana Commission for Higher Education. (2008). *Reaching higher strategic initiatives for education in Indiana*. Retrieved from http://www.in.gov/che/files/2012_RHAM_8_23_12.pdf

Indiana Tech. (n.d.). *About us*. Retrieved from http://www.indianatech.edu/Pages/Default. aspx. Accessed on February 8, 2012.

Lehrfeld, M. (2009). Using virtualization to aid student learning in traditional, hybrid, and online courses. In *2009 ASCUE proceedings*. Available online http://www.ascue.org/ files/proceedings/2009/p124.pdf

Leitner, L. J., & Cane, J. W. (2005). A virtual laboratory environment for online IT education. *Proceedings of the 6th conference on information technology education*, ACM, Newark, NJ, USA.

LibreOffice. (n.d.). Retrieved from http://www.libreoffice.org/features/. Accessed on February 9, 2012.

Livermore, J. (2007). What are faculty attitudes toward ethical hacking and penetration testing? In *Proceedings of colloquia for information systems security education (CISSE)*.

Luce, T. (2007). Virtualization in the classroom. *Issues in Information Systems, 3*(1), 174–178.

Martin, F., & Klein, J. (2008). Effects of objectives, practice, and review in multimedia instruction. *Journal of Educational Multimedia and Hypermedia, 17*(2), 171–189.

McCrea, B. (2010). The lowdown on virtualization. Journal. Retrieved from http://thejournal. com/articles/2010/04/22/the-lowdown-on-virtualization.aspx. Accessed on January 12, 2012.

Mendicino, M., Razzaq, L., & Heffernan, N. T. (2009). A comparison of traditional homework to computer-supported homework. *Journal of Research on Technology in Education, 41*(3), 331–359.

Microsoft DreamSpark. (n.d.). *DreamSpark for academic institutions*. Retrieved from https:// www.dreamspark.com/. Accessed on February 2, 2012.

Nance, K., Hay, B., Dodge, R., Wrubel, J., Burd, S., & Seazzu, A. (2009). Replicating and sharing computer security laboratory environments. In *Proceedings of the 42nd Hawaii international conference on system sciences*.

Open Web Application Security Project (OWASP). (n.d.). *OWASP Projects*. Retrieved from https://www.owasp.org/index.php/Category:OWASP_WebGoat_Project. Accessed on February 2, 2012.

Owens Community College (OCC). (n.d.). *About Owens*. Retrieved from http://www.owens. edu. Accessed on February 9, 2012.

Padman, V., & Memon, N. (2002). Design a virtual lab for information assurance education and research. In *Proceedings of 2002 IEEE workshop on information assurance and security*. United States Military Academy, West Point, NY, June 17–19, 2002.

Partnership for 21st Century Skills. (2006). *Results that matter: 21st century skills and high school reform.* Retrieved from http://www.p21.org/storage/documents/RTM2006.pdf. Accessed on January 6, 2012.

Pheils, D. M. (2010). *Remodeling: Building on the strengths of existing course development models to present a student centered model for online learning for community colleges.* Capella University. Retrieved from ERIC database (ED523529).

Project Honeypot. (n.d.). Retrieved from http://www.projecthoneypot.org/. Accessed on February 16, 2012.

Shinder, D. (2008). *Security through virtualization.* WindowsSecurity.com. Retrieved from http://www.windowsecurity.com/articles/security-through-virtualization.html. Accessed on December 11, 2011.

Simpson, T. (2008). *Virtual machines companion.* Boston, MA: Thomson Course Technology.

SWEET. (2012). *Secure web development teaching modules.* Retrieved from http://csis.pace.edu/~lchen/sweet/. Accessed on January 27, 2012.

Ternus, M. P., Palmer, K. L., & Faulk, D. R. (2007). Benchmarking quality in online teaching and learning: A rubric for course construction and evaluation. *Journal of Effective Teaching, 7*(2), 51–67.

U.S. Department of Education. (2007). Affordability, accessibility, and accountability in higher education. In *Proceedings of the community college virtual summit.* Retrieved from http://www.ed.gov/about/offices/list/ovae/pi/cclo/ccvirtualsummitsummary.pdf

VirtualBox. (n.d.). *Welcome to VirtualBox.org!* Retrieved from https://www.virtualbox.org/wiki/VirtualBox. Accessed on December 30, 2012.

VMware Academy. (2012). *VMware IT academy program.* Retrieved from http://www.vmware.com/partners/programs/vap/academy-program-participants.html. Accessed on January 4, 2012.

Xen. (n.d.). *What is Xen?* Retrieved from http://xen.org/products/xenhyp.html. Accessed on April 1, 2012.

APPENDIX A. SPECIFIC COURSE LISTINGS

Specific networking and OS courses included in the various concentrations and in the networking degree include CS 1200 (*Introduction to Computer Science*); CS 1500 (*Introduction to Server Systems*); CS 3200 (*Operating Systems*); IS 1150 (*Principles of Information Systems*); MIS 1500 (*Computer Systems and Hardware*); MIS 2100 (*Networking and Infrastructure*); MIS 2150 (*Component Analysis and Design*); NET 1200 (*Network Design I*); NET 1250 (*Network Design II*); NET 2000 (*Windows Networking*); NET 2500 (*Linux Networking*); NET 3200 (*Wireless and Mobile Communication*); NET 3400 (*Directed Studies in Networking*); NET 4000 (*Networking Seminar*); NET 4100 (*Network Design and Administration*); NET 4200 (*Advanced Server Systems*); NET 4300 (*Voice and Video Systems*); and NET4900 (*Networking Project/Internship*).

The courses focused on fully functional programming languages and concepts include IST112 (*Introduction to Computer Programming*), IST135 (*Introduction to VB.Net*), IST140 (*Advanced VB.Net*), IST260 (*Introduction to C#*), IST261 (*Advanced C#*), IST265 (*Introduction to Java*), and IST269 (*Advanced Java Programming*). The web development courses that focus on code and website development include IST126 (*Introduction to X/ HTML*), IST128 (*Introduction to XML*), IST228 (*Web Imaging*), and IST267 (*Web Development Tools*).

The variety of application and special purpose courses that could potentially benefit from virtualization, and in some cases, the use of open source applications include CS 1600 (*Project Management Seminar*), CS 2100 (*Introduction to Computer Systems*), CS 2500 (*Database Systems*), IS 2200 (*Developing Business Solutions*), MIS 1300 (*Software Tools*), MIS 3100 (*Database Management*), MIS 3150 (*Database Application Development*), MIS 4000 (*Enterprise Resource Planning*), MIS 4200 (*Systems Analysis and Design*), and MIS 4400 (*MIS Project Management*).

The courses proposed for virtualization include IST131 (*Computer Concepts and Apps*) covering the Microsoft Office Suite, IST235 (*Spreadsheet Applications*) detailing advanced Microsoft Excel functionality, IST236 (*Database Applications*) detailing advanced Microsoft Access, IST238 (*Peachtree Accounting*), and IST239 (*QuickBooks Accounting*).

USE OF OPEN SOURCE SOFTWARE AND VIRTUALIZATION IN ACADEMIA TO ENHANCE HIGHER EDUCATION EVERYWHERE

Maurice Eugene Dawson Jr. and Imad Al Saeed

ABSTRACT

As costs around the world continue to rise for education, institutions must become innovative in the ways they teach and grow students. To do this effectively, professors and administrative staff should push toward the utilization of Open Source Software (OSS) and virtual tools to enhance or supplement currently available tools. In developing countries, OSS applications would allow students the ability to learn critical technological skills for success at small fraction of the cost. OSS also provides faculty members the ability to dissect source code and prepare students for low-level software development. It is critical that all institutions look at alternatives in providing training and delivering educational material regardless of limitations going forward as the world continues to be more global due to the increased use of technologies everywhere. Doing this could provide a means of shortening the education gap in many countries. Through reviewing the available technology, possible

Increasing Student Engagement and Retention using Immersive Interfaces: Virtual Worlds, Gaming, and Simulation
Cutting-edge Technologies in Higher Education, Volume 6C, 283–313
Copyright © 2012 by Emerald Group Publishing Limited
ISSN: 2044-9968/doi:10.1108/S2044-9968(2012)000006C013

implementations of these technologies, and the application of these items in graduate coursework could provide a starting point in integrating these tools into academia. When administrators or faculty debate the possibilities of OSS, gaming, and simulation tools, this applied research provides a guide for changing the ability to develop students that will be competitive on a global level.

INTRODUCTION

This book chapter will cover the utilization of virtualization, Open Source Software (OSS), and simulation tools that are also OSS. OSS can be defined as software that is made available in source code form. This is important as this source code may fall under the General Public License (GPL) which is a widely used free software license that is managed under the GNU Not Linux (GNU) Project (GNU, 2007). Virtualization is important as this is an effective method to reproduce system learning environments as a virtual instance reducing the overall hardware footprint and need to for a massive lab. This chapter will also cover two simulation tools to include correlating published research on how these items were integrated into graduate systems engineering coursework.

VIRTUALIZATION

In terms of virtualization, there are available tools to create a virtual version of a system. In terms of educational resources this provides a method for institutions to train on virtual machines (VMs). This allows a university to teach students complex techniques to computer science, engineering, or information technology (IT) such as networking, programming, system administration, and Information Assurance (IA). There are multiple types of virtualization such as hardware, desktop, memory, storage, data, and network. In Fig. 1 displayed is a screenshot of Ubuntu 11.10 running in a VM on the Windows 7 desktop.

For institutions that would like the opportunity to provide a cloud-like environment, tools such as Oracle Virtual Box and Vmware Player provide that ability. However, it should be noted that new Linux distributions running that require GNOME 3 will have issues running on older hardware. With older hardware as a constrain, there are bare minimal Linux

Fig. 1.   Screenshot of Ubuntu VMware VM Running on Windows 7 Desktop.

distributions such as Puppy Linux and Damn Small Linux (DSL). VMs provide the ability for a student to experiment with hundreds of Operating Systems (OSs) without installing uninstalling the base OS.

Additionally, this allows for the creation of baseline OS images for classes. For example, a marketing course would have an OS created with all the software, case studies, etc. preloaded. This baseline OS for marketing would have statistics software, graphic design software, social marketing tools, case studies, eBooks, links to online course management tool, etc. This would allow an institution to have image ready for every class to ensure consistency, and that the students have all required tools needed. In the case for a more technical course such as software engineering, the students would have a baseline OS image with all the programming software, the integrated development environment (IDE), quality testing tools, etc. preloaded.

For professors, this virtualized environment would allow for the monitoring, distribution, and quicker deployment of available tools. This environment would be a cloud computing solution. Cloud computing is based on concepts of virtualization, distributed computing, and networking and is underpinned in the latest web and software technologies (Vouk, 2008). A useful definition of cloud computing is that it is a way of delivering applications as services over the Internet as well as a way of providing for the hardware and system software that act as platforms for these applications and services (Armbrust et al., 2009). Cloud is also used to refer to a network of computers that are linked together and distribute processing capacity and applications to different systems (Johnson, Levine, & Smith, 2009). Cloud computing lets organizations add on to their IT and computing capacity without having to invest in new architecture, software, or hardware or in training and developing personnel (Glotzbach, Mordkovich, & Radwan, 2008). A cloud environment could prove to be a cost-effective implementation of which would allow for scalability if these right tools are utilized.

ADDING AND EXPANDING CAPABILITIES WITH LINUX

In terms of virtualization, the most cost-effective method is with the use of Linux as the OS. As institutions around the world look to provide their students and faculty with the ability to work in highly technical or large demand fields, it is imperative that all institutions have the ability to provide a simulated environment to teach the necessary concepts such as program management, design, and engineering. However, to do this at a fraction of the cost, Linux and other OSS are vital for implementation.

Why We Need to Consider Linux Essential in Higher Education

Linux is a Unix like OS that is built on the Linux kernel developed by Linus Torvalds with thousands of software engineers. As of 2012, there are over 200 active Linux distributions. The majority of the kernel and associated packages are free and OSS. This type of software provides a license that allows users the right to use, copy, study, change, and improve the software as the source code is made available. Providing source code allows developers or engineers to understand the inner workings of development. Imagine being able to study Mac or Windows by viewing all the source code to replicate similar developments. This exercise would be great for a developer to learn low-level coding techniques, design, integration, and implementation.

In terms of associated cost the majority of Linux distributions are free. However, some distributions require a cost for updates or assistance that related to specific needs such as OS modifications for server hosting. In software, there is a packet management system that automates the process of installing, configuring, upgrading, and removing software packages from an OS. In the Linux OS builds, the most common packet management systems are Debian, Red Hat Package Manager (RPM), Knoppix, and netpkg. Below are a list of some Linux distribution and potential uses in education (Table 1).

Other countries are supporting the OSS movement as well. In China, Red Flag Linux commands over 30 percent of the market (Pan & Bonk, 2007). China is actively looking for an OS to combat Windows OS, thus the momentum for OSS continues to grow. In Russia, Linux may become a national OS by 2015 as they are as well looking for lower cost solutions in all levels of education. The Edubuntu OS, which has roots in South Africa, is being utilized by the Republic of Macedonia in all K-12 schools. With software packages such as LibreOffice students and faculty have the ability to perform similar functions as those found in the Microsoft Office suite without having to spend any money to obtain the software (Fig. 2).

Since the early 2000, there has been significant encouragement for the use of Linux in the Spanish public school system (Munoz et al., 2012). This use has been at the K12 level; however, the university level has yet to fully integrate this technology into the classroom. However, in a survey conducted by Accenture over 300 large blue chip organizations utilize OSS (Accenture, 2010). This indicates that there is a growing need for organizations to have employees familiar with OSS tools for development to include those for management.

OSS to Assist with the Development of Project Management Concepts and Tools

The need and presence of project management knowledge has developed to become a necessity in many organizational industries, while project management methods, processes, and certifications have become accepted standards in many industries (PMI, 2010). In 2008, *Global Knowledge* and *Fortune Magazine* listed project management in their top 10 career of choice, while in a recent salary survey conducted by ZDNET's Tech Republic organization, the PMP (Project Management Professional) certification was listed as the highest paying certification to have in the technology industry, while other project management certifications governed by the International Project Management Association (CPD, CPM) and Office of Government Commerce (PRINCE2) are highly sought after in European industries.

Table 1.   Linux Distributions and Potential Uses.

Linux Distributions	Description and Potential Use	Packet Management System
Ubuntu	One of the most popular Linux OS developed to be a complete OS that can be an easily replaced for other comparable OSs	Debian-based
Edubuntu	OS targeted for grades K12. Contained in OS are tons of software applications that are useful to those who are education majors	Debian-based
Damn Small Linux	This OS is designed as a small OS to be utilized on older hardware. This OS is great for institutions that have old computers and want to revitalize them for use. OS is also great for VMs as DSL requires a low amount of memory	Knoppix-based
BackTrack	OS based on Ubuntu for digital forensics and penetration testing. Great tool for students majoring in technology fields. As cyber security is becoming a hot topic around the world, this tool provides students the ability to learn from over 30 software applications that aid in penetration testing and more	Debian-based
Fedora	This OS is supported by the Fedora Project and sponsored by Red Hat. This OS provides a great resource for learning Red Hat Enterprise Language (RHEL). As there are thousands of jobs requiring expertise specifically with Red Hat, this OS is a great tool to prepare students for employment in IT. Fedora has over six Fedora Spins such as Design-suite, Scientific-KDE, Robotics, Electronic-lab, Games, and more	RPM-based
CentOS	This OS is derived entirely from RHEL. The source code is developed from Red Hat, which allows a student to learn RHEL with a small number of differences. CentOS can be used for teaching IT students on how to set up, administer, and secure a server	RPM-based
Ubuntu Studio	This OS is derived from Ubuntu. This OS is developed specifically for multimedia production such as audio, video, and graphics. Departments for multimedia could use this OS for multimedia instruction and the development of projects. As many of the tools for multimedia production are expensive, this alleviates large license costs for institutions	Debian-based

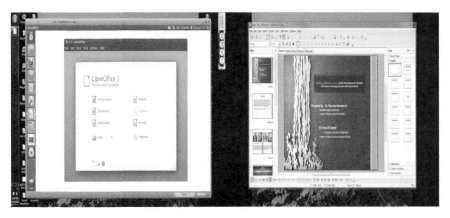

Fig. 2.   LibreOffice Running in VMware Virtual Machine.

Fig. 3.   OSS Project Management Tool Project Planner.

Communication and IT has also developed rapidly within this decade. With the enhanced role of IT, project managers must also prepare themselves to face the challenges of the future, both in the industry of project management as a whole and in the IT sector in particular. The increasingly important role of IT is undoubtedly the effect of rapid globalization that requires companies to have a larger capacity, timelier and more accurate information management within their decision-making system.

In project management part of a project manager's toolkit is the Microsoft Office Project software suite. One of the many available OSS is Project Planner which allows the creation of Gant Charts, ability to manage resources, and ability to track tasks created. Using Linux-based software allows institutions and organizations to teach this critical skillset at a fraction of the cost (Fig. 3).

Additional OSS tools that are present can be found on websites such as Open Source as Alternative (OSALT), which provides open source alternatives for items such as Microsoft Windows Suite, Araxis Merge, Bea Weblogic Server, and more (OSALT, n.d.).

DESIGN COLLABORATION WITH LINUX

In many graduate and undergraduate programs, institutions teach techniques for collaboration and system processes such as the Capability Maturity Model Index (CMMI). In teaching these techniques, OSS is the perfect platform as one of the key pillars for development is essentially coloration. With websites such as SourceForge, there are over 3.4 million developers participating in the development of over 324,000 projects. With these projects there is a group of developers that develop, deploy, and maintain these projects. For institutions this provides a method for students to understand the Software Development Life Cycle (SDLC) first hand.

Teaching and Understanding SDLC with the Aid of OSS Tools

The success of OSS demonstrates the alternative form of software and systems development processes. Software development is undergoing a major change from being a fully closed software development process toward a more community driven OSS development process (Deshpande & Richle, 2008). As a significant number of the information system (IS), computer science, or systems engineering students worldwide need to understand the SDLC, the OSS environment provides a great opportunity to learn all facets of the lifecycle (ACM, 2008). The SDLC known as the Waterfall Method (Fig. 4) is composed of six key phases that entail completing one phase and moving to the next without going back to the previous phase in the development cycle. The first phase is the requirements phase. During this phase of developments requirements are gathered for development. This allows developers and customers to capture requirements such as software functionality to user authentication requirements. The second phase of the SDLC is the design phase. In this phase the requirements become design specifications and developers develop the system. In the third phase, which is implementation, systems and subsystems are integrated to

Fig. 4. SDLC Process.

function as an entire system. For example, a software application may be composed of multiple subsystems developed independently. At this phase they are integrated together for a final implementation of the system. In the four-phase verification, a final test of the software or system is conducted before the final release. In the fifth-state deployment the software application is installed after it has passed a rigorous check in the fourth stage. The last state is maintenance which consists of maintaining the software or system. It is important to also note that in this stage the decision to retire a software application or system is also made.

THE OPEN SOURCE LEARNING MANAGEMENT SYSTEM

Many studies suggest the traditional way of teaching, through books and static figures, appears to be inadequate in bringing across the complicated ideas of scientific concepts (Guimaraes & Murray, 2006). The current emerging media technology revolution supplemented the traditional face-to-face learning process with various e-learning communities as one of the fastest moving trends in today's education to assist in preparing the students for more in-depth in interactive instructional environments could lead to enhance their learning opportunities in both online and on ground mixed-learning courses (Cole & Foster, 2007; Ko & Rossen, 2004; Rice, 2007; Waterhouse, 2005). Institutions around the world used various commercial teaching and learning applications such as Blackboard (http://www.blackboard.com) and WebCT to provide 24/7 communications between instructors and their learners. Those commercial applications could be very costly to buy their licensing.

In 2005, Munoz and Van Duzer mentioned that Humboldt State University paid approximately $8,600 for Blackboard license and they also pointed out that California State University system paid approximately 1 million dollars for licensing all the universities in the system. That could be huge amount of money for many institutes to licensing such educational systems. The best solution for such cost problem may lie in OSS (Wheeler, 2007). There are many open source programs available which are designed to solve numerous problems, but the most robust open source program is called Moodle.

Moodle is one of the most famous emerging media tools and widely known learning management systems (LMSs) in the U.S. universities, and other educational organizations (Martin-Blas & Serrano-Fernandez, 2009) used to develop a professional and more interactive educational (e-learning) environment especially for the higher education. Nowadays, Moodle comes as a first answer to the academic voracious demands for a professional and inexpensive tool for creating professional educational environment particularly by higher education and further education.

Moodle Overview

Moodle is one of the most user-friendly and flexible open source programs for electronic or e-learning (CoSN, 2010), identified as LMS, online interactive environment (OIE), and virtual learning environment (VLE) (Martin-Blas & Serrano-Fernandez, 2009), which has a large social framework of education support, and competitive alternative to many commercial applications. The word Moodle stands for "Modular Object-Oriented Dynamic Learning Environment, which is mostly useful to computer programmers".

Moodle was developed from the ground zero by Martin Dougiamas who has great experience in both education and computer science (Cole & Foster, 2007) as an innovative e-learning tool designed to assist educators to easy build and share their courses online. Moodle was developed as an alternative approach to costly systems available in the market. It has variety of features and a relatively quick learning curve make it very popular tool among U.S. universities for creating online dynamic web-based teaching, and learning environment could be used as a stand-alone online teaching and learning environment or as a supplement tool to their face-to-face traditional courses.

Dougiamas made the decision to make Moodle a copyrighted open source model to allow users to use, modify, add features, and distribute software package without modifying or removing the original license and copyrights (Melton, 2008). Originally, Moodle was developed for Linux OS but currently it is compatible with various OSs such as Windows and Mac. The first version of Moodle (Ver 1.0) was released on August 20, 2002. After the first release, there were many programmers all over the world starting exploring and examining the Moodle code, adding and removing features, and fixing the possible bugs if available.

Currently, there are many universities all over the world that adopted Moodle to build custom educational environments for their courses. Table 2 shows the list of top 10 countries prepared from registered sites in 223 countries.

Within academic environments, instructors can build their course specifying their course settings including the course format, course title, starting date, finish date, etc. Instructors can use Moodle to create stand-alone online courses by managing web-based content for their courses including course segments, lessons, focused technology, and so on. Additionally, they can use it to complement their traditional courses to facilitate complex courses' concepts with limited face-to-face interaction, or they can use it to augment their traditional courses.

Moodle has many features including:

- easily managed courses;
- real-time collaboration and communication environment;

Table 2. Top 10 Countries Using Moodle (Moodle.com).

Country	Registrations
United States	12,710
Spain	6,558
Brazil	5,384
United Kingdom	4,199
Germany	3,011
Mexico	3,007
Portugal	2,259
Colombia	2,154
Australia	1,808
Italy	1,758

- simple integrated quizzes and easy grade books;
- unlimited class size;
- unlimited enrollments;
- unlimited number of courses per school; and
- unlimited number of courses per teacher in particular.

In addition, Moodle provides many benefits such as

- 24/7 access from anywhere in the world to its learning environment;
- Upload and download course material including audio, video, .doc, . docx, PDF, image, and so on;
- Link to resources anywhere on the Internet;
- Easily create rich courses without need to learn HTML knowledge;
- Access files/papers/resources by a computer;
- Provide the ownership to the course content;
- Manage course content from year to year and never lose any work;
- Handle secure payments through using PayPal.

System Requirements and Obtaining Moodle

In particular, Moodle needs the most recent version of PHP, web application (one programming language), and SQL database such as MySQL or PostgreSQL. These tools could be found in one open source OS called LAMP. LAMP stands for the Linux OS, the Apache web server, MyQSL, and PHP. In addition, Moodle should run an automated Cron process every 5 minutes or so (Melton, 2008). The host of the Moodle should include one. It is good to note that the Moodle website (http://docs.moodle.org/en/Install) has detailed information and complete instruction about how to install Moodle for the first time.

There are two options to obtain Moodle; the first option is that Moodle need to be downloaded and installed on a local installation on a personal server as part of a local network at the institution. This option could require highest maintenance. The second option is a remote hosting by a commercial web server. A user can contact one of the Moodle companies listed as a hosting at the Moodle services website (http://moodle.com). This process includes buying a domain name, and install Moodle software application on one of their servers (Melton, 2008). Those companies offered easy used tools for installing, upgrading, and maintenance. In this way, users will not have a highest amount of maintenance instead they will have a mid of low-level amount of maintenance, but those companies will charge a fee for doing that.

Moodle Organization

Moodle could be set up according to its needs to deliver the information to the audience. For example, it could be used either as a networking environment or for handling course purposes. Instructors need to choose the format of the course by having only one screen that either contains the course material or consists of semester, term, or even year. In addition, the right and left sides of the main central course content could be arranged to include upcoming events, open forums, course members, latest news, search, recent and upcoming activities, etc. (Fig. 5). Moodle organization's layout could be edited by administrators who have skills with Hyper Text Markup Language or HTML code and cascading style sheet or CSS. In 2008, Melton explained Moodle setup items as follows.

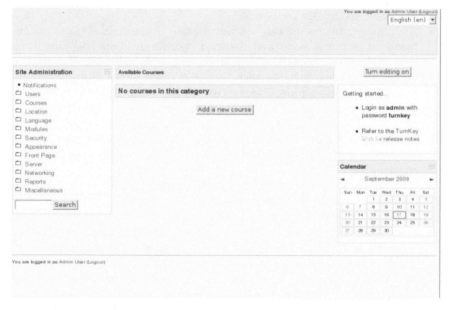

Fig. 5. Screenshot of Moodle Course Page.

Moodle organization's layout can be edited by administrators who have skills with HTML code and CSS. In 2008, Melton explained Moodle setup items as follows:

1. Forum: It is asynchronous module. Instructor can set up four types of forums such as standard forum, a question and answer forum, a forum for each member, and a forum for just one discussion. Instructor can use these entire forums to generate discussions, set for grading, assigning deadlines, attachment files, block attachment, email, and more.

2. Group: Instructor can make team tasks by combining a certain number of students to do a certain project(s) or any other course work. Instructor can hide the group work from other group and make it visible for the other group members by the end of the course. This allows students to learn how to work in virtual groups which according to a survey by Wainhouse, 72 percent of the respondents are more interested in alternatives to travel since the September 11, 2011 event (Wainhouse, 2002).

3. Grading: The latest version of Moodle allowed educators to assign grades for students and export the grades in different formats. These tool can be utilized to allow the student and the instructor to track progress throughout the course.

4. Assignment: Instructor can use this area to organize his course assignments in different ways and assign a specific deadline for submitting each assignment. Moodle allows students to submit their assignment in different formats such as text file, PDF file, Word document, and PowerPoint presentation, Excel sheet, pictures with various formats, etc.

5. Quiz: Instructor can set up their quizzes for each student individually or in groups. Instructor can open and close each quiz in specific day and time, send a customize feedback for each student, and so on. Quizzes can also be developed from a random test bank to minimize cheating.

6. Chat: It is a synchronous module for communication allowing the instructor to announce chat times, groups, and session logs. Student can use chat for real-time communication with or without their instructor for specific discussion issues. These chats can also be archived to be viewed at a later time to review the communication to ensure the message was understood or relayed appropriately.

7. Message: It provides both synchronous and asynchronous benefits. For example, a message window will pop up when the student change his web page during sending the message process. On the other hand,

a user will receive an email message in this registered email addresses when he is not online. Also, the user will see a pop-up message at the time he or she log in to the Moodle course.

8. Blog: A communication modules located on a user's profile. User can use their blogs for personal publications, read and write current entries' purpose, and access popular topics easily. The publications appear in reverse order, so the most recent post appears first.

9. Wiki: A communication module could be used in a different ways. Normally users use Wiki to collaborate with each other on coursework and projects. They can use it as a brainstorming session to exchange their thoughts about ascertaining subject. Wikis can also be exported to reside on a student's or professor's desktop. Wikis can serve a living document which can be updated at any time to include serving as configuration management systems for manuals or books.

10. Lesson: Instructor can use this module to prepare lessons in multimedia or PDF file forms. Also, the instructor can add questions to the content to check his or her understanding to the subject.

11. Glossary: This is very important module that can help the instructor to explain the difficult vocabulary word to the students and add new concept to the content to facilitate the concept of the course content.

12. Gathering feedback and data: Instructors can use this module to gather student's feedback and/or other types of data in three different ways: database, survey, and choice. This module can be exported for a review or to provide a synopsis of issues to administration.

13. Administration issues: Site administration panel contains many tools that allow the instructor to create and organize his course(s) with respect to the privacy and security issues. For example, they can create new courses and share them with the others and store them if necessary. In addition, they can make a manual or automatic backup for their courses including course data and student data (Melton, 2008).

Moodle has associated weakness. Moodle does not have the ability to reorganize courses into functional groups for each user. It only has a few related organizations by the topic of the current and previous courses and weekly course descriptions. The user would be blind and does not have the ability to see his courses' organization and could miss his opportunity to reorganize his courses.

Moodle does not have any link for advanced conferencing features such as a whiteboard conferencing feature. Sometimes chatting with the professors alone does not have the ability to convey the exact meanings like visual information always do. So this facility allows the professor to visu-ally share information in real time and allow the other students to watch the professor's movement and discuss with him.

Summary

The Moodle is great online learning software or course management sys-tem used by a wide variety of users and allows professors and students to conduct and participate in an electronic classroom. Students have the abil-ity to post their discussion items, submit their assignments, and post jour-nals and resources as attachments.

Moodle has a simple interface, uses a minimum of words, and includes simple icons with the words to aid users and show them the direction to where he can find the information they looking for.

REVIEW OF VIRTUAL WORLDS IN THE CLASSROOM

Emerging technologies offer exciting new teaching options for teachers and new learning options for students (Al Saeed, 2011a). For example, open source as one of the emerging media popular tools offered free innovative base to develop new teaching tools for instructors and new learning envi-ronment for students. In 2011, Dawson argued, "Simulation-based training provides many benefits to education, commercial, and military industries, allowing trainees to test and hone their skills in a safe virtual environ-ment"(Dawson, 2011).

Financing could be the main driving forces behind utilizing open-source software development especially for the institutions of higher education (Miro International Pty Ltd, 2006; Wang, 2004; Rooij, 2007). Open-source virtual simulator software applications such as Second Life (SL) and Open Simulator (OpenSim) as one of the most popular virtual world environ-ments might be considered as a potential solution to eliminate financial restrictions could face any higher education institution (Pan & Bonk, 2007). Al Saeed argues that "SL and Open Simulator (OpenSim) provide an opportunity to create innovation space educational simulations and allow students to become immersed in the learning process and help in convert them from passive to more active learners to become hand-on operators in more interactive environment. In other words, simulation environment could be designed using emerging virtual technology for educational purpose such as space education purposes. It may turn students to be active leaners by engaging them in an immersive virtual environment" (Al Saeed, 2011a). University can easily access to source code, modify it, save the license fees could be chard by the vendor to develop and provide the institution with the flexible and cost efficient learning environments (Pavlicek, 2000; Weber, 2004; Williams, 2002).

Virtual world such as SL is a public utility for digital media that includes many features such as 3D graphics and simulation technology, text chat, voice chat (VOIP), and advance digital media for online collaborative courses and classrooms' environment.

Based on the emerging global distribution for web and computerized technologies, all types of virtual worlds were designed on the existing web standards to create a global virtual social network for socializing, messaging, media delivery, storage, and processing. It is an open and extensible platform that enables of Immersive education and distance for a wide range of variety students.

SL as one of the most popular virtual world provides a unique and secure teaching and learning environment for instructors and students. This learning environment could be designed to be private for a specific school where each avatar assigned to a unique name could include the name of the university, collage, or any other educational institution that the individual belongs to.

Many advances are incorporated into the design of such educational environment using virtual world such as SL. For example, the universities that host their own servers have complete control over who

1. Has access to their educational virtual worlds and has the ability to restrict access to those worlds at their discretion. For example, there were no anonymous access allowed for virtual worlds hosted on the Education Grid. Universities can also provide student rosters, and teacher rosters, from which authenticated avatars may be provisioned.
2. Has the ability to keep their virtual worlds for education private, or make them available to some other learners.
3. Has the ability to make separate copies of a virtual world simultaneously available for few levels of learners, where appropriate security measures are applied to enable students and teachers to work together in safe and secure learning environments.
4. Has to ability to have a single virtual world be utilized, simultaneously by multiple universities. Additionally each school can be provided with

Fig. 6.   The Virtual Campus for Colorado Technical University.

its own private audio channel, which prevents lectures and discussions from being heard by anyone outside of that particular class.

Higher education technologists especially for those in the doctoral/research institutions utilized the efficiencies of open source. Colorado technical university is one of the first universities who realized the importance of using virtual worlds in teaching. They designed their own virtual campus as new teaching and learning environment in SL (Fig. 6). Additionally this institution has developed new degree programs at the graduate levels to teach emerging media and technology (Al Saeed, 2011b).

SL OSS Educational Competitor

One of the virtual world education grid competitors is OpenSim. OpenSim is an open source multi-user 3D application server designed by taking the advantage and make a reverse-engineering to the published application programming interface (API) functions and specific Linden Lab open source parts of the SL code. One of the strength for creating any virtual environment is making it accessible by a variety of users through using various protocols. OpenSim offers a great opportunity for the virtual world developers to create customized virtual worlds easily extensible through using the technologies that fit with their needs.

One of the weaknesses is that this kind of virtual worlds are susceptible to attacks by regular web clients. It is actually easier to copy assets with a web-based client. The weakness is that asset servers are connected to the public Internet, and the protocol for interacting with them is public.

The Virtual World Education Grid will result in an improvement over the OpenSim because it has a great potential in language learning and teaching, projects turn out to be motivating both for the students and instructors, task-based activities are favored over other methodologies. On the other hand, OpenSim is high technological requirements and hard user interface compared to the virtual world grid.

Virtual World Educational Grid

Demand for online or non-traditional classes is increasing day after day. Technology is providing more tools in which schools can enhance performance of their learning model. The Virtual World Educational Grid is considered a free environment developed upon existing web standards in order to emerge a unique environment for virtual world delivery.

Virtual World Educational Grid has many powerful features including interactive and collaborative 3D graphics, game technology, audio, video, simulation technology, VoIP, text chatting, web cameras, and so forth with collaborative online course environments. The educators and students will fell themselves are physically attending a class session even that is not possible and that will cut any cost associated with attending class sessions in real world. Students from all over the world can communicate with each other in a way they can enhance their learning experience process. It will engage the instructors, educators, and students with the teaching and learning process in the same way they can collaborate within the traditional teaching and learning process. Virtual World Educational Grid supports individual-based learning process as well as group-based learning environments where the interactive lessons could inject into larger bodies of course material in order to enhance the education learning and teaching experience.

Identified Baseline Requirements

1. Accessible: The Virtual World Educational Grid should be designed in a way to be accessible to all users and institutes thought to previously set up a specific procedure and open usage policy, but also preserve the right to make the server private for events.

2. Open Application Programmer Interface functions and a portion of the code: The Virtual World Educational Grid should be flexible and extensible for virtual world developer to make customized virtual environments, and that would be possible by publishing open API functions, protocols, and a portion of Virtual World Education Grid code.
3. Open and interoperable file formats: Software configuration and files should be transferable to other environments and platforms with respect to the minimum hardware needed.
4. Open hosting with conformance and compatibility: The Virtual World Educational Grid should be designed with the relevant educational and operational standards to achieve the conformance and compatibility standards.
5. Support multiple content formats: The Virtual World Educational Grid should support 3D content in addition to other content formats such as gaming, audio, video, text, etc.
6. Quality control: The Virtual World Educational Grid content should be reviewed and categorized by using metadata in order to meet the standard and be accepted into the Virtual World Educational Grid. That includes qualitative analysis, rating, and tagging by educators, students, and expert people of the subject matter.
7. Security and privacy of the learning environments: Developing Virtual World Educational Grid requires variety levels of protection. Learning environments could be created with some levels of security and access procedures for those only who are authorized in order to provide safe and private learning environment for the learners.

UTILIZATION OF VIRTUAL WORLDS IN ACADEMIA

Currently, virtual worlds are widely used for training and education purposes to facilitate trainees' learning activities (de Freitas, 2008; Dobson et al. 2001; Granlund 2001; Robert et al. 1996). Virtual worlds allow users to create their own avatars, which are referred to their residents and offer them the platform they need to interact with each other easily. Virtual world is a playground for imagination and expands the boundaries of users' creativity in exploring, defining, creating, designing, modeling real environments, building, coding, document sharing and recording facilities, performing, and collaboration (Chen et al., 2008). Virtual worlds can be very effective and cost-efficient environment that can provide a new methodological framework that supports training purposes to include serving as a tool for collaboration. Virtual worlds are a playground to simulate real-world applications for training purposes, but there is a chance it may not be able to simulate overall scenarios with small details that could be involved in real system because of the limitation boundaries of virtual worlds (Stolk et al., 2001). This chapter lays out the strategic use of virtual worlds for training purpose and provides a framework based on existing methodologies could be employed to facilitate modeling and testing process.

SL is an associated free client program known as the viewer which allows the users, known as residents, to interact with other individuals through avatars. Students created avatars which were representative of their personality and how they best felt to interact with other residents. This environment can be described as environments created by technology that have incorporated virtual representations of elements found in the real world (Kock, 2008). This course allowed students to develop virtual objects with limited knowledge of the Linden Scripting Language. As the Linden Scripting Language has syntax familiar with the C programming language, the students were able to jump right into developing scripts. Fig. 7 is an example of the Linden Scripting Language that would be utilized to have an object display text when they are five meters near the object. In terms of SL the most common method to gather information is through blogs and special journals as this knowledge base is constantly growing (Kern, 2009).

OpenSim is an OSS application that can be utilized to simulate virtual environments. This would allow architects and designers the freedom to develop their own virtual representation of an environment. However, an architect would need to have knowledge of the .net framework and programming in order to develop or modify items without any support. Furthermore, this competition not only developed a health care facility, but also created an entirely new vernacular by approaching this with SL virtual design capabilities. The introduction of a new form of instant communication beyond words and diagrams but in a full on demonstration of ideas creates a platform for creative designs. The implication of SL into competitions will provide user with a clear path to think creatively. The ideas can then overflow into a multi-faceted direct source, instead of just using one or two types of devices to demonstrate ones ideas, such as through email, telephones, video, or webcasting. The impact the SL has had will grow into a more influential design world.

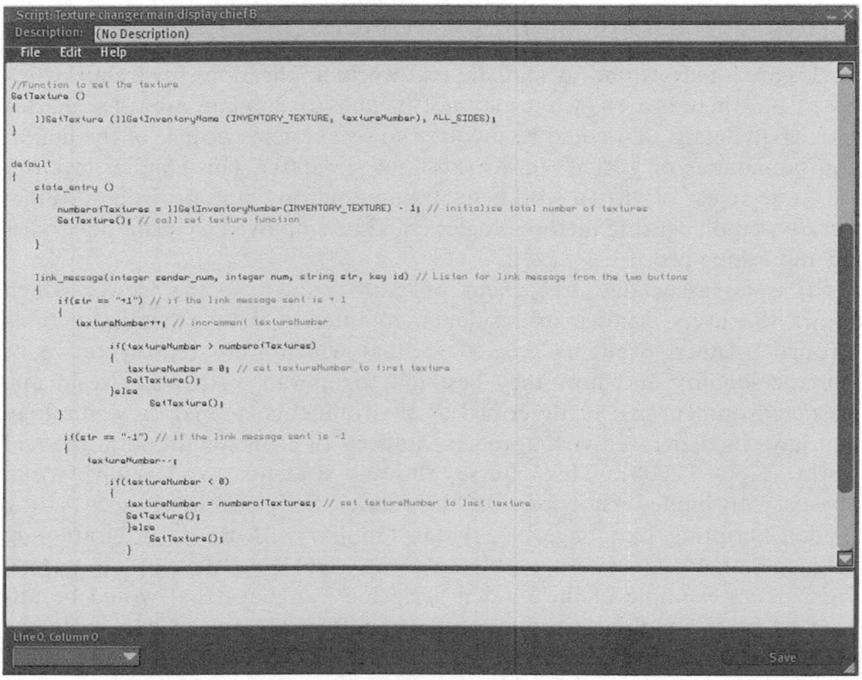

Fig. 7. Example of Second Life Linden Script.

University Graduate Projects Using Virtual Worlds

The introduction to Advanced Systems Engineering course at Morgan State University's School of Engineering graduate students participated in a group project that consisted of creating a virtual education center using SL, a virtual world developed by Linden Lab (Dawson, Burrell, & Emanuel, 2011). This project permitted students to apply their systems engineering concepts and skills learned as a result of the provided course materials (Dawson, Burrell, & Emanuel, 2011). The initiation of this course project was through a Request for Proposal (RFP) provided by the course professor who acted as the end customer. Displayed in Fig. 8 is a screenshot taken of the IEGR 501 SL Class during a live session in a virtual world during the Fall 2010 semester.

The goal of the virtual education center was to foster learning allowing for the development of engineering capabilities, and to hold large

Fig. 8. IEGR SL Class.

conferences of approximately 100 researchers. The land consisted of multi-ple regions. The first portion of the land was required to provide a large conference center that allowed authentication to occur for all entering per-sonnel. The second portion of the island was to act as an engineering development ground. This development ground was to consist of objects available for testing. Also, in the engineering, development ground was a rapid prototyping center for developing many applications related to the present world. The third portion was to be a classroom environment for three classes to be held simultaneously without hearing the other classroom during the lecture.

Throughout the semester, every student worked diligently to adhere and produce to the list of requirements proposed by the professor. Small groups were developed within the team to formulate a list of items needed and their pricing. The necessary items ranged from land to office equipment. After all of this preliminary research has taken place, the professor chose the most feasible items presented from each group, purchased them, and put together this virtual education center using SL.

Systems Modeling Using Virtual Worlds

Beginning from the initial problem definition and users' requirements, a High Level Systems Analysis (HLSA) was proposed resulting into graphically modeling the system with high-level and low-level system diagrams. This allowed the developers to capture the main important entities within this project.

Once analyzing the problem and system, a plan for design was implemented into Enterprise Architect (EA) using the SDLC OOAD methodology. The idea then leads to purchasing objects from the SL market to use as prototypes within the environment of SL. Difficulties aroused while using the software SL, such as programming objects as well as receiving objects from the market; some objects were unable to be modified and required to purchase other objects that would cooperate with the proposed system and environment.

The overall experience was interesting in learning to plan a development of a graphical user interface (GUI). Future work will be to present the development process of the research project as well as further enhance knowledge within SL to use an effective tool in simulation work.

Optimizing Student Participation in the Design Process

A widely held principle in the field of systems engineering is that the success of a system is directly proportional to the extent of user participation in developing the system. The results of this are that when an end user has a higher level of perceived meaningfulness task this would positively impact subjects' attitude and performance. The other result is that when the user has a perception of control and procedural justice then the user's outcome is satisfaction and their performance increases for the subjects as one increase the user's mode of participation. Perception of user control with procedural justice yields an outcome that increases the performance of a project as the user is given more opportunity to voice their opinion. It is interesting that when the users are given the choice to establish boundaries in the decision-making process there are increasing gains in user participation attitudes and performance. When the user's meaningfulness task is increased then procedural justice and control task commitment and performance also increase. The user participation positively influence perceived control even though none of the users received their preference. Perceived control influence perceptions of procedural justice. The direct path from decision control to outcome satisfaction reinforces the fundamental importance of perceived control. Path analysis demonstrates a direct effect of task meaningfulness on performance. Meaningful task evokes feelings of inclusion and increase perceptions of control.

Modeling and Designing Using Virtual Worlds

In this section, two design projects shall be described in detail. The first design project shall be a military training facility and the second shall be a modern student building. Both projects were designed as part of graduate level coursework in computer science and systems engineering programs where the students had limited knowledge on architecture and design principles. The students were allowed to use script generators to develop code for objects to include purchasing some of the materials needed from the SL marketplace.

The utilization of SL for these graduate students provided them the ability to develop concepts with the larger picture in mind. As many new computer science and system engineer graduate students are new to the concept of systems thinking, these projects provided them the ability to understand how design concepts are essential to the larger picture. Many of the students thought that job was only important for architecture, civil, or design students; however, they quickly realized the importance of understanding these design concepts themselves in order to provide a full solution to the end users or customers.

Virtual Military Training Facility

This design project was to develop a military training facility that would be the virtual representation of a training facility that could be utilized in

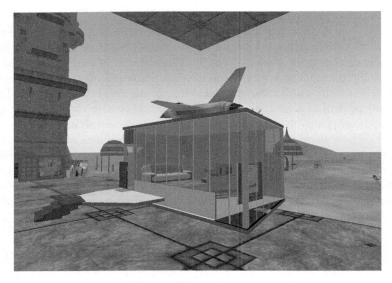

Fig. 9.   Virtual Military Training Facility.

the real world (Dawson, 2011). This virtual prototype was developed to test the usability of a proposed military training facility. The facility required a passcode to enter to include a presentation viewer that displayed training on national security. This design project went through the systems development process. Requirements were captured and tested during the design of this system to include a significant number of tests conducted with live participants. Fig. 9 displays the end result of the completed military training facility.

This design project proved that SL was a viable place for designing military training facilities. SL also proved to be a cost-efficient tool for testing the system's design concepts and usability with end users to include stakeholders.

Modern Student Building Project

The main objective of the modern student building project was to research and clearly understand the requirements of an automated teller machine (ATM) system, as well as understand the application model requirements for integration with an ATM system simulation. The goal of this research design project was to discuss the planning, analyzing, designing, implementing, testing, and evaluating phases of the development of a GUI of an ATM machine model using the software SL; virtual world (Davis & Dawson, 2012).

To accomplish this design project the researchers had to plan the path in which a developer will take to follow for production. This meant properly analyzing requirements and literature review to understand the entities within the system. The use of Object Oriented Analysis & Design (OOAD) to graphically model users, use cases and scenarios, data and flow diagrams was implemented.

The Object Oriented (OO) model was implemented into SL by constructing an environment in which the system will possibly be able to operate in (Davis & Dawson, 2012). Programmed objects to function when virtual users wants to perform a task. Fig. 10 displays the system modelling done for the project.

Beginning from the initial problem definition and users' requirements, a High Level Systems Analysis (HLSA) was proposed resulting into graphically modeling the system with high level and low level systems diagrams. This allowed the developers to capture the main important entities within this project.

Once the program was analyzed and system a plan for design was implemented into Enterprise Architect (EA) using the SDLC OOAD methodology. The idea then leads to purchasing objects from the SL Market to use as prototypes within the environment of SL. Difficulties aroused while

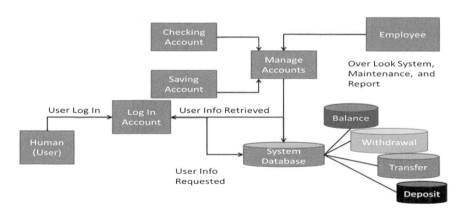

Fig. 10. Low Level Systems Diagram.

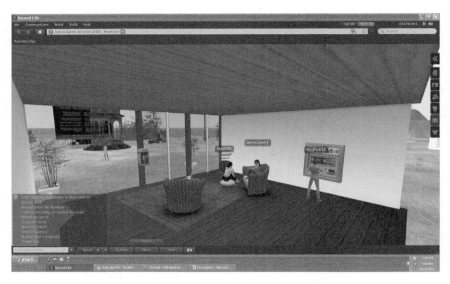

Fig. 11.   Virtual Modeling of Modern Student Building with ATM.

using the software SL. Difficulties such as programming objects as well as receiving objects from the market; some objects were unable to be modified and required to purchase other objects that would cooperate with the proposed system and environment.

The overall experience was interesting in learning to plan a development of a GUI. Future work will be to present the development process of the research project as well as further enhance knowledge within SL to use an effective tool in simulation work. Fig. 11 displays the finished design project in which live participants utilized the system to capture valuable data to test the hypothesis.

FINAL REMARKS

This chapter discussed the utilization of Linux, OSS, and virtualization tools that are currently available. Also discussed was how OSS virtual tools have been applied at the university level in graduate course projects to teach SDLC. We have described the benefits and challenges of OSS implementation to include how some countries are currently using OSS.

It is important that we as educators utilize these tools to allow students everywhere the opportunity for creativity and learning. As we realize that every institution worldwide does not receive the same level of funding, it is imperative that these tools become part of a technological arsenal to raise educational experiences with minimal impacts to funding.

ACKNOWLEDGMENTS

We would like to recognize Dr. Cynthia Calongne who is a Professor and Chair of Emerging Media in the Doctor of Computer Science and Doctor of Management degree programs at Colorado Technical University who provided great mentorship in the development of virtual worlds. We would also like to recognize the system engineering graduate students at Morgan State University and faculty member Dr. LeeRoy Bronner. Lastly, we would like to thank our families for having patience during the completion of this submission.

REFERENCES

Accenture. (2010). *Investment in open source software set to rise, Accenture Survey Finds.* Retrieved from http://newsroom.accenture.com/article_display.cfm?article_id = 5045. Accessed on May 1, 2012.

ACM (2008). *Computer science curriculum 2008: An interim revision of CS 2001.* Retrieved from http://www.acm.org//education/curricula/ComputerScience2008.pdf. Accessed on May 1, 2012.

Al Saeed, I. (2011a). Important of emerging technology in society for futuring and innovation. *Journal of Applied Global Research, 4*(11), 12–22.

Al Saeed, I. (2011b). Emerging technology as a degree option. *Proceedings of Intellectbase Conference, 18,* 421.

Armbust, M., Fox, A., Griffith, R., Joseph, A., Katz, R., Konwinski, A., ... Zaharia, M. (2009). Above the clouds: A Berkeley view of cloud computing. October 10, 2009. Retrieved from http://www.eecs.berkeley.edu/Pubs/TechRpts/2009/EECS-2009-28.pdf. Accessed on October 11, 2010.

Chen, Y-F., Rebolledo-Mendez, G., Liarokapis, F., de Freitas, S., & Parker, E. (2008). *The use of virtual world platforms for supporting an emergency response training exercise.* In *Proceedings of the 13th international conference on computer games: AI, animation, mobile, interactive multimedia, educational & serious games.* Wolverhampton, UK, November 3–5 (pp. 47–55). ISBN: 978-0-9549016-6-0.

Cole, J., & Foster, H. (2007). *Using moodle: Teaching with the popular open source course management system* (2nd ed.). Sebastopol, CA: O'Reilly.

Davis, L., & Dawson, M. (2012). Systems modeling a graphic user interface with using virtual worlds. *Academy of Information and Management Sciences Proceedings*, *16*, 1–6. Available at http://sbaer.uca.edu/research/allied/2012-new%20orleans/AIMS%20Proceedings%20Spring%202012.pdf.

Dawson, M. (2011). Applicability of web 2.0: Training for tactical military applications. In *Proceedings of global TIME 2011* (pp. 395–398). AACE.

Dawson, M., Burrell, D. & Emanuel, W. (2011). Utilization of e-learning tools, virtual machines, & open source software to enhance graduate systems engineering Programs. In S. Barton, et al. (Eds.), *Proceedings of global learn Asia Pacific 2011* (pp. 2088–2091). AACE.

de Freitas, S. (2008). *Serious virtual worlds: Scoping study*. Bristol: Joint Information Systems Committee.

Deshpande, A & Richle, D. (2008). The total growth of open source. In *Proceedings of the fourth conference on Open Source Systems (OSS 2008)* (pp. 197–209). Milan, Italy: Springer Verlag.

Dobson, M., Pengelly, M., Sime, J., Albaladejo, S., Garcia, E., Gonzales, F., & Maseda, J. (2001). Situated learning with cooperative agents simulations in team training. *Computers in Human Behavior*, *17*, 543–557.

Glotzbach, R., Mordkovich, D., & Radwan, J. (2008). Syndicated RSS feeds for course information distribution. *Journal of Information Technology Education*, *7*. Retrieved from http://informingscience.org/jite/documents/Vol7/JITEv7p163-183Glotzbach293.pdf. Accessed on October 11, 2010.

GNU. (2007). *GNU general public license*. Retrieved from http://www.gnu.org/copyleft/gpl.html. Accessed on April 25, 2012.

Granlund, R. (2001). Web-based micro-world simulation for emergnecy management training. *Future Generation Computer Systems*, *17*, 561–572.

Johnson, L., Levine, A., & Smith, R. (2009). *The 2009 Horizon report. One year or less: Cloud computing*. Austin, TX: The New Media.

Kern, N. (2009). Starting a second ife. *English Teaching Professional*, *61*, 57–59.

Ko, S., & Rossen, S. (2004). *Teaching online: A practical guide*. Boston, MA: Houghton Mifflin.

Kock, N. (2008). E-collaboration and e-commerce in virtual worlds: The potential of Second Life and world of warcraft. *International Journal of e-Collaboration*, *4*(3), 1–13.

Martin-Blas, T., & Serrano-Fernandez, A. (2009). The role of new technologies in the learning process: Moodle as a teaching tool in physics. *Computers & Education*, *52*, 35–44.

Melton, J. (2008). Need an LMS? Try the open source package moodle. *Journal of Instruction Delivery System*, *22*(1), 18–21.

Miro International Pty Ltd. (2006). *Application of open-source software in chinese schools. OS School*. Retrieved from: http://www.osschool.org/index.php? option=com_content&task=view&id=1&Itemid=1. Accessed on February 1, 2006.

Munoz, J. V., Nofuentes, G., Garcia-Domingo, B., & Torres, M. (2012) Customizing distributions based on linux. A new software tool to stimulate and design integrated circuits. *INTED2012 Proceedings*, 3209–3214

Murray, M. C. & Guimaraes, M. (2006). A review of the first phase of a project to develop and utilize animated database courseware. In *Proceedings of the 2006 Southern Association for Information Systems conference* (pp. 259–264). Jacksonville, FL USA: Southern Association for Information Systems. Available at http://sais.aisnet.org/2006/Murray-SAIS2006-paper.pdf.

OSALT (n.d.). *Development*. Retrieved from http://osalt.com/development#. Accessed on April 16, 2012.

Pan, G., & Bonk, C. (2007). The emergence of open-source software in North America. *The International Review of Research in Open and Distance Learning, 8*(3), 1492–3831.

Pavlicek, R. G. (2000). *Embracing insanity: Open source software development*. Indianapolis, IN: SAMS.

PMI. (2010). *Handbook of accreditation of degree programs in project management* (3rd ed.). Newton Square, PA: Project Management Institute. Retrieved from http://www.pmi.org/~/media/PDF/Professional-Development/GAC_handbook_2010.ashx

Rice, W. H., IV. (2007). *Moodle teaching techniques*. Birmingham: Packt.

Rooij, S. (2007). Perceptions of open source versus commercial software: Is higher education still on the fence? *Journal of Research on Technology in Education, 35X4*, 433–453.

Robert, B., Gamelin, C., Hausler, R., & Jarry., V. (1996). Training concept for environmental emergency measures structuring knowledge. *Journal of Contingencies and Crisis Management, 4*(3), 175–183.

Stolk, D., Alexandrian, D., Gros, B., & Paggio, R. (2001). Gaming and multimedia applications for environmental crisis management training. *Computers in Human Behavior, 17*(5), 627–642.

The Consortium for School Networking (CoSN). (2010). *CoSN K12 open technologies implementation study #3 Moodle: An open learning content management system for schools*. Washington, DC: CoSN K12 Open Technologies Implementation Study.

Vouk, M. A. (2008). Cloud Computing – issues, research and implementations. *Journal of Computing and Information Technology, 16*(4), 235–246.

Wainhouse. (2002). *Survey results: Usage trends of collaboration technology by business travelers*. Duxbury, MA: Wainhouse Research.

Wang, G. (2004) The role of Linux in the development of campus network. *Red flag linux*. Retrieved from: http://www.redflag-linux.com/upfiles/solution/aa.doc. Accessed on February 1, 2006.

Waterhouse, S. (2005). *The power of elearning: The essential guide for teaching in the digital age*. Boston, MA: Pearson.

Weber, S. (2004). *The success of open source*. Cambridge, MA: Harvard University Press.

Wheeler, B. (2007). Open source 2010: Reflections on 2007. *EDUCAUSE Review, 42*(1), 48–67.

Williams, S. (2002). *Free as in freedom: Richard stallman's crusade for free software*. Sebastopol, GA: O'Reilly.

ACTIVE LEARNING IN A ROBOTICS LABORATORY WITH UNIVERSITY STUDENTS

Lorella Gabriele, Assunta Tavernise and Francesca Bertacchini

ABSTRACT

Educational Robotics is a research field aimed at promoting an active engaging learning through the artifacts students create and the phenomena they simulate. In fact, designing, building, and programming a small robot, users discover and learn in a playful and joyful way. Moreover, the constructivist approach fosters the development of creative and critical skills, as well as problem-solving, communication skills, cooperation, and teamwork. This chapter presents the results of a research with university students, carried out at the Università della Calabria (Italy): an Educational Robotics laboratory has been integrated in a Cognitive Psychology Course in order to examine the kind of learning, workgroup retention, and engagement. Outcomes show that engaging experiences can remarkably enhance students' learning efficiency and retention of the acquired materials. Moreover, a rich interaction can provide

Increasing Student Engagement and Retention using Immersive Interfaces: Virtual Worlds, Gaming, and Simulation
Cutting-edge Technologies in Higher Education, Volume 6C, 315–339
ISSN: 2044-9968/doi:10.1108/S2044-9968(2012)000006C014

entertaining and appealing experiences capable of promoting learning and understanding.

INTRODUCTION

In recent years, learning researchers have underlined the great challenge that teachers and educators have to face up to in order to understand, evaluate, and promote an effective and appropriate technology integration in instructive field (Barreto & Benitti, 2012; Adamo, Bertacchini, Bilotta, Pantano, Tavernise, 2010; Bertacchini, Bilotta, Pantano, Tavernise, 2012; Chitiyo & Harmon, 2009; Davies, 2011; Hsu, 2011; Jonassen, Howland, Marra & Crismond, 2008; Loveless, Burton & Turvey, 2006; Martinovic & Zhang, 2011; Sánchez & Alemán, 2011). Their main theory of reference has been constructivism (Harel & Papert, 1990; Honebein, 1996; Joldersma, 2011; Martin, 1994; Papert, 1984, 1986; Piaget, 1971; Resnick, 1989, 1994; Sklar & Eguchi, 2004) that conceives learning as the result of subjects' active construction through action in the world. Cognitive functions are mediated by tools usually namely artifacts, which embody, expand, and combine human capacities (Parricchi, 2004; Bilotta, Pantano, Bertacchini, Gabriele, Mazzeo, Rizzuti, Vena, 2007). However, if our ancestors have been able to build artifacts randomly, the complexity of today's technological artifacts is indicative of the fact that they are not the result of a random process, but of a precise culture (Corbellini, 2007). Thus, technologies as "mental cognitive artifacts" are capable of supporting, guiding, and extending users' thinking process. They do not make a task easier, but facilitate the construction and learning of meanings, favoring the development of critical thinking, and actively engaging subjects. Moreover, new knowledge reflects a real understanding of the information presented by the teacher, rather than a replica of the contents.

In this scenario, Educational Robotics artifacts have acquired a very important role, demonstrating that the building and programming of small robots, as well as the simulation of robotic behavior, enable students to develop advanced cognitive skills in problem solving, in thinking strategies, and in the acquisition of new concepts (Bilotta, Bertacchini, Gabriele & Tavernise, 2011; Garbati, 2010; Herold, 2010; Lund & Pagliarini, 2001; Rutten, van Joolingen, & van der Veen, 2012).

In this chapter, the research carried out at the Università della Calabria (Italy) is presented. In the educational Robotics laboratory held in a

Cognitive Psychology Course, behavioral robot functionalities have been implemented, simulating race performances in an arena. Higher order thinking skills as problem solving, setting of goals, plan strategies, decision-making, and different modalities of cooperative/collaborative work have been investigated. Retention has been analyzed quantitatively; engagement has been examined qualitatively. In particular, in next sections the main researches in the educational Robotics field are introduced, as well as some laboratory arrangement connected to Robotics learning; after an analysis of the MindStorms kit, the case study is presented. The last section concerns final remarks.

EDUCATIONAL ROBOTICS RESEARCH

The Educational Robotics field applies Piaget's theories on cognitive development and Papert's constructivism, focusing on the active role of students in learning process thanks to the increasing of knowledge through the manipulation and construction of objects or artifacts. In particular, according to Piaget (1967, 1971), cognitive development consists in the progressive reorganization of mental processes as a result of maturation and experience. Thus, children construct an understanding of the world through a process of assimilation of new knowledge, as well as the "accommodation" (rearrangement) of what they already know and what they discover in their environment. Starting from Piaget's theories, Papert (1984, 1986, 1991) affirms that learners are active creators of their own knowledge and they learn better and more when they are engaged in constructing personally meaningful artifacts (such as computer programs, animations, or robots). Nowadays, small robots are commonly used as learning tools (Bilotta, Gabriele, & Servidio, 2001; Bilotta, Gabriele, Servidio, & Tavernise, 2007; Martin, 2001). In particular, using a simple Robotics kit, users can design and build real robots able to move and behave as animals. In fact, these kits are endowed with a sensory system (sensors that are sensitive to light or heat), a motion structure (e.g. mechanical arms controlled by motors or wheels), and a "brain" (a computer capable of controlling the motion structure using sensory system). The programmed artifacts have already been used both for educational and research purposes in several fields including psychology, ethology, electronics, computer science, and evolutionary Robotics (Barbero, Demo & Vaschetto, 2011; Bers & Portsmore, 2005; Lund & Pagliarini, 2001; Miglino, Lund & Cardaci, 1999).

Moreover, Robotics have been used in research in different school grades: in primary (Bilotta, Gabriele, Pantano, & Servidio, 2002; Bertacchini, Bilotta, Gabriele, Pantano, & Servidio, 2003; Bilotta, Gabriele, Servidio, & Tavernise, 2007a, 2011; Caci, D'Amico, & Cardaci, 2002) and high school (Elmore & Seiler, 2008; Kiss, 2010; Sklar & Eguchi, 2002, 2004), as well as in university courses (Arcella, Bertacchini, Bilotta, & Gabriele, 2003; Bertacchini, Bilotta, Gabriele, Pantano, & Servidio, 2006; Bertacchini, Bilotta, Gabriele, & Servidio, 2010; Behrens et al., 2010; Gabriele et al., 2005a, 2005b; Kim & Jeon, 2009; Karp, Gale, Lowe, Medina, & Beutlich, 2010). At this latter level, Robotics fosters the teaching/learning of some disciplines, such as Computer Science, Programming Languages and Software Engineering. Moreover, it is also used in the rehabilitation of autistic subjects and/or those with cognitive deficit (Cardaci, Caci, & D'Amico, 2004; Cook, Howery, Gu, & Meng, 2001; D'Ambrosio, Mirabile, & Miglino, 2003; Kronreif, Prazak, Kornfeld, Hochgatterer, & Fürst, 2007; Kronreif, 2009; Legof & Sherman, 2006; Owens, Granader, Humphrey, & Baron-Cohen, 2008). Therefore, Educational Robotics is an ideal bridge between the real experience and the study programs (Jadud, 2000; Miglino et al., 1999). Many studies have demonstrated that students achieve results such as acquisition of concepts, development of logical reasoning and creativity, learning by doing, understanding of phenomena by their own activities (Bilotta et al., 2001, Bilotta, Gabriele, Servidio and Tavernise, 2009; Moshe & Yair, 2009). Panadero, Román, and Kloos (2010) have described the research carried out in three different scholar contexts: an elementary course on Programming, an advanced-level course on Artificial Intelligence and a third first-level course on Robotics. They have aimed at demonstrating that collaboration, competition, and peer learning in laboratory activities can have the following results: (a) promotion of motivation, (b) improvement of transversal and specific skills in problem solving, (c) enhancement of team work and leadership. Kato and Tominaga (2010) have also proposed some exercises for beginners on robot control programming and game projects using LEGO® Mindstorms®, with the objective to promote problem-solving skill and learning motivation during group collaboration works. Maia, Silva, de S Rosa, Queiroz-Neto, de Lucena (2009) have demonstrated that the use of Educational Robotics kits allows students to develop creative designing and planning skills as well as motivates students to assimilate the abstractions of Computer Science with playful and practical actions. Tekerek (2009) has highlighted the development of abilities on planning applications: Robotics education does not aim to allow students to learn the elements of a robot, but to experience mechanic construction and laboratories which improve in befitting to future settings. It has been demonstrated that experiencing Educational Robotics represents a highly motivating activity for the promotion of socialization, collaboration, and cooperation (Cerezo et al., 2009; Filippov & Fradkov, 2009; Jardón, Paloma, de la Casa, & Giménez, 2008; Karahoca, Karahoca, & Uzunboylu, 2011; Mitnik, Recabarren, Nussbaum, & Soto, 2009).

Other researches have been focused on learning motivation. As a meaningful example of these studies, Chang, Lee, Wang, and Chen (2010) used RoboStage, a mixed-reality learning environment, in an experimental study with 36 high school students, examining the difference in motivation with either physical or virtual characters. Differences in research include the kind of robot implemented. For example, Makrodimitris, Nikolakakis, and Papadopoulos (2011) designed a mobile robots acting like a "pacman," able to simulate a prey-predator behavior. They observed the enthusiastic children's efforts in understanding the game rules and improving their gaming skills. Gonzalez-Gomez, Valero-Gomez, Prieto-Moreno, and Abderrahim (2011) realized "Miniskybot," a robotic platform for educational purposes that allows the students to learn robot programming and to easily customize the robot skeleton and its parts.

Regarding engagement, Robotics kits have been used in educational contexts in order to promote fruitful feelings of participation and appealing experiences in instructive process. In this view, the term "Edutainment" (education plus entertainment) has been used to designate a specific use of Robotics as a provider of enjoyable hands-on activities, especially to children and young people (Bilotta et al., 2009). Hence, Robotics artifacts have become essential in the design of specific stimulating settings and experiences that can generate a mental state of joy/serenity/relaxation, but also concentration/deep reasoning in the subjects. As a consequence, researches have demonstrated that the retention of content increases both in the short- and long-term memory (Custers, 2010; Upadhyay & De Franco, 2008), and the development of transversal skills and competences between different disciplines is improved (Mitnik, Nussbaum, & Soto, 2008).

ROBOTICS LABORATORIES: AIMS AND PERSPECTIVES

Robotics laboratories are advanced learning environments in which students carry out activities aimed at acquiring and sharing knowledge, promoting collaboration and reflection. Moreover, the promoted hands-on approach transforms users into active co-authors of their artifacts, or "intentional learners" (Bereiter & Scardamalia, 1989; Sinatra & Pintrich, 2008). Thus, as Bertacchini, Gabriele, and Tavernise (2011) have demonstrated, laboratories have a great potential for teaching/learning practices and can be easily integrated into the traditional school context.

The construction of a small robot in a laboratory is presented in Fig. 1.

The educational approach adopted is called project-based learning (PBL) (Bell, 2010; Chu, Tse & Chow, 2011; Hudson, 2010; Larmer & Mergendolle, 2010; Nari, 2010). In general, all PBL environments are characterized by cooperative and individual activities, focused at building, manipulating, or creating a product or an artifact (Bransford & Stein, 1993). This methodology refers to the constructionist approach and new learning theories, where the "doing" and "build to learn" take place inside of a well-defined social context. Students' efforts are concentrated on the finding of answers to complex questions, or the solving of a problem, or the dealing with a challenge (Bell, 2010; Chu et al., 2011; Hudson, 2010). This method foresees the utilization of a detailed work dossier that specifies the following data: (a) duration; (b) project objectives; (c) identification and definition of the problem; (d) details on educational strategy to be implemented; (e) identification of the technologies; (f) list of useful resources (websites, learning objects, books, magazines, media) that can

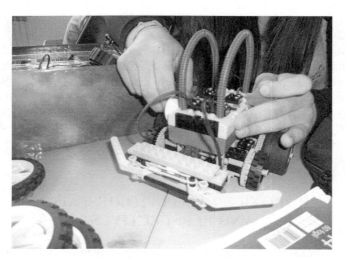

Fig. 1.   A Student Working in Robotics Laboratory.

stimulate students to do further research; (g) detailed planning of the work documentation modalities.

PBL enhances the experience of self-learning in educational contexts, allowing students to share ideas, and build knowledge through exchange activities and discussion. According to Blanchard, Freiman, and Lirrete-Pitre (2010), we can speak of Robotics-based learning, that is a set of activities that can develop a strong critical thinking in young people and is oriented to the development of important cognitive/meta-cognitive skills. Moreover, RoboDidactics aims at creating a European methodology for introducing Robotics in didactics in order to advance teaching and learning processes of scientific and ICT-oriented subjects that are critical for equipping young generations of students with a set of skills that is increasingly required by the job market.

Regarding students' work, daily reports provide important detailed descriptions of decision-making, and the strategies applied to solve the assigned task. In particular, they analyze the changing of the competence level related to the proposed activities and the objectives that subjects decided to achieve. For example, in some cases, students can choose to decompose the problem into many small parts in order to reach the general resolution (Arcella et al., 2003).

LEGO® MINDSTORMS® KIT

Currently, different Robotics kits have been designed and are available on the market. Among them, Lego® MindStorms® kit 2.0 (Fig. 2) is one of the most used commercial systems that allow user to build and program a robot without specific knowledge in Robotics or Computer Science. The kit includes more than 700 traditional Lego pieces, the RCX (Robotics Command System), an infrared transmitter, different types of sensors (such as light and touch sensors), motors, gears, a guide called Constructopedia™, and the Lego Mindstorms RIS 2.0 software.

Lego pieces are characterized by differences in shape, color, and functionalities. There are pieces that their functions are basically because they attend/serve in to constructing typical Lego objects, in order to construct legs and robot arms, robot body in different, and so many ways. Others are pieces that serve to build wheel, carriage, trap in order to build robot that can run. Others pieces serve to create some humanoid characterization (like robot eyes), and other pieces that are like some ornamental embellishment, in order to stimulate users' fantasy.

Fig. 2. Some Pieces of the Lego® Mindstorms® Kit.

The building guide, called Constructopedia™, helps students to build working robots, as well as it is a source of inspiration for more complex robotic inventions models. It provides small hints for the building of the robot as well as models. The RCX is a microcomputer that allows the robot to receive input from the environment through sensors, processes data, and then transfer the output to the motors. Different programming languages to program the robot behavior exist both for beginners and experts. The RCX code, supplied with the Lego® MindStorms® kit, is a visual programming language very easy to use and winning, where each statement consists in blocks; logically assembling sticks of blocks (Fig. 3), the user define the robot behavior and using an infrared transmitter he can download the program in the robot and run it.

THE CASE STUDY

Objective

The objective has been the examination of students' learning/workgroup, retention, and engagement. In fact, students without a specific and/or specialist knowledge have had the opportunity to experience, learn, and understand the specific Robotics topic by simulating and observing robot behaviours.

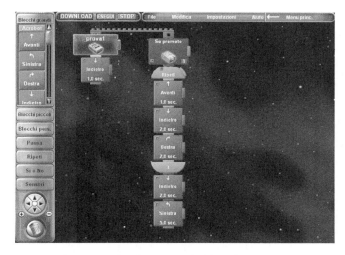

Fig. 3. An Example of Program Built Using the RCX Code.

Methodology

Experimental group of 38 subjects has

1. compiled an entry assessment of students' information on Robotics;
2. manipulated Lego pieces, programmed the artifact, and simulated robots behavior;
3. compiled reports on the progress of the workgroup, the distribution of the tasks in the group, and the positive/negative opinions on the experience;
4. filled a Robotics knowledge questionnaire; and
5. compiled a retention questionnaire (8 months after the closing of Robotics laboratory).

Laboratory had a duration of 12 hours.

Control group of 38 subjects has

1. compiled an entry test on Robotics knowledge;
2. attended 12 hours of traditional lessons using only textbooks and still-pictures; visual documents (PowerPoint slides) were used by the teacher;
3. wrote positive/negative opinions on the experience;
4. completed the Robotics knowledge questionnaire; and
5. completed the retention questionnaire (8 months after the 12 hours of traditional lessons).

Finally, the acquisition of high cognitive skills by the experimental group has been analyzed according to the data presented in the reports, and retention results by the experimental group have been compared to those obtained by control group by using SPSS version 18.

Sample

The experimental group consisted of 38 students ($N = 38$), aged between 19 and 23. Only four students were comfortable with computers, and none had used technology applications in other instructional activities. They did not have previous knowledge in a programming language or Lego® Mind-Storms® kit. They were organized to work in six workgroups of five, and two workgroups of four subjects.

The control group consisted of 38 students ($N = 38$), aged between 19 and 23. The research has been carried out in the structured context of the educative environment to which the students belonged, delimiting the research field to the specific area of the Laboratory in Psychology and Cognitive Science (experimental group) or a lecture hall (control group).

Materials

Both the entry test and the Robotics knowledge questionnaires consisted of 15 questions. Regarding the first one, it has been designed to collect some personal data (age, class), and assesses the level of Robotics knowledge possessed by students before the experimentation. Regarding the Robotics knowledge and retention questionnaires, knowledge questions were not identical to the pre-test but very similar, with the aim to ensure that students did not learn from the previously asked questions. Fifteen multiple-choice questions addressed both factual knowledge and application questions. Regarding the score, 1 point was attributed for each correct answer and 0 for each incorrect answer, for a maximum of 15 points. Regarding the reliability of the questionnaire, the test had an alpha value of 0.65.

The following materials were used by experimental group:

- Eight Lego® MindStorms® kits version 2.0 (one for each group)

- Eight personal computers with a monitor 17″ (one for each group), endowed with the operative system Microsoft® Windows XP, and a 1280×1024 screen resolution

- Eight board diaries, pens, pencils, and rubbers

- An arena (100 ⇒ cm × 70 ⇒ cm) to test the robot performance. The path was signaled by a red strip, the black line represented the border, and two obstacles were present

- A camera and a camcorder to record the building tests and the robot behavior.

Experimental Group

The research included five stages for the experimental group. In the first stage (2 hours), students compiled an entry assessment of students' information on Robotics and met the laboratory coaches, who introduced the laboratory activities. In particular, general information about Robotics, the construction of robots, and functional characteristics of the Lego® MindStorms® system was given by visual documents (PowerPoint slides). Materials and equipment have been shown; the tasks of second and third stages were assigned.

In the second stage (four hours), the sample was organized to work in groups, in order to explore the electronics elements and understand how to collect and merge them to develop robots. Then each group was supplied with a MindStorms® kit and a computer, in order to build a Lego robot. Group members had to build robots and provide them with tactile and light sensors.

In the third stage (4 hours) three tasks were assigned. The tasks' aims were to program and test three different behavioral sequences:

1. The robot had to move from a casual point of the arena twirling twice, first to the right and then to the left. The robot also had to produce a melody (Fig. 4a)
2. The robot had to move from a casual point and cross the arena avoiding two obstacles. This task involved the programming of tactile sensors (Fig. 4b)
3. The robot had to move from a casual point and cross the arena, avoiding the obstacles and stopping before a black line. In order to solve this task, the students had to program tactile sensors and a light sensor (Fig. 4c)

Each robot had 2 minutes to complete each task.

In both stages 2 and 3, students had to document each phase of their work through reports, schemas, photos, and videos. In particular, they had to write accurate daily laboratory reports describing the different work phases which included problem finding, problem setting, and problem solution. In addition, students had to report the adopted methodologies of

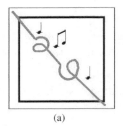 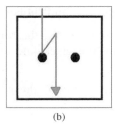 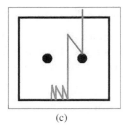

(a)   (b)   (c)

Fig. 4. The Three Sketches Represent the Schemes of the Tasks Assigned at the Students: (a) Scheme of the First Task; (b) Scheme of the Second Task; (c) Scheme of the Third Task.

programming, the number of the executed tests to evaluate the robot behavior, the modalities of work subdivision in the different groups, as well as the positive/negative aspects of their experience. Regarding this latter description, the nuance of personal opinions on perceived competence and interest/enjoyment in students' own words has been requested in order to enrich the research, recording the different grades of students' engagement.

In the forth stage (1 hour), robot's performance related to students' tasks took place. Then, students compiled a Robotics knowledge questionnaire.

In the fifth stage (1 hour), or retention stage, a new Robotics knowledge questionnaire was given 8 months after the fourth stage, in order to measure the retention of the contents learned during the research period.

Results: Building Methods

Both reports and programs have been analyzed as indicators of students' comprehension in order to detect the following cognitive abilities:

1. Work strategies during the designing and building of the artifact
2. Programming strategies to create a successful robot behavior
3. Work distribution during the different tasks

Students have selected a basic structure among the different suggestions present in the Constructopedia™, designed and built the robot, and learned how to use the pieces of the Lego kit. The manipulation of the various pieces of the kit has allowed students to organize their work and to discover the importance of pieces and connections. Making the good connections and error correction was an important and long process.

Many students were observed using their own personalized design. In particular, results showed that the groups adopted two different building methods:

1. Bottom-up approach (Sun & Zhang, 2002): Subjects built the basic structure and then added sensors and anthropomorphic features. This building/working method was adopted by the large majority of teams (six groups).
2. Top-down approach (Sun, Merrill & Peterson, 2001): Subjects assembled the sensors on a smaller structure or have created special anthropomorphic features, building the basic structure of the robot later in the task. This building/working method was adopted by two of the eight groups.

Moreover, 50% of the working groups preferred to build the artifact with the complete components necessary to implement the three different tasks, while the others preferred to build a robot with a basic structure modifying it later, according to the tasks. Fig. 5 shows an example of a robot built by a group.

Results: Programming Strategies

Regarding the programming activities, students have learned a programming language that has allowed them to control the robot's behavior. Results show that all the groups programmed a robot able to carry out the first and the second tasks, and seven groups of eight succeeded in programming the third one.

Regarding the number of tests carried out by each group for first task, three workgroups (C, E, G) modified the program only once before a working performance, four workgroups (A, D, F, H) modified it twice, and one workgroup five times (B). With regard to the structure revision, two workgroups (B and H) adopted this solution after the testing phase. These results are shown in Fig. 6.

Regarding the number of tests carried out by each student group for the second task (Fig. 7), two workgroups (B, F) modified the program only once before a working performance, five workgroups (A, C, E, G, H) modified it twice, and one group three times (D). Moreover, two workgroups (C and E) revised the structure and modified the program.

Fig. 5. An Example of Robot Assembled by a Team.

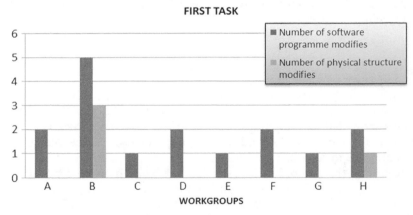

Fig. 6. Number of Tests (First Task).

Regarding the number of tests carried out by each student group for the third task (Fig. 8), three workgroups (B, C, E) modified the program once before a working performance, five workgroups (A, C, F, G, H) modified it twice, and one workgroup (C) revised the robot structure.

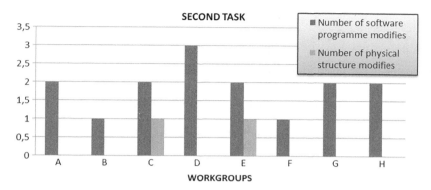

Fig. 7.   Number of Tests (Second Task).

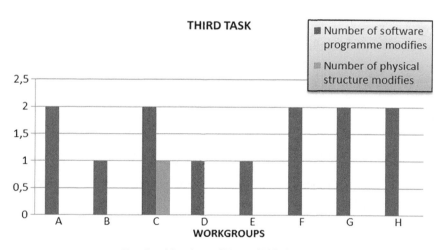

Fig. 8.   Number of Tests (Third Task).

Regarding the work subdivision in groups, three strategies have been adopted:

1. Cooperative work (A and G)
2. Clear division of the work in two different activities: half the group built the robot and the other has programmed it (E and H)
3. Clear division of the roles in both the building and programming activities (B, C, D, F).

DISCUSSION

Results show that students have been stimulated in

- problem finding – the subjects identified problems and formulated ideas to solve them;
- problem solving – the subjects elaborated and explored some possible solutions to reach the objective; and
- checking procedures – the subjects valued the artifact properties from a functional point of view.

The repetition of each of these phases allowed the students to modify and improve a structure that reflected their own mental model of the artifact in relation to the assignment. Construction has mostly been embodied in a cooperative and collaborative work.

In particular, from the analysis of the reports, it emerged that the activity of realization of the artifact has been carried out by the following well-defined phases (Fig. 9):

1. Analysis of the problem (the analysis of the task)
2. Brainstorming and conceptualization of the problem
3. Building of the robot
4. Programming of the robot
5. Test

The subjects also had the opportunity to come back to the preceding phases for the revision of the work. Moreover, the analysis of the reports highlighted that the subdivision of the main problem into small sections represented a great advantage in problem solving.

Regarding the building and programming stages, according to the principles of constructivism, in this phase the manipulation of Lego pieces was fundamental for cognitive processes. Students became skillful in exploring, combining, and recombining Lego pieces in different structures, according

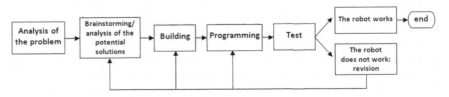

Fig. 9. Stages in the Realization of the Robot.

to a mental design of the artifact. Finally, the Constructopedia™ models were used as inspiration to build more advanced artifacts.

Retention Results

Retention of Robotics content among university students was analyzed using a repeated-measure ANOVA with entry/Robotics knowledge questionnaire scores (entry test, posttest, retention) within subject factors, and treatment versus control between subject factors. In this research, all statistical analyses have been set at $p = 0.05$. According to Mauchly's test, assumption of sphericity was met at $p > 0.05$. The main effect of time on the retention was significant between control and treatment groups, $F(1, 36) = 4.67$, $p = 0.037$.

The scores (entry versus Robotics knowledge questionnaire and Robotics knowledge questionnaire versus retention) of treatment and control groups have been analyzed using paired sample t-tests to determine if the ANOVA main effect was because of the treatment. For the experimental group, the knowledge score has increased from a mean of 1.5 (SD = 1.55) at entry assessment to a mean of 13.58 (SD = 1.08) immediately following the treatment, $t(37) = -39.308$, $p < 0.01$. With respect to the Robotics knowledge score, the retention score decayed to a mean of 11.92 (SD = 1.65) and $t(37) = 8.417$, $p < 0.01$.

In the case of the control group, the paired sample t-test showed a significant increase of score in the entry/traditional lessons course. The Robotics knowledge score significantly increased from the entry mean score of 2.24 (SD = 1.3) to a mean of 11.6 (SD = 1.62) and $t(37) = -28.05$, $p < 0.01$. The retention mean score decayed to a mean of 5.76 (SD = 1.92) and $t(37) = 14.938$, $p < 0.01$.

Table 1 shows students' mean score and standard deviations.

ANOVA provided a significant interaction between scores over time and treatment, $F = 5.163$, $p < 0.01$. Also, between subjects ANOVA showed that the treatment factor was significant, $F = 38.100$, $p < 0.001$. Therefore, there was a remarkable increase in Robotics knowledge both in experimental and control group from entry questionnaire to knowledge questionnaire: the kind of treatment (manipulation, construction, and programming of the robot for experimental group; traditional lesson for control group) didn't produce much of a change in knowledge results. However, after 8 months, the rate of knowledge related to Robotics contents is much higher in experimental group students compared to control group students.

Table 1.   Students' Mean Score and Standard Deviation.

	Experimental Group			Control Group		
	N	Mean (0–15)	SD	N	Mean (0–15)	SD
Entry	38	1.5	1.55	38	2.24	1.3
Robotics knowledge	38	13.58	1.08	38	11.6	1.62
Retention	38	11.92	1.65	38	5.76	1.92

Enjoyment and Edutainment: Qualitative Data Findings

Some questions asked students' opinions on positive and negative aspects of Robotics learning experience. In particular, subjects answered open ended questions on what they thought were the positive and negative aspects of the laboratory setting. The answers have been mostly brief, ranging from enthusiastic to moderately positive. Several subjects from the experimental group highlighted the socialization ("We liked workgroup"), or the engaging nature of the proposed activities ("We enjoyed the construction of the robot," "the programming activity was appealing"). Moreover, students mentioned different reasons for liking Robotics, such as hands-on activities or the possibility to present the work to parents and friends through pictures. Some students from a particular group did not like the approach used to learning, because they were not "good at using computers for programming." However, in general, the comments were very satisfied.

On the other hand, students in control group class agreed that lessons on Robotics were interesting, but nobody declared that the activity has sustained entertainment. Some of the comments were the following: "the topic was interesting," "the subject was too hard," "the explanation of programming has been quite long," "I think I have missed some explanation, because I am quite confused," "I hope the examination will not be too difficult," "I disliked the lessons, because I don't know how this can be useful in my life," "these Robotic contents are not functional in a course of Cognitive Psychology."

Hence, thanks to the qualitative analysis of results, this research has showed what secondary school students find engaging and motivating in the laboratory setting: problem solving, play, and socializing. In fact, regarding this latter, results show that subjects are interested in collaborative work groups. Therefore, designers of new educational settings (especially those devoted to science learning) should consider the incorporation of this feature for the improving of retention. Moreover, a great effort should be provided to the arrangement of a coherent Edutainment path from grammar school to university based on the construction of tools, as well as a reasoned, rational, and articulated concurrence with school contents. Finally, the present research results are in alignment with the outcomes obtained by using other learning environments, even if the arrangement of other Edutainment settings has often foreseen only the manipulation of virtual objects.

FINAL REMARKS

Many studies have underlined the important and precise add-value of Educational Robotics laboratories in school curriculum, from primary education to university courses. Recently, in Italy, different institutions (schools, universities, and companies) working in the Robotics field have signed a memorandum of understanding for the creation of a long-term national strategy aiming at a rational use of Robotics in educational contests. In particular, the memorandum of understanding considers Robotics as a key tool in the fostering of the twenty-first century education and in fighting students' low interest for science. In the learning field, "Educational Robotics" has become "Edutainment Robotics": Robotics has begun to be taught in educative contexts as hands-on laboratories at school, in order to create entertaining and engaging experiences that support active learning and understanding.

Taking into account the importance that Robotics has gained today from an educational and research point of view, this chapter has focused on the analysis of the cognitive strategies adopted by university students attending a Robotics Laboratory Program, and retention of Robotics contents. In particular, subjects had to build and program basic robots and their reports on the laboratory activities have been analyzed in order to gather information on their experience. A Robotics knowledge questionnaire has been administered in order to quantitatively determine students' understanding of the scientific concepts linked to Robotics, and results have been compared to those obtained thanks to an entry assessment. Then, a retention questionnaire measured the maintenance of Robotics contents after a precise period of time. Control group subjects did not manipulate robotic artifacts.

Results showed that the use of Robotics tools in the proposed educational contexts encouraged and stimulated students. In particular, they have adopted cognitive processes that have allowed them to analyze problems, to select only the information relevant for the task solution, and to develop suitable strategies for the problem solving. Therefore, subjects have been encouraged/stimulated to master new ways of thinking (creative thought), not linked to a specific domain of knowledge. This aspect cannot be measured quantitatively through questionnaires, nor engagement, interest, and enjoyment in the field. Thus, students replied to some questions in the laboratory report on positive and negative aspects of Robotics learning experience. In the experimental group, the majority of the answers have been positive, highlighting the socialization in workgroup, the engaging nature of the proposed activities, and the possibility to take pictures and show the work to university friends. The negative answers regarded the difficulty of some subjects to use technological tools since, as the entry questionnaire has underlined, only few students were comfortable with computers. In the control group, subjects studied diligently the contents explained by the teachers (so their questionnaire results have been similar to experimental group students), but in the anonymous brief answers to the questions regarding their involvement in the course, they declared that the traditional lessons were interesting, but also underlined the difficulty of the subject. Moreover, they declared a confusion related to the topic or the functionality of studying Robotics for students who chose a Cognitive Psychology Course. Therefore, it is possible to affirm that, in this research, Robotics activities have positively affected learning motivation, increased the retention of contents, and enjoyed the participants.

REFERENCES

Arcella, A., Bertacchini, P. A., Bilotta, E., & Gabriele, L. (2003). Progettare il comportamento di un robot: un esperimento didattico. In P. A. Bertacchini, E Bilotta, S. Nolfi & P. Pantano (Eds.), *Proceeding del I° Workshop Italiano di Vita Artificiale*. Arcavacata di Rende.

Barbero, A., Demo, B., & Vaschetto, F. (2011). A contribution to the discussion on informatics and robotics in secondary schools. In *Proceedings of 2nd international conference on Robotics in education (RiE 2011)*. INNOC – Austrian Society for Innovative Computer Sciences, Vienna, Austria, September (pp. 201–206).

Barreto, F., & Benitti, V. (2012). Exploring the educational potential of robotics in schools: a systematic review. *Computers & Education, 58*(3), 978–988.

Behrens, A., Atorf, L., Schwann, R., Neumann, B., Schnitzler, R., Ballé, J., et al. (2010). MATLAB meets LEGO Mindstorms – A Freshman introduction course into practical engineering. *IEEE Transactions on Education, 53*(2), 306–317.

Bell, S. (2010). Project-based learning for the 21st century: Skills for the future. *The Clearin House: A Journal of Educational Strategies, Issues and Ideas, 83*(2), 39–43.

Bereiter, C., & Scardamalia, M. (1989). Intentional learning as a goal of instruction. In L. B. Resnick (Ed.), *Knowing, learning, and instruction: Essays in honor of Robert Glaser* (pp. 361–392). Hillsdale, NJ: Lawrence Erlbaum.

Bers, M. U., & Portsmore, M. (2005). Teaching partnerships: Early childhood and engineering students teaching math and science through robotics. *Journal of Science Education and Technology, 14*(1), 59–73.

Bertacchini, F., Bilotta, E., Gabriele, L., & Servidio, R. (2010). Using LEGO Mindstorms in higher education: Cognitive strategies in programming a quadruped robot. In The 18th international conference on computers in education, ICCE 2010, Putrajaya (Malaysia): 29 November 2010 through 3 December 2010.

Bertacchini, F., Gabriele, L., & Tavernise, A. (2011). Bridging educational technologies and school environment: Implementations and findings from research studies. In J. Hassaskhah (Ed.), *Educational theory* (pp. 63–82). Hauppauge, NY: Nova Science.

Bertacchini, P. A., Bilotta, E., Gabriele, L., Pantano, P., & Servidio, R. (2003). Investigating cognitive processes in robotic programmers developed by children in educational context. In M. Roccetti & M. R. Syed (Eds.), *Proceeding of international conference on simulation and multimedia in engineering education/western multiconference on computer simulation (ICSEE/WMC '03)* (pp. 111–116). Orlando: SCS.

Bertacchini, P. A., Bilotta, E., Gabriele, L., Pantano, P., & Servidio, R. (2006). *Apprendere con le mani. Strategie cognitive per la realizzazione di ambienti di apprendimento-insegnamento con i nuovi strumenti tecnologici.* Milano: Franco Angeli.

Bilotta, E., Bertacchini, F., Gabriele, L., & Tavernise, A. (2011). Education and technology: Learning by hands-on laboratory experiences. In *3rd annual international conference on education and new learning technologies — EDULEARN11.* Barcelona, Spain.

Bilotta, E., Gabriele, L., Pantano, P., & Servidio, R. (2002). Robot, Bambini e apprendimento. *Congresso Nazionale della Sezione di Psicologia Sperimentale dell'AIP,* Bellaria-Rimini, September 16–18, 2002.

Bilotta, E., Gabriele, L., & Servidio, R. (2001). Robotica e Creatività: una ricerca empirica in bambini di scuola elementare, Quaderni del Centro Interdipartimentale della Comunicazione, 10, UNICAL, Cosenza.

Bilotta, E., Gabriele, L., Servidio, R., & Tavernise, A. (2007b). Moto-manipulatory behaviours and learning: An observational study In *Proceedings of interactive computer aided learning — ICL2007,* September 26–28, 2007, Villach, Austria.

Bilotta, E., Gabriele, L., Servidio, R., Tavernise, A. (2009). Edutainment robotics as learning tool. In Z. Pan, A. D. Cheok, W. Müller, & M. Chang (Eds.), *Transactions on Edutainment III. Lecture Notes in Computer Science* (Vol. 5940, pp. 25–35). Berlin Heidelberg: Springer-Verlag. DOI: 10.1007/978-3-642-11245-4_3.

Bilotta, E., Gabriele, L., Servidio, R., & Tavernise, A. (2007a). Investigating mental models in children interacting with small mobile robots. In *Proceedings of interactive computer aided learning — ICL2007,* September 26–28, 2007, Villach, Austria.

Blanchard, S., Freiman, V., & Lirrete-Pitre, N. (2010). Strategies used by elementary school-children solving robotics-based complex tasks: Innovative potential of technology. *Procedia Social and Behavioral Sciences, 2*(2), 2851–2857.

Bransford, J. D., & Stein, B. S. (1993). *The ideal problem solver.* New York, NY: Freeman.

Caci, B., D'Amico, A., & Cardaci, M. (2002). Costruire e Programmare Robots. Resoconto di un'Esperienza Pilota. In Tecnologie Didattiche, 27-3, Genova.

Cardaci, M., Caci, B., & D'Amico, A. (2004). *La robotica nella riabilitazione di soggetti autistici e con deficit cognitivi.* Retrieved from Tecnologie digitali e l'Intelligenza Artificiale al servizio dei disabili, C.I.T.C, Università di Palermo, http://www.siptech.it/giornatabis. html.

Cerezo, A. G., de Gabriel, J. G., Lozano, J. F., Mandow, A., Munoz, V. F., Vidal-Verdu, F. et al. (2009). Using LEGO Robots with LabVIEW for a Summer School on Mechatronics. In *Proceedings of the 2009 IEEE international conference on mechatronics*, April 2009, Malaga, Spain.

Chang, C., Lee, J., Wang, C., & Chen, G. (2010). Improving the authentic learning experience by integrating robots into the mixed-reality environment. *Computers & Education, 55* (4), 1572–1578.

Chitiyo, R., & Harmon, S. W. (2009). An analysis of the integration of instructional technology in pre-service teacher education in Zimbabwe. *Education Technology Research and Development, 57*(6), 807–830.

Chu, S. K. W., Tse, S. K., & Chow, K. (2011). Using collaborative teaching and inquiry project-based learning to help primary school students develop information literacy and information skills. *Library & Information Science Research, 33*(2), 132–143.

Cook, A., Howery, K., Gu, J., & Meng, M. (2001). Robot enhanced interaction and learning for children with profound physical disabilities. *Technology and Disability, 13*(1), 1–8.

Corbellini, G. (2007). Un disegno tutt'altro che intelligente. *Sistemi intelligenti, 19*(1), 149–156.

Custers, E. J. F. M. (2010). Long-term retention of basic science knowledge: A review study. *Advances in Health Science Education, 15*, 109–128.

D'Ambrosio, M., Mirabile, C., & Miglino, O. (2003). Uno studio pilota sull'impiego di giocattoli robotici nella riabilitazione cognitiva. In P. A. Bertacchini, E. Bilotta, S. Nolfi & P. Pantano (Eds.), *Proceeding del I° Workshop Italiano di Vita Artificiale. Arcavacata di Rende.*

Davies, R. S. (2011). Understanding technology literacy: A framework for evaluating educational technology integration. *TechTrends: Linking Research & Practice to Improve Learning, 55*(5), 45–52.

Elmore, B. B., & Seiler, E. (2008). *Using LEGO robotics for K-12 engineering outreach.* Presented at the ASEE Southeastern Section Conference 2008.

Filippov, S. A., & Fradkov, A. L. (2009). Cyber-physical laboratory based on LEGO mindstorms NXT. In *First steps, 18th IEEE international conference on control applications, part of 2009 IEEE multi-conference on systems and control*, Saint Petersburg, Russia, July 8–10, 2009.

Gabriele, L., Arcella, A., Servidio, R. C., & Bertacchini, P. A. (2005a). Investigare strategie di problem solving attraverso la robotica: un'esperienza con studenti universitari. *2° Workshop Italiano di Vita Artificiale*, Istituto di Scienze e Tecnologie della Cognizione, CNR, Roma, 2−5 Marzo, 2005. In Baldassarre, G., Marocco, D., & Mirolli, M. (Eds) CNR:Roma, 2005.

Gabriele, L., Servidio, R., & Tavernise, A. (2005b). Acquisire concetti complessi attraverso l'uso di strumenti: un'indagine empirica. *Congresso Nazionale della Sezione di Psicologia Sperimentale dell'AIP*, September 18−20, 2005.

Garbati, M. (2010). *Robotica Educativa.* Milano: Boopen editore.

Gonzalez-Gomez, J., Valero-Gomez, A., Prieto-Moreno, A., & Abderrahim, M. (2011). A new open source 3D-printable mobile Robotic platform for education. In *Proceedings of the 6th international symposium on autonomous minirobots for research and Edutainment,* May 23−25. Bielefeld, Germany.

Harel, I., & Papert, S. (1990). Software design as a learning environment. *Interactive Learning Environment, 1*(1), 1–32.

Herold, D. K. (2010). Mediating media studies: Stimulating critical awareness in a virtual environment. *Computers & Education, 54,* 791–798.

Honebein, P. (1996). Seven goals for the design of constructivist learning environments. In B. Wilson (Ed.), *Constructivist learning environments* (pp. 17–24). Englewood Cliffs, NJ: Educational Technology Publications.

Hsu, S. (2011). Who assigns the most ICT activities? examining the relationship between teacher and student usage. *Computers & Education, 56*(3), 847–855.

Hudson, R.A. (2010). *Statistical argumentation in project-based learning environments.* PhD Disseration, Indiana University.

Jadud, M. (2000). Teamstorms as a theory of instruction. In Proceedings of IEEE systems, cybernetics, and man 2000 (SMC2000). October 8−11, 2000, Nashville.

Jardón, A., Paloma, Z., de la Casa, S.M., & Giménez, A. (2008). CEABOT: National wide little humanoid robots competition; Rules, experiences and new challenges. In *Workshop proceedings of Simpar 2008, international conference on simulation, modeling and programming for autonomous Robots.* November 3−4, Venice, Italy.

Joldersma, C. W. (2011). Ernst von Glasersfeld's radical constructivism truth as disclosure. *Educational Theory, 61*(3), 275–293.

Jonassen, D., Howland, J., Marra, R. M., & Crismond, D. (2008). *Meaningful learning with Technology* (3rd ed.). Upper Saddle River, NJ: Pearson Education.

Karahoca, D., Karahoca, A., & Uzunboylu, H. (2011). Robotics teaching in primary school education by project based learning for supporting science and technology courses, WCIT-2010. *Procedia Computer Science, 3*(2011), 1425–1431.

Karp, T., Gale, R., Lowe, L. A., Medina, V., & Beutlich, E. (2010). Generation NXT: Building young engineers With LEGOs, 80. *IEEE Transactions on Education, 53*(1), 80–87.

Kato, S., & Tominaga, H. (2010). *A style and tool for group exercise of introductory programming with LEGO robot control as pre-education event.* Paper presented at the 9th International Conference on Information Technology Based Higher Education and Training, April 29−May 1, 2010. Cappadocia, Turkey.

Kim, S. H., & Jeon, J. W. (2009). Introduction for freshmen to embedded systems using LEGO Mindstorms. *IEEE Transactions on Education, 52*(1), 99–108.

Kiss, G. (2010). Using the Lego-Mindstorm kit in German Computer Science education, SAMI 2010. In *8th IEEE international symposium on applied machine intelligence and informatics,* January 28−30, 2010. Herl'any, Slovakia.

Kronreif, G. (2009). Robot systems for play in education and therapy of disabled children. *Studies in Computational Intelligence, 243,* 221–234.

Kronreif, G., Prazak, B., Kornfeld, M., Hochgatterer, A., & Fürst, M. (2007). Robot assistant "PlayROB" − User trials and results. In *Proceedings − IEEE international workshop on Robot and human interactive communication,* 4415063 (pp. 113−117). Lucca.

Larmer, J., & Mergendolle, J. R. (2010). 7 essentials for project-based learning. *Educational Leadership, 68*(1), 1–4.

Legof, D. B., & Sherman, M. (2006). Long-term outcome of social skills intervention based on interactive LEGO© play. *Autism, 10*(4), 317–329.

Loveless, A., Burton, J., & Turvey, K. (2006). Developing conceptual frameworks for creativity, ICT and teacher education. *Thinking Skills and Creativity, 1*(2006), 3–13.

Lund, H.H., & Pagliarini, L. (2002). Edutainment and robotic games for children. In *Proceedings of 2nd IFAC conference on mechnatronic system*, Elsevier.

Maia, L., Silva, V., de S Rosa, R.E.V., Queiroz-Neto, J.P., de Lucena, V.F. (2009). An experience to use robotics to improve computer science learning. In *TX 39th ASEE/IEEE frontiers in education conference*. October 18–21, San Antonio.

Makrodimitris, M., Nikolakakis, A., Papadopoulos, E. (2011). A robot-based semi-autonomous color line-following educational robots: Design and implementation. In *International conference on advanced intelligent mechatronics (AIM2011)*, IEEE/ASME, July 3–7, Budapest, Hungary.

Martin, F. (1994). *Circuits to control: Learning engineering by designing LEGO robots*. PhD thesis. MIT, Boston.

Martin, F. (2001). Interviste. In E. Bilotta (Ed.), *In ONDE, Periodico di Comunicazione e Innovazione Tecnologica della DATEL, Quadrimestrale di approfondimento scientifico*. Catanzaro: Abramo Editoren. 1 (gennaio 2001).

Martinovic, D., & Zhang, Z. (2011). Situating ICT in the teacher education program: Overcoming challenges, fulfilling expectations. *Teaching and Teacher Education, 28*(3), 461–469.

Miglino, O., Lund, H. H., & Cardaci, M. (1999). Robotics as an educational tool. *Journal of Interactive Learning Research, 10*(1), 25–48.

Mitnik, R., Nussbaum, M., & Soto, A. (2008). An autonomous educational mobile robot mediator. *Autonomous Robots, 25*(4), 367–382.

Mitnik, R., Recabarren, M., Nussbaum, M., & Soto, A. (2009). Collaborative robotic instruction: A graph teaching experience. *Computers & Education, 53*, 330–342.

Moshe, B., & Yair, Z. (2009). Robotics projects and learning concepts in science, technology and problem solving. *International Journal of Technology & Design Education, 19*(3), 289–307.

Nari, L. (2010). *Effects of project-based Learning on critical thinking: Focusing on class of environmental design in first-grade high school students*. Master's thesis. Ewha Womans University.

Owens, G., Granader, Y., Humphrey, A., & Baron-Cohen, S. (2008). LEGO® therapy and the social use of language programme: An evaluation of two social skills interventions for children with high functioning autism and Asperger Syndrome. *Journal of Autism and Developmental Disorders, 38*, 1944–1957.

Panadero, C.F., Román, J.V., & Kloos, C.D. (2010). Impact of learning experiences using LEGO Mindstorms® in engineering courses, IEEE EDUCON Education Engineering 2010 – The Future of Global Learning Engineering Education, Madrid, Spain, April 14–16.

Papert, S. (1984). *Mindstorms, Bambini Computers e creatività*. Milano: Emme edizioni.

Papert, S. (1986). *Constructionism: A new opportunity for elementary science education*. Cambridge, MA: MIT, Media Laboratory, Epistemology and Learning Group.

Papert, S. (1991). Situating constructionism. In I. Harel & S. Papert (Eds.), *Constructionism* (pp. 1–11). Norwood, NJ: Ablex Publishing.

Parricchi, M. (2004). *Tecnologie della comunicazione e metodologie e-learning in università. Un processo evolutivo per le scienze umane*Milano: Vita e Pensiero.

Piaget, J. (1967). *Lo sviluppo mentale del bambino*. Torino: Einaudi.

Piaget, J. (1971). *L'epistemologia genetica*. Roma-Bari: Laterza.

Resnick, M. (1989). LEGO, logo, and life. In C. Langton (Ed.), *Artificial life* (pp. 397–406). Redwood City, CA: Addison-Wesley.

Resnick, M. (1994). *Turtles, termites, and traffic jams: Explorations in massively parallel microworlds*. Cambridge, MA: MIT Press.

Rutten, N., van Joolingen, W. R., & van der Veen, J. T. (2012). The learning effects of computer simulations in science education. *Computers & Education, 58*(1), 136–153.

Sánchez, J. J. C., & Alemán, E. C. (2011). Teachers' opinion survey on the use of ICT tools to support attendance-based teaching. *Computers & Education, 56*(3), 911–915.

Sinatra, G. M., & Pintrich, P. R. (2008). *Intentional conceptual change*. Mahwah, NJ: Lawrence Erlbaum.

Sklar, E., & Eguchi, A. (2002). Examining team robotics through RoboCupJunior. In *Annual conference of Japan Society for Educational Technology*, Nagaoka, Japan, November 2002.

Sklar, E., & Eguchi, A. (2004). Learning while teaching robotics. In *AAAI spring symposium 2004 on accessible hands-on artificial intelligence and Robotics education*. Westin Peachtree Plaza Atlanta, Georgia, USA. July 11–15, 2010

Sun, R., Merrill, E., & Peterson, T. (2001). From implicit skills to explicit knowledge: A bottom-up model of skill learning. *Cognitive Science, 25*(2), 203–244.

Sun, R., & Zhang, X. (2002). *Top-down versus bottom-up learning in skill acquisition. Proceedings of the 24th annual conference of the cognitive science society, Fairfax, VA*. Mahwah, NJ: Lawrence Erlbaum.

Tekerek, M. (2009). A human robot interaction application for robotic education, WCSE2009. *Procedia, 1*(1), 2164–2169. *Social and Behavioral Sciences, 1*(1), 2164–2169.

Upadhyay, B., & De Franco, C. (2008). Elementary students' retention of environmental science knowledge: Connected science instruction versus direct instruction. *Journal of Elementary Science Education, 20*(2), 23–37.

UTILISING THE VIRTUAL LEARNING ENVIRONMENT TO ENCOURAGE FACULTY REFLECTION AND IMPROVE THE STUDENT LEARNING EXPERIENCE

Tiffany M. Winchester and Maxwell K. Winchester

ABSTRACT

Student evaluations of teaching (SETs) are the most frequent form of faculty performance in the classroom, though they tend to be used as summative rather than formative evaluations. In this chapter, a project involving the use of a virtual learning environment for formative, weekly SETs is explored from both the student and faculty point of view at a rural university college in the United Kingdom. This project encouraged student participation in creating the learning environment and faculty reflection on how to improve the student experience. From the student

Increasing Student Engagement and Retention using Immersive Interfaces: Virtual
Worlds, Gaming, and Simulation
Cutting-edge Technologies in Higher Education, Volume 6C, 341–368
Copyright © 2012 by Emerald Group Publishing Limited
All rights of reproduction in any form reserved
ISSN: 2044-9968/doi:10.1108/S2044-9968(2012)000006C015

perspective, the weekly anonymous evaluations were useful for providing feedback; however, students tended to only respond if they were not satisfied with the faculty member. The exception to this was that some students were more motivated to complete the evaluation forms if they believed the faculty member was utilising their feedback. From the faculty perspective, the feedback was not as detailed as they had expected, and some questioned whether it was worth the effort of conducting formative evaluations if the response rate was so low. Others used the feedback for reflective purposes, and it was found that those that reflected on their work at higher levels tended to receive a greater year-on-year increase in their end of year teaching evaluations.

INTRODUCTION

Years ago, the quality of a university was solely judged by its research output (Massy, 1994). Although the informal introduction of student evaluations of teaching (SETs) occurred in the 1960s, the practise was formalised in the 1980s and 1990s when there was a push to recognise the value of the quality of the teaching students received (Hittman, 1993). Student evaluations of teaching quality are now the most frequent form of evaluation of faculty performance in the classroom (Becker & Watts, 1999; Davis, 2009; Lill, 1979; Onwuegbuzie, Witcher, Collins, & Filler, 2007; Parayitam, Desai, & Phelps, 2007; Read, Rama, & Raghunandan, 2001; Yao & Grady, 2005). Now higher education institutions not only seek student views, but also attempt to act upon them; the institutions that report the outcomes of changes publicly have achieved high scores in quality assurance (QA) reports (Leckey & Neville, 2001).

With the implementation of formalised SETs over the last few decades, it is easy to assume that the quality of teaching should have improved. However, what qualifies as 'good teaching' is subjective and has caused disagreement in the literature (e.g., Carmichael, Palermo, Reeve, & Vallence, 2001; Kember, Leung, & Kwan, 2002). Even though the definitions vary, it could be assumed that most academics in higher education seek to improve their teaching quality. Some literature suggests that the best form of response on which to encourage consideration about teaching quality is student feedback (Beaty, 1997). Beaty (1997) notes, however, that finding efficient ways to understand the student perspective is crucial and the best strategy is to use a method that requires the least amount of effort from both the faculty member and the student while still gathering useful information. It could be argued that SETs are an efficient method of gathering such information, and possibly why they have such great acceptance across universities.

The rationale for implementing such a QA system in universities was to ensure that faculty members were engaging in good teaching practices. The principle that university teaching not only can be improved, but should be improved is widely accepted (e.g. Ramsden, 1992); however, the reliance on SETs to measure the success of this has been widely criticised (Anderson, Cain & Bird, 2005; Cahn, 2011), questioning the aforementioned 'usefulness' of the information they provide. This information collected at the end of semester or degree via the SETs is used for a variety of purposes. The most obvious is that SETs provide an academic with feedback, which they may utilise to improve their teaching methods (Chen & Hoshower, 1998). While "such evaluations are . . . the most important, and sometimes the sole, measure of an instructor's teaching ability" (Wilson, 1998, p. A12, cited in Becker & Watts, 1999), given they are usually administered at the end (summative) rather than during (formative) a semester, there seems to be a more retrospective QA practice. This focus, common in most universities across Australia, New Zealand, the United States, and the United Kingdom, SETs may be more concerned with "quantifying some of the presumed indicators of good teaching and good management" (Biggs, 2001, p. 222) rather than focusing on the actual quality of teaching and learning. In this sense, they may be useful for administrators, but of limited value to the faculty member (Becker & Watts, 1999; Onwuegbuzie et al., 2007; Yao & Grady, 2005).

CRITICISMS OF STUDENT EVALUATIONS OF TEACHING

A few educational researchers have questioned whether SETs have any direct impact on the overall quality of teaching (Kember et al., 2002). In some instances, it is argued, SETs can actually have a negative impact on teaching quality due to the increase in stress or pressure to perform (Brown, 2008; Mercer, 2006). Such criticisms of using SETs include

- Grading leniency bias (higher ratings when higher grades are expected, and therefore vice versa);

- Adapting unit[1] difficulty (e.g., reducing the amount of homework or dumbing materials down to keep students happy, or even reducing or eliminating the fail rate of students);
- Decreasing the likelihood that teachers discuss controversial ideas or challenging questions because of the fear that students will decrease their scores on the SET, thus the SET becomes a threat to academic freedom (Braskamp & Ory, 1994, cited in Parayitam et al., 2007);
- Decreasing the chances that the teacher be willing to challenge the student, thus actually decreasing the learning in the classroom (Pritchard & Potter, 2011);
- Other factors over which the faculty member has little control may influence the SET score, such as cosmetic factors (such as faculty member's gender, race, sense of humour, and/or physical appearance);
- Whether the unit is a required unit or an elective, student effort and student interest in the unit (McPherson, 2006; Onwuegbuzie et al., 2007; Parayitam et al., 2007; Scriven, 1995; Weinberg, Hashimoto & Fleisher, 2009).

In spite of these criticisms, empirical research has shown some SET tools directly measure quality of instruction (Barth, 2008). If this is so, there is an argument that those who benefit most from any improvement in teaching quality would be best to provide such information: "Learners are perceived by many to be the most reliable source of data about the relationship between teaching and learning on the grounds that they are witness to the teaching across time and the best judge of its effects on their achievements" (Pratt, 1997, p. 35). From a customer service perspective, it has been argued students are in fact customers of universities and therefore it is important to ensure they are satisfied, though there have been debates about whether students should be seen as 'paying customers' and therefore treated as such. One might suggest that some of the criticisms of SETs have come about because one begins to think of the student as a customer. However, since students are stakeholders who are intricately involved in the classroom, it is reasonable that they should have some sort of voice in its outcome, and help to shape the learning environment.

A major issue with the current implementation of SETs is that they are most commonly administered at the end of the semester or degree programme in a summative manner. Since students who typically complete such SETs have finished the unit of study, or their degree, they cannot experience the positive outcome of these evaluations (Winchester & Winchester, 2011). Such summative SETs are of limited benefit to the students completing them. The current system of only using summative SETs also risks a decrease in student motivation to correctly fill in evaluation forms, therefore possibly reducing their meaningful input. It is important for students to see that the information leads directly to changes in teaching or curriculum, as students tend to doubt this when completing end of semester evaluations.

Response rate for summative SETs seems to vary depending on how they are administered. One study noted that students attending an Open University course were mailed the questionnaire with a postage-paid envelope, along with two or three reminders. The response rate to this SET was around 60% (post-exam) and 50% (if done within the unit of study) (Kirkwood & Price, 2005). Others have noted that the response rate to SETs seems to be declining over the years (their data cited 44% and 39%), possibly due to student fatigue and disinterest (Leckey & Neville, 2001). To address this issue, one study encouraged student response by tying it to grade release, increasing the response rate to near 80%, though they did acknowledge this may have biased the results of the SET (Pan et al., 2009). Oliver and Sautter (2005) reviewed the literature from the late 1990s and early 2000 and noted that most research found that online SET response rate was much lower than in-class ones, though their own research found that with continual assurance of student response anonymity, there was no significant difference between the methods of eliciting response. More recent work found that participation in an online survey with e-mail solicitation had only a 20% response rate (Kidwell & Kidwell, 2008), and one Australian university which made the switch from paper-based to online SETs found that the overall response rate across the university was initially 5%, though with changes to the design as well as faculty promotion of the SET, the result increased to 21% (Hamilton, Sibley, & Hawkins, 2011). Overall, some researchers note that with the decrease in response rate in shifting from paper-based to online SETs, the overall mean rating of the SET doesn't change (Stowell, Addison, & Smith, 2011) though there would be a decrease in the overall amount of qualitative feedback from the students.

Most importantly, given the possible focus on organisational rather than faculty objectives in interpreting results of SETs, it appears that Ramsden's original hope for teaching evaluation in many cases has not been taken on board: "Evaluation is not at heart about collecting evidence to justify oneself, nor about measuring the relative worth of units or teachers. It is about coming to understand teaching in order to improve student learning" (Ramsden, 1992, p. 241). This point of view is consistent with other views that the main purpose of teaching evaluation should be to allow the faculty member to use it as part of their reflective practice (Trigwell & Shale, 2004). This suggests evaluations would be more useful for students if they were conducted formatively, rather than summatively as is the common practice. A formative evaluation would allow the faculty member to utilise feedback to improve their lectures as they happen, rather than waiting until the end of a year or semester when what they actually did in a particular class may be difficult to recall. However, as mentioned earlier by Beaty (1997), finding an efficient system that works for both the faculty member as well as the student may be a challenge. As well, in light of the changing response rate for SETs, asking students to complete more than one SET and also provide meaningful feedback also may be problematic.

DEVELOPING A FORMATIVE FEEDBACK SYSTEM

In light of this, a system of formative evaluations needed to be developed that was efficient for both faculty and students. The project came about serendipitously after conducting mid-unit feedback forms with open-ended questions. The responses of the students were positive and detailed, concurring with previous research on mid-unit evaluations where students perceived they reflected positively on the instructor's commitment to teaching and performance (Brown, 2008). This observation led to the idea that it might be worth doing continuous formative evaluation throughout the life of a unit. However, these mid-unit feedback forms were paper-based and conducted during the class-time, and the results then needed to be entered into a spreadsheet in order to look at the overall results. The thought of conducting more than one of these, or even progressing to doing them on a weekly basis, was a daunting task from the faculty members' perspective. As well, from the student perspective, this used up valuable class time, and while some might consider the reduced lecture time a benefit, overall there would be a decrease in the amount of learning time available each week.

It was important to recognise that different student groups at different levels of education may have different needs and styles of learning, and therefore the same teaching style may not be appropriate for all units, nor each time the unit was run. It was hoped that an outcome of this project was that knowledge gained would assist in the continual improvement of each unit, and potentially adapting each unit's presentation to that particular group of students.

Therefore, the aim of the overall project was to explore the feasibility of weekly online evaluations of lectures both from a student and faculty point of view. The objective of using the virtual learning environment (VLE) for conducting the formative evaluations was two-fold. First, it allowed anonymous student feedback in a convenient, easily accessible manner, which was tied in with activities the students were already involved in via the VLE, and therefore added to their learning experience. Second, it allowed the faculty to gain weekly feedback without 'putting themselves out there and asking for it' and utilise that feedback to improve their teaching as it happened. Most student evaluations were previously conducted by the students in the classroom setting (Becker & Watts, 1999), and recommendations are that the teacher be absent in order to reduce biases (Lill, 1979). Conducting SETs electronically is not a common practice, though with the increase in student numbers across many universities and constantly updated technologies, this practice is becoming less unheard of, especially in the sciences (Peat & Franklin, 2002) and online learning programmes (Ogunleye, 2010). However, with this switch from paper-based to online SETs, survey nonresponse is increasing (Adams & Umbach, 2012).

Though there are other more intensive forms of evaluation, such as peer reviews, teaching portfolios, and qualitative feedback from students, Read et al. (2001) noted these place a greater demand on those doing the evaluation, as well as the institution, as they are more time consuming. This study addresses the time consumption demand by conducting the evaluations both online and weekly in order to gain ongoing quantitative and qualitative feedback. As well, such formative objectives eliminate the need to consider many of the aforementioned criticisms of SETs outlined earlier, as the purpose of using formative SETs is for personal development only.

SETTING UP STUDENT EVALUATIONS OF TEACHING THROUGH THE VIRTUAL LEARNING ENVIRONMENT

Prior research indicates that there are limited criteria of effective teaching that students can evaluate effectively and therefore provide useful feedback to (Green, Calderon, & Reider, 1998). Therefore, it was important to research what types of questions were both assessable by the students, and also useful for feedback to the faculty member. Calderon, Gabbin, and

Green (1996, cited in Green et al., 1998) noted that students were unable to effectively assess items beyond their scope of knowledge, including

- sufficiency of unit content;
- whether unit materials are current;
- instructors knowledge of the subject matter;
- appropriateness of unit objectives and content;
- appropriateness of technology used in the unit.

Another issue for questionnaire design was the use of opened- or closed-ended questions. While closed-ended questions make the questionnaire quicker to fill out from the student perspective, open-ended questions provide the opportunity for students to provide explanatory feedback. Mostly close-ended questions were used, as this practice is most common (Becker & Watts, 1999; Lill, 1979; Onwuegbuzie et al., 2007), usually with an arbitrary rating from 1−5 Likert scale, anchored by Strongly Agree and Strongly Disagree on either end. There has been concern in previous research about reducing the 'complex teaching process to series of numbers on a teaching form' (Mercer, 2006, p. 24), but it facilitates easy interpretation and was less time-consuming for the faculty member to assess the evaluation forms. One open-ended question was added at the end of the questionnaire to allow for any other feedback the student wished to make.

A list of possible questions was compiled using a variety of literature (Becker & Watts, 1999; Lill, 1979; Onwuegbuzie et al., 2007; Parayitam et al., 2007) and faculty feedback before the final questionnaire was assembled. This questionnaire was pilot tested during the first few weeks of study by the students before being finalised for use throughout the year. This common questionnaire was administered to each faculty member to use as a guide, though they were encouraged to add questions that were more specific to their unit. The final SET included the following questions based on themes (note: the themes were not visible to the students):

LECTURES PITCHED AT THE RIGHT LEVEL
1. The material covered in the class was aimed at a level that I understand.

MATERIAL PRESENTED IN AN INTERESTING AND CHALLENGING MATTER
2. The lecturer presented the subject material in a way that was interesting.

3. The lecturer presented different viewpoints on the subject.
4. I have learned a great deal in this class.
5. The lecturer encouraged me to broaden my understanding of the subject material through additional study.

BALANCE BETWEEN ACTUAL FORMAL LECTURING AND OTHER DISCUSSION-BASED ACTIVITIES
6. The lecturer encouraged relevant questions or comments.
7. The lecturer raised challenging questions.
8. The lecturer managed classroom discussions that they were useful.

PARTICULAR CLASS MATERIALS LINKED WELL TO MATERIALS PREVIOUSLY TAUGHT IN EARLIER WEEKS (OR OTHER MODULES) (OR REAL WORLD)
9. The lecturer related the subject matter among the topics in this module.
10. The lecturer related course material to real-world situations whenever possible.

LECTURER'S COMMUNICATION ABILITY
11. The lecturer organised the subject matter of this course in a logical manner.
12. The lecturer communicated clearly and effectively.
13. The lecturer inspired interest in this subject material.

There was not any formal criterion for the selection of faculty and units, though it was hoped that the participants might come from diverse backgrounds so a broad range of data could be collected (Yao & Grady, 2005). Faculty from different departments, seniority, gender, and experience were asked to volunteer for the study, and the eLearning department also gave recommendations on what faculty members might be interested, based on their engagement in the VLE previously. Nevertheless, as the study was exploratory, representativeness was not a major criterion for the selection of participants. Each faculty member was given a set of instructions and a training session on how to set up the SET within their unit's VLE, and how to access the feedback each week.

Initially, it was proposed that students would have to fill in the questionnaire as a condition of downloading their class notes off the VLE, thus creating a 'roadblock' before they could access the materials. However, the

British Educational Research Association deemed this unacceptable practice: 'researchers must not use coercion or duress of any form to persuade participants' to provide feedback (BERA, 2004, p. 7). It was agreed by the researchers not to use the questionnaire as an immovable caveat to downloading the unit materials, and instead, it would need to be linked to the VLE in a different manner.

Each faculty member was therefore able to choose what technique they would like to use for eliciting feedback from the students, as long as they complied with BERA guidelines. Half of the faculty members did not normally provide printed out notes in class and the students were responsible for downloading them from the VLE. In these cases, the evaluation tool was linked to the notes, and the students were faced with a 'speed bump' of the evaluation tool each week prior to getting their notes (though they could by-pass the evaluation tool and not answer the questions). Another faculty member linked them to activities, which the students will re-visit once the lectures are all completed. One faculty member did not link the evaluation tool to any VLE items, and simply reminded the students to fill it in each week.

PHASE ONE: FACULTY PERSPECTIVE ON UTILISING THE VIRTUAL LEARNING ENVIRONMENT TO RECEIVE FEEDBACK

The faculty members represented a number of departments within the overall university college, representing Business, IT, Veterinary Nurses, and Environmental Studies. Four of the faculty members were from British backgrounds, one Canadian, and one Australian. Most of the respondents had only been teaching for a year or two, and two of the respondents had over ten years' experience. Two of the respondents were males, and four were females, and the ages varied from earlier teaching career (20s) to later teaching career (50s).

Qualitative interviews were conducted with the faculty members about half way through the yearlong project, once they had received approximately 12 weeks of feedback (note: the units for this particular study were run on a 25 week basis). All of the faculty members had experience with the typical end of year evaluations conducted university wide by the university's QA department. These evaluations tended to rate the overall unit on a score of 1−5, and that information was fed back to the faculty leader of the unit. Most of the faculty members expressed frustration with the current system of summative evaluations in terms of implementing changes to their teaching method, so were interested in the idea of using weekly feedback via the VLE. One expressed a great deal of interest in using the VLE for weekly feedback, as 'If you got immediate feedback at the end of that session, you can actually do something about it in the beginning of the next session'. A few of the faculty members had tried to do their own formative evaluations in previous units, and one attempted to do this via the VLE, stating they were too shy to ask for feedback during the class time. However, they found the experience frustrating: 'I think out of a 104 students I think I had about 10 actually fill it in, having given them about sort of 4 weeks. So I wouldn't bother with that again'.

Based on the experience that the volunteers had previously with student evaluations, the researchers queried what made them want to get involved in the project of weekly SETs via the VLE. One faculty member wanted to get involved in projects with like-minded faculty and was interested in further developing as a reflective practitioner. A few mentioned they were really interested in getting more detailed feedback from the students as perhaps they were not confident enough to ask for it in class, or lacked experience in 'reading' the students during the unit: 'realised that I had no idea what kind of level I was talking to and if the students were getting anything out of it.... I wasn't experienced enough to really get that verbal feedback during class'. Others noted that the context of the feedback, being via the VLE, was interesting as the feedback would be easily accessible, but were concerned that while the students valued the VLE, 'they value it for revision and that's their primary source for all the links'.

One interesting find was that regardless of the method used for eliciting feedback from the students, all faculty struggled with a lack of response rate from students. All participants were disheartened by this factor: '... that ends up being a 25% response rate for the overall class ... makes you wonder if that was representativeness enough to be able to do anything with the feedback ... those students that respond, is there a reason they're responding?' The literature on expectancy theory suggesting that students will be motivated by seeing their input into the lecture being taken seriously may have led some students to keep using the evaluation tool, but didn't seem to inspire new students to sign up, supporting the work of Chen and Hoshower (1998).

Some questioned the students' ability to be critical when evaluating a lecture, as most of the feedback was very positive. 'I've gone into class and actually shown them the results from the previous week, and made the comment that everything seems to be fine again ... try to encourage them that way .... I'm not sure how you get students to make more comments'. However, one new faculty member commented that even if there were not many comments made or many students participating, you still had an overall view of how the lectures were going, consistent with research finding that students are 'discerning evaluators who are sensitive to different qualities of courses' (Remidios & Lieberman, 2008, p. 112).

When asked about their barriers to using the evaluation tool, the respondents tended to agree that one impediment was the lack of student response. While they were positive about the evaluation tool itself, they questioned its usefulness in light of a small number of students actually utilising the tool. Another comment made by a number of the respondents was the lack of critical evaluation of each lecture. 'I think the problem is the students are apathetic, I just don't think they care enough to make comments that are useful... their view on the way teaching works is, maybe they don't see it as a two way communication'. This is consistent with the research by Chen and Hoshower (1998) on the essential components of meaningful and active participation (p. 532) when looking at the link between motivation and outcome. In this case, that type of participation did not seem to be elicited by the overall student responses to the evaluation. One respondent agreed with this, and even taught some non-updated lectures to see if the students would respond, 'almost like a test to see if they were doing it right, and found that the feedback didn't actually change as much as I would have thought that it should'. This is consistent with research by Divoky (1995) in that students generally became more uninterested with the evaluation tool because it was too familiar.

There were some serendipitous findings to the study. One faculty member, when questioned on what they did with the feedback noted:

> To be fair I think it's not so much what have I been doing with the feedback tool, for me it was the fact that I knew that feedback was coming, I consciously changed my lecture before.... I had been evaluated on it ... knowing those were the questions they were going to be answering I actually changed the lectures that I ran from last year so that they would be able to answer those questions positively.

Thus, the evaluation tool provided a sense of motivation, and the questions themselves provided scope for what elements should be changed. Another faculty member noted:

> One of the questions in particular asked if they were inspired to go and learn more, perhaps wasn't something that I'd identified as a key thing that I should be doing ... which is of course in a final year group is something hopefully very important. I think

> I was quite interested to find out whether I had done enough of a push to get them to go out and look for themselves at the end of a lecture.

Regarding the usefulness of the VLE for conducting feedback, the results were varied. There were a few comments about how frequently they would use the tool, and most agreed that weekly was possibly too often, and a more flexible approach would be worthwhile. 'I'm keen to actually evaluate…this focuses very much on what went on in the session … there are some other things I'm keen to experiment with…… I thought our students would be more digitally natured than they are'. A few mentioned that perhaps the inclusion of more qualitative comments around each question would allow for more detailed feedback, but they questioned the student's likelihood of responding to more detailed questionnaires. Others thought that there wasn't a strong culture of using the VLE at this particular university, and therefore the students were not used to accessing the VLE on an ongoing basis, which may have impacted the response rate. Therefore, the second study focused on the research question: Are weekly online evaluations of lectures viable from a student perspective.

PHASE TWO: STUDENT PERSPECTIVES ON UTILISING THE VIRTUAL LEARNING ENVIRONMENT FOR PROVIDING FEEDBACK

This study considers student perspectives on the viability of filling in the evaluations both online and weekly. The evaluation tool was available to all students enrolled in each unit that was part of the study, a total of 192 students. From this population of students, the total number of participants in this study was limited to seven so the amount of qualitative feedback from the interviews would not be overwhelming. Again, as the study was exploratory, representativeness was not a major criterion for the selection of participants. The sample was drawn to ensure males and females were interviewed, along with students of different year level and unit. Five of the students interviewed were local UK students while two were final year international students from China.

The interviews took place towards the end of the year, after the students had an opportunity to fill in approximately 18–20 weekly evaluation forms (out of a total of 25).

An aide-mémoire was developed which included the following points for conversation:

1. What has been your previous experience with evaluating lecturers?
2. How often did you fill in the evaluation tool? If not, why not?
3. Did you see any results from your lecturer/classes from your evaluation? Or, what do you think they did with the evaluations?
4. Did this response (or lack of response) inspire you to continue/start the evaluations?
5. Were there any barriers to you filling in the evaluation tool?
6. What changes, if any, would you suggest to this tool?
7. Would you like to continue using this tool?

All students indicated they had experience in filling in the common end-of-unit summative feedback forms. Their feelings were mixed as to how they believed traditional evaluations were utilised by faculty members. Some students were confident that faculty took on board feedback they had received, though others were less convinced. Even when they believed that the lecturers would take on board comments given in summative evaluations, some students were concerned that being at the end of a teaching period, they would not benefit from any changes made.

When asked about the formative evaluation tool, the results were also mixed. Some students expressed they were happy about the tool in the early weeks, but their motivation dwindled as the year went on. Others thought it was a real benefit having the evaluation tool, as they believed that any problems that arose could be dealt with quickly. This led to a discussion on their perceptions of whether or not the faculty member was using the feedback tool. Some were positive that their lecturer was using the feedback, and they were positive about the changes being made. Others noted that if they were not able to see changes, this might make the evaluation tool useless. One of the British students aired a similar thought: 'I wouldn't have put the same effort into doing the questionnaire if I wasn't sure there would be a payoff'. These comments led the interviewers to understand the importance of ensuring that students were aware that faculty were taking on board the feedback coming from the evaluation tool. When this question was probed for further information, some students commented that since they had only put agree or strongly agree on the feedback form, they hadn't expected to see any changes. Though this being said, they did comment that the lecturer brought up the feedback form each week, and therefore if there were changes that needed to be made, they were confident that the lecturer would take them on board.

The students were then asked about using the VLE for conducting feedback, and the overall results were positive. Students thought it was a useful tool for providing anonymous feedback, and appreciated having an outlet where they could express their views at any place and any time. The faculty concerns about response rate were also brought up, and some students commented that this should not be a concern, as they might only comment if there was a problem: '. . . no news is good news'. Students seemed to be more inclined to comment on negative issues, rather than provide constructive positive feedback.

A theme that arose around the timing of the tool was probed further. There was a conflict in feelings on this issue. Respondents almost unanimously did not want to fill out a survey every week: 'I think it would be redundant ... I don't think it would work. Having to do it for every class people will get very fed up of it very quickly'. Others commented that if the questions were different, or more tailored to the materials being covered, this might help. Others suggested reducing the questionnaire to 4–5 questions, with the inclusion of more open-ended questions for the opportunity to expand on the feedback.

The overall comments on the use of the feedback brought up a discussion on the type of faculty member who would be willing to receive weekly feedback via the VLE. Some students commented that the faculty members who were using the tool were those who would be willing to receive feedback. They also commented that they would have liked other faculty members to use the tool so that they could comment directly to them and ensure that faculty member received the feedback. This was confirmed by another student who saw the evaluation tool as an opportunity to give anonymous constructive feedback to other lecturers, knowing that feedback would go directly to the lecturer in question rather than via someone else. This may be related to the type of lecturer who would be willing to stand up to scrutiny and implement such a tool voluntarily, calling upon future research to explore this topic further.

PHASE THREE: IMPROVING THE LEARNING EXPERIENCE THROUGH FACULTY REFLECTIVE PRACTICE

The next study considered faculty use of information gathered by weekly formative SETs for reflective purposes. While previous research has shown that formative SETs are one form of information that can be utilised to encourage reflection (Beaty, 1997), there is limited research on the depth of the reflection that is undertaken using such information.

Being a reflective practitioner is considered a pinnacle of teaching practice and its desirability is assumed in the literature (Moon, 1999). The level of journal articles on reflection or reflective practice is phenomenal. A simple search using those terms will turn up hundreds, if not thousands, of articles looking at reflection as something that all teachers in higher education should aspire to, if not already be doing. At the time of writing, a simple search in Google Scholar using the search words 'reflective practice' and 'higher education' turned out 20,100 scholarly articles. Simply put, reflective practice involves a teacher realising that learning to teach is something that happens throughout their career, not just when they are taking their teaching qualification (MacFarlane & Ottewill, 2001; Zeichner & Liston, 1996).

Although much of the literature alludes to the use of journals, peer observation, notes or other qualitative forms of data (Beaty, 1997; Bolton, 2005; Loughran, 1996; Moon, 1999), 'the process of becoming a reflective practitioner cannot be prescribed' (Larrivee, 2000, p. 296). Although some literature suggests that the best form of response with which to encourage reflection is student feedback, it has also been noted that finding efficient ways to access this student perspective is a crucial element (Beaty, 1997). Such an efficient method has been developed and trialed by conducting formative SETs using the Internet or the university's VLE in both the United States and the United Kingdom (Ravelli, 2000; Winchester & Winchester, 2010).

Though the aim may be to improve the quality of teaching, there is little evidence that SETs alone improve teaching (Rindermann, Kohler, & Meisenberg, 2007). However, if formative SETs can facilitate reflection by academics (Bolton, 2005; Norton, 2009) and formative SETs via the VLE are an efficient way to conduct such an evaluation (Winchester & Winchester, 2010), weekly formative SETs should then facilitate reflection. The type of reflection that could take place using week on week student feedback could be 'reflection-on-action', where faculty members review what happened the week before, possibly leading to 'reflection-for-action', where the faculty members identify what could succeed in future lectures (Killion & Todnem, 1991; Schön, 2009). In these cases, the faculty members are 'generating reflection by means of evaluative techniques' (Moon, 1999, p. 211). The level of reflective practice taking place will vary depending on what the feedback is and how open the faculty are to the information.

'In most cases, feedback from students gives us much to think about. ...
Don't ask questions if you are not prepared to hear the answers' (Beaty,
1997, p. 18).

Reflective practice is something that can occur during a unit, at the end
of a unit, or over a complete programme of study (Brown, Fry, &
Marshall, 1999). A formative SET as proposed in this project is quite com-
plementary to the idea of reflective practice during a unit. For example,
Brown et al. (1999) suggest some areas that an academic could reflect on,
including the success of particular activities, the pace of the delivery and
the success of student engagement, noted as surface-level or content reflection (Kreber, 2004; Larrivee, 2008). Such information can be gleaned from
a formative SET that could allow the academic to reflect on how to modify
the class material week-on-week. Such information could also be very valuable in a teaching portfolio, as student evaluations are highlighted as a key
component of such portfolios (Fry & Ketteridge, 1999). Most of all, however, such formative SETs provide a straightforward process to support
faculty in their efforts to be reflective practitioners.

Previous research on reflection has noted that there are three distinct
levels of reflection. The three levels, as outlined by Larrivee (2008), are

1. an initial level focused on teaching functions, actions or skills, generally
   considering teaching episodes as isolated events;
2. a more advanced level considering the theory and rationale for current
   practice;
3. a higher order where teachers examine the ethical, social, and political
   consequences of their teaching, grappling with the ultimate purposes of
   education.

Put simply, level 1 focuses on what the faculty member is doing, level 2
on why they are doing what they do and level 3 on to what purpose or to
what end. The SET tool is therefore most likely to induce the first level of
reflection, with the possibility of second-level reflection. At the highest
level of reflection, teachers move from initially asking 'Am I doing it
right?' to eventually asking 'Is this the right thing to do?' (Larrivee, 2008,
p. 344). Therefore, the aim of this part of the study was to explore whether
the introduction of weekly evaluations of lectures via the VLE encouraged
active reflection about classes and units.

The same six faculty members were re-interviewed at the end of the 25
weeks of ongoing feedback once the formal summative evaluation form
administered by the university's QA department was completed. The

interviews were conducted within a week of these results, thereby increasing the validity of the results (Bryman & Bell, 2003).

What is not surprising is that not all faculty members moved on from the surface reflection to pedagogical reflection. This phenomenon has been noted in previous research by Chappell (2007) when conducting teaching observations as a means to reflect. He noted that 'the absence of pedagogic knowledge and reflection in the latter academics' response to the teaching observations appeared to reaffirm the conventional lecturer-centred approach' (Chappell, 2007, p. 263). Those who did have higher levels of reflection recognised that though the student response rate was not as high as they would have liked, they could still reflect over the course of the unit: 'Using the evaluation itself made me reflect on what I was doing, the results of the evaluation, not so much'.

Those faculty members who engaged in pedagogical reflection were much more positive about using the evaluation tool, but for different reasons. Although two participants used the tool as an ongoing gauge of the students' engagement with the class, or to assess their level of understanding, most used the tool as a reminder, or friendly nudging, as to what constitutes 'good teaching practice': 'What's interesting is the literature that backs up what the questions were based on makes sense, you know, "this is what you should be doing as a lecturer". So it made me think about, you know, if these are the things I should be doing as a lecturer, am I doing them, is there any way I can improve, before I even go into class'.

It was also interesting to note the acceptance of blame, or recognition of an internal factor, which did not appear in those faculty members who only facilitated surface level reflection. While the discussions on why the results were the way they were varied for a number of reasons, it was interesting to note that many times those faculty members pushed the focus back on the students instead of internalising the issues: 'Final year module I knew didn't feel as good as it had done the previous year. Mostly I don't put that down particularly to any different particular approach from me, different group of students, different reactions, different dynamics ... some of the exercises just didn't work as well from that point of view'.

Revisiting the different levels of reflection, it is interesting to note that the level of reflection (surface, pedagogical) and the type of reflection (reactive, proactive) determined how the faculty utilised the weekly SETs. For the reactive surface-level practitioners, the weekly online SETs provided structure within which they could think about the classes and/or unit, but the reflection stopped at that level. For the proactive higher-level reflection practitioners, the frame provided a base from which to work, but did not enclose the levels of reflection, or stop them reflecting further. Those faculty members that were more involved in this student evaluation used the feedback to improve their teaching and as an incentive to improve future classes.

In the past it has been assumed that reflective practice relies on journals, peer evaluations and other qualitative data, but the formative SETs used for this study have provided an efficient and possibly effective tool that can encourage faculty to reflect on what they are doing — again, depending on the nature of the faculty member involved. This tool does not necessarily help academics become reflective practitioners, but it is useful as a tool for collecting data upon which reflection-on-action can lead to reflection-for-action taking place (Winchester & Winchester, 2011).

Kreber (2004) suggests that reflection is valuable only if its outcomes are valuable; in this case, improved teaching. While there is an abundance of literature on the importance of reflective practice, there have been very little, if any empirical studies to date examining or even searching for the evidence that reflective practice increases teaching. As well, there is no empirical evidence that the student recognises the value in the faculty member's reflective practice. This begged the question: does faculty reflection on their teaching improve teaching quality, at least in the minds of those on the receiving end — the students?

PHASE FOUR: STUDENT REACTION TO IMPROVED TEACHING QUALITY

The 11 units taught by the six faculty members from four different departments within the institution were used for the study. From 11 units reviewed, 4 units had surface reflection level instructors and 7 had pedagogic reflection level instructors. Some students from three of the units may have completed the evaluation form on more than one unit within that year; however, overall the students were different for each unit. The total number of students that completed the summative evaluation for these units in 2008–2009 was 212, and in 2009–2010 was 192. For the purposes of anonymity and privacy, the specific unit titles are not used, and instead we have given anonymised titles based on the school the module was based. For example if we had an introductory marketing unit, so that the particular academic could not be identified, we would have labelled it 'Business X'. The Year column indicates the main year of study that the

Table 1. Units and Student Numbers.

Unit	Year	Total Student Response	
		2008−2009	2009−2010
Business A	1	16	19
Business B	2	8	12
Business C	3	14	24
Business D	2	15	26
Business E	2	9	13
Business F	1	10	10
Countryside and environment A	3	17	26
Countryside and environment B	2	80	20
Extended foundation degree A	0	5	4
Extended foundation degree B	0	39	26
Veterinary nursing A	3	8	12
Total		221	192

students are in, ranging from year 0 (extended foundation students), year 1 (first year students), year 2 (second year students) and year 3 (final year students). A full breakdown of the student numbers by unit is outlined in Table 1.

Once all the results were generated via the compilation above, a table of averages across all units was brought together. The initial results indicated a positive change between the average 2008−2009 results and the 2009−2010 results. As the analysis involved a simple comparison of two mean scores, the most appropriate statistical analyses to establish a significant difference was a two tailed *t*-test (Bryman & Bell, 2003). A two-tailed *t*-test was then run to demonstrate if the difference between the two sets of results was significant for each unit.

The results for all units from both 2008−2009 (prior to the evaluation tool being used) and 2009−2010 (using the evaluation tool) are outlined in Table 2. The units are sorted in ascending order of the summative evaluation score from 2009−2010.

From Table 2, it would appear that using the VLE tool to encourage reflection had, on average, a significant impact on the SETs collected from the QA department.

However, as noted earlier, there were two distinct groups of reflective practitioners found within the group, and the following two tables outline those results.

From Tables 3 and 4, it seems as if those that participate in more advanced levels of reflection (i.e. pedagogic as opposed to surface) tend to

Table 2.   Results Across All Units.

Unit	2008–2009		2009–2010			
	Total Student Response	Overall Score	Total Student Response	Overall Score	Change	t-Test
Business A	16	2.89	19	3.16	0.27	0.444
Countryside and environment A	17	3.40	26	3.31	− 0.09	0.832
Extended foundation A	5	3.40	4	3.50	0.10	0.798
Countryside and environment B	80	3.49	20	3.55	0.06	0.856
Business C	14	4.06	24	3.88	− 0.19	0.705
Business B	8	2.76	12	4.00	1.24	0.046**
Extended foundation B	39	2.60	26	4.04	1.44	0.000**
Business D	15	3.98	26	4.19	0.21	0.160*
Business F	10	3.32	10	4.20	0.88	0.009**
Veterinary nursing A	8	3.51	12	4.33	0.82	0.029**
Business E	9	3.43	13	4.54	1.11	0.000**
Total	221		192			
Total average		3.35		3.88	0.53	0.000**

*indicates significance ($p < .20$).
**indicates high significance ($p < .05$).

Table 3.   Results of Units with Surface Level Reflection.

Unit	2008–2009		2009–2010			
	Total Student Response	Overall Score	Total Student Response	Overall Score	Change	t-Test
Countryside and environment A	17	3.40	26	3.31	− 0.09	0.832
Extended foundation A	5	3.40	4	3.50	0.10	0.798
Countryside and environment B	80	3.49	20	3.55	0.06	0.856
Extended foundation B	39	2.60	26	4.04	1.44	0.000**
Total	141	3.22	76	3.60	0.38	0.002**

Table 4. Results of Units with Pedagogic Level Reflection.

Unit	2008–2009		2009–2010			
	Total Student Response	Overall Score	Total Student Response	Overall Score	Change	t-Test
Business A	16	2.89	19	3.16	0.27	0.444
Business C	14	4.06	24	3.88	−0.19	0.705
Business B	8	2.76	12	4.00	1.24	0.046
Business D	15	3.98	26	4.19	0.21	0.160[*]
Business F	10	3.32	10	4.20	0.88	0.009[**]
Veterinary nursing A	8	3.51	12	4.33	0.82	0.029[**]
Business E	9	3.43	13	4.54	1.11	0.000[**]
Total	80	3.42	116	4.04	0.62	0.000[**]

not only score higher on average, but also have a greater positive change between last year and this year's evaluation scores.

As summative SETs directly measure the quality of instruction (Barth, 2008), and those who benefit most from any improvement in teaching quality are the best to provide such information (Pratt, 1997, p. 35), the results of this study indicate that faculty members involved in reflective practice show improvements in their teaching quality, as indicated by the summative student evaluation scores. This is a positive finding, as the goal of both reflective practice and SETs is to improve teaching. It is clear from the results above that, on average, there was a significant increase in SETs from one year to the next. It is also demonstrated, using Tables 3 and 4, that on average, deeper (pedagogic) reflective practices also generated a greater increase in student evaluations.

The results from the unit Extended Foundation B within Table 3 stood out as a unit whose results were different than the other units from within that group. The transcripts for this faculty member were reviewed to ensure that this unit was placed within the correct category. It was found that this faculty member used the weekly SET tool to gauge the students grasp of the information each week, and any lecture that the students indicated they struggled with was reviewed the following week to ensure the students then understood the material. While the students made no qualitative comments on the summative evaluations about this unit, it could be assumed that their positive response to the unit was because of the faculty member's increased time spent on making sure they understood the material. This is particularly important to these types of students, as they are often younger students who have struggled with classroom materials academically, as it is a bridging programme for entrance to the university.

Overall, the results suggest that the quality of teaching improved, on average, for all reflective practitioners, as demonstrated by increased year-on-year summative SETs, and improved even more significantly in those faculty members who demonstrated higher levels of reflection.

SUMMARY

The chapter has discussed the use of weekly SETs in a formative fashion via the VLE at a rural university college in the United Kingdom. The researchers have outlined some of the arguments for and against the use of summative SETs, and the benefits of using them formatively. Finding an effective and efficient means of collecting student feedback from both the student and faculty perspective is crucial, and it was proposed that collecting feedback via the VLE addressed this. Such an evaluation conducted utilising the VLE also provided a 'safe' environment for continual feedback for faculty members who felt uncomfortable asking for feedback in the classroom environment, or who perhaps felt they were not experienced enough to gauge student response.

From the student perspective, they found the tool a useful means to communicate and provide immediate anonymous feedback directly to the faculty member, and were motivated by seeing the results of their feedback incorporated into the lecture. In this way, the students were a part of the learning environment, and were positive about the impact that they might make. However, they were demotivated partly because of the lack of variation in the evaluation tool, and partly because they felt if the faculty member was doing a good job they did not need to positively comment via feedback. Students were, overall, more inclined to comment on negative issues, rather than provide constructive positive feedback.

This research started out as a means to continually access student feedback and serendipitously found it was also an efficient means to collect data for reflection-on-action. Being a reflective practitioner is considered a pinnacle of teaching practice, but often the process of collecting information upon which to reflect can be very time consuming. The VLE provided an efficient platform off which to reflect, leading to further investigation on what impact this reflection had on the students within the classroom.

The results suggest that not only does reflection encourage faculty members to improve teaching, but that this improvement can be observed by the students as shown by a significant increase in student summative evaluations. As students perceive the main benefit of conducting evaluations of teaching is an increase in teaching quality, it would seem that faculty reflection on their teaching is beneficial in the minds of those on the receiving end — the students. This is a positive finding, as the goal of both reflective practice and SETs is to improve teaching, and the use of the VLE facilitated both in this learning environment.

Further research should be conducted to see if these findings can be generalised across different universities, as well as different countries or cultural groups. It would be desirable to replicate the research in a setting with larger unit that have a lot more student enrolments to get a more robust sample size. Other future research could investigate if other means of encouraging reflection, other than formative SETs, also improve summative evaluations.

NOTE

1. "unit of study" in Australia is equivalent to a "course" in North America and "module" in the UK.

ACKNOWLEDGEMENTS

This study began as part of the work of the *Aspire* Development Fellowship Award at Harper Adams University College, and partially funded by the *Aspire* Development Award Scheme which aims to enhance teaching and student learning. The authors are particularly grateful for the support of the eLearning team, especially the eLearning Coordinator Dr. Henry Keil's counsel and comments, as well as the volunteers who participated in the year-long study, without which this project would not have been possible. The authors would also like to thank Dr. Stephen Bostock of Keele University for his advice and mentoring during the duration of the project.

REFERENCES

Adams, M. J. D., & Umbach, P. D. (2012). Nonresponse and online student evaluations of teaching: understanding the influence of aalience, fatigue, and academic environments. *Research in Higher Education, 53*(5), 1–16.

Anderson, H. M., Cain, J., & Bird, E. (2005). Online student course evaluations: review of literature and a pilot study. *American Journal of Pharmaceutical Education, 69*(1), 34–43.

Barth, M. M. (2008). Deciphering student evaluations of teaching: a factor analysis approach. *Journal of Education for Business, 84*(1), 40–46.

Beaty, L. (1997). *Developing your teaching through reflective practice*. Birmingham, UK: SEDA.

Becker, W. E., & Watts, M. (1999). The state of economic education: how departments of economics evaluate teaching. *American Economic Review, 89*(2), 334–349.

BERA. (2004). *Revised ethical guidelines for educational research*. London: British Educational Research Association. Previously available from http://www.bera.ac.uk/files/guidelines/ethical.pdf.

Biggs, J. (2001). The reflective institution: assuring and enhancing the quality of teaching and learning. *Higher Education, 41*(2), 221–238.

Bolton, G. (2005). *Reflective practice: Writing and professional development* (2nd ed.). London: Sage.

Braskamp, L. A., & Ory, J. C. (1994). *Assessing faculty work*. San Francisco, CA: Jossey-Bass Publishers.

Brown, M., Fry, H., & Marshall, S. (1999). Reflective practice. In H. Fry, S. Ketteridge & S. Marshall (Eds.), *A handbook for teaching and learning in higher education: Enhancing academic practice* (pp. 190–199). London: Kogan Page.

Brown, M. J. (2008). Student perceptions of teaching evaluations. *Journal of Instructional Psychology, 35*(2), 177–181.

Bryman, A., & Bell, E. (2003). *Business research methods*. Oxford, UK: Oxford University Press.

Cahn, S. M. (2011). *Saints and scamps: Ethics in academia*. Lanham, MD: Rowman & Littlefield.

Calderon, T. G., Gabbin, A. L., & Green, B. P. (1996). Summary of promoting and evaluating effective teaching. *Journal of Accounting Education, 14*, 367–383.

Carmichael, R., Palermo, J., Reeve, L., & Vallence, K. (2001). Student learning: 'The heart of quality' in education and training. *Assessment & Evaluation in Higher Education, 26*, 449–463.

Chappell, A. (2007). Using teaching observations and reflective practice to challenge conventions and conceptions of teaching in geography. *Journal of Geography in Higher Education, 31*(2), 257–268.

Chen, Y., & Hoshower, L. B. (1998). Assessing student motivation to participate in teaching evaluations: An application of expectancy theory. *Issues in Accounting Education, 13*, 531–549.

Davis, B. G. (2009). *Tools for Teaching*. San Francisco, CA: Josey-Bass.

Divoky, J. (1995). Eliciting teaching evaluation information interactively. *Journal of Education for Business, 70*, 317–320.

Fry, H., & Ketteridge, S. (1999). Teaching portfolios. In H. Fry, S. Ketteridge & S. Marshall (Eds.), *A handbook for teaching and learning in higher education: Enhancing academic practice* (pp. 213–222). London: Kegan Page.

Green, B. P., Calderon, T. G., & Reider, B. P. (1998). A content analysis of teaching evaluation instruments used in accounting departments. *Issues in Accounting Education, 13*(1), 15–30.

Hamilton, D., Sibley, J., & Hawkins, K. (2011). Measuring of factors contributing to student performance at university: new approaches and new insights to inform quality teaching and learning. In W. Broucek, J. Wegleitner, & H. Schacht (Eds), *Proceedings of the 18th annual South Dakota international business conference*, September 29–October 2, Rapid City, SD, USA, Northern State University, USA.

Hittman, J. A. (1993). TQM and CQI in postsecondary education. *Quality Progress, 26*(10), 77–80.

Kember, D., Leung, D. Y., & Kwan, K. P. (2002). Does the use of student feedback questionnaires improve the overall quality of teaching? *Assessment & Evaluation in Higher Education, 27*(5), 411–425.

Kidwell, L. A., & Kidwell, R. E. (2008). Do the numbers add up to different views? Perceptions of ethical faculty behavior among faculty in quantitative versus qualitative disciplines. *Journal of Business Ethics, 78*(1), 141–151.

Killion, J. P., & Todnem, G. R. (1991). A process for personal theory building. *Eudcational Leadership, 48*(6), 14–16.

Kirkwood, A., & Price, L. (2005). Learners and learning in the twenty-first century: What do we know about students' attitudes towards and experiences of information and communication technologies that will help us design courses?. *Studies in Higher Education, 30*(3), 257–274.

Kreber, C. (2004). An analysis of two models of reflection and their implications for educational development. *International Journal for Academic Development, 9*(1), 29–49.

Larrivee, B. (2000). Transforming teaching practice: Becoming the critically reflective teacher. *Reflective Practice, 1*(3), 293–307.

Larrivee, B. (2008). Development of a tool to assess teachers' level of reflective practice. *Reflective Practice, 9*(3), 341–360.

Leckey, J., & Neville, N. (2001). Quantifying quality: The importance of student feedback. *Quality in Higher Education, 7*(1), 19–32.

Lill, D. J. (1979). The development of a standardized student evaluation form. *Academy of Marketing Science, 7*(3), 242–254.

Loughran, J. (1996). *Developing reflective practice: Learning about teaching and learning through modelling*. London: Falmer Press.

MacFarlane, B., & Ottewill, R. (2001). Reflection and evaluation. In B. MacFarlane & R. Ottewill (Eds.), *Effective learning and teaching in business and management* (pp. 67–76). London: Kogan Page.

Massy, W. F. (1994). Measuring performance: How colleges and universities can set meaningful goals and be accountable. In J. W. Meyerson & W. F. Massy (Eds.), *Measuring institutional performance in higher education* (pp. 29–54). Princeton, NJ: Peterson's Guides.

McPherson, M. A. (2006). Determinants of how students evaluate teachers. *Journal of Economic Education, 37*(1), 3–20.

Mercer, J. (2006). Appraising higher education faculty in the middle east: Leadership lessons from a different world. *Management in Education, 20*(1), 23–26.

Moon, J. (1999). *Reflection in learning & professional development*. London: Kogan Page.

Norton, L. S. (2009). *Action research in teaching and learning: A practical guide to conducting pedagogical research in universities*. Abingdon, Oxford: Routledge.

Ogunleye, A. O. (2010). Evaluating an online learning programme from students' perspectives. *Journal of College Teaching and Learning, 7*(1), 79–90.

Oliver, R. L., & Sautter, E. P. (2005). Using course management systems to enhance the value of student evaluations of teaching. *Journal of Education for Business, 80*(4), 231–234.

Onwuegbuzie, A. J., Witcher, A. E., Collins, K. M. T., & Filler, J. D. (2007). Students' perceptions of characteristics of effective college teachers. *American Educational Research Journal, 44*(1), 113–160.

Pan, D., Tan, G. S. H., Ragupathi, K., Booluck, K., Roop, R., & Ip, Y. K. (2009). Profiling teacher/teaching using descriptors derived from qualitative feedback: Formative and summative applications. *Research in Higher Education, 50*(1), 73–100.

Parayitam, S., Desai, K., & Phelps, L. (2007). The effect of teacher communication and course content on student satisfaction and effectiveness. *Academy of Educational Leadership Journal, 11*(3), 91–105.

Peat, M., & Franklin, S. (2002). Supporting student learning: The use of computer-based formative assessment modules. *British Journal of Educational Technology, 33*(5), 515–523.

Pratt, D. D. (1997). Reconceptualizing the evaluatino of teaching in higher education. *Higher Education, 34*, 23–44.

Pritchard, R. E., & Potter, G. C. (2011). Adverse changes in faculty behavior resulting from use of student evaluations of teaching: A case study. *Journal of College Teaching & Learning (TLC), 8*(1), 1–17.

Ramsden, P. (1992). *Learning to teach in higher education*. London: Routledge.

Ravelli, B. (2000). *Anonymous online teaching assessments: Preliminary findings*. Paper presented at the The Annual National Conference of the American Association for Higher Education, Charlotte, NC.

Read, W. J., Rama, D. V., & Raghunandan, K. (2001). The relationship between student evaluations of teaching and faculty evaluations. *Journal of Education for Business, 76*(4), 189–192.

Remidios, R., & Lieberman, D. A. (2008). I liked your course because you taught me well: The influence of grades, workloads, expectations and goals on students' evaluations of teaching. *British Educational Research Journal, 34*(1), 91–115.

Rindermann, H., Kohler, J., & Meisenberg, G. (2007). Quality of instruction improved by evaluation and consultation of instructors. *International Journal for Academic Development, 12*(2), 73–85.

Schön, D. A. (2009). *The reflective practitioner: How professionals think in action*. London: Maurice Temple Smith.

Scriven, M. (1995). Student ratings offer useful input to teacher evaluations. *Practical Assessment, Research & Evaluation, 4*(7). Retrieved from http://pareonline.net/getvn.asp?v=4&n=7

Stowell, J. R., Addison, W. E., & Smith, J. L. (2011). Comparison of online and classroom-based student evaluations of instruction. *Assessment and Evaluation in Higher Education, 37*(4), 465–473.

Trigwell, K., & Shale, S. (2004). Student learning and the scholarship of university teaching. *Studies in Higher Education, 29*(4), 523–536.

Weinberg, B. A., Hashimoto, M., & Fleisher, B. M. (2009). Evaluating teaching in higher education. *Journal of Economic Education, 40*(3), 227–261.

Wilson, R. (1998). New research casts doubt on value of student evaluations of professors. *Chronicle of Higher Education, 44*(19), A12.

Winchester, M. K., & Winchester, T. M. (2011). If you build it, will they come? exploring the student perspective of weekly student evaluations of teaching. *Assessment & Evaluation in Higher Education(iFirst Article)*, 1–12.

Winchester, T. M., & Winchester, M. K. (2010). *Exploring the utility of using a VLE for weekly student evaluations of teaching.* Paper presented at the *International Conference on Information Communication Technologies in Education (ICICTE)*, Corfu, Greece.

Winchester, T. M., & Winchester, M. K. (2011). Exploring the impact of faculty reflection on weekly student evaluations of teaching. *International Journal for Academic Development, 16*(2), 119–131.

Yao, Y., & Grady, M. (2005). How do faculty make formative use of student evaluation feedback?: A multiple case study. *Journal of Personnel Evaluation in Education, 18*(2), 107–126.

Zeichner, K. M., & Liston, D. P. (1996). *Reflective teaching: An introduction.* Mahway, NJ: Lawrence Erlbaum.

ABOUT THE AUTHORS

Jonathan Becker is an assistant professor in the Department of Educational Leadership of the School of Education at Virginia Commonwealth University, Richmond, Virginia, USA. Jonathan's teaching and scholarly endeavors occur at the intersection of educational technology, policy, law and leadership. Currently, Jonathan is serving as the evaluator of a multi-million dollar, multi-year grant program funded by the U.S. Department of Education to develop simulations and to support leadership preparation and is a co-investigator of an NSF-funded grant targeted at research and development of science curriculum modules for students in underserved areas.

Francesca Bertacchini is a Ph.D. student in Psychology of Programming and Artificial Intelligence, at the Department of Linguistics, Università della Calabria, Italy. Her research interests are Edutainment, Virtual Storytelling and Communication of Science. She designed and wrote the script "Plexus" for a performance based on the small world network theory; then she realized the editing of videos in augmented reality for the realization of the performance in a storytelling system. Moreover, she worked on to develop the 'ImaginationTOOLS' (TM) software, and of ideas, concepts and proto-types of games to use also on mobiles. Currently she is working on different topics relative to the communication of science using media as books, videos, exhibitions and installations of virtual reality. In particular, she is completing a book-interview on Chua's circuit as paradigm of contemporary science, with an unpublished interview to Professor L. O. Chua.

Patrick Blessinger is the founder and executive director of the International Higher Education Teaching and Learning Association and a research fellow at the School of Education at St. John's University in Queens, New York, USA. He has taught over 150 college and university courses and he has served as a program chair at colleges and universities in the United States and Eurpean Union. He consults with HE institutions in the areas of technology innovation and internationalization and serves as an academic and accreditation advisor for HE institutions. He is the co-founder and co-director of the Institute for Meaning-Centered Education. He is the

369

founder and editor of the *International HETL Review* and co-editor of the *Journal of Applied Research in Higher Education*. He is co-editor of several volumes within the *Cutting-edge Technologies in Higher Education* book series (Emerald) and co-editor of the book, *Meaning-Centered Education: International Perspectives and Explorations in Higher Education* (Routledge: 2013). He attended Auburn University, Georgia Tech, and the University of Georgia. He is a peer-recognized expert and thought leader in the field of teaching and learning and he has received several academic awards including a Fulbright Scholarship from the US Department of State and a Governor's Teaching Fellowship from the State of Georgia, USA.

Jon Cabiria is currently one of only a small number of people worldwide who hold a doctorate degree in media psychology. He also holds a master's degree in organizational dynamics from The University of Pennsylvania. He is on the leading edge of an increasingly important field that looks at the relationships between human behavior and technology. His interests and research include online social sites, virtual worlds, and augmented reality technologies and their uses in education, the practice of psychology, business, and identity control. He is also CEO and principal of Teksylos, a consulting company that assists other companies in their new technology initiatives. He is an active public speaker, traveling worldwide to present on topics about the positive benefits of online social engagement, online and hybrid education, and augmented reality. He teaches in the media psychology master's program for Walden University, and in the media psychology and social change program for Fielding Graduate University, where he developed the popular course "Identity in the Virtual Age." He currently serves as an executive board member for Division 46 (Media Psychology) of the American Psychological Association, and chairs their Website Development Committee and the News Media, Public Education, and Public Policy Committee.

Maurice Eugene Dawson, Jr. currently serves as an assistant professor of Management Information Systems at Alabama A&M University and chief information officer (CIO) of Reynolds Research & Technology Corporation in Huntsville, Alabama, USA. Dawson is a graduate of the College of Engineering and Computer Science at Colorado Technical University with a Doctor of Computer Science (DCS) with a concentration in Enterprise Information Systems. Also obtained from this institution is a Master of Science in Management (MSM) in Information Systems Security, Master of Business Administration (MBA) to include multiple graduate certificates.

Dawson is also the editor-in-chief for *the Journal of Information Systems Technology & Planning* (JISTP) – ISSN: 1945-5259, advisory board member for *the Indian Journal of Commerce and Management Studies* (IJCMS), and a board member for the Intellect Base International Consortium. Maurice's primary research is focused on cyber security software assurance, systems engineering. In terms of industry experience, Dawson has over 11 years in defense and aerospace within cyber security and intelligence.

Stayc DuBravac is associate professor of French and Linguistics at the University of Kentucky, USA, and director of the MA in Teaching World Languages. He earned his Ph.D. in Second Language Acquisition from The Pennsylvania State University. He is the author of *Technology in the L2 Curriculum* and a variety of foreign language multimedia projects such as *Interaction: Critical Analysis and Pedagogical Presentation of Ten Literary Texts* and the video program to accompany *Dicho y Hecho*. He has published articles on issues in language teaching and learning with technology including topics such as activity theory and human-computer interface, second language literacy, and L2 task design for electronic media. He has led numerous workshops to educators worldwide on assessment, project-based instruction, use of blogs, wikis, video, and gamification.

Lorella Gabriele is a Ph.D. in Psychology of Programming and Artificial Intelligence, and collaborates with the Laboratory of Psychology at Università della of Calabria (Italy) since 1999. Her research interests lie within psychology of programming, educational technologies and their use in didactic context, e-learning systems, techniques of human computer interaction, communications systems, and their use for educational purposes. She published different papers in conferences, workshops, and referred journals, both in Italian than in English language; moreover, she participated in different conferences and workshops in Italy and abroad. From 2009 till now, she is referee for *the Journal of Computers & Education* and *Scientific Research and Essays*. She collaborates at the coordinating and writing work of different national and international projects. Currently she holds a 3 years fellowship at the University of Calabria, with a project titled "Robot for Thinking: Cognitive Strategies to Experiment the Use of Evolutionary and Educational Robotics in Classroom."

Steve Gove is an assistant professor of Management at Virginia Tech's Pamplin College of Business, USA. He received his Ph.D. in Business Administration from the W. P. Carey School of Business at Arizona State

University. His research has been published in *Strategic Management Journal*, *Academy of Management Journal*, *Journal of Management Studies*, and *Journal of Management Education*, among others. He received the 2011 Sage Publications/Robert McDonald Advancement of Organizational Research Methodology Award by the Research Methods Division of the Academy of Management. He has authored multiple case studies on strategic management. His work has been presented internationally at the Annual Meeting of the Academy of Management, the Strategic Management Society Annual International Conference, and Babson College Kauffman Foundation Entrepreneurship Research Conference among others. His research interests include the role and effect of top managers in strategy and corporate governance, intersections of philosophy of science and faculty productivity, research methods, particularly measurement error, and management education. He currently serves on the editorial board of *Academy of Management Journal* and *Corporate Governance: An International Review* and has reviewed for various journals including *Strategic Management Journal*, *Organizational Research Methods*, *Academy of Management Review*, *Journal of Management*, and *Journal of Management Education*. He has received multiple Outstanding Reviewer Awards from the Management Education and Business Policy divisions of the Academy of Management, been recognized as Virginia Tech's Scholar of the Week, and is the recipient of Virginia Tech's 2011 Pamplin Excellence in Teaching Award.

Scott A. Johnson is professor and director of the Department of Business and Accounting at the College of Idaho, USA. His primary teaching and research interests are in the intersection of leadership development and experiential learning, positive organizational behavior, service management, identity and identification processes, and social entrepreneurship. Scott earned his Ph.D. in Management, jointly supervised by Center for Services Leadership, at Arizona State University. His research has been published in outlets such as the *Journal of Organizational Behavior* and *Journal of Marketing Management* (funded by the Society for Human Resource Management), several book chapters, and multiple proceedings and presentations at international conferences, including the annual meetings of the Academy of Management.

Jing Luo is a visiting lecturer in the Business School, University of Greenwich, UK, conducting leadership seminars and simulation labs and supervising undergraduate dissertations for Chinese students. Jing earned her Ph.D. in Management Science from the Huazhong University of Science and Technology (HUST) and joined the International Survey and Research Project on Changing Academic Profession (funded by Ford Foundation). Jing's research interests lie in the field of human resource management and organizational behavior. She has been involved in several research projects funded by the National Natural Science Foundation of China (NSFC), and also in charge of several consulting projects in China.

Dale Mann is professor emeritus at Columbia University (Teachers College and the School of International and Public Affairs), New York, USA, and managing director of Interactive, Inc. Since 1985, he has concentrated in e-learning, a field in which he has been identified as one of America's 10 most influential leaders. At Virginia Commonwealth University, he serves as a collateral professor responsible for the design and delivery of the first virtual school to train school administrators. "Project ALL: Authentic Learning for Leaders" is an immersive, interactive, and individualized web-enabled simulated replication of a middle school with day-in-the-life scenarios that must be dealt with by school principals on a real-time and scored basis. He has been involved with school improvement since the 1960s when his Washington service included responsibility as Special Analyst for Education in the Executive Office of President Lyndon Johnson. He is the author of *Policy Decision Making in Education* and *Making Change Happen?* At Teachers College, he chaired the Department of Educational Administration. He is the founding chair of the International Congress for School Effectiveness, an organization with members from 66 countries focused on improving schools for the most-needy children. With the Soros Foundations and the World Bank, he created networks to reform the school systems of 8 countries of the former Soviet Union and has worked in 25 countries.

Grace May has a doctorate in Interdisciplinary Studies in Human Development from the University of Pennsylvania, USA. She is associate professor of Education, led the teacher certification special education program for 12 years, helped the college through initial and continuing National Council for Accreditation of Teacher Education (NCATE) accreditation as NCATE coordinator, served as the associate dean of Assessment and Accreditation, and is now the dean of the College of Education and Human Services at Seton Hall University. Grace has been an eager user of technology in all of her roles. Recognizing that faculty must model the use of technology in their own teaching, she has been an early adopter of many of the trainings, software, and devices made available through the Teaching

Learning Technology Center. Her specific interest in simulated learning environments stemmed from teacher candidate's struggle with classroom organization and behavior management. The use of Second Life provided an opportunity to apply theory to practice without affecting the lives of real K-12 students. Additional areas of research include the utilization of flexible and comprehensive assessment strategies for field placement, creating a feedback loop for teacher candidates, field supervisors, and university faculty. Recently, the College of Education and Human Services has explored the use of iPads to support teacher candidates in their coursework as well as in their student teaching placements.

Danielle Mirliss is an associate director at Seton Hall University's (New Jersey, USA) Teaching, Leaning and Technology Center. She is responsible for overseeing the Instructional Design and Training team in a variety of faculty and student technology support initiatives. She has been part of the Instructional Design team at Seton Hall for 10 years and has a broad range of experience in mobile computing, pen-based computing, course redesign, online learning, virtual worlds, and assessment. She is an early adopter of the use of virtual worlds in higher education, integrating this platform into her own teaching in 2006, and manages Seton Hall's Second Life presence, Pirate Island. In addition, she has been published on the use of virtual worlds for experiential learning and simulation training. Virtual world projects include the creation of collaboration activities to promote team work, emergency preparedness training, and teacher candidate classroom management exercises. Before coming to Seton Hall, she worked as an instructional designer at The Distance Learning Project, an online division of Columbia University. Currently Danielle is a doctoral candidate at Teacher College, Columbia University in Instructional Technology and Media. She earned her Ed.M. in the same program and has M.A. in Industrial and Organizational Psychology from New York University.

Denise M. Pheils earned her Ph.D. in Education specializing in Online Teaching and Training from Capella University, USA. Her training in IT includes an MBA in Information Systems of Management and a BBA in Management Information Systems and 18 professional certifications including the Certified Information System Security Professional (CISSP) and Project Management Professional (PMP). Prior to entering academia, she was an analyst for several national and global companies in a career spanning 19 years. She is adjunct faculty at Indiana Tech and a trainer for the Center for System Security and Information Assurance (CSSIA).

Previously, she was a Professor at Owens Community College for almost 15 years. During that time she developed many courses including the core System Security and Information Assurance degree courses, mapped the content to the NSA's 4011 and 4012 curriculum standards, and sought and was awarded the NSA's accreditation of Center of Academic Excellence for 2 Year Schools (CAE2Y). She is on the Board of Directors for the Northwest Ohio Infragard Chapter and several college and secondary school advisory boards. She was 2010 Teacher of the Year for ACBSP region 4.

R. Martin Reardon is an assistant professor in the Department of Educational Leadership of the School of Education at Virginia Commonwealth University (VCU), Richmond, Virginia. He has taught instructional leadership, data-driven decision-making, and systems thinking courses at the master's and post-master's level in both Wisconsin and Virginia since 2001. As chair of the Leadership Studies Department at Marian University, he was instrumental in the creation of an innovative cross-disciplinary Ph.D. program and taught the first two cohorts of students. Since arriving at VCU in 2005, he has taught courses focused on policy and leadership in the Ph.D. in Educational Leadership strand. In 2011, he became the director of the Education Doctorate program – a program which was established in 2009 in conjunction with the Carnegie Project on the Education Doctorate (CPED) initiative. He received the VCU School of Education's Award for Distinguished Teaching in 2011. His research interests span three areas: learning-centered leadership, educational quality and equality, and technology-infused learning. A particular recent interest has been the implementation of systemic models of change at the small rural school district and local school levels. He is the past chair of the School-University Collaborative Research Special Interest Group (SUCR-SIG) of the American Educational Research Association (AERA), and maintains a strong belief in the importance of such collaborations as laboratories of practice.

Michael R. Reich is the senior developer at "Project ALL: Authentic Learning for Leaders," the first virtual school to train school administrators at Virginia Commonwealth University, USA. He oversees all technical aspects of the simulation, including planning, software construction, graphic design, quality assurance, deployment, and data reporting/analytics.

Margarida Romero holds a Ph.D. in Psychology by Universitat de Toulouse UMR CNRS in France and Universitat Autònoma de Barcelona in Spain, where she was awarded with the Extraordinary Ph.D. Award in Psychology. Her research is focused on the study of the use of educational technologies in face-to-face, blended learning, and online learning modalities. In the context of computer supported collaborative learning (CSCL), she studies how students, in long-term collaborative learning tasks, perceive, allocate, and regulate their learning times at the individual and group level. She is leading the Euro-CAT-CSCL research project within the FP7 Marie Curie IAPP actions, and created the Spin Off Ouak in France aiming to transfer the scientific knowledge to international organizations (ITIN Paris, IUFM French Guyana, Educational Ministry of Algeria). In 2007, she won the 3rd price on Technology Transfer from the EU Network of Excellence Kaleidoscope. In 2006, she won ex-aequo the Artificial Intelligence French Association Award (Prix de l'Association Française d'Intelligence Artificielle). Since 2007 she collaborates with the European Commission as an expert evaluator of the EACEA and FP7 call and has participated in the European Research Area Board (ERAB) aiming to define the 2030 Agenda.

Imad Al Saeed is a graduate of the College of Engineering and Computer Science at Colorado Technical University with a Doctor of Computer Science (DCS), USA, with a concentration in Emerging Media. He also obtained a Master of Science (MS) degree in Software Engineering and a Bachelor of Science (BS) degree in Computer Engineering. For more than 13 years, he has been faculty member within higher education, having taught undergraduate courses in information technology (IT), computer science, computer networking, and software engineering. In addition, he is currently responsible for providing multiple universities' leadership with operational and instructional support for the development of courses using virtual worlds. He has professional experience in virtual worlds' simulations Second life and OpenSimulator. In addition, he has additional professional skills in NVIDIA's Graphics Processing Unit (GPU) architecture and compute unified device architecture or CUDA interface programming models.

Charol Shakeshaft is professor and chairperson, Department of Educational Leadership of the School of Education at Virginia Commonwealth University, Richmond, USA. Her research focuses on leadership and gender, educator sexual misconduct, and technology and learning. She is currently PI of a $5.2 million grant to develop simulations to support leadership preparation.

Wei LianTan is currently attached as a lecturer at the School of Business, Taylor's University, Malaysia. She has a track record of 12 years of teaching experience and her passion has always been in seeing active learning take place in the fun way. This passion had also led her to explore and use technologies to enhance teaching and learning based on the belief that technologies opened up the opportunities for making learning fun and enjoyable. In line with this vocation, Wei Lian committed herself to the university-wide e-learning initiative as an *eLITE* (e-Learning Implementation Team) member to drive e-learning in the School of Business. Her primary role as an eLITE member is to facilitate the transformation of teaching and learning from conventional approach to e-learning in the business school by taking active role in planning and leading, conducting trainings, initiating and implementing e-learning projects, and research. Wei Lian is also pursuing Ph.D. in education specializing in the area of instructional technologies. Her thesis is looking at educational game as a medium for promoting engagement, problem solving, and critical thinking skill among business students. Wei Lian's research interests include instructional technologies, instructional design with technologies, computer games in education, and problem-based learning.

Assunta Tavernise is a Ph.D. in Psychology of Programming and Artificial Intelligence, and collaborates with the Laboratory of Psychology at Università della of Calabria (Italy) for the realization of technological tools able to improve learning. Her research interests concern various scientific topics from an interdisciplinary point of view and comprise the following areas: educational technology, human computer interaction, edutainment, virtual worlds/games, virtual agents, ICT for cultural heritage. She has worked on the constructivist approach to Robotics, carrying out laboratories with students from grammar school to University. Moreover, her researches have involved virtual worlds and virtual theatres as learning environments by the design of educational paths for different (also personalized) target of users. She is also an expert of Edutainment (education through entertainment). Currently her studies are focused on the nonverbal communication of virtual agents for the realization of didactic tutors. She has worked in national and international projects, and is editor/referee of international scientific journals.

Charles Wankel, professor of Management at St. John's University, New York, earned his doctorate from New York University. Charles is on the Rotterdam School of Management Dissertation Committee and is

Honorary Vice Rector of the Poznań University of Business. He has authored and edited about 46 books including the bestselling *Management*, 3rd ed. (Prentice-Hall: 1986), 11 volumes in the IAP series Research in Management Education and Development, the *Handbook of 21st Century Management* (SAGE: 2008), and the *Encyclopedia of Business in Today's World* (SAGE: 2009), which received the American Library Association's Outstanding Business Reference Source Award. He is the leading founder and director of scholarly virtual communities for management professors, currently directing eight with thousands of participants in more than ninety nations. He has been a visiting professor in Lithuania at the Kaunas University of Technology (Fulbright Fellowship) and the University of Vilnius (United Nations Development Program and Soros Open Society Foundation funding). Fortune 50 consulting clients include McDonald's Corporation's Hamburger University and IBM Learning Services. International consulting includes TNK-Nizhnevartovsk (former ChernogorNeft) Oil Company, Siberia.

Maxwell K. Winchester is a senior lecturer in Marketing at Victoria University, Melbourne, Australia. He is also currently the deputy director of Learning and Teaching in the School of International Business at Victoria University. Maxwell teaches master's level units in consumer behavior, marketing communications, and marketing management and holds a Ph.D. in Marketing from the esteemed Ehrenberg-Bass Institute for Marketing Science. He has consulting experience as a marketing researcher in Australia, Asia, North America, and Europe. His clients have included Astra Motor Company, Cartier Asia, BHP, Pernod Riccard, and a number of government agencies. He has also held a senior management position in one of Australia's largest companies and held political seats in the United Kingdom. In addition to his industry experience, he has many years of academic teaching experience globally, having held permanent faculty positions in Australia, Canada and the United Kingdom. In addition to these, he has been a visiting professor in China, Singapore, Malaysia, France, Germany, Kuwait, and Austria. His research interests include reflective learning and reflective practice, qualitative and quantitative research methods, empirical generalizationalist research methods, and behaviorist consumer behavior theories. He has published articles on student evaluations of teaching and reflective practice, as well as negative brand beliefs, luxury and premium brands, and wine marketing.

Tiffany M. Winchester is a lecturer in Marketing and a Ph.D. scholar in the Graduate School of Business at Deakin University in Australia where she teaches MBA level units in research design and analysis, marketing management, and strategic customer service. Prior to moving to Australia, she was a Senior Lecturer at Harper Adams University College in the UK, where the focus of this chapter's research project took place. She has also been a visiting professor at Fachhochschule Bingen – University of Applied Sciences, in Germany, the Beijing Agricultural College in China, and Ecole Supérieure de Commerce de Dijon in France. After completing a postgraduate course in teaching and learning in higher education, she has been very engaged in researching reflective learning and reflective practice, specifically as it applies to her own work and practice. Her more recent research interest is in the application of marketing theory to political voting behavior, the topic area of her Ph.D. She is currently involved with many aspects of learning and teaching, including the promotion of paperless marking using the GradeMark system, as well as ways of eliciting formative student feedback for improvement of the learning environment and faculty reflection. Recently she was involved in a collaborative project on constructively aligning learning outcomes of higher-level units to assessment tasks across the course of study.

Mary Zedeck is an instructional designer with the Teaching, Learning, and Technology Center at Seton Hall University, New Jersey, USA. Mary supports faculty members in the design, integration, and assessment of technology resources for courses and programs. Mary's primary interest is in researching and implementing existing and emerging technologies with a special interest in social media to facilitate teaching and learning. She has designed and supported the use of virtual worlds in a variety of academic fields including gothic literature, teacher education, and writing. She has published and presented on her work supporting student interpretations of the novel House of the Seven Gables using Second Life as the canvas. Additional projects include the creation of a classroom management simulation for teacher candidates and a virtual writing center integrating collaborative Web 2.0 tools to support tutoring. Mary received a BA in Biology from Lafayette College, Easton, PA. After several years working in biological research, Mary decided to pursue a degree in adult and corporate education and received her Ed.M. from Loyola University, Chicago. Before joining Seton Hall, Mary provided technology training and instructional design services to K-12 educators, administrators, and corporate clients. Mary has supported the use of technology to support teaching and learning in K-20 for over 20 years.

INDEX